𝕮𝔥𝔢 𝔑𝔢𝔴 𝔜𝔬𝔯𝔨 𝔗𝔦𝔪𝔢𝔰
PRACTICAL
TRAVELER

The New York Times
PRACTICAL
TRAVELER

PAUL GRIMES

Times
BOOKS

All rights reserved under International and Pan-American Copyright
Conventions. Published in the United States by Times Books,
a division of Random House, Inc., New York, and simultaneously
in Canada by Random House of Canada Limited, Toronto.

Library of Congress Cataloging in Publication Data

Grimes, Paul.
  The New York Times practical traveler.

  Includes index.
  1. Travel. I. New York Times. II. Title.
III. Title: Practical traveler.
G151.G75   1985   910.4   84-40431
ISBN 0-8129-1152-0

Designed by Marjorie Anderson

Manufactured in the United States of America

9 8 7 6 5 4 3 2

This book is dedicated to my wife, Mimi, who steadfastly encouraged me to complete it despite many agonizing periods when I felt sorely overworked and was strongly tempted to give up. But Mimi also did much more than that. She offered many practical ideas that simply never occurred to me, and she was frequently available to chat with other travelers about their experiences, providing grist that otherwise might never have come my way.

Acknowledgments

I give special thanks to a few people whose guidance and encouragement helped greatly. The first is Robert W. Stock, whom I sought out when he was travel editor of *The New York Times* and who has since become a close personal friend. He got me into travel writing and encouraged me to write a column that eventually became—unfortunately after his departure for another *Times* assignment—the *Practical Traveler*. Bob Stock, now a senior editor of *The New York Times Magazine*, is one of the finest editors I have known.

I also give special thanks to Abe Rosenthal, executive editor of *The Times*, who approved the creation of the column, provided its name, and, despite some early misgivings, encouraged its continuance. I thank Arthur Gelb, a source of substantial and lasting support; Joyce H. Jack, who long encouraged me to write a book; Margaret Zellers, one of the most honest, painstaking and authoritative travel writers I know; Kathleen Moloney, my editor at Times Books; and Lynn Waggoner, who helped keep my information up to date.

I am grateful too to Robert S. Crandall, who succeeded Bob Stock as travel editor and in whose incumbency the *Practical Traveler* began. His immediate successor, Michael Sterne, proved a tough but fair editor with perception of how a column should be executed that often exceeded mine. My thanks also go to Mike Sterne's two deputies, Betsy Wade, a friend for more than a quarter century, and Michael J. Leahy, who followed her and is the travel editor as this is being written, and to Tom Bodkin, who arranged for art that invariably enhanced my written words. On the Travel section staff, present and former, I am grateful to Robert J. Dunphy, Suzanne Donner, Stanley Carr, and Paul Freireich, who often copyedited my work, to Judy Miceli, who provided invaluable logistical help, to Nora Kerr, John Brannon Albright, Sarah Ferrell, and Phyllis Goldblatt, who provided ideas and encouragement, to Ursula

Mahoney, always a congenial office mate, and to Larry R. Shannon, who was one of the first to encourage me and who has long been a special friend.

Finally, this book could never have been produced if not for the patient, generous technical support given me by Howard Angione, technology editor of *The New York Times*, and Jed Stevenson, one of his assistants. Most of the *Practical Traveler* columns were originally written on a computer, and getting them into book form involved computer gymnastics that I could not have accomplished without Angione & Company's support. My thanks, too, to my good friend Don Caswell, who copyedited the manuscript in its final form.

If, due to oversight, I have omitted anyone from mention here who deserves to be on the list, please forgive me. And finally, let me express deep gratitude to the thousands of readers who wrote or phoned me in response to columns or who had complaints or travel questions on their minds. If I had not known they were out there, I would have given up long ago.

Contents

PART II: ON THE ROAD 227

Introduction: Practical Traveling

This book is dedicated to the belief that travel should be fun. Whether you go for business or for leisure, travel should be as free of hassle as possible, and when something does go wrong, you should understand why. As far as possible, expectations should be met and promises fulfilled. What you pay should generally be in direct proportion to what you receive.

In the last generation, the growth of jet travel and the widespread construction and improvement of airports and highways have sharply narrowed the time gap between distant places and have made more and more of them readily accessible. Only twenty-five years ago, for example, I was among the first American journalists to be permitted into the Himalayan kingdom of Bhutan. At that time it took six days to travel the sixty-five miles from Phuntsholing, on the frontier with northeastern India, to Paro, then Bhutan's capital, and most of the way we had to go on muleback because there were no roads. Most Bhutanese whom we met along the way and in Paro had never even heard of the wheel.

Today, however, the wheel has indeed arrived in Bhutan, and electricity and many modern conveniences have arrived with it. Roads and airports link much of the country, and it has been opened to tourism for virtually any foreigner who can pay the price. In fact, Bhutan maintains an official travel bureau in midtown New York.

Just about the only large areas of the world that are barred to Americans today are those closed for political or military reasons. Because the Soviet Union won't allow Americans into Vladivostok, for example, the United States won't let Soviet citizens visit Atlantic City. Americans are not permitted to visit Cambodia, Afghanistan, Iran, or Albania and are discouraged by the State Department from visiting Cuba, even if the Castro government will let them in. But one can travel through the jungles of Papua New Guinea, on the barren high plateaus of Ladakh in Kashmir, in the

Australian Outback, in the heart of central Africa, and far up the Amazon in Brazil.

Meanwhile, technological advances have provided the travel industry with the ability to make travel easier. Modern hotel construction has made it possible to spread American-style comfort throughout the world. Computers have allowed instantaneous confirmation of reservations to many places and in many facilities. Wherever you may think of going and whatever you may think of doing there, you can probably find a tour to take you or, at least, a package combining transportation with accommodations at a rate substantially lower than if you bought the components separately.

It sounds, indeed, like a great, thrilling world. The trouble is, however, that travel in the mid-1980s often does not work out the way technology and the travel industry promised. If it did, there would be no reason for this book. The truth is that much of travel has become a sharply honed business in which an entrepreneurial urge to make money often prevails over any inclination to provide gratifying service.

The founder of what became one of the biggest tour operations in the Americas once commented acridly to me that he could not understand why I wrote about delays at airports, jammed jetliners with meager service and inferior meals, about vacationers being "walked" by overbooked hotels, about surly service, about the common difficulty in finding an appropriate official who would listen sympathetically to a complaint, about the frequent extreme difficulty in getting a refund when one was clearly warranted. A lot may go wrong in travel, the tour operator conceded, but why, he asked, do people rarely seem outraged by delays on commuter trains from Scarsdale to New York City, for example, or on the subway?

My reply was simply this: Delays in commuting are part of one's daily routine, something that a traveler becomes conditioned to bear, until they become too frequent, too great, and, therefore, intolerable. But distress on a vacation, I said, is something much more painful, because it intrudes on a dream. For some, it impairs a once-in-a-lifetime opportunity for which thousands of dollars have been squirreled away over many years and then spent. "Look at your own brochures," I said. "You are openly advertising dreams, and you have a responsibility to assure that, to the best of your ability, they are delivered. If something goes wrong, you also have a responsibility to see that your passengers are appropriately assuaged."

This book is being published around my tenth anniversary as a professional travel writer. I became one at the age of fifty, which makes me a sort of Grandpa Moses of the field. My first major effort was a two-part series on travel agents, which Robert W. Stock, then the travel editor of *The New York Times*, featured on his section's front page. My reporting took six months and included not just extensive interviews and research but also completion of a fourteen-week travel-agent course at a New York career school.

While acknowledging that there were many competent, industrious, and highly considerate travel agents, I wrote that many others sold from brochures on their office rack rather than from personal familiarity with destinations and hotels, and many seemed to care more about which suppliers paid the highest commissions than about pleasing clients.

In September 1977 I began the *Practical Traveler* column in *The New York Times*. It appeared every other week until March of 1979, and it has been weekly since then. I was the sole writer for the first five years and have been the principal writer since then. It is from that column that most of the material for this book has been drawn.

Writing the column involves relatively little traveling. My ideas come from a variety of sources: letters from readers, luncheon conversations with colleagues and members of the travel industry, and a careful reading of the trade press, especially of the advertisements in my own newspaper's Travel section. These tell a lot about where the trade thinks people ought to go this year, and, based on the number of midseason price cuts, whether the public agrees. Most of my investigating is done by telephone, many hours of it every week.

I do travel at least five times a year, though, usually several brief trips and one of three or four weeks. I inevitably return home with dozens of ideas that one can glean only from experience or from talking with people along the way. Even a few hours of observation at a major airport will produce material that I would not have been aware of if I had stayed home. I travel as unassumingly as possible, although I do always use my own name. Unless asked, however, I do not identify myself as a travel writer, and I neither seek nor accept any favors that, under the same circumstances, would not be available to the general public. Occasionally *The New York Times* helps with my expenses; otherwise I pay my own way.

All my life I have loved to travel and have done so widely and often, so it is ironic that the extent and frequency of my traveling have diminished substantially since I became a professional travel writer. The primary reason is that I have other duties that take precedence and keep me largely in the office. For nearly four years I was an editor on the foreign desk. Then I became an assistant business and financial editor, responsible for news production. In early 1981 I moved again, this time to become head of the copy-editing staff for the daily Style page and the weekly Living and Home sections.

Such office responsibilities meant that my travels were confined principally to weekends and vacations. Weekends meant Amtrak between New York and Philadelphia, my family home, and in the mid and late 1970s I saw the government-subsidized rail passenger service deteriorate to a point where it was a distinct disservice, although it has markedly improved since. Rarely in those days did I ride a train in the vital Northeast Corridor that was on time or even close to it. Delays of fifteen minutes to half an hour seemed more the rule than the exception for trains between Philadelphia and New York that originated in either city; those that began farther away, such as in Boston or Washington, were frequently an hour late or more.

En route, it seemed as if almost anything might happen. In winter, trains stalled because switches were frozen. In summer, coaches overheated and air-conditioning failed, but windows were sealed closed and could not be opened, so passengers dripped with perspiration. To steel myself for whatever, I always made certain to carry a paperback novel that I knew would interest me and of which enough remained unread to keep me distracted from reality for at least a three-hour journey (although the typical scheduled run from Penn Station to 30th Street in those days was about an hour and fifty minutes). Once, we had just left Penn Station and I settled back with my novel when suddenly the lights went out and remained that way all the way to Philadelphia—a trip that took two and a half hours that night because the crew tried to repair the power line in Newark and again in New Brunswick but failed. Around Princeton Junction I groped my way to the cafe car for a cold beer—foolish aspiration because the same power failure that turned off the lights and air-conditioning had turned off the refrigeration, too.

Gradually Amtrak upgraded its equipment, completely refurbishing some of its old coaches built before World War II and adding new red, silver, and blue oval-shaped cars called Amfleet.

When they were introduced, however, they seemed at least as susceptible to breakdowns as their older relatives. The windows never seemed to be washed, and washrooms in the coaches, old and new, lacked running water or soap or paper towels or toilet paper or a combination of these things or all four.

Amtrak officials explained many of the operating delays by saying they were laying all new tracks, which would be able to carry trains at much higher speeds. "We've been working on the railroad!" Amtrak advertisements proclaimed. For one long stage this obviously had to include the Hudson River tunnel between New York and New Jersey, which is only two tracks wide, compared with four tracks for most of the New York-Washington corridor. Since it had to keep tunnel service operating, Amtrak sometimes resorted to what it called single tracking, which meant running trains in both directions on one of the tracks while the other, piece by piece, was replaced.

When single tracking was in effect, most passengers might easily have been able to adjust if they had been forewarned, but usually they were not. So I sometimes faced a frustrating experience such as this: My train from Philadelphia would arrive in Newark on time, sometimes even a few minutes early. We would leave on time and cross the bridge over the Passaic River to Harrison, New Jersey, then would stop. We would wait perhaps twenty minutes while several trains passed in the opposite direction. Then we would move forward perhaps four or five miles and the delay would be repeated. Our final delay would be just before the tracks narrowed from four to two—one of which was not in service. Finally we would reach Penn Station in New York, fifty minutes to an hour late.

If only I had known, before leaving Newark, that single tracking was in effect, I could have changed my plans.

If only I had known. Those few words alone say a lot about the frustrations that pervade much of the travel business today. I am convinced that one of the biggest sources of passenger complaints is not being informed of travel problems. Much less anger (and much less legal action) would be directed against airlines and tour operators if they had competent personnel on duty to explain delays and arrange simple amenities (even as little as a hot cup of coffee) to help alleviate discomfort. Many passengers are willing to tolerate substantial discomfort if they know the reason and if the reason seems to make sense, but lack of information or lack of gestures of compassion often make them much angrier than the discomfort itself.

Many travelers complain that airlines, tour operators, bus companies, cruise lines, hotels, or whatever do not really care about their customers—just about the money the customers pay. That view is understandable, but it is really not true. The providers of travel facilities actually care very much about their customers, because for most people in the industry the key to success is repeat business, and unless you have a monopoly, repeat business is impossible if your customers are unhappy.

Of course, many problems can be avoided if you, the traveler, think before you travel. There is a Latin expression for it: *caveat emptor*—let the buyer beware. Instead of being carried away by a misleading brochure, use your intelligence and apply a little common sense. Even when the dollar is strong and the economy of Greece is ailing, can a tour there really be top quality for only a hundred dollars a day, including round-trip transportation from the United States? If another operator is charging twice as much for a similar itinerary, it does not necessarily mean that his tours are twice as good, but it may prove highly worthwhile to compare the two brochures with the help of an expert travel agent, one whom you trust. A careful examination will probably bring out the differences in quality of hotels, meals, sightseeing and other ingredients of the tours.

Similarly, it is unreasonable to expect that a Caribbean cruise that costs an average of $125 a person per day will be as high in quality as one that costs $275. Yes, occasionally there are "distress" sales in which prices are slashed to fill unsold berths, but in general in travel, as in any other business, you get what you pay for. This does not mean that cheap is bad. Rather, many charter tours (for example, seven nights in Peru for $380 a person, including round-trip transportation from New York) are hundreds of dollars less than the cheapest noncharter tours to the same destinations. But don't expect luxury for that price, and do be prepared for flight delays or for the fact that you will not be offered a refund if inclement weather blocks that optional side trip to the magnificent Inca citadel city at Machu Picchu.

My files are loaded with letters of complaint from readers who feel they have been grievously shortchanged in buying everything from bare-bones transportation to complete tours. Few such letters surprise me. As a result of a decade of studying advertisements and brochures, I can usually predict which operators will draw complaints. And some of them draw dozens of complaints, year after year after year, indicating either that they do not depend much on repeat business or, more likely, that most of their tours work reasonably well, so they are willing to absorb the flak from the relatively few that bomb. The truth is that many tour operators are high rollers: They take heavy risks and usually win. But when they occasionally lose, it is often disastrous, with a badly delayed flight resulting in lost vacation time and possibly a loss of hotel space and the forced cancellation of sightseeing, etc.

A few caveats should be kept in mind when you read this book. The first is that prices are always subject to sudden change—some times up and, in foreign travel, sometimes down because the dollar's value fluctuates. Prices mentioned in this book should be taken as examples of what something might cost now or might have cost when the situation occurred. Prices as such are not important to this book; the main point about them is what sort of value they indicated for the service or travel facility that was provided, and I have attempted in all cases to make this clear.

Second, offerings in the travel industry are constantly changing, which means that what is highly popular today may not even be available tomorrow. For example, when I began writing about travel, there were no such things as public charters, only charters for so-called affinity groups. Now anyone can buy seats on charter flights to dozens of destinations from dozens of American gateways—sometimes, to borrow the name of one organization that sells them, literally on a "moment's notice." A few years ago, accompanied children under eighteen years old could fly free between New York and southern Florida; at this writing they cannot, but tomorrow they may be able to again. Sometimes all the major hotels in a city offer weekend bargain plans to fill rooms. Later such offerings may abruptly be withdrawn because rooms are filled without them. In the next season, however, the weekend plans may be back again.

Therefore, what you read in this book should not be taken as gospel for what exists in travel at the moment you read it. I would prefer, instead, that you look upon the book as containing illustrations of what may exist: in other words, as a guide to the sort of possibilities you should keep in mind or discuss with your travel agent or with airlines, hotels, cruise lines, etc., when you begin your planning.

Third, it should be emphasized that travel in general is not nearly so perilous as some of the examples in this book may make it seem. According to the thousands of accounts I have heard over the years, most travel works at least reasonably well, and my personal experiences substantiate that. But there are indeed many pitfalls out there, and they are disturbing enough that they should be exposed as fully as possible and that the ways to avoid or alleviate them should be explained. That, to a large extent, is what the *Practical Traveler* column and this book are all about.

The more we travel, the more we learn. We learn for ourselves what a good journey is made of and why some fail. So let this book be your primer, your guide to practical traveling as you start out, and refer to it from time to time to compare your experiences with some of those discussed here. And if you find you have something worthwhile to share, please write me about it at *The New York Times*.

Meanwhile, have fun!

—PAUL GRIMES

PART I
BEFORE YOU GO

If you must travel to a particular place at a particular time—for business, say, or to attend a friend's wedding or because of a family emergency—your options are obviously limited. Your destination has been selected for you, so your attention can focus primarily on getting there as expediently as possible.

If, however, you are planning a vacation and the choice of where you go is up to you, the options are more complicated. But before you even start thinking of destinations, it is important to do a bit of thinking about yourself.

What do you like to do? What would you enjoy most when traveling and is it consistent with what you enjoy at home? Do you visit museums a lot at home? If not, why focus on a destination where museums and archaeology are the major attractions? Would you like an active vacation—lots of sightseeing, skiing, tennis, golf, or water sports, shopping, night life—or would you prefer a total escape, simply lying on a beach all day and going to bed early? Do you enjoy beaches at all? Or are you perhaps extremely sensitive to the sun?

What kind of accommodations best suit your taste? Do you need a private bathroom? Can you tolerate pensions or guest houses, or do you prefer the more impersonal atmosphere of hotels? Is the type and quality of food very important to you, or does that not have a high priority in your list of vacation requirements? Do you enjoy trains? Do you get seasick? Can you tolerate poverty? If not, do not go to Calcutta. Do you enjoy resorts, or do they bore you? What sort of climate do you prefer?

Do you prefer to travel alone or with just your spouse, or do you prefer being part of a group, with all the pampering of an escorted tour? If you are thinking of traveling with one or two other couples from home, how much togetherness do you plan or can you tolerate? Are you willing to do all your sightseeing, eating, and shopping

3

together, for example. And what happens if you and your spouse are always punctual but the other people always are not?

Actually, do even you and your spouse have the same travel tastes? Perhaps one of you likes to shop and the other detests it. If you differ, is it really necessary to be together all the time, or should you arrange periods when each of you goes separately? In fact, have you ever considered completely separate vacations? Perhaps one of you cannot take the sun and the other cannot get enough of it. If you are on a motoring vacation and one likes to stop at every garage sale, flea market, or farm stand along the way, should the other perhaps be sure to have a good book along to be able to tolerate the delays? In short, you have to know, in travel, both what you can tolerate and what you will really enjoy.

After such introspection, it is time to begin planning. What more interesting and challenging way to spend fall and winter evenings than planning for your vacation or vacations next year? You may ultimately decide to have a travel agent make the detailed arrangements, but many vacationers have found that the more advance homework they do themselves, the better those arrangements are likely to be.

1 . Doing Your Homework

If you prefer to do most or all of your trip planning and arranging, you should know about tools of the trade. The public tools are guidebooks and articles in newspapers and magazines. In your public library, check the *New York Times Index* and the *Reader's Guide to Periodical Literature* for articles on destinations and types of vacations you are considering. Also check the advertisements in your newspaper's travel section, if it has one. In many travel sections, the hardest and most significant news is in the ads. They tell you where the bargains lie and give some idea of what destinations are likely to be the most popular. Notably, however, they tell little or nothing about the poshest and most exclusive resorts because those places often have no need to advertise or do so in slick magazines aimed at upscale audiences.

Be careful, however: Ads can be terribly misleading. Even some of the biggest travel suppliers and tour operators—especially in the air charter and auto rental fields—are noted for promises they often cannot fulfill and for severely restricted offerings. So before you commit yourself to advertised travel that sounds too good to be true, be aware that it may not be true. Ask lots of questions, preferably of a travel agent who deals heavily in the type of travel you are considering. Check out the advertiser with your nearest Better Business Bureau. Read the fine print in the ad and in the followup brochure carefully. What, for example, do the asterisks mean?

Guidebooks

There are five basic types of guidebook. The first, not strictly a guidebook, delves into the history, lore, character, and drama of a place or region; it gives you a feel of what a place is like and can be extremely important in helping you decide whether you will like it. It often gives an excellent overview of what there is to do there. Much of Mark Twain's writing falls into this category and will never become outdated. More recent examples are the writings of Jan Morris and Paul Theroux.

The second type is the sightseeing guidebook, such as the Michelin Green series, the Blue Guides, and the Nagels. There are also many excellent individual guidebooks to countries, parts of countries, cities, and special interests, such as sailing, hiking, bicycling, etc.

The third type is essentially the meat-and-potatoes book for hotel, restaurant, and entertainment suggestions, including price range. These include the Fielding, Fodor, Frommer, and Birnbaum series, and the Let's Go series of the Harvard Student Agencies. Some guidebooks combine meat and potatoes with excellent descriptive evaluations of prominent sights; among them are Robert Fisher's Annotated Guidebooks and the diligently researched works of Robert S. Kane.

Fourth is the directory type of meat-and-potatoes book, some with rating systems, such as the Michelin Red series, the Mobil series, Egon Ronay's Lucas guides, the American Express Pocket

Guides, the outspoken Gault-Millau books, individual country directories, and specialty directories, such as to campgrounds and the use of recreational vehicles, to farm vacations, to adventure travel, and so on.

Fifth is the specialty critic's guidebook, such as to restaurants, country inns, architectural sites, or museums.

A problem in finding good guidebooks is that some of the worst are among the most readily available in stores, and some of the best are issued by small regional publishers with weak means of distribution. Therefore, if you want something out of the ordinary, it is best to shop first at the largest general bookstores in your area, then look for stores that specialize in travel books. There are perhaps two dozen across the United States, including the Complete Traveller, 199 Madison Avenue, New York, New York 10016; phone (212) 685-9007; the Traveller's Bookstore, 22 West 52nd Street, New York, New York 10019; (212) 664-0995; Sandmeyer's Bookstore, 714 South Dearborn Street, Chicago, Illinois 60605; (312) 922-2104; Book Passage, 57 Post Street, Suite 401, San Francisco, California 94104; (415) 982-7866 or, outside California, (800) 321-9785; Travel Books Unlimited, 4931 Cordell Avenue, Bethesda, Maryland 20814; (301) 951-8533; and Travel Bound, 2020 Smallman Street, Pittsburgh, Pennsylvania 15222; (412) 281-2665.

Many travel bookstores also handle mail orders, which are the principal business of the Forsyth Travel Library, Post Office Box 2975, 9154 West 57th Street, Shawnee Mission, Kansas 66201; (913) 384-0496; Wayfarer Books, Post Office Box 1121, Davenport, Iowa 52805; (319) 355-3902; Around and About Travel, 931 Shoreline Drive, San Mateo, California 94404; (415) 573-7998; World Wide Products, 401 NE 45th Street, Seattle, Washington 98105; (206) 634-3453; and the Armchair Traveler, Post Office Box 152, West Roxbury, Boston, Massachusetts 02132. Offbeat guidebooks and maps, particularly on Latin America, are the mail-order specialty of Bradt Enterprises Inc., 95 Harvey Street, Cambridge, Massachusetts 02140; (617) 492-8776.

Catalogues are usually available for mail orders. Most companies charge extra for postage and handling; some will not accept personal checks, but many will accept major credit cards.

Some of the most popular meat-and-potatoes guidebooks are sold at substantial markdowns by discount chains in some cities, such as the Barnes & Noble sales annexes in New York and the Encore bookstores in the Philadelphia area. Also, you may have to pay only a small fraction of the original price if you buy an out-of-date guidebook in a remainder sale; in many cases, the only differences from current editions are restaurant and hotel prices, which frequently fluctuate while the current year's edition is on sale anyway. In addition, some budget-wary publishers severely restrict the number of pages on which they allow changes each year.

Excellent literature can sometimes be obtained free from domestic and foreign governments tourist offices, although the quality varies substantially. Most foreign countries that encourage tourism have official tourist offices in New York, and some are also represented in Chicago and San Francisco or Los Angeles. Check the appropriate *Yellow Pages* under "tourist information." Some bureaus are staffed by travel experts, but others are directed by political appointees who are being rewarded for their connections or past favors by being assigned to the United States.

Expect a wealth of informative literature from the bureaus of Britain and Switzerland, for example, but not much of practical use from some other countries. They may not have extra copies to give you, but the tourist offices of countries such as Italy, where hotels are officially rated by the government, have up-to-date directories with these ratings. So if you want the names and addresses of five-star hotels in Rome or a couple of modest pensions in Siena, the government tourist bureau should be able to help. A note of caution, however: Government rating standards and Michelin's, for example, may differ, although probably not that much that often. So whose word do you take? Personally, I'd lean toward Michelin.

Every state in the United States has an official department of tourism or a tourism section of some other department, such as commerce or economic development. Very few have offices outside their state, such as in New York, but the six New England state governments jointly sponsor the New England Vacation Center, which has a storefront on the lower concourse of the International Building in Rockefeller Center, 630 Fifth Avenue, New York, New York 10020; phone (212) 307-5780. As with foreign government publications, what the states publish can vary sharply in quality depending on the size of the travel promotion budget. Most state governments have their own free road maps, however, and they usually are as good as what you can buy or better.

Besides maps, the best literature available from those states that publish them are leaflets suggesting auto tours of varying lengths.

Those of Texas, Georgia, Illinois, and Pennsylvania, among others, are excellent. State lists of parks and public campgrounds are generally comprehensive, stating what facilities are offered by each. Sometimes this information is on the back of the official map. Lists of private overnight accommodations, restaurants, and sightseeing attractions may give such information as facilities (a heated indoor pool at a hotel, for instance), operating hours, prices, type of food served, dress code, etc., but usually there is a dearth of qualitative information because of pressure to be unbiased and treat everyone equally. Thus, a privately published guidebook is generally of much more help in advising you on where to eat and sleep.

What the Travel Agents Use

Do-it-yourself travel planners will also benefit from familiarity with some tools of the trade, which you can often use on the premises in airline ticket offices or sometimes in travel agencies if the agent knows you and has reason to believe he or she will do your booking and receive commissions. For example, with an *Official Airline Guide* (semimonthly for North America and monthly worldwide) you can work out a jet itinerary and determine all the direct and connecting services between two points, which will help when you seek the lowest fare. *Russell's Guide* (monthly) contains all domestic long-distance bus schedules, and the *Official Railway Guide* tells all about North American trains, including fares and the rules that govern them. For foreign rail travel, the monthly *Thomas Cook Continental Timetable* has comprehensive schedules for Europe and the *Thomas Cook Overseas Timetable* for the rest of the world. The *Continental Timetable* is sold at travel bookstores or through the Forsyth Travel Library; at this writing the price is $16.95, which includes postage for mail orders. The *Overseas Timetable* is available in the United States only from Forsyth at $19.95 plus $1 for postage and handling.

Among other things, the *Official Steamship Guide* and the competing *OAG Cruise and Shipline Guide*, either of which is commonly used by travel agents, contain comprehensive directories of cruises everywhere and include relatively obscure river services and ferry services in the United States, Europe, and across the Mediterranean.

For hotels, the road gets rockier. The best guide I know is the *Official Hotel and Resort Guide*, a three-volume product of the Ziff-Davis Publishing Company, but ratings often are ambiguous or inadequate. Next best is probably the *Hotel and Travel Index*, also by Ziff-Davis. For qualitative assessments in the Caribbean, a candid newsletter for travel agents called the *Star Report* seems the best.

For air-land packages in the United States, first check the *Consolidated Tour Manual*, then ask for individual brochures. The annual sales directory of the National Tour Association is good on land-only packages, as are the annual sales guides issued by states, although they are usually limited to what's available in the issuing state. The *OAG Travel Planners*, in North American and European editions, provide a wealth of information about destinations, such as airport diagrams, addresses and phone numbers of hotels and motels, and maps of metropolitan areas.

For local sightseeing, a travel agent should have the comprehensive Gray Line and American Sightseeing annual directories. For auto rentals, the homework road is rough. I could find no directories of auto-rental rates beyond those issued individually each month by the major rental companies, and they often do not show special bargain offerings and sometimes are out of date by the time they are distributed. You will get some idea from them, however, of how sharply rates vary from city to city and sometimes in the same metropolitan area, depending on whether you pick up and drop the car off at an airport, in the suburbs, or in the heart of the city. The best homework you can do on auto rentals is to ask the 800-number reservations operator as many questions as you can think of and be sure to write down the confirmation number of your reservation and the name of the clerk—she may tell you only her first name. Then, if there is any possibility that you will be dealing with a franchisee rather than the company itself—a strong possibility with anyone but Hertz or Avis—call the pick-up point directly, using its local number. This may cost you the price of a long-distance call, but it is the safest way to verify the price you will pay and whether you are likely to get the type of car you ordered.

Once you, as a do-it-yourselfer, have worked out a detailed itinerary and know exactly what to order, you can save yourself countless hours by letting a travel agent do the actual booking. At best, airline and tour-operator reservation numbers are often hard to reach, and why make all those phone calls yourself anyway? It costs no more to go through an agent than to book yourself, and any sensible agent will be delighted to handle your arrangements under such circumstances because he or she will receive all the commissions while you have done all the ground work. With computers, ticket-writing machines, and special telephone numbers to travel suppliers, agents can, in most cases, arrange bookings and ticketing with speed. If overseas phone calls or telex messages are necessary or desirable, expect to pay extra for the cost of the message, although some agents will absorb the cost for a good customer.

2. Travel Brochures

A typical way that Americans begin to plan vacations is to scour advertisements and collect brochures. Some will get the happy holidays they are seeking, but others will be misled and disappointed.

Because of increasing vigilance by state legislators and prosecutors, travel advertising is generally more honest these days than it was a few years ago. Some resort areas, hotels, transportation companies, and tour packagers are extraordinarily explicit about what the traveler can and cannot expect. But there is still so much confusing fine print, so much florid language, so many modifications to stated prices, and so much focus on insignificant frills that consumer vigilance is still required.

By all means read brochures, but remember that almost always it is necessary to supplement what they tell you with information from your travel agent or someone else whom you trust who has taken the tour or recently been to the destination. You should ask many pointed questions and leave virtually nothing to chance.

Because facilities and service can deteriorate rapidly, the word *recently* is particularly important. If you want to go, say, to southern Mexico, and your travel agent simply gives you a handful of brochures and says, "Here, pick out a hotel, and I'll make the reservation," it's time to change agents.

One January, a stack of fliers appeared in the staff cafeteria of *The New York Times* advertising a four-day, three-night excursion to Bermuda from February 28 to March 2. On the surface, the price—$339 a person, double occupany, including air fare—seemed excellent, and perhaps it was. But let us look at the flier closely.

Among other things, it advertised "free chaise lounges/towels poolside." Doubtless they were there, but anyone familiar with Bermuda might doubt that the climate would be warm enough at that time of year to do much outdoor lounging, unless the pool was sheltered and the water heated. The leaflet advertised accommodations at the "deluxe Princess Hotel in Hamilton or Southampton." To those who know them, both Princesses are top drawer, but they have three grades of rooms: standard, superior, and deluxe. The flier did not say which grade was part of the package.

It did say "American breakfast and dinner daily." That meant that lunch, because it was not mentioned, was not included. In the travel trade, "American breakfast" is quite explicit: It is at least juice, bacon and eggs, toast and coffee. But "dinner" can mean your choice of anything available or it can mean a restricted set menu with selected items unavailable or costing extra.

The leaflet promised a "welcome rum swizzle party," "afternoon tea daily," baggage tags, and travel wallets. Pleasant, perhaps, but in dollar terms, how much are they worth? It made no mention of sightseeing or entertainment, which meant they cost extra—factors that should be considered when deciding whether a tour is really within your budget.

A newspaper advertisement on Hong Kong, meanwhile, offered "14 day complete springtime charter-value vacations" for an "unbelievable" $999.94. Reading the smaller print, however, one learned that while the entire tour, going nearly halfway around the world, lasted fourteen days, only twelve nights were in Hong Kong. This meant that one night was spent in the air and much of two days was spent getting to and from the destination.

The ad promised a "welcome get-together with refreshment" (what kind of refreshment?), "Oriental fashion show," "Chinese handicraft exhibition," "jade-cutting demonstration," "Chinese cooking lecture and recipe guide." It did not indicate whether those frills, except the welcome get-together, would be arranged especially for members of the tour or were open to the public, possibly at no charge.

The ad also offered a "specially written walking tour of Aberdeen," a section of Hong Kong. That could involve no more than being given a single sheet of paper telling you how to do something yourself. Of course, it could mean more, but nothing in the ad guaranteed that.

When studying an ad or brochure, one of the first things to look for is an asterisk or dagger next to a price. One or the other (sometimes both) is usually there. Be sure you understand exactly what it means. In cruise advertising, an asterisk often means that the minimum rate, although advertised boldly, may no longer be available. On many liners there are very few minimum-rate cabins and those that exist are highly undesirable—small and in a bad location, for example. In hotel and resort advertising, an asterisk or dagger often means minimum-rate room, off season. In airline advertising, an asterisk commonly indicates that the quoted fare is restricted by season, day of the week, time of day, or number of seats per flight.

A tour operator once advertised a "complete vacation" in Cartagena, Colombia, for $299.95, including air fare. But a small asterisk next to the price led the vigilant to learn that it did not include "a current air increase of $33.62," which meant that the rate was not $299.95 at all. In many advertisements of vacation packages using chartered planes, an asterisk has referred to a footnote that 15 percent is added to all prices to cover taxes and service charges, including added compensation to the tour operator.

A brochure promoting "the ultimate" excursion to Hong Kong spoke of accommodations at "the beautiful New World Hotel, Lee Gardens Hotel, or equivalent." There was an asterisk after the word "equivalent," and a reference to an inset lower on the page in which the hotels were described as "exquisite." The inset said hotel ratings were based on those in a respected trade manual, but no ratings were given except for the words "beautiful" and "exquisite."

What, by the way, does "equivalent" mean? Equivalent in quality but not necessarily in convenience, or vice versa, or neither? In recent years, the switching of hotels has been a prime cause of consumer complaint.

Obviously, the romantic language in brochures is far less important than what is left out. You may be proved wrong, but you should start out by assuming that what is not mentioned is not included. A responsible tour operator will specify which meals are included, for example, and will make it clear that you are on your own for the others. His brochure will also tell you whether the included meals are "run of the menu" or set dishes that allow you no choice.

These are some other points to watch for in brochures:

- What sightseeing is offered in a tour package, and is it included in the price or as an optional extra? If it is an extra, is there any indication how much it will cost?
- How much free time is there? Almost anything you do during that time probably will cost something unless you sit around the hotel.
- If you are going to Europe, you will probably take an overnight flight, and most of the day of arrival will probably be free. Interpret that as time to sleep to recover from jet lag. And remember that most of the last day of the tour probably will be used getting to and from airports and flying home. Also, is the day you leave home counted as one day of the tour even if you take off late at night? If so, a sixteen-day tour of Europe may actually amount to thirteen days when you subtract the night of departure, the day of overcoming jet lag and the day of traveling home.
- Will there be a "tour desk" in your hotel? If so, will it be staffed from early morning until evening by someone competent to deal with nuisances, emergencies, and requests for information, or will someone be there just once in a while and primarily to sell theater tickets, dine-around plans and sightseeing?
- What are the requirements for paying for your vacation, and what are the penalties for cancellation? Are the penalties sufficiently severe to warrant your buying insurance against them? Be careful, however: Trip-cancellation insurance has its own fine print and can usually be invoked only in case of a well-substantiated medical emergency or death.

Be especially wary if you plan to visit a small, remote resort, as many are in the Caribbean, where it can be very expensive in time and money to leave if you do not like the place. If you are unhappy with your hotel in a big city such as London, Paris, Hong Kong, or New York, it is often easy to move somewhere better, but not in the far islands of the South Pacific or the Bahamas.

Toward the end of almost every tour brochure, in the fine-print section that is typically headed "general information," you will find what the trade calls a disclaimer. It absolves the tour operator of legal responsibility for most things that can go wrong. Despite the disclaimer, some major tour operators will promptly assume responsibility for mishaps that cause clients severe discomfort. But others may blame airlines or hotels, which may pass the blame back to the operators or to insurance companies, neither of which may compensate you, on the ground that the law relieves them of liability.

If you feel that enough is at stake, however, consider suing. Often disclaimers have not proved as unbreakable as tour operators or travel agents said they were.

A lot of frustrating litigation can be avoided if the traveler asks all the pertinent questions that come to mind before signing a contract and paying a deposit. Above all, ask about the tour operator who is offering the package. What is his reputation in the trade? Check him out with the Better Business Bureau as well as with your travel agent. If your travel agent seems unsure, ask him to make sure or take your business somewhere else.

Between the Lines

Some vacationers learn the hard way how misleading a resort brochure can be. Such was the experience described here, which was real, including the name of the vacationers to whom it happened. The name of the resort, which was published in my original column on the subject, has been omitted here because the situation there has improved.

Mark H. Mirkin, then a student at Duke University, and his friend Bruce Goldstein, who was attending Tulane University, decided to take a winter vacation in the Bahamas. Through a travel agency in Durham, North Carolina, they bought a seven-night package offered by Caribbean Holidays of New York, a leading wholesaler of resort space.

Armed with a Caribbean Holidays voucher for which they had paid $256 each for a double room, without meals, they took off for a small resort off the island of Abaco, a plane flight and ferryboat ride from Miami.

The two young men had chosen the resort on the basis of its brochure. It spoke of "pampered relaxation," a variety of water sports, and a pool amid "magnificent natural settings of privacy and solitude."

Mr. Mirkin recounted that this happened instead: "We were

placed in a shack about ten feet square that contained one too-soft bed for both of us. There was no restaurant facility and, as there was no way of getting around the island, no alternative to dining except for the dining room right there. Not only did we not have any choice of food, we had no choice of seat or even price.

"And to top it off, we had to eat when they were quite ready. That night, they were ready to serve 'dinner' at ten P.M. It consisted of hors d'oeuvres, nothing else, and they demanded fifteen dollars a person."

"Next morning," Mr. Mirkin continued, "we found to our dismay and shock not only no pool but no beach. True, the adventuresome could hike a few miles to a beach somewhere but, for me, spending a supposedly leisurely vacation traipsing around some unsettled island has no appeal."

Mr. Mirkin and Mr. Goldstein checked out immediately to return to Miami. They refused to surrender their prepaid Caribbean Holidays voucher, so they had to pay the resort $74.80 in cash for one night and dinner plus tax. Eventually they received a refund from Caribbean Holidays, but their vacation was abortive.

When I tried to telephone the manager of the resort, he was reached through a Bahamian telephone operator who had to use citizens band radio to summon him to a phone, because he had none. The absence of a phone was not mentioned in the resort's brochure. If indeed the two students were required to share one bed, the manager said, "it was because we didn't have anything else," although their Caribbean Holidays voucher clearly specified twin.

"We don't pretend to have a restaurant," he said, "but we have a preset meal plan."

To advertise that the club has a swimming pool, he said, was a mistake. "We have no swimming pool," he commented, "but we have a pool table." He insisted that there was at least five hundred feet of private beach in front of the club—a stretch that Mr. Mirkin admitted was waterfront but insisted was unsuitable for pleasure swimming.

The students' experience was similar in many ways to those of many visitors to many resorts. Travelers are constantly lodging complaints about nonexistent beaches and swimming pools, inedible food, inadequate transportation, slovenly service, and, perhaps most frustrating of all, the unavailability of any sympathetic official to whom one can complain and who has the authority to take remedial action. Although only a small fraction of vacation travel by Americans generates such complaints, they have been numerous enough to warrant state and Federal investigations.

Even at resorts where most facilities are excellent, a guest can be disappointed if he does not make sure in advance that his particular interests can be satisfied. For example, at the Treasure Cay Beach Hotel, a luxury resort in the Bahamas where facilities for swimming, fishing, golf, and tennis were first class, my wife and I were disappointed one winter to find that the bicycles mentioned in one of the hotel's brochures were rarely available to transients. Furthermore, the sightseeing excursions listed by the hotel were nonexistent—unless one took the initiative of forming a group and chartering a yacht or taxi at considerable expense, often several days in advance.

William Carey, an executive of Caribbean Holidays, was asked what criteria his company applied before agreeing to act as the wholesaler for a resort. "They must all belong to their national or regional hotel association," he said, "and our own president, John H. Keller, visits most of them in his extensive travels. But we deal with eight thousand hotels, so one man or ten or eighteen obviously can't visit every hotel listed in our brochures. We send questionnaires to the hotels and we ask every question under the sun, but if someone lies, we may not catch up with it until we get consumer complaints. Then we investigate promptly and, if a complaint is justified, send a 'stop sell' order to retail travel agents."

Later, Mr. Keller said he was sending inspectors to re-evaluate resorts listed in the Caribbean Holidays brochure.

Accommodations at the resort that Mark Mirkin visited were also sold through Gogo Tours of Paramus, New Jersey, another long-established, prominent travel wholesaler. Steven Heydt, Gogo's vice president for advertising, sales and marketing, said that in some countries, such as the Bahamas, a wholesaler who works through the local hotel association must offer space in all member hotels unless complaints against a particular hotel can be substantiated. He noted that Gogo's listings for the Abaco area of the Bahamas were in order of price (those of Caribbean Holidays were alphabetical), and he said this gave some indication of quality. For Abaco, the rates of the Mirkin-Goldstein resort were the lowest listed.

The resort's listing in the three-volume *Official Hotel and Resort Guide,* which their travel agent consulted, called the place an "informal clublike sports lodge." But the guide, a worldwide basic source book for travel agents, gave little clue to quality. It described the accommodations as "comfortable" and said that among other facilities were a swimming pool and private beach. The Caribbean Holidays brochure told virtually nothing about the club except its rates and that the room type was "standard."

At that time, the *Official Hotel and Resort Guide* had ten ratings for the places it listed, ranging from "superior deluxe," which was "exclusive and expensive," to "moderate tourist class," which was "often quite old and may not be well kept." But many listed resorts were not rated at all.

"Sometimes we have not seen a place, and we don't have enough information to make a judgment," said Dorothy H. Rubin, associate publisher of the guide and for long its editor. "Over the years we try to develop a body of knowledge and we try to give travel agents as much guidance as we can, but it is really impossible for us to do it thoroughly. We don't have enough staff, time, and money."

3. Travel Agents

How do you select a travel agent? In Kerrville, Texas, where John J. B. Miller runs Magic Carpet Travel, the answer until recently was simple: The twenty thousand people of his community had little choice. When Mr. Miller bought the agency in 1973, he had no competitors in Kerrville, although he now has several.

In the New York metropolitan area, however, the number of travel agencies is estimated at 2,700. The majority are full-service agencies, presumably prepared to take on most types of travel requests. Some, however, specialize in particular modes of travel, such as cruises or escorted tours, particular destinations, or particular types of clients, such as individual vacationers, affinity groups, or corporate executives who travel frequently on business. So in most big cities and suburbs, selecting the best possible travel agent to meet one's needs can be difficult indeed.

Few travel subjects evoke greater sensitivity and controversy than those dealing with agents and the services they perform. Many travelers consider their agent among their wisest, most helpful, and most trustworthy friends. Other travelers, perhaps soured by only one misfortune, vow never to use an agent again. Between these two extremes lie two broad questions: Do you need a travel agent, and, if so, how do you find one who is good?

There is much to be said for putting a trip together yourself. If your vacation consists simply of flying from New York to San Francisco, spending a week there at the home of Aunt Thelma, then flying home, you could as easily deal with the airline directly as through an agent. But it is conceivable that in the seemingly simple process of buying a New York-San Francisco air ticket, the agent may know of bargain fares that will elude you unless you know exactly what questions to ask and where and how to ask them.

A long and complicated trip or one requiring many decisions could be very intricate to set up yourself. Arranging a two-week cruise may seem simple because one ticket covers almost everything: transportation, a cabin, meals, entertainment, and use of recreational facilities. But on second thought you will realize that you must decide—before you buy that one ticket—what sort of cabin will meet your needs and budget, what sort of dining arrangements you prefer, and, above all, how one cruise compares with another. If you have taken many cruises, you may have the answers; if not, you could benefit from an agent's advice.

A buff who likes to spend long evenings poring over guidebooks, brochures, and timetables and constructing itineraries may be able to put a trip together without help. But remember, there will be many phone calls to airlines and a lot of letters to distant hotels before all arrangements are complete. Is handling all this an economical use of your time? So you opt for an agent. What then?

"You find a good one just as you would find a good doctor or lawyer," Arthur L. Schiff, former staff vice president and general manager of the American Society of Travel Agents (ASTA), said, giving a typical industry reply. It is hardly that simple. Travel agents rarely have anywhere near the degree of training and testing that most professionals have. Only four states—California, Hawaii, Ohio, and Rhode Island—plus Puerto Rico license travel agents.

And even in the fields of medicine and law, there is substantial malpractice.

More than a dozen travel experts were asked how they would select an agent. They did not agree on everything, but the consensus was that an important first step was to solicit recommendations from relatives, friends, and business associates—people whom you trust—as you might in selecting a physician, a lawyer, or even an auto mechanic. "Personal reference is the backbone of this industry," Richard Knodt, a recent president of ASTA, said.

Most also agreed with Sarah Marquis, who has been an agent more than sixty years, that establishing a long-term compatible relationship with one agency would both benefit the agency and help assure the traveler of close attention by someone familiar with the client's likes, dislikes, and habits.

"Personal likes and dislikes are extremely important," said Harriett Emerson, former president of the New York chapter of ASTA and owner of a small agency in mid-Manhattan. "One man's tea is another man's poison."

When you first visit an agency, look around. Are you greeted promptly and courteously, even if you must wait for service? Are there brochures to examine while you wait? Is the agency an accredited agent of airlines? Plaques on the walls and seals on the front window will tell. Is it a member of the American Society of Travel Agents? If it is, it will display the ASTA decal, which is evidence that it has been in business at least three years under its present ownership or control.

Better still, look at the desk nameplate or calling card of the agent who is serving you, and see if the name is followed by the initials C.T.C., which stand for certified travel counselor. This means that the agent has had at least five years' experience and has, in his or her spare time, completed a two-year graduate-level program with examinations that was developed and supervised by the nonprofit Institute of Certified Travel Agents (ICTA) in Wellesley, Massachusetts. The designation C.T.C. may not imply as much know-how as the C.P.A. label implies for a certified public accountant, but it arises from the best educational program the travel industry offers.

In your first interview, be as specific as possible about your desires, tastes, and budget. If possible, do a little homework beforehand by reading guidebooks or appropriate brochures. Then note the questions the agent asks you. Does he or she really seem interested in satisfying you rather than simply selling a package off the brochure rack? Ask whether he or she has been to the country or resort you hope to visit and whether he or she personally knows the hotels recommended. Be wary of any recommendation that is not based on an agent's personal knowledge or at least the expertise of a close colleague.

If an agent tries to steer you toward Chichén Itzá, the spectacular ancient Mayan city in southeastern Mexico, without first determining that archaeology and history interest you, it is time to interrupt the conversation and shop elsewhere. "As a starter, if you are interested in the Caribbean," said Don Alto, manager of a Liberty Travel branch in mid-Manhattan, "a good agent will ask whether you want a casino. Whichever way you answer will quickly eliminate a lot of islands."

On both the agent and client sides, frankness seems mandatory. "You should level with the agent," said Milton A. Marks of the Marks Travel Service of Dayton, Ohio, who is chairman of ICTA and a past president of ASTA. "Don't play games. Every once in a while we get someone who wants to go to Tokyo, then a few minutes later to Scandinavia, and then to South America. We stop him right there. The client may complain, 'You cut me short,' but who's got time to go waltzing around the world? He would do better to say 'I've got two weeks vacation in October, and I don't know where I want to go.' "

Ask an agent about tour packages and cut-rate air fares. A package is not necessarily a group tour; rather, it may simply mean that if an individual traveler buys a certain combination of transportation, accommodation, meals, and frills, the cost of each element is substantially lower than if arranged separately.

Do not hesitate to check out the agency with ASTA, whose national headquarters are at 4400 MacArthur Boulevard N.W., Washington, D.C. 20007; phone (202) 965-7520, or with your local Better Business Bureau. Such organizations will at least tell you whether any complaints are outstanding against the agency.

Determine what fees, service charges, or cancellation penalties may be faced. While agents depend largely on commissions, they frequently charge clients for telex messages and long-distance telephone calls and sometimes for preparing a complicated individual itinerary.

If you plan to travel far, find out what service the agency can provide you when you get there. American Express and Thomas

Cook have their own offices in many countries, but many smaller companies have capable representatives in distant places who will treat the traveler from afar as ably as they treat their own clients.

If you feel the least bit uncomfortable, go someplace else. Shop around. It may take a lot of time, but in the end it could mean the difference between a costly disaster and the fulfillment of a dream. Things can go wrong on the best-planned trips, and sometimes even the best travel agents, like all human beings, goof. But if, after you return home, the agent seeks you out for your frank assessment of what was good and bad, at least you know that you are on to someone who is trying hard and who cares.

Most travel agencies, whether large or small, perform a wide variety of services. They arrange transportation, accommodations at hotels or resorts, sightseeing, auto rentals, participation in all-inclusive escorted tours, admissions to theaters and sporting events, and even meals at leading restaurants. They sell insurance to cover person, baggage, or penalties if you have to cancel a trip because of illness or an immediate relative's death. They help obtain passports and visas, and they advise on what clothes to take along, where to shop, and whom to tip and how much.

Most of these services are free because the travel agent receives a commission from the vendor. The overall benefit to the traveler, therefore, can be tremendous. One visit of perhaps half an hour to a travel agency can set the process of arranging complicated vacation plans in motion. All the phoning around for reservations and the preparation of tickets and vouchers are the agent's responsibility.

But as the travel field expands, as it has been doing almost steadily in recent years, it becomes more and more difficult for agents to know everything they feel they should to provide sound advice. Many complain bitterly, for example, of the problem, even with computers, of keeping abreast of the persistent and ever-changing rash of cut-rate air fares.

Yet besides personal knowledge, an agent has many sources of information, and a competent one uses them. They are not simply the brochures on the rack, which are essentially advertisements that do not always give a balanced picture. The best tools, rather, are computer systems, an assortment of costly directories and qualitative reference materials, trade publications, attendance at meetings and seminars, and participation in "familiarization trips" that are arranged for the trade at nominal rates.

Sarah Marquis is a firm believer in "fam trips." When she was eighty years old, she toured the Dordogne region of southwestern France, where, she says, she gained ten pounds on pâté and other delicacies. Earlier that year she visited India and Sri Lanka on such trips.

Opinions of the experts differed substantially about whether the average traveler should use a small agency or a large one or one that specializes or one that does not. Some said a small agency tended to give more personalized service, often because the owner deals directly with clients.

Gilbert Harouche, president of the Liberty chain, contended, however, that only a large agency such as his with highly computerized resources could zero in on the most popular destinations and have specialists who assembled all available material on those places and how to get there at the lowest fare. He said such material, in constantly updated manual form, is provided to all Liberty salespeople.

Some smaller agents conceded that they could not always muster as much influence as they would like. "If a client decides at the last minute to go to Barbados at Christmas," one said, "it helps if the agent has clout with the airline that flies there. Sometimes you can get favors. It's not supposed to be that way, but it's true."

A travel agent is often referred to as he. In fact, more are shes. Situations differ, but a newcomer to an agency is often a recent high school graduate, hired as a receptionist and typist. The hope that she may soon qualify for the free or cut-rate travel accorded agents often compensates for long hours and a relatively low salary, perhaps $8,500 a year to start.

Eventually she graduates into ticket-writing, counseling clients, and making reservations. She learns how to use trade directories and computers. An enlightened agency that can afford it may encourage, even require, her to take courses to improve her knowledge and expertise. Typically, after two years in an agency or perhaps with an airline, she is considered qualified to call herself an agent.

Some women and men start as outside sales representatives— usually part-time and often without salary—generally selling tour packages. The agency that employs them writes the tickets and makes their reservations, splitting the commissions with them. In two years, they, too, may be considered qualified by the trade.

Two years of agency experience is commonly ample for a person of good character to qualify for official appointments by air and cruise lines to sell their tickets. Agents with such appointments are in demand, often to manage agencies for entrepreneurs who buy into the field but lack the experience to be accredited on their own.

Agents take advantage of free or subsidized travel as much as they can—often to enhance their familiarity with distant places more than to enjoy—but office chores tend to limit their time. Many of them continue studying in their spare time and eventually earn the designation certified travel counselor.

But all this does not necessarily make a good agent. Sometimes the owner of an agency is especially well informed and astute, but not necessarily all his employees are. And sometimes it is the other way around.

I once had an agency arrange three months of complicated travel for me in Eastern Europe. Because I am a travel writer, the owner insisted on carefully tailoring my itinerary and making all the reservations herself. She performed admirably. But when she insisted on writing my tickets herself—the sort of chore she almost always delegated to others—she erred badly. She transposed flight numbers for one leg of my journey, an error I caught at the Kennedy check-in counter but barely in time to prevent my baggage from being shipped to Buenos Aires instead of Budapest.

How a competent and imaginative travel agent can help with the complexities of foreign travel was illustrated when a colleague of mine decided to go to Israel as part of a month's vacation. She found that at that time she could go from New York to Tel Aviv and back on El Al for $649. When she asked her travel agent to arrange a stopover in London, however, she learned that this would put her in another category and the fare would be $940. Two stopovers—one going and the other returning—would have raised her fare to $1,479, and greater flexibility would have cost $2,514.

With the help of her agent, however, she found that she could fly by charter to Europe for as little as $175 one way. She could go by train to Ancona, Italy; take an Adriatic ferry from there to Piraeus, the port for Athens; tour Greece and the Aegean islands at leisure for a week or so; then take another ferry to Haifa. She could be just as flexible on the way home. Her total transportation cost would probably approach a thousand dollars, but she would see more of the world than she could for that price by air alone.

The bottom line for the traveler is that an agency is only as competent as the skills of the particular counselor with whom you deal, and these can vary widely in the same office. Also, it is always prudent to examine tickets and hotel vouchers with great care; after all, it is you who are taking the trip, not your agent.

Modern Times

A few years ago you could walk into most travel agencies, plot a detailed itinerary for an extensive overseas vacation, and expect an expert to make all the arrangements for you for the same price you would pay if you did it all yourself. The agent would get commissions on sales but nothing else. Today, however, you may have to do it yourself because many agents lack the wherewithal to help or are unwilling unless you are a regular customer who provides them with substantial business.

"The newer agents usually sell package deals," said Walter Plaut, a Manhattan agent who was deeply involved with travel from the time he first piloted a plane in Germany in 1913 until he died in 1984. "You have to go to someone with experience in working with details. Many newer agents don't know these details. And unfortunately, preparing a detailed itinerary can take a long time."

Time is probably the most important factor for travel agents today. Most of them simply do not have enough of it. Until the United States Government embarked on airline deregulation a few years ago, it was relatively simple, for example, to calculate air fares: They were uniform on most routes. Today there are all kinds of fares and all kinds of rules and restrictions to govern them. Some fares are here today and gone tomorrow, and, based on the degree of competition, it is sometimes much cheaper to fly a long distance than a short one.

Computers are supposed to deal with such complexities, but they often lack up-to-the-minute information, and they cannot make judgments. Therefore, many agents spend an enormous proportion of their time writing air tickets and often rewriting them so clients can benefit from sudden fare reductions such as those offered recurrently on flights between the Northeast and Florida.

"I ask myself, what is my time worth?" said Doris Dichek of Better Travel in Mamaroneck, New York. "It can take two or three hours to price an itinerary. And for how much commission, seven or ten percent?"

Interviews with a dozen agents produced this pattern:

- Although it is still uncommon for agents to charge, more of them are adding $10 or $15 per booking to your bill for making arrangements such as reservations at small foreign hotels that do not provide much if any commission. Telex or long-distance telephone charges are commonly charged to the customer.

- If you are not a repeat client or are not prepared to commit yourself immediately, you may be asked for a nonrefundable deposit of $50 to $100. "We have to weigh whether someone who walks in or calls in is serious or simply shopping," Mrs. Dichek said.

- If you walk into an agency where you are not known and ask for help with a complicated itinerary, you are more likely to get short shrift from agencies in the midtown areas of Manhattan, Chicago, and other cities than you are from those in suburbs or small towns. Some midtown agencies will accept clients only on the recommendation of other clients. Also, many downtown agencies concentrate on lucrative commercial accounts and are wary of time-consuming individuals who may not be prospects for repeat business.

Asked what American Express would do in Manhattan, Hugh Gallagher, former vice president in charge of the company's retail travel operations in the East, said: "If someone comes in off the street and says, 'Hey, I want a super el cheapo, stripped-down vacation,' we'd probably discuss it a bit to determine what you want to do, then suggest that you call on the appropriate government tourist offices to get folders and write directly to the people abroad."

John J. B. Miller, who runs Magic Carpet Travel in Kerrville, Texas, said the attention he would pay to a walk-in's complicated request would depend on "how busy we are."

"If I have the time," he said, "I might sit down with maps, because I like to do it. But if we're busy in here, I don't have the time to deal with it." Mr. Miller added: "But Kerrville is a small town and good will is important. Here in Kerrville, if we make someone mad, they'll spread it all over town."

The American Society of Travel Agents, according to a spokesman, "has tried to make agents as customer-responsive as humanly possible." But he added: "There aren't two agents alike in the country. What one will do, others won't do."

In Manhattan and other urban centers, some of the most respected agencies do not advertise widely but add clients through personal recommendation. The Hardach Travel Service, on the 30th and 36th floors of 500 Fifth Avenue in New York, is "locked up where nobody can find us," as the general manager, J. Henry Riefle, puts it. Hardach is essentially a highly computerized specialist in commercial accounts, but its vacation department, Mr. Riefle said, has "our most experienced agents, those less addicted to a computerized operation."

4. The Air-Fare Maze

Few things can be more frustrating than trying to find the lowest possible air fare to suit one's needs and taste. It is a bigger challenge than most individuals and even many travel agencies can successfully meet, even with highly sophisticated computers. Even the experts often produce different answers, and to become an expert requires a rare combination of skill at the computer plus intimate, up-to-the-minute information on rules, restrictions, and meet-the-competition offerings that have not been entered into the computer systems. You have to know—or know how to find out—which airlines go where, at what points they interconnect, and whether they are actually operating the flights they promise.

Let's concentrate here on travel in the United States. A few years ago, before airline deregulation began during the Carter Administration, buying a ticket was relatively easy. What you paid was usually in direct proportion to the distance flown. Every change in price or route had to be approved in advance by the Civil Aeronautics Board.

Where more than one airline served the same route, each had to charge the same fare for the same category of service. For example, American's one-way fare between New York and Los Angeles had to be the same as United's and T.W.A.'s. If American offered a reduced-rate round-trip for passengers who paid for their tickets at least three weeks in advance and agreed to stay away at least seven days, its competitors were committed to the same rate and same restrictions if they offered such passage.

About the only competitive edge that airlines could have in those days was in amenities. This meant that if Delta chose to serve steak and free champagne to coach passengers between New York and southern Florida, Eastern did not have to follow suit, although it probably would.

But since passage of the Airline Deregulation Act in 1978, all this has gradually changed. Except in a few areas, such as aircraft safety, how to handle overbooking, and how to control smoking aboard planes and protect the rights of nonsmokers, the airlines have been virtually freed of government regulation. The C.A.B. went out of existence at the end of 1984, and the airlines are free to set their own fares and add or drop routes, the only exception being that certain routes that the government considered essential must be maintained. Rules can be changed at will, although every carrier is supposed to have its current ones readily available at ticket counters for public inspection.

Even under deregulation, however, airlines that fly within the United States and from this country abroad have held to the custom of protecting passengers against any price increase between the time a ticket is paid for and the time of departure. It behooves you, therefore, not just to reserve early but also to pay for your ticket as soon as you can. If the price is reduced before you fly, you are entitled to a refund. But if you try to change your itinerary in any way after buying your ticket, your price protection ends.

Price protection, however, does not necessarily mean that your ticket provides the cheapest way to get from Point A to Point B. Rather, the burden is heavily on you or your agent to sleuth out the most convenient routing and the most economical fare and determine whether they jibe with your plans. If not, it is up to you or your agent to find the most appropriate compromise.

An airline may advertise that you can go from Washington to Houston, say, for $99 one way, but when you read the small print you may find that the fare is good only Tuesdays and Wednesdays on flights leaving after eight P.M., that seats are "limited" (which means there may be only a handful at that price), and that the fare expires in two weeks. Because seats at bargain prices are usually limited, it often happens that one economy-class passenger is seated next to another who has paid three times as much.

Five days before Mother's Day in 1983, sorely ailing Continental

Air Lines, badly in need of cash, announced that any woman who bought a round-trip ticket anywhere on its system before the next Sunday could do so at half price. The ticket would be good any time before December 15. The offer meant, for example, that a woman who planned a round-trip between Philadelphia and Seattle, a new Continental route that already was being promoted with bargain fares, could do so for only $168. How many travelers seized upon the offer is not known. What is known, however, is that before many of them took their trips, Continental sought protection under Chapter 11 of the Federal bankruptcy law and temporarily suspended service, rendering many of the tickets useless.

In these days of deregulation, marrying a low fare to the needs of a traveler can be delicate. By no means is cheapest always best. A lot depends on what time of day and which day of the week you are willing to fly and whether you mind a few stops en route or even a couple of changes of plane. No expert suggests that to save a dollar you spend two days on a journey that otherwise might take two hours. But if a couple of hours more or less do not make that much difference and you do not have a lot of luggage to haul from one plane to another, you can sometimes save a lot with a creative trip design.

The more competitive a route is, the more likely you are to find bargains on it. Fares are likely to seem sky high (no pun intended) where there is no competition. (One of the principal shortcomings of deregulation is that many American cities lost air service completely because carriers felt the amount of business did not justify service by even one of them.) Sometimes, however, you will see the most intensive price cutting when a carrier begins service on a route that had previously been the monopoly of another.

Unfortunately, creative trip design is not a feasible do-it-yourself exercise unless doodling with air fares is your passion. Some travel writers suggest that you ask a travel agency or airline ticket office to let you browse through the latest North American edition of the *Official Airline Guide,* a semimonthly compendium of domestic timetables. With the *OAG,* you can match your departure city with your destination and find schedules covering most ways to get from one to the other—nonstop, multistop on the same plane, or with connections. It is suggested that you then phone the airlines involved and compare fares.

Even the *OAG,* however, has difficulty keeping abreast of frequent route changes. And it won't tell you, for example, that if you are going from Los Angeles to Dallas, it might be cheaper—as it once was because of a temporary promotional fare—to buy a ticket from Los Angeles to Miami on a plane that stops at Dallas on the way and simply get off there. And any suggestion that you phone the airlines yourself presumes, of course, that you can quickly get through, which you often cannot.

In late 1983, I asked "Maggie" at Air Florida by phone for the cheapest one-way fare from White Plains, New York, to Miami that would be in effect on Wednesday, January 11. She quoted $139 for two direct flights that day, both via Washington. A travel agent had tipped me off, however, that it might be cheaper via La Guardia in New York, and after checking further, Maggie agreed that for travel after December 15 on three days each week, including Wednesdays, I could buy two Air Florida tickets, one from White Plains to La Guardia for $15 and the other on a convenient connecting flight from La Guardia to Miami for $109, or a total of $124.

The tip about this had come from Richard Russo, a fare specialist for Traveltron of Irvine, California, a nationwide service that specializes in helping clients, many of them travel agents, get the best deal possible. According to Thomas Davis, vice president, the company uses the computer systems sponsored by American Airlines and Trans World Airlines and the Airline Tariff Publishing Company, an independent concern that monitors fare and rule changes. In addition, he said, Traveltron's fare specialists maintain personal contacts with other agents across the nation.

Considerably more sophisticated are the electronics at the disposal of Gelco Travel Services, a rapidly growing network of agencies based in a suburb of Minneapolis. James F. Hare Jr., senior vice president, described the company's Fare Automated Search Technique—FAST, for short—which has access to all the major airline computer systems plus other sources of information on possible fare and route changes and steps that airlines may be thinking of taking but on which they have not yet announced plans. Because of its size, a company such as Gelco can sometimes coax seats out of an airline that a smaller concern cannot.

Some agencies have joined in cooperatives or consortiums through which they exchange information, but many small travel agencies are not computerized at all. Unless they specialize in certain destinations and certain types of trips, such as cruises or group tours, the lack of automation can severely impair their service. Most computerized agencies have only one system—generally Apollo, which is sponsored by United Airlines; Sabre by American; or PARS, T.W.A.'s Passenger Automation Reservations System. Most systems also have co-hosts, such as smaller airlines or auto rental companies, and until recently a travel agent often had to scroll through many screenfuls of listings of schedules and fares on the computer to get beyond those for the sponsors. This, obviously, took time, and many agents resented it.

Computers often lag days behind on fare changes—occasionally even by host lines—or show that seats at certain fares are sold out on nonhost airlines when actually some are available because of cancellations. "That's when you have to phone the airline," said Sarah Marquis, the longtime Manhattan travel agent. "But sometimes you can phone and get several rates from the same company. You need experience in this field to know if a rate sounds too high and to question it."

The figures that follow are out of date, but they illustrate what experts might produce. Mr. Russo of Traveltron and Shelly Bormes of Gelco recommended "best possible" fares and routings for leisure travelers between several pairs of cities specified at random.

To get from Monroe, Louisiana, to Chicago, for example, Miss Bormes said the best published routing was from Monroe to Dallas via Delta for $80 and from Dallas to Chicago via Midway for $99 for a total fare of $179.

But she added from her personal knowledge that Republic and Delta had heavily restricted round-trip excursion fares of $229 between Chicago and Monroe, and that under an unpublished "match the competition" offering, Republic would fly a passenger one way from Monroe to Chicago at half that, or $114, with almost no restrictions. Mr. Russo's best Monroe-Chicago fare was $175, but his suggestions seemed the more appropriate on other routes.

For the leisure traveler in search of the best deal, several points should be kept in mind:

- Be as flexible as possible in your tour requirements. Some fares may be valid Thursday but not on Wednesday, for example, so give your travel agent maximum latitude.
- If you can book far enough in advance and stay away long enough to meet the requirements, do not overlook "super saver" and other restricted fares because they are often

cheaper than anything else. But remember that such fares are typically "blacked out," or unavailable, during holiday periods when travel is heavy anyway. Also, if you cancel a restricted ticket, you may be subject to a penalty. If you cancel and later change your mind and want the ticket back, chances are the bargain fare will no longer be available because either your place has been taken by somebody else or the airline has decided not to reoffer it at that price.

- If you are considering a stopover or two on the way to or from your destination, ask whether they are permitted at all at the proposed cheapest fare and, if they are, whether they are free or at additional cost. Also, remember that some round trips permit a stopover or two in one direction but not in the other.

- Ask about standby fares. They are not always offered and not always the cheapest way to fly, but sometimes they are substantial bargains. They typically involve going to the airport several hours in advance without a reservation and being permitted to fly at a reduced rate if seats are available. If you plan to go standby, however, beware. Only a small proportion of seats may be available on that basis, and airline secrecy has made it difficult for travelers to learn the exact number.

- Sometimes it is cheaper and less trouble to go by road for one leg rather than fly. From White Plains to Miami, for example, you can sometimes do best to take a minibus or drive to Kennedy or Newark and fly nonstop from there, depending on promotional fares in effect.

- If you find, as Mr. Russo said you once could, that the cheapest way to get from Los Angeles to Dallas, say, is to buy a ticket to Miami and get off en route, be careful about your baggage; you probably will have to carry it on board to keep it from being sent to Miami.

- If you plan to use multiple airlines, be sure they have an interline agreement before you try to check bags from your point of origin to your destination; you may have to reclaim and recheck when you change planes.

Changes

With air fares subject to dramatic change, the prudent traveler keeps two points in mind. First, if a fare is reduced after you have paid for your ticket but before you fly, you are usually entitled to a refund. Second, once your reservations are confirmed and the ticket is purchased, you are usually protected against any increase in price before you go.

The word *usually* is important, because there are exceptions. And as Rosemary Cole found, getting a refund is not always straightforward.

Miss Cole, whose home is in Leonia, New Jersey, was a student at Evergreen State College in Olympia, Washington, when her problem arose. To bring her home one Christmas, her father paid the Landesman Travel Service of Fort Lee, New Jersey, $299 for a round-trip ticket on Western Airlines between Seattle and New York. He mailed the ticket to his daughter.

Before her departure, however, Western lowered the fare to $249. Miss Cole called Western's toll-free number and was told she could get the refund from the airline in Seattle or, because she was sixty-five miles away, could try a travel agent in Olympia. So she went to Act Travel there, where she was told that under trade regulations, an agency could not refund a ticket that it did not sell. The agency was right and the airline wrong.

Western, however, quickly gave her $50 in cash when she checked in at Seattle Airport for her flight. But at a very busy time, she might have had to arrive at the airport perhaps two hours early and wait in line. Even then, the counter clerks might have been too busy to deal with refunds, and she might have been left with the sole alternative of seeking her money by mail—a process that a spokesman for Western said could have taken two months.

When you warrant a refund, be aware that the initiative is usually up to you. Sometimes an alert and considerate check-in clerk will point out that you paid more for your ticket than you should have and will help you obtain an adjustment. Often, however, clerks are much too preoccupied with verifying your flight number and destination, checking your baggage, and issuing a boarding pass and perhaps a seat assignment. If you spot a newspaper ad or article about reduced fares, do not wait for the airline to call you and volunteer a refund.

"Once you become aware of a lower fare than you paid, call the airline and see if you can get it," William D. Berry, then manager of public relations for Delta, said. "I remember one day on which we made almost a hundred fare changes across our system. We're just like a major department store now."

Processing a refund may require substantial paperwork, including voiding your old ticket and issuing a new one. For example, it might have delighted you to take advantage of the "kids fly free" programs that Trans World and Eastern Airlines offered briefly a couple of winters ago. But every child's ticket on those lines that you bought before the offering but had not yet used had to be rewritten.

Harriett Emerson of Emerson Travel in Manhattan, a national director of the American Society of Travel Agents, estimated that it cost $7 to $9 in time and labor to adjust an air ticket. "It's an unconscionable mess," she said, "and a burden that can't be productive."

Ronald A. Santana, head of two travel agencies in the New York suburbs and president of the Association of Retail Travel Agents, said many agents, unlike the airlines, take the initiative to go through their files when a fare is reduced and track down clients who are entitled to refunds—a chore he termed "above and beyond the call of duty." He said the airlines' "lack of foresight in setting fares and rules is a major problem."

Ellie Fine of Fine Travel in Providence, Rhode Island, said many of her clients are "snowbirds," who winter in Florida condominiums and summer in the North. They typically order their air tickets in early fall, she said, and one year she pointedly collected payment and issued them all before December 1, when a 5 percent fare increase was to take effect. Then the major airlines abruptly reduced their fares to Florida to $99 one way, and all the tickets had to be rewritten.

Experiences such as these distress travel agents greatly. To add to their discomfort, some airlines send debit memos to agents, downgrading commissions to the applicable percentage of the lower fare.

However, getting a refund when a reduced fare carries restrictions can be tricky. For example, Delta once advertised: "Just show us any published fare on any other major airline to any domestic U.S. Delta city or San Juan. We'll sell you a Delta seat at the same price, with the same qualifications, as long as the supply of our discount fare seats lasts."

Read that one carefully. It meant that if you already held a Delta ticket and learned that another carrier advertised a lower fare to the same destination, the flights had to be equivalent, such as both nonstop or both one-stop, both at the same time of the week, and both at roughly the same time of day.

It also meant that only a certain, undisclosed number of seats on each flight would be available under the offer. So you might well have been denied a Delta refund. It could have been too late, meanwhile, to switch to the cheaper airline.

If you are convinced that you merit a refund because of a fare change, call the airline to find out the best way to get one. If the line permits it and it is convenient, it is often best to take your ticket to an in-town office of the airline and be reticketed while you wait.

If you originally paid in cash, you can often obtain a cash refund or a check. If you paid by charge card, a credit form will be prepared for the card company, with a copy to you. If you paid by check, you may receive a cash refund on the spot if the amount is under $25, but sometimes the refund must be processed through the airline's accounting office to be sure your check has cleared.

If your air ticket involves several flights and different airlines, and especially if it includes foreign travel, the refund procedure is more complicated because of the way interline rates, particularly international fares, are calculated and prorated. In such case, you will probably have to file a refund application and wait three weeks or more for a check by mail.

Under existing practice (until January 1, 1983, it was a Civil Aeronautics Board rule), all United States carriers protect you against fare increases between the time you pay for your confirmed reservations and the time you fly, provided you make no change in your itinerary. This is also generally true across the Atlantic, but ask the appropriate airline about it to be sure.

Elsewhere abroad, however, a different general rule applies. Under this, you are subject to whatever fares are in effect on the day you begin your journey. If you are ticketed for a series of flights, all the fares are protected from that first takeoff day, even if many airlines are involved, but not before. Among other things, this means that unless you keep abreast of fare changes after you buy a ticket abroad, you could be hit by a whopping additional bill when you check in at the airport. Ponder what this might mean if you do not have the money or a charge account to cover it.

Extras

The day may be approaching when many arrangements that air travelers have traditionally taken for granted decrease sharply or disappear.

For example, on some trips it may not always be possible to do these things:

- Work out with a travel agent or airline a detailed itinerary involving three or four carriers, have the agent or originating airline make all your reservations for you, and have all your flights covered by the same book of ticket coupons.
- Check your bags at the airport where you begin your journey and forget about them until you collect them at your destination, even if you have changed airlines on the way.
- Have a flight coupon quickly endorsed for use on another airline flying the same route, should a departure be delayed or should you decide that the other airline's schedule is more convenient.
- Expect that, if you are aboard a flight that is just late enough for you to miss a scheduled connection, the airline will ask the connecting carrier to delay its departure a few minutes so you can catch up.
- Take advantage of what the trade calls joint fares, under which the total cost of flights from A to B on one airline and from B to C on another is less than the sum of the fares for each leg.

All these conveniences result from interlining, the term applied to the use of more than one airline to reach a destination or complete a journey. But the cooperative arrangements that make such amenities possible are imperiled by deregulation and by sharpened competition among airlines and their need to cut costs.

It is extremely doubtful that all such amenities will disappear, but it is likely that arranging interconnecting air travel will become more complicated, for your travel agent, at least, if not for you, and that travelers will have to make sure they understand carriers' rules about such things as checking baggage and connecting with other airlines.

It is clear—from testimony before the Civil Aeronautics Board in the last year or so before it went out of business, and from interviews with airline executives—that some form of interlining will remain, especially on major routes. But on some heavily used short routes, such as in the Northeast Corridor, some airlines are already avoiding it.

For example, People Express, based in Newark, operates without interline agreements, saying the saving from this policy helps it keep ticket prices low. The same policy is followed by the Muse Air Corporation, an airline operating between Texas and the Far West, and Southwest Airlines, which serves the Southwest and pioneered the opposition to interlining, to simplify procedures and cut costs.

Your benefit in this trade-off is lower prices. In some cases—for example, if you are making a one-day round-trip from New York and have no baggage—this may be highly beneficial. People Express, which has undercut or forced down the fares of its competitors, says it keeps costs down by issuing its tickets aboard the aircraft, charging $3 for each checked bag (while providing larger-than-usual space for carry-on luggage), putting more seats on each plane (meaning, of course, less leg and shoulder room), and serving no hot meals, only beverages and light snacks for which it charges extra.

"An airliner is not a flying restaurant," Gerald Gitner said when he was president of People Express. He now is a vice chairman of Pan American.

Mr. Gitner and other executives of airlines that cater primarily to passengers who go from embarkation to destination on only one flight say interlining adds to basic overhead expenses and, therefore, fares. They cite the costs of setting up and maintaining the systems—no matter how much or how little they are used—to arrange multiflight reservations and multicoupon tickets, to transfer baggage, and to apportion fares among more than one carrier.

"Why," Mr. Gitner asked, "should the person going to Boston for a two-hour lunch have to pay so you can take your baggage on an overnight trip?"

On the other hand, defenders of interlining say, a lessening of amenities may place a heavy burden on those baggage-laden travelers who have to make one or more connections on a single journey. It could be increasingly important to plan travel carefully: to find out exactly what ground services can be expected from specific airlines and to alter travel habits to make any increased hassle as light as possible.

Suppose your trip involved travel on both a carrier that participated in interlining and one that did not. Suppose you took People Express, which does not subscribe to interlining agreements, from Newark to Washington, had a luncheon meeting there, and flew to

Charlotte, North Carolina, by Eastern in the late afternoon. If you arranged your trip through a travel agent, he probably would have used a standard multicoupon ticket of the type approved within the industry for interlining. People Express would have accepted a coupon made out to it, and you would not have had to get a new ticket in Washington for the Eastern portion.

You would, however, have had to reclaim any baggage upon arrival in Washington, take it to Eastern to see if it could be checked in early or arrange to store it during lunch and check it with Eastern later. You might have been able to pay a skycap to do some of this for you, if you could find one.

If you boarded your Newark-Washington plane without a ticket, as many passengers do, People Express would have accepted payment for only its flight; it would not have sold you an interline ticket with a coupon good on Eastern. You would have had to be reticketed in Washington for the leg to Charlotte.

If you returned to New York the same way, with another meeting in Washington en route, you might have been able to check your baggage through from Charlotte if Eastern agreed to deliver it to People Express in Washington, but this is unlikely and risky. Some airlines at some airports will do this; others will not unless both connecting carriers participate in interlining.

Central to interlining is the system of joint fares, under which connecting carriers agree on how much will be charged for two or more legs of a journey and how the revenue will be apportioned among them. Under the Airline Deregulation Act of 1978, Congress actually tightened one aspect of Federal control by requiring that a joint fare system imposed by the Civil Aeronautics Board be available to commuter airlines as well as larger carriers.

One reason that a joint fare on a journey with three legs, for instance, is less expensive than the total cost of the three legs if purchased separately is the limitation on what are called terminal fees. Each time you buy a separate air ticket, a terminal fee—an accounting device that covers such overhead items as processing, rent for waiting rooms, and use fees imposed by the airports on the airlines—is built into the price. For an interline ticket, however, you pay only the terminal fee of the airport where your trip begins, not of the connecting ones. Thus, the more legs to your interline trip, the greater your probable savings compared with buying each leg separately.

Penny-Wise Planning

Perhaps nothing better illustrates the recurrent competitive confusion in the travel business than air fares between the Northeast and Florida. The confusion illustrates the need to shop around exhaustively or to consult The Best Travel Agent in the World. It illustrates the strong advantage of examining the fares not just for the fastest routes but also for indirect routes that may take a little longer but save you a lot of cash.

Unfortunately for Irwin Alters, an eighty-five-year-old retired physician who lives in Hollywood, Florida, he could not be flexible enough. He and his wife, Beatrice, planned to attend a wedding in Philadelphia and they wanted to fly Eastern, which had nonstop service from and to Fort Lauderdale, a short car ride from home. They could stay away only a few days, however—not long enough to qualify for a round-trip excursion fare.

When they phoned Eastern and then Delta, which had one-stop service between the two cities, they were told that the economy fare was $270 each way—or $71 more than Arrow Airways, a small carrier, was charging at that time between Miami and New York in first class. Airline clerks suggested, however, that the couple could fly from Fort Lauderdale to Newark for only $109, and rent a car to drive to Philadelphia. If they had been younger they might have, Dr. Alters said, but such a trip would have been too taxing. Ultimately they settled on the now-defunct Air Florida, which offered them one-stop evening service to Philadelphia for $125 one way midweek and $133 on a weekend.

Because of the heavy competition and volume of travel, there is almost always a "special" between somewhere in the Northeast and somewhere in Florida—perhaps five or six cities at each end at the same time. In one period of price-cutting, a New Yorker could have flown to leading Florida destinations in any coach seat on any flight of any major airline from any of the three big metropolitan-area airports for $99, or $9 less than Eastern was charging for a comparable unrestricted coach ticket from New York to Richmond, Virginia, which is a quarter of the way to Miami.

Each year the major airlines that ply the Atlantic seaboard try to restrict the deep discounting to off-season, such as in the late spring, in the fall, and the period between the week after New Year's and around the second week of February, when peak season begins. Despite all such intentions, one carrier, big or small, usually breaks the price line at the height of season when it is supposed to be a seller's market, and the competitors scramble to slash fares, too, not to be left behind.

Similar situations exist elsewhere in the country—between San Francisco and Los Angeles, for example, or between California and Hawaii. But nowhere does the recurrent zaniness seem as intense as between the Northeast and Florida. Often the distance you travel has absolutely no relationship to price. And sometimes if you are flying from or to New York, the fare can vary depending on which airport you use and the day of the week on which you fly.

For example, in August 1983 Pan American would have carried you nonstop between Miami and Newark for $99 any day of the week, between Miami and Kennedy International for $119 midweek or $139 weekend, and between Miami and La Guardia for $139 or $159. Eastern's minimum matched Pan Am's for Kennedy and La Guardia but was $139 or $159 for Newark. Delta was not flying directly between the New York area and Miami but had nonstop service to and from Fort Lauderdale. Minimum fares were $109 to or from Newark any day, but from $10 to $20 more to or from La Guardia or Kennedy, depending on the day of the week.

Air Florida, meanwhile, was charging $139 or $159, depending on the day of the week, between Miami and La Guardia, but only $135 or $149 between Miami and White Plains, its other gateway in the New York area. Piedmont, however, would have flown you between Miami and either Newark or La Guardia for only $99 one way any day, but you would have had to make one or two stops on the way and sometimes change planes. Or, between Newark and West Palm Beach, you could have flown People Express for $99 during peak hours and $69 off-peak.

Because of such low-cost service and the possibility that People Express would expand, the major airlines were reserving their biggest bargains for routes that they considered the most competitive with that maverick carrier. "The fares right now have no logic to them as far as relationships between them are concerned," James R. Ashlock, director of the news bureau of Eastern, said at the time. "The only factor today is to try to gain a competitive edge. Eastern has markets where the yield per mile is twenty-five to twenty-seven cents; in other markets it's seven cents—all because of unbridled price competition." William D. Berry, then manager of public relations for Delta, was even more explicit. "Newark is the base of

People Express," he said, "and if Delta's going to stay in the marketplace and compete against People Express, we're going to have to take a more competitive position at Newark than at La Guardia or Kennedy. It's simply the competitive marketplace."

You can almost always expect deeply discounted fares to be suspended around major holidays, when many people feel a need to travel, regardless of price. A couple of years ago, for example, you could have gone from New York to Miami for $99 on, say, December 10 or January 11, but if you had gone southbound within three days before Christmas or northbound within three days before New Year's, your coach fare would have been $269 each way.

For the winter leisure traveler to Florida, one lesson is obvious: the more flexible your vacation dates, the greater potential benefit for your purse. Here are some pointers to consider:

- Avoid traveling around holidays if you possibly can.
- In seeking air bargains, look beyond the major lines. Several new small companies have entered the scene, some of them operating from relatively small airports, such as MacArthur Field near Islip, Long Island, and Atlantic City. Also, check newspaper travel section advertisements and ask your travel agent about charters.
- If you have the time, consider going by train or even by bus, preferably with stopovers to ease the trip and allow you to enjoy cities such as Charleston and Savannah en route.
- Examine family plans; some airlines and Amtrak allow a head of household to be accompanied by spouse and children at reduced rates.
- Investigate auto rental offerings, many of which are part of packages that include air fare. But be aware that sometimes you can go cheaper without obligating yourself to rent a car and that the Florida auto rental market is so competitive that you may do better when you get there than by committing yourself in advance.
- Weigh the possibility of driving your own car. Based on figures provided by Peyton E. Hahn, vice president for public information of the Automobile Club of New York, a couple could drive from New York to Miami for about $400 one way, including all expenses, on a trip taking three days. With a couple of children and perhaps a grandparent or two

along, the per-person cost diminishes sharply, and the opportunities for sightseeing on the way are limited only by your available time.

- If you contemplate a long Florida stay, consider shipping your own car with one of the many Northeastern companies that specialize in that service. They send it by rail or highway carrier or have someone drive it. Check the *Consumer Yellow Pages* under "Automobile Transporters and Drive-Away Companies."
- Consider package plans that include air fare and accommodations at your Florida destination. They have proliferated, particularly in the Orlando area, where lodgings of all sorts have likewise spread rapidly in recent years.
- Consider combining a Florida vacation with one to the Bahamas or the Caribbean. The Bahamas are readily accessible from Florida by both air and sea, and it is easier and cheaper for a Northerner to reach some islands there or in the Caribbean via Miami than directly from New York. Also, most winter cruises from the Eastern seaboard originate and end in southern Florida.

5. "Creative" Air Travel

It does not happen very often, but sometimes it is cheaper to buy a round-trip air ticket even if you are going only one way. Such would have been the case not long ago if you had flown United Airlines between Sacramento, California, and Raleigh, North Carolina. The normal one-way coach fare was $427. But for passengers who could travel on a Tuesday or Wednesday and buy their tickets at least fourteen days in advance, United also offered a round-trip for

$328. Thus, a one-way traveler could have thrown away the return portion of the ticket and saved $99.

This is only one of many examples these days of unorthodox ways to save money on air travel. They are perfectly legal, although the airlines obviously do not advertise them. Neither do many carriers seem to be trying very hard to stop them, however, because they bring in at least some revenue.

"There is really no way to police it and really no way to track it either," said David Lobb, director of public relations, marketing, for American Airlines. What is happening is primarily an outgrowth of airline deregulation. Competition among carriers, both large and small, has grown intense in many parts of the United States. Routes are being realigned frequently, and the introduction of a new service is typically accompanied by temporary promotional fares intended to attract business. In international travel, the savings can be much larger than on domestic flights. This is partly the result of different fare structures in different countries and partly of being able to pay for some travel in foreign currencies, a distinct advantage if the dollar is strong. As always when dealing with air fares, be warned that specific fares quoted below—both international and domestic—are given only as illustrations and will undoubtedly be outdated by the time you read this.

The round-trip saving between Sacramento and Raleigh was turned up by Richard Russo of Traveltron in Irvine, California. Another example he cited was between Sacramento and Madison, Wisconsin. The lowest one-way fare on United was $347, requiring purchase of your ticket at least three days before departure. But if you could buy your ticket at least fourteen days in advance, travel on a Tuesday or Wednesday and stay away seven to fourteen days, Frontier Airlines would sell you a round-trip for only $329.

While no one says you have to use the return portion of a round-trip ticket, you could not get a refund because refunds are usually the difference between the round-trip and one-way fares, and in this case the one-way fare was higher. And giving the return portion to someone else to use is illegal because the ticket is in your name.

A more common way to save money on domestic flights is to take advantage of what the trade calls flyover, point-beyond or hidden-city ticketing. For example, not long ago the normal one-way coach fare between San Francisco and Atlanta was $420 on nonstop flights of Delta or Eastern. But Delta was selling seats on the same flight to Tampa, Florida—a point beyond Atlanta—for $179. Thus, a San Franciscan bound for Atlanta could have saved $241 by buying a ticket to Tampa and simply leaving the plane at its first stop.

Such a passenger could have had only carry-on luggage, however; anything else would have had to be checked through to Tampa and could not have been claimed in Atlanta. Also, if the passenger wanted to return to San Francisco, he could not buy a ticket originating in Tampa, because he would not be embarking there.

These were other recent alternatives:

- A one-way ticket on USAir from Dallas-Fort Worth to Pittsburgh cost $270. But on the same flight, you could have been ticketed to Grand Rapids, Michigan—a point beyond the first stop at Pittsburgh—for only $129.
- One way on a United nonstop flight from Los Angeles to Chicago cost $389, but to Tampa, a point beyond, the price was only $209.
- One way from Hartford, Connecticut, to Philadelphia on USAir cost $112, but to Baltimore, a point beyond via a connecting flight of an affiliated commuter line, it could be as low as $49, depending on day of the week and availability of seats.

Seat availability is important if you want to play the point-beyond game. The lowest-priced seats on many flights are capacity-controlled, which means that only a limited number are available. If that category is sold out but the entire plane is not, you have the option of paying a higher price or going some other time.

Some major travel agencies shun point-beyond travel. "We think it's unethical," said David K. Hillman, vice-president, finance and administration, of Thomas Cook Inc. in New York. "We do provide the lowest possible domestic fares in a timely and reasonable way, but we really don't promote getting around the system. If the airlines condoned flyovers, they would have a regular fare to match the advantage." Mr. Hillman said that if a customer asked for a $129 Dallas-Grand Rapids ticket via Pittsburgh, Thomas Cook would sell it, but would not volunteer the information that a Dallas-Pittsburgh passenger might save $141 by being ticketed to Grand Rapids.

But Paul Cardoza, general manager of the Palo Alto, California, office of the nationwide Gelco Travel Services, took a different view.

"We're not here to cheat the airlines," he said, "but we must dig out the best fares for our clients. Sometimes cheapest is best, but sometimes it's the convenience of the route."

To some fare sleuths, what is called hidden-city ticketing for international flights is even more intriguing. At one time not long ago, a one-way ticket from New York to Frankfurt cost $739 in economy class on Trans World Airlines. But you could have bought a New York-to-Zurich ticket on a flight via Frankfurt for $600 and simply have gotten off in Germany at a saving of $139.

The saving can be even greater in business class, which many companies use for employees traveling abroad on their behalf. For example, in early 1984 it cost $1,034 to fly T.W.A. from New York to Paris in business class but only $702 to go New York-Paris-Brussels, theoretically switching in Paris to Air France.

When the dollar is strong in relation to major European currencies, it can pay to take advantage of what is called reverse ticketing. For example, instead of buying a round-trip ticket between New York and London, payable at the dollar rate, you buy two one-way tickets, paying in dollars for the outbound trip and in British pounds to return home. The lowest one-way dollar fare on British Airways in January 1984, for example, was $388, but the British fare of 199 pounds converted to only $284. A computerized travel agency could have gotten that return ticket for you before you left home.

A note of caution, however: If you can comply with restrictions on advance purchase and length of stay, you can usually do better with the lowest possible round-trip fare payable in dollars. Also, fares from the United States are protected against any increase between the time you pay for your ticket and the time you travel; fares from Europe usually are not.

Price Wars

Here is how a major price war developed after deregulation freed the nation's airlines from most government control:

The major trunk routes between East and West Coasts—those between New York and Los Angeles and New York and San Francisco—had long been dominated by three airlines: American, United, and Trans World. Until early 1980, there usually was enough business to please all.

As an outgrowth of deregulation, however, there suddenly were seven carriers in the field, the newcomers being World, Capitol, Eastern, and Pan American. Cutthroat price reductions began to develop early in the spring of 1980, with World, which advertised itself as David fighting Goliath, in the lead in an attempt to recoup losses from a long strike. The rest of the pack quickly followed, and other lines began to take initiatives.

The biggest jolt came from Eastern, which entered the New York-California market that June 1 with several flights a day. It offered all its coach seats unrestricted at $99 each way through June 30. Its "big three" competitors—American, United, and T.W.A.— quickly matched this fare, but they balked when World lowered its fare to $88.

For the airlines, such warring was potentially disastrous. June is the beginning of high season for coast-to-coast travel, and in previous years airlines did not have to offer bargains in that month to attract traffic. So it was not a question of filling planes.

Rather, for the big three it was a matter of maintaining their position in the market. For the newcomers, it was a matter of establishing a position. For all lines, as their officials readily admitted privately, the cost was intolerable, but so was the thought of losing out to the competition.

For most travelers that June between New York and California, the minimum fare was the cheapest in twenty years on a major airline on that route. For those who had bought their tickets in advance at what was then a nonpromotional, unrestricted fare of $195 one way, it meant getting a substantial refund. A few June travelers lost out, however, and in an odd way.

They were people who had bought "super saver" round-trips, which have usually been the cheapest form of domestic air travel and were heavily promoted as such. They required advance purchase and had minimum and maximum restrictions on how long you might stay.

Some New Yorkers went to California on "super saver" tickets before the $99 fare was introduced. While away, the unrestricted $99 fare suddenly came in, and they found themselves holding restricted tickets that cost $70 to $90 more, depending on whether they traveled by day or night, than a round-trip at the unrestricted $99 one-way fare.

To cash in the return portion of a "super saver" ticket and buy a $99 ticket to get home, however, would have involved paying a penalty that might have raised the total price of the round trip as much as $26 above the original "super saver" fare.

When a Group Isn't

When Michael Michaud got his immediate family to go to France for two weeks to celebrate his parents' fortieth wedding anniversary, he did exactly what he would have done if he had been going alone. There were twelve adults and eight teen-agers in the party, so he went to an airline ticket counter and bought twenty round-trip excursion tickets between Detroit, their home city, and Paris.

He did not know—because nobody had told him and it had not occurred to him to ask—that the party was entitled to a group fare that could have saved him several hundred dollars. He also did not know that as an alternative he would have been eligible for a cut-rate tour-basing fare if he had arranged for hotel accommodations in France at the same time that he bought the tickets.

Group fares are not always available; they come and go in different marketplaces, depending on how airlines, their home governments, and their trade associations view the possible ways to fill planes. In the United States, you can usually do as well if not better with individual advance-purchase round-trip excursions. If at least four people are traveling together, however, it is worth asking about group travel.

Similarly, you will commonly find that major resorts, urban hotels, and car rental companies have arrangements under which, if you buy your flights and at least some land arrangements as a package, you are probably entitled to a tour-basing fare, even if you are traveling alone. In almost every brochure of a major tour packager, such as Gogo Tours, Caribbean Holidays, and Travellers International, you will find that each offering has a code number preceded by the capital letters *IT* for *independent tour*. This means that a purchaser of the offering is entitled to some sort of tour-basing fare.

Some airlines will not discuss such fares with travelers directly because they consider it more efficient to let a travel agent or wholesale tour packager deal with the details of putting a group together or selling an air-land combination. Question your travel agent carefully about what is available; if you have put together a group, many thousands of dollars may be at stake, and you deserve utmost value and quality. Even if you do not have a group of your own, your travel agency or one of its wholesalers may have enough people going to the same place on the same day to qualify for a group rate. Often you do not all have to return home together.

When you think of group travel, you may conjure an image of "If It's Tuesday, This Must Be Belgium" in which thirty or forty dazed tourists are hustled on and off buses by impatient guides. Some groups are like that, but many others are virtually invisible. On some flights you will have no way of knowing who is traveling at a group rate unless you ask every passenger, and even then, some may not know what you are talking about. Sometimes the creation of a group is simply a bookkeeping device to enable the airline to fill empty seats by establishing a category in which remaining space can be offered at a bargain rate.

6. Charter Flights

Travel by chartered jetliner has become an increasingly significant fixture on the American vacation scene. It is not to everyone's taste, and when something goes wrong, the dreams of several hundred passengers can quickly turn to acute distress. But with each added year of experience, charter operations in general become smoother and offer some of the best travel bargains around.

In short, charter travel, predicated on cramming a plane with the fullest load possible and thus minimizing the price each passenger must pay, has made it possible for hundreds of thousands of Americans to afford vacations that previously were far beyond their means.

For example, in early 1983 it became possible to go from New York to Rio de Janeiro and back on a DC-10 chartered from Pan American World Airways and spend seven nights at a Rio hotel, all for $499, plus 15 percent for service charges and most taxes, or a total of $573.85. If you went on a Pan Am scheduled flight, however, your round-trip from New York at that time would have cost $1,412 for economy-class transportation alone unless you were prepared to stay at least fourteen days in Brazil and paid for your ticket at least three weeks before leaving home, in which case you could have taken advantage of a $1,059 excursion rate.

How could the charter operator do it?

"Rio was never a mass market for American tourists," Arthur Berman, president of Vacation Travel Concepts of New York, said. "We were never able to talk to the hotels there to get a rate that would allow a mass market to develop. But in 1983 things were different. Many Argentines used to come up to Rio for vacations, but then the inflation in their country prohibited it. This meant that many hotels in Rio faced a grim year."

So, Mr. Berman said, he was able to negotiate tremendous hotel bargains. As for transportation, the charter operator pays a flat negotiated rate to the airline for a series of round-trips. The plane that takes one load to Rio takes home the load that it brought a week earlier.

"They gave us a tremendous break," Mr. Berman said of Pan Am. "We were taking a whole plane and guaranteeing income to them, regardless of how many seats we sold."

Lewis Robinson, originally a part owner of V.T.C. and now president of the Carefree David Travel Company, a major charter operator, said the per-seat cost to a tour operator, predicated on a full planeload, might be only 30 to 35 percent of the normal economy fare. On that basis, a round-trip seat from New York to Rio in 1982 and 1983 might have cost the charter operator as little as $420. Any loss leaders that were offered to the public were supported by the substantial profits the charter operator could make from selling packages that included luxury accommodations at much higher than minimum tour rates.

Charter travel is not arranged by the airline that flies you but by middlemen such as Mr. Berman and Mr. Robinson, who are known as tour operators. The tour operator charters the plane from the airline and handles the marketing himself. He decides how much to charge you, how far in advance you must book, what penalties to levy if you cancel, and what kinds of meals, drink, and other amenities the airline will provide in flight. Sometimes the tour operator even handles the check-in procedures at the airport and is the one to whom you must turn with any questions. This practice generates many consumer complaints that representatives of the tour operator are often hard to find or that there are much too few of them to handle check-ins efficiently.

Charter travel to foreign countries cannot be arranged at the whim of the tour operator, however. His programs, landing rights for the airline that flies them, and often the fares must be approved by authorities at the destination. This can involve substantial negotiation, resulting in considerable difference from country to country.

Until recently, Scandinavia and Japan were among the popular tourist destinations that did not permit American charters at all. But Britain, France, and Greece have let charters undercut scheduled fares sharply, although recently the trend has changed. Ask a travel agent for comparisons.

Because most charter flights operate only once a week, they can attract full loads on routes that a scheduled airline could not possibly fly every day at charter rates.

"We determine what day the passenger is both going and returning," one major charter operator said. "This is something that cannot be done on scheduled flights. So our control over seat utilization can save the passenger fifteen to twenty-five percent on air fare alone. In addition, mass purchasing permits us to obtain hotel rooms at twenty-five to forty percent below normal daily rates, and the greater part of this saving goes to the passenger."

The pricing formula of charters obviously calls for virtual sell-outs. If many seats go empty, an operator can face financial difficulty and even ruin. For this reason, some charter operators drastically reduce prices a few weeks before departure if seats are not selling well. Some, such as International Weekends of Boston, openly advertise "sales" in newspaper travel sections. Others quietly notify travel agents of the reductions, since most charter seats are sold through agents, or offer blocks of seats to "consolidators," subwholesalers who sell them through travel clubs (to which members pay perhaps $25 to $50 a year) or directly to the public. A few operators will even sell tickets to airport standby passengers at even greater reductions on the theory that no matter how little you get for a seat, it is better than leaving it empty.

Such practices have been responsible for substantial ill feelings toward charter operators by fraternal, religious, and social organizations that committed themselves to substantial blocks of seats perhaps a year or more in advance of a charter's departure. To obtain a large block and market it successfully to members, they had to commit themselves far ahead of time. Sometimes, however, as departure date nears, the charter operator cuts the price to below what organization members paid but gives no refunds. A common excuse to organizations that complain is that when an auto dealer or clothing dealer cuts prices, it always affects only future sales, not past ones—although the way charters are marketed is obviously far different.

The lesson in all this is clear: In charters, at least, buying later may be better than buying earlier. There is a risk, of course, especially around holidays and at the beginning and latter part of summer, that a charter will quickly sell out, but often space is available at the last minute to either your preferred destination, or a comparable one. If you can make vacation plans on short notice and your departure and return dates can be flexible by a few days, so much the better.

The term *charter* can evoke diametrically opposite feelings among air travelers. To some, it means taking a chance: risking late changes in departure arrangements, arrivals at unexpected airports, switches in hotels, misdirected baggage, no responsible person to whom to complain, and little or no recourse after returning home. There is no question that such problems do occasionally arise; in fact, almost all have been known to occur on the same trip. And when four hundred people are simultaneously suffering the same plight, word of their collective misery often gets noisily around.

To other travelers, however, a charter means a sound bargain—an opportunity for travel that otherwise might be far beyond their means. Millions of Americans—nobody knows exactly how many— have flown charter since a change in Federal regulations in 1978 made them available to the general public rather than just to selective groups. Most charter trips go relatively smoothly, and the aficionados of that sort of travel are increasing rapidly.

In summer, the principal focus is Europe and Israel, although Japan and other Asian points may enter the market soon. In the winter, the main focus is the Caribbean. Mexico and Hawaii are popular—the latter especially from the Midwest and West Coast— much of the year.

Unlike scheduled flights, charters are subject to cancellation by the operators up to ten days before departure because of inadequate participation. "No one is able to guarantee departures," said Arthur Frommer, a pioneer in the charter business. "But we are all aware that to maintain our position as tour operators, we have to keep cancellations to a minimum."

In summertime, many problems have resulted from the unruly nature of the European charter business. In wintertime charter travel to the Caribbean or Mexico, passengers usually go and return in the same group, typically staying away for one week. Summer charters to Europe, however, are often tailored to demand, with different passengers arranging to return from one to ten or twelve weeks after departure.

Even with computers, this practice complicates the problem of coordinating planeloads, especially for the trip home. According to trade reports, overbooking problems and long delays have arisen in midsummer when a great many passengers seemed to be returning home much earlier than charter operators had predicted.

Colleen Zarich, deputy executive director of the nonprofit Council on International Educational Exchange, which operates a major charter program, said it takes "fairly sophisticated planning, beginning very early in the year," to predict summer loads and determine how many planes to charter. She said airlines were often lenient in adjusting charter contracts, for example, allowing a smaller plane to be substituted for a larger one or permitting the number of departures in a week to be cut from, say, three to two. As an example, she said C.I.E.E. might have contracted to fill three 250-seat DC-8's from Paris to New York in one week but might have sold only 580 places. So, she said, it might reduce the flights to two and put eighty passengers on the charter of another operator or even on a scheduled flight.

It is this sort of change that frequently causes problems at airports. The more responsible charter operators have ample staffs to handle them quickly and have competent representatives in Europe to keep returning passengers well informed.

When you ask a travel agent about charters, be aware that while different operators' programs to the same destination have inevitable similarities—in fact, sometimes they share the same chartered plane—there are always differences. Some will sell air only—an advantage for vacationers who prefer to stay in small guesthouses or condominiums—while others insist that you also buy hotel packages.

If you want a land package, you should know that at some

destinations some charter operators have more impact than others and that a lot depends on the clout and efficiency of the local ground operator, or representative upon whom they depend for airport-hotel transfers, sightseeing if included in the package, and maintaining a presence to whom travelers can turn if something goes wrong. Few charter operators have their own staffs at the destinations to which they fly.

Buying a charter package, incidentally, does not necessarily tie you to a group, although some are escorted tours. Other packages allow you to buy only transportation and lodging; otherwise, you are on your own. On some charters you must go and return with the same group. On others you have the option of staying away from a few days to many weeks or months.

Some European countries, such as Britain and Italy, have forbidden one-way charters because they do not want their own residents to use them to go to the United States instead of taking a scheduled flight on the national carrier. Some charter operators openly defy this rule, however, and sell one-way tickets from the United States, though often not at half the round-trip rate, but at $50 or so above that, just in case the seat cannot be sold for the return trip. A few operators allow you to "mix and match"—fly to one European city and return from another—but sometimes this practice is responsible for substantial overbooking at some airports and long delays for passengers waiting to get home.

While some operators will deal with you directly, many deal only through travel agents, although they lean toward eye-catching advertisements in the press. From your standpoint, it is best to work through a travel agent who is familiar with charters and is willing to shoulder the often frustrating burden of trying to reach the operators on the telephone (unlike scheduled flights, charters normally cannot be booked through computers). Many agents say they do not deal with charters at all because of the nuisance involved and because some clients insist on traveling with the least reliable operators because of price. Many bigger travel agencies readily sell charters, however, and the wise traveler will heed their advice.

Here are some questions worth asking your agent. What is the charter operator's record? How long has he been in business, and how well has he fulfilled his promises? Does he seem financially sound? Exactly what will you get for your money? If you buy a package, what sort of accommodations are available at minimum rate? Can you upgrade for a higher charge, and if so, how will the price then compare with what you would pay for a package by scheduled flight?

Here are other questions to ask the agent, along with probable answers.

Which airline—major or supplemental—will operate the flight?

This could make a difference, since the bigger the line, the better the prospects for servicing and substituting planes if necessary and the smaller the risk of long delays. You need have little worry about safety, however; charter flights must conform to the same safety regulations as scheduled services. In any event, the flight crew does not want to be killed any more than you do.

But despite whatever initial information you get, airlines, aircraft, or both are often substituted within a few days of departure if it becomes clear that consolidation of flights is advisable. Under Federal charter regulations (subject to amendment by the time you read this), schedule changes of less then forty-eight hours in international charter flights can be made right up to departure time.

Another possibility in the consolidation process is the scrapping of plans to operate separate charters to London from, say, New York and Philadelphia. Instead, they may be combined to use one plane, which would take off from one city first and stop to pick up additional passengers at the other. Still another possibility is that if there are still many empty seats when it is too late for the operator to cancel a charter departure, the operator may make a deal with the airline and switch the passengers to a scheduled flight.

What happens if your departure is delayed by an act of God?

An example was the big East Coast snowstorm in February 1983 at the height of the Caribbean, Mexican, and Brazilian tourist season. Will you be compensated for loss of time? Probably not. If your return is delayed because an act of God kept the charter plane from picking you up on schedule, will you have to pay extra to keep your hotel room? Probably yes, if the room is available at all.

Federal rules at this writing say that under more normal circumstances, an international charter departure may be delayed up to forty-eight hours and a domestic charter flight up to six hours before the airline must produce substitute transportation or you must be offered a refund. In some cases when a long delay seems likely, the airline alone or together with the charter operator pays any added cost of getting you aboard a scheduled flight, reasoning that this is cheaper than paying refunds.

Do not automatically assume, however, that if an international delay is less than forty-eight hours you are not entitled to compensation, even though the charter operator need not offer it. Court action in at least two New York cases—*Irving Trust Company* v. *Nationwide Leisure Corporation* and *Feuer* v. *Value Vacations*—has determined that a charter operator may be liable for many failings, including flight delays, though not for physical injury or property damage.

What happens if the return flight is canceled when you are far from home?

Charter operators have gone bankrupt at awkward times. Under rules at this writing, you could be placed on a scheduled flight at no extra expense to you. However, this could be subject to long delays and delicate negotiations unless the scheduled carriers flying the route have many empty seats. No airline will willingly bump paying passengers to make room for you, who must be carried free.

What are the penalties if you cancel shortly before departure?

On some charters, they are 100 percent. Ask what sort of cancellation insurance you can buy; what it will cover and under what circumstances you can collect.

If you take two small children with you, will they get a reduced fare, as on a scheduled flight?

Probably not, because charter bargains are predicated on filling as many seats as possible at full rate.

What protection, if any, do you have against surcharges, whatever the reason?

Under charter rules at this writing, surcharges are permitted ten or more days before departure, and they have sometimes been imposed when fuel prices have been rising. But if the surcharge is more than 10 percent you have a right to cancel and get a refund. Passengers have sometimes complained, however, that although the charter operator contended that a surcharge had been announced well in advance, they knew nothing about it until they checked in for departure.

If a flight is delayed, will the tour operator assume responsibility for feeding and lodging you and keeping you well informed until takeoff, or is the buck likely to be passed between him and the airline?

Probably the latter. And if the delay is long, will the tour operator assume the cost of sending you instead on a scheduled flight, an alternative that was sometimes permitted by the Civil Aeronautics Board? If not, the alternative may be a severely impaired vacation.

Because of the uneasy economic situation of most major airlines, the gap has narrowed considerably between the type of service you can expect in the economy section of a scheduled flight and on a charter flight. On both flights, the seating will probably be as tight as possible, the principal difference being that charters rarely have a first-class section.

As for in-flight service, a lot depends on how much the charter operator is willing to pay. The major carriers insist, however, that they cannot afford to serve inferior meals on charters because it would reflect on their overall image. On some charters, movies and drinks are on the house, while on scheduled flights, passengers in bargain seats have to pay extra for movies and drinks. If it matters much to you, ask your travel agents about such amenities before you commit yourself.

If business is so bad that the operator cancels a charter a couple of weeks before departure, you will be entitled to a full refund. It may be too late, however, to get on another charter, if there is one, to the same destination or to meet the advance-purchase restrictions of the lowest scheduled fare. This emphasizes the importance of finding out as much as possible about the operator's record before you part with your cash.

7. Escorted Tours

To many travelers, the ultimate tour is one on which you do not have to worry about anything.

Someone else is concerned with all your long-distance transportation; getting you to and from airports and on and off buses, cruise ships, and trains; providing you a room with bath and many if not all meals; carrying and keeping track of your luggage; making sure you see all the prominent sights and the best local shows; steering you toward the best shops; and, occasionally, allowing you time to rest.

Such is the promise of the escorted tour, and so it has been for generations. These days, however, there are so many of them, often advertised in thick, colorful brochures that you can pick up free at travel agencies, that it can be difficult to choose. At first glance, many of them seem similar—and some are. But if you read the brochures with an incisive eye and ask a travel agent about anything unclear, you will quickly find that differences can be tremendous.

The backbone of most escorted tours is a deluxe bus. Most tour operators prefer to call it a motor coach, but to me the word *bus* is hardly pejorative and is much easier to express. Short bus tours are discussed in the section on buses. They tend to be relatively simple, but longer tours—a week to a month, say—can be extremely elaborate and expensive. Some tour operators also use other forms of transportation: rail, ship, airplane, even helicopter, and sometimes a combination of several of them on the same vacation.

As a general rule you will find that in escorted tours, as in almost anything you buy, you get what you pay for. This does not necessarily mean that expensive is good and cheap is bad; what matters is to get the best value for your dollar, according to your taste. Prices on European tours range from about $30 to $270 a person a day plus transatlantic air fare, which is usually at the lowest available scheduled rate but sometimes by charter.

You may want to be pampered and may have the money to afford it. Or you may find some of the frills on the costliest tours to be much more than you could possibly want or need. Some hotels may be much too lavish for your budget or taste. Some sightseeing may be too rigorous or too steeped in a cultural pursuit that barely interests you—or, at the other extreme, it may be too once-over-lightly.

Many travelers disdain any hint of being shepherded around—the "If It's Tuesday, This Must Be Belgium" syndrome. Some of them, however, can afford and insist upon the best of two worlds. One experienced New York travel agent, who asked not to be identified by name, told of clients who use escorted tours as the framework for individual travel.

"They don't want to be bothered with any of the detail," she said, "and they also don't want to pay for independent travel, which often costs more. So they go with the tour from city to city and stay at its hotels, but within each city they float around on their own.

"Of course," she added, "they don't get any refunds for those tour services that they don't use."

Augustus Bullock Jr., president of East Norwich Tours and Travel on Long Island, said older travelers are especially attracted to escorted tours. "It isn't just the ease," he said. "Many of them are afraid that if they go alone they may be right next door to something that they should see but miss it because nobody told them about it."

Pegge Hlavacek of TV Travel in Omaha said more women than men take escorted tours. "The main thing to them is a good tour guide," she said. "Maybe he will agree to take six of them out at night, and they'll go to some nightclub, and they'll just love it. Never mind all the museums, just get the single women out at night."

Hundreds of companies run European tours from the United States—from very big operators with wide varieties of tours to one-person shops in which the owner also does the escorting, often to different destinations each year to encourage repeat business. Bookings are usually made through travel agents, although some of the small operators use mailing lists or advertise in magazines or newspapers read by the type of people they hope to attract.

Among the big names that are usually found at or near the top of travel agency lists are Maupintour, Travcoa, Swan, Hemphill-Harris, Caravan, and Olson-Travelworld. American Express tours and Trans World Airlines's Getaway are often cited because they have different choices for different budgets and, in the case of T.W.A., because of the exceptional clarity in the brochure describing what you get and what you don't.

"Lifeseeing, not sightseeing—that's kind of our philosophy," said a spokesman for Maupintour. "We feel inclined to show a lot more of all those little places that people might not know about, such as lunch at a little vineyard out in the country, dinner at a floating restaurant, or coffee and homemade rolls at a country home in Switzerland."

Among other big operators—those that chip at frills and therefore charge less—are Travellers International, Cosmos, Globus-Gateway, Trafalgar, T.W.A. Super Saver, and Frames.

"People today are buying down," Jeffrey Joseph, executive vice president of Cosmos and Globus-Gateway, said. "They don't see the necessity of spending a lot on food, accommodations, and such. They want to spend the same amount of time and see the same things as anybody else, but they find they can go on a tourist-class tour and see just as much." He said the hotels used by Cosmos were often family-owned and quite small.

Some operators specialize geographically, such as Perillo, CIT Travel Service, and Central Holidays in Italy, although Perillo has recently expanded to Ireland and the Greek islands; Esplanade in Britain, France, and European cruises; Homeric and Tourlite in Greece; General Tours in Eastern Europe and the Soviet Union; and Bennett, Tumlare, and Four Winds in Scandinavia. Others focus on special interests, such as Dailey-Thorp in opera and music festivals, Swan in art treasures and Serenissima of London in history and exotica. Special-interest tours are often accompanied by guest lecturers—some of them prominent in their fields—as well as by professional tour managers.

The European escorted tour market is so crowded that those mentioned here are just a small sampling. At least as crowded is the market in the United States, where such already-mentioned names as Maupintour and Four Winds are joined by, among others, Tauck, Johansen, and Cartan. Other prominent operators specialize in Asia, Africa, and Latin America. To help you make a choice, the best advice can come from travel agents or from friends who have taken a similar tour.

"There are really very few companies that I would recommend sight unseen," said Sarah Marquis, the New York travel agent.

Of the half-dozen agents I asked about escorted tours to Europe, all agreed that the quality of the tour manager—the escort who accompanies the group throughout the European portion of the trip—was the most important factor in the trip's success. Many tour managers are professional teachers with long vacations; others are from a variety of backgrounds, but all the good ones have a deep, sincere interest in people. Good escorts are considered vital to repeat business; many experienced travelers often ask where a favorite escort will be next summer so they can go with him or her again.

A good travel agent will question you carefully about your budget, likes, and dislikes before recommending a tour; an agent you have used before and one you trust will already know some of the answers and probably a lot more about you that can help. Before you visit an agent, however, it is best if you define your interests, wishes, and limitations as closely as you can. It's foolhardy to talk about an art tour, for example, if you almost never visit a gallery or museum at home.

Question the agent and study the brochures for specifics on what is included and what is not, such as number and quality of meals. Ask about types and locations of hotels and whether you can check in immediately upon an early-morning arrival after a transatlantic flight. Ask about tipping, about whether all sightseeing is included or whether, in free time, you will be pushed into taking extra-cost "optional" tours. Ask whether shopping will be on your own time or whether a lot of the included "sightseeing" will actually be at stores selected by a guide. Ask about penalties if you cancel or interrupt a tour and insurance to defray the cost.

And find out the maximum number of people the tour will carry. Smaller tours usually cost more, but they will probably be more enjoyable.

Packages and Tours

Many people do not understand the differences between a vacation package and a tour.

A package, essentially, is any combination of two or more elements that go into travel. It can consist of only your air transportation and a rental car to use at the destination. Or it can consist of transportation and several nights at a hotel, or transportation and accommodations and car. To get more elaborate, it can include transfers to and from the airport at your destination and selected meals or a full dining plan. It can include a few hours of sightseeing or a cocktail party or both or a full range of events. It can even include a bus for travel from place to place as a group, with an escort to attend to your needs and show you around. At that point it becomes a full tour.

Therefore, a tour is a package, but a package is not necessarily a tour.

The person or company who puts together a travel package is commonly called a wholesaler. He acts as a middleman between the suppliers who provide the rental cars, hotel rooms, or whatever, and the travel agent, who sells the package to you. He is also commonly called a tour operator, however, even though he may primarily be a packager who operates nothing himself. But the people who actually conduct group tours, as well as package them, are called tour operators, too.

The main point to absorb from all this is that even if you abhor the idea of group tours, don't automatically rule out a package. It can leave you quite free to come and go as you wish but can be much cheaper than if you buy each element of your vacation separately.

The secret lies obviously in mass marketing. As an individual, you would probably be negotiating with a hotel for only one room; a wholesaler negotiates for hundreds, even thousands, throughout a season. His patronage alone may determine whether a hotel has a profit or loss for the year, so it behooves a hotel to discount its rates to him in exchange for his business. After adding a markup that allows for profit and a commission to your travel agent, the operator passes part of the reduced rate to you. The operator can also probably arrange with the appropriate airline to fly you to and from the destination at a reduced fare if you buy transportation and accommodations as a package.

Prepaid hotel packages priced in dollars have proliferated in recent years and can produce a substantial saving. They are available in many parts of the world, most notably Europe, the Caribbean, Mexico, and, of course, convention and resort centers in the United States. Most packages can be booked through travel agents, and some can be bought from major airlines and Amtrak as well. In the United States, many packages for stays of a weekend or longer are offered directly to the public by hotels; although advance reservations are usually required, you do not always have to prepay.

While prepaying for a package can sometimes save you much

money, it can have pitfalls as well. There may be a heavy penalty, often depending on whether your room can be resold, if you cut your visit short or cancel it at the last minute. Sometimes this creates a dilemma.

"What if you can't stand the hotel?" a Houston travel agent said. "I just came back from the Orient, and they said the hotel where I was booked in Singapore was one of the finest there. But I didn't like it, and I moved out after the first night. If I had had to remain there, it would have colored my whole view of Singapore, which, as it turned out, I thought was a really fine city."

Travel agents have plenty of hotel packages available in such cities as London; in fact, some relatively spartan but modestly priced and convenient hotels—the Tavistock in Bloomsbury, a central area of London, is one example—are almost impossible to book except through a travel agent. The reason: Virtually all their rooms are allocated to wholesalers.

Many hotel offerings, however, include all sorts of frills, such as extensive sightseeing and Elizabethan banquets. "If someone wants a full package, I have them," said Bernice Rosmarin of Edison Travel in Edison, New Jersey, "but I try to take the package apart and look at the components separately." Too many unwanted components, she and other agents said, can make the overall price uneconomical.

Conversations with travel agents, wholesalers, airline officials, and hotel representatives evoked near unanimity: While you might save money with accommodations that can be booked only through agents or airlines, you should carefully consider your own needs. These are some questions you should ask yourself:

- Does the hotel offering require that you fly one-way or round-trip on a given airline, and if so, must you commit yourself in advance to a specific itinerary?
- Must you pay the entire hotel bill in advance?
- Is your prepaid rate guaranteed if the dollar weakens? Might you get a refund if the dollar gets stronger?
- What happens if you do not like the hotel and want to change, or if you decide to leave the city early? Must you pay a penalty? How difficult will it be to obtain a refund for unused days?
- Does the hotel offering cover any room in the hotel, or is it limited to a specific type or price range? If you pay extra, can

you have a larger or more comfortable room or one with a better view?

Christmas Offerings

For most of us, Christmas is a time for home, family, and close friends. But for others it can be an especially rewarding time to travel. Many options designed to help travelers enjoy the ritual and traditions of the season are available at Christmas. They range from the very modest to the extremely posh. Some are particularly attractive to singles, others to couples and traditional family groups who want a different sort of Christmas.

Here, to give you a rough idea of what is usually available, are examples of tours and Christmas destinations that have been popular in the past. Wherever you are, your travel agent can probably help you find something similar this year.

The simplest and cheapest of the offerings is a one-day bus tour on Christmas itself. Such tours are not so numerous as might be expected because many bus drivers, guides, chefs, waitresses, and entertainers do not want to work on Christmas Day if they can avoid it.

In the New York area, however, and undoubtedly around other major cities, too, buses chartered by tour operators usually leave home base around eight or nine o'clock in the morning and return in early evening. For about $40 a person, a typical New York-based tour might go first to a year-round resort in the Poconos for use of its indoor and outdoor recreational facilities and for a holiday buffet luncheon that is included in the price. Then the tour might go to a ski area to walk around or sit in the lodge and watch others ski—there probably would not be time to ski yourself—and then back to New York with a wine and cheese party aboard the bus.

If Christmas falls on or adjacent to a weekend, a tour bus might pick you up a day or two before the holiday for a four-day excursion to a country inn near a ski area in Vermont—or Utah or Colorado, say, depending on where you live. Besides having a "traditional Christmas dinner," you might join in a tree-trimming party, be visited by Santa Claus with gifts, have a chance to roast chestnuts over an open fire, and enjoy entertainment ranging from a ride in a horse-drawn sleigh to a magic show and bingo. The cost of $250 or so would include transportation, lodging for three nights, and all meals.

Here are more ambitious samplings.

Colonial Williamsburg—The Christmas season at this seventeenth-century restoration in southern Virginia usually begins about December 15, and from then until January 2 or 3 there is no way you can forget what season it is. Every day has a round of Christmas entertainment that includes parades, concerts, exhibitions, and plays. A community tree is usually lighted on Christmas Eve, followed by music and entertainment in the Governor's Palace and your choice of a "Yuletide Supper" for $20 to $25, including entertainment, wine, tip, and tax, and subject to change, or a Christmas party with food, drink, and entertainment for about $25.

For many Christmas-season meals at Colonial Williamsburg, reservations must be made far in advance, preferably by December 1. For details, write to Colonial Williamsburg, Williamsburg, Virginia 23187; phone (800) 446-8956, or consult a travel agent.

Estimate your costs carefully. The restoration appeals especially to family groups, and although there are many budget-type hotels and motels off the premises, the overall cost for four, including lodging, meals, admissions, and transportation to and from home, can easily exceed $500 for three days.

Pennsylvania Dutch Country—The rolling hills of this prosperous farming area in southeastern Pennsylvania, about a five-hour drive from Manhattan, are replete with Christmas activities, but your choices can be simplified if you send $1 for a holiday information package to the Pennsylvania Dutch Visitors Bureau, 1799 Hempstead Road, Lancaster, Pennsylvania 17601; phone (717) 299-8901.

The Homestead and the Greenbrier—These two gracious resorts usually offer Christmas packages that lean heavily on traditional Americana, including lots to eat, drink, and do, both indoors and out. They commonly require three-day minimum stays in a period that begins December 21 or 22 and ends January 2 or 3. On Christmas Day they have holiday activities from early morning until midnight. Rates per person are in the $85 a day and up range, including meals but not tips and taxes. Addresses: The Homestead, Hot Springs, Virginia 24445; (800) 336-5771; The Greenbrier, White Sulphur Springs, West Virginia 24986; (800) 624-6070.

Mohonk Mountain House—This massive nineteenth-century inn and surroundings, popular among nature lovers, is two hours north of Manhattan. From just before Christmas through just after New Year's, in addition to caroling, burning the Yule log, and trimming the tree, you can hike nearby trails, ice skate, ski if there's snow, and go along on the annual Christmas bird census. Rates begin at about $65 per day, including meals, with a two-night holiday minimum. For details: Mohonk Mountain House, Lake Mohonk, New Paltz, New York 12561; (914) 255-1000 or (212) 233-2244.

Cruises—Some lines operating out of Florida and California and sometimes New York have Christmas cruises. Ask your travel agent for details. If you are single and want company or do not want to pay a supplement to occupy a cabin alone, Gramercy's Singleworld can help for a membership fee of $18 a year regardless of how many trips you take. The company has space on most Christmas and other major cruises. The address: 444 Madison Avenue, New York, New York 10022; (212) 753-7595.

International—Lavish holiday tours are available from some of America's most respected tour operators and travel agencies. Maupintour, an operator that sells through travel agencies, has in the past offered a two-week Vienna Christmas Gala and a Britain Christmas Gala from about December 19 to January 3. Both tours, which were fully escorted, left from New York at rates running upward from $3,000 a person plus air fare.

Dailey-Thorp Travel, 654 Madison Avenue, New York, New York 10021; (212) 486-9555, has offered holiday tours to Europe that have included tickets to musical performances, with rates beginning at about $2,700 plus air fare. Olson-Travelworld, which sells through agents, has had a sixteen-day Christmas tour to South America for $2,000 and up and a twenty-four-day tour through the South Pacific for about $3,500 and up, both plus air fare.

Meanwhile, the Catholic Travel Office, Suite 520, 1019 19th Street N.W., Washington, D.C. 20036; (202) 293-2277, has sponsored pilgrimages to the Holy Land with Christmas in Bethlehem, led by a priest-educator, for about $2,000, including air fare.

Doing It Yourself

In traveling abroad, situations occasionally arise in which, because of changing values of currencies, it is cheaper to make your own arrangements than to buy a package. These situations, however, may be difficult to predict.

Such was the case in Western Europe in recent years, when the value of the dollar was increasing in relation to local currencies. If you had made your own hotel reservation in Paris, for example, you might have had to pay an advance deposit, but your final bill would have been calculated in local currency at the time you checked out. Only then would you have had to convert dollars into francs to pay it—or you might even have been able to use a credit card and thereby defer payment until the dollar was even stronger (or weaker; it's hard to tell).

But travel wholesalers commit themselves to hotel rates many months before their packages are offered to you. The packages are priced in dollars, and those prices reflect the value of the dollar when the commitments were made. If the dollar strengthens after that, it means that the price advantage of your buying a package could be wiped out unless the hotel relieves the wholesaler of his commitment.

To illustrate: Suppose a wholesaler contracts for a block of Paris hotel rooms at a price to you of 480 francs per night per room. If the dollar is then worth 6 francs, the price to you becomes $80. At the time you use the room, the dollar may be worth 8 francs, which means that 480 francs is the equivalent of only $60. If you had not bought a package, you probably could not have gotten the room for the equivalent of $60, but you might have gotten it for $70, or $10 less than you, through your travel agent, paid the wholesaler.

In such situations, many European hotels have cut prices to wholesalers to retain their business, but because of the time necessary to adjust advertising and notify travel agents of changes, such cuts have usually lagged behind the increase in the value of the dollar.

It could work the other way, of course. If the dollar weakens between the time the wholesaler makes a commitment and the time you use the hotel room, your cost could be a lot less than if you had made arrangements yourself. Commonly, but not always, wholesalers' dollar prices are guaranteed.

8. American Rail Travel

To those who complain that rail travel in the United States is nothing like it used to be, Amtrak's reply, in effect, is, "Who cares?"

Under the leadership of its septuagenarian president, W. Graham Claytor Jr., who formerly headed the Southern Railway, the idea has been not to restore the past but to build a new type of rail network. Except for the 455-mile Northeast Corridor from Boston to Washington and the 128-mile stretch from Los Angeles to San Diego, Amtrak has virtually given up to the airlines the long-haul travelers who simply must get somewhere in the most expedient way possible.

Yet long-haul travel is essentially what Amtrak, the popular name for the government-subsidized National Railroad Passenger Corporation, is all about. Amtrak operates nearly all the long-distance trains in the United States. Its accent in rebuilding intercity rail service from the shambles of the 1950s and 1960s, when it all but collapsed under pressure of airline competition, has been on wooing the vacationer. In brief, the idea is this: Suppose it takes three days to go from New York to San Francisco, think of all you can see if you have the time. Or perhaps you can even take longer and visit a few major cities and national parks along the way.

Amtrak's biggest challenge has been in providing sufficiently comfortable service that vacationers will want to take the extra time. Although its on-time record has improved markedly in the last few years, some of its New York-Florida, New York-Chicago and Boston-Washington trains are subject to frequent delays. Food-service managers are persistently struggling to improve menus, both for snacks and full meals, but it is still often a guessing game as to how palatable your order will be. Some stations have been or are slated to be modernized—including Penn Station in New York, at a cost of $13.2 million, even though it was rebuilt less than twenty years ago.

For the present, however, to use the main men's rest room at Penn Station, a hangout for loiterers who obviously are not traveling anywhere, is like diving into a cesspool of perversion. At the North Philadelphia station, which Amtrak officials say they would like to close, much of the rest-room plumbing is perennially out of order and the escalators to the train platforms have not worked in years. In the waiting rooms of most large stations, keep close watch on your belongings, and do not turn them over to anyone who isn't clearly a Red Cap attendant.

As Amtrak copes with its shortcomings—and it seems to be progressing despite a rash of accidents in 1984—there are some gratifying lessons for vacationers who might consider seeing America by rail. Although you will be dealing with one unified network instead of a wide variety of airlines, there is a lot that you ought to know before you buy a ticket.

Unlike air fares, Amtrak's rates are not subject to sudden change, although increases have been common once or twice a year. On some routes, however, promotional fares make it important to consider the alternatives before buying a ticket.

For example, recent Amtrak tariffs showed fourteen different fares between Boston and New York. The basic one-way coach fare, good any time, was $35.50. At most times, however, you could do better. Except for certain blackout days around the Thanksgiving and Christmas-New Year holidays, Amtrak offered a one-way fare of $25 Mondays through Thursdays and $19 Fridays through Sundays. The same fare was also valid to or from Newark.

Amtrak also offered a thirty-day round-trip Boston-New York excursion fare of $45. Mondays through Thursdays it was cheaper for a round-trip traveler to buy this than two one-way tickets at $25 each. On weekends, however, it was cheaper to buy two one-way tickets at $19 each. In addition between one and seven P.M. on Fridays and Sundays the excursion fare was blacked out. During the holiday blackout periods, the round-trip rail traveler going alone had no choice but to buy two one-way tickets at $35.50 each.

For families, however, there was a loophole because family-plan fares were good any time. The head of a family traveling together paid the full one-way fare and the spouse and any children twelve or older paid half fare; younger children were charged one-quarter fare.

This meant that around Thanksgiving, when most discounted fares were blacked out, a family of four members over twelve could have made a round-trip from New York to Boston for $179—Amtrak rounds off certain figures in calculating discounts—or $105 less than the basic coach fare.

When there was no blackout, it was a toss-up whether to go by family plan, which was valid for a year, or thirty-day excursion. The family plan cost $1 less for four people than the excursion. The family plan was $21 cheaper on a round-trip for four people than using the special $25 midweek one-way fare but $27 more than using the $19 weekend fare.

If you are at least sixty-five years old and can prove it with a driver's license, Medicare card, etc., you can qualify for discounted fares on most Amtrak services. Using the Boston-New York example, the round-trip fare was $54 at this writing, but there were holiday blackout periods.

Most discounted fares are not valid on the New York-Washington Metroliners and some other popular trains where reservations are required. Check with Amtrak or a travel agent.

Amtrak recently reduced by $25, to $150, its All Aboard America fare, which allows a round-trip within one of the three north-south geographic regions into which it has divided the country. A round-trip embracing two adjoining regions was still $250, and a trip across the country and back was still $325. Tickets were to be sold at least through May 31, 1985, for travel through June 30. These fares were valid in sleeping cars as well as coaches, but accommodations charges were extra.

If you want to take your car from the Northeast to Florida and back but do not want to drive all the way, ask about the Auto Train, which Amtrak operates between Lorton, Virginia, near Washington, and Sanford, Florida, near Orlando. Also worth checking, depending on your plans, are the Week of Wheels auto rental tie-in in Florida and, in several parts of the country, circle-trip fares, which allow you to go via one route and return home via another. Through arrangements with tour operators, Amtrak also offers discounted hotel and sightseeing packages in many cities and even escorted tours by rail. Ask a travel agent about them, or write to get free brochures and, if you wish, a copy of Amtrak's national timetable, from the Amtrak Distribution Center, Post Office Box 7717, Itasca, Illinois 60143.

Beginning in late October 1984, Amtrak restored a long-gone

service intended to promote overnight travel between New York and Washington. Passengers in either direction are able to board sleeping accommodations at 9:30 P.M. for trains that leave much later. Sleepers may be occupied until 7:15 A.M. in New York—long after the train has left there for Boston—and until arrival in Washington, scheduled for 8:22 A.M.

There is a lot more to know about travel by Amtrak, and much of it is in the paperback *America by Train* by Ira Fistell. It contains practical information on the major cities served by Amtrak and tells, very briefly, what you will see along selected routes. The 463-page 1984-85 edition retails for $8.95 at larger bookstores and is published by Burt Franklin & Company, 235 East 44th Street, New York, New York 10017; phone (212) 687-5250.

If you really want to dig deeply into timetables, fares, services, and the rules that govern them, *The Official Railway Guide* gives it all plus comprehensive rail timetables for Canada and Mexico. It is issued eight times a year by the National Railway Publishing Company, 424 West 33rd Street, New York, New York 10001; (212) 563-7300. The price is $18 for one issue and $64 for a year.

Two paperbacks on what you will see from Canadian trains are Bill Coo's *Scenic Rail Guides*—one to central and Atlantic Canada and the other to western Canada. They retail for $9.95 each in larger bookstores and are available by mail from New York Zoetrope, Suite 516, 80 East 11th Street, New York, New York 10003; (212) 254-8235 or 420-0590.

9. The Eurailpass

The Eurailpass was twenty-five years old in 1984, and its sponsors say that more than two million people have bought it. The price has quadrupled since the first pass was issued March 1, 1959, but the options for using it have broadened substantially, and it remains one of the best bargains for the traveler in Western Europe.

The pass is a single ticket that, within a stipulated time period, is valid for more than 100,000 miles of first-class rail travel in sixteen countries. It is also good on many boat and intercity bus services. The longer the validity of the pass, the more you pay: fifteen days for $260, twenty-one days for $330, one month for $410, two months for $560, and three months for $680. If you are under twenty-six years old, you can buy a Eurail Youthpass for second-class travel: one month for $290 and two months for $370. Children four through eleven are charged half the first-class fare and those under four go free.

You can cover a lot of Europe in fifteen days. But as many travelers have found, a marathon on rails is rarely what an enjoyable vacation is all about. The secret to enjoyment is usually planning. This does not mean that you should commit yourself to an inflexible itinerary, but that you should ponder where in general you want to go, how much time you can afford to get there, who and what you plan to take with you, and whether a Eurailpass will provide the easiest and cheapest way to go.

These are some questions to consider:

Where can the pass be used?
It is valid on most rail lines of the sixteen sponsoring countries: Austria, Belgium, Denmark, Finland, France, West Germany, Greece, Ireland, Italy, Luxembourg, the Netherlands, Norway, Portugal, Spain, Sweden, and Switzerland. It is not valid in Britain, which has its own BritRail Pass with a choice of first-class or economy travel. Basic adult prices in Britain begin at $115 for seven days, with lower rates for younger people and those over sixty-five. Extensions of the BritRail Pass, at additional cost, permit you to sail between Britain and Ireland or the Continent.

Eurail travelers to and from Ireland can skirt Britain by using the pass to sail between Ireland and France, although they must pay extra to use a cabin. The pass is also good on many other sailings, such as across the Adriatic Sea between Brindisi, Italy, and Patras, Greece; between Helsinki, Finland, and Stockholm; and on lakes of Switzerland. The pass is not good on all such sailings, however, only on certain lines, so choose carefully. Also, port taxes are usually extra, and there is often a surcharge during peak travel periods.

The pass does offer reduced fares on many boat services and on certain Europabus routes, such as between Antwerp, Belgium, and Barcelona, Spain. But it is not valid on some private mountain railroads in Germany and Switzerland, such as the scenically dazzling Swiss cog line from Interlaken to Jungfraujoch, at 11,332 feet the highest rail terminal in the world, for which the round-trip fare is about $45, depending on the day's rate of exchange.

Where can the pass be bought?

The pass is intended to encourage rail travel by foreigners who might not otherwise use trains, so it is sold throughout the world except in Europe and North Africa. For Americans this usually means buying it in United States dollars before leaving home. You can get one through a travel agent or from any office in the United States of the French National Railroads, German Rail, Italian State Railways, or Swiss Federal Railways. All have offices in New York; check the Manhattan telephone directory for addresses and phone numbers or get numbers from directory assistance for the 212 area code. Also sold in the United States are the BritRail Pass, which has its own New York office, and unlimited-mileage passes for travel solely within Finland, France, West Germany, Ireland, Italy, and Switzerland. Ask a travel agent or the national railroad or tourist office in New York of any of those countries for details. Many European countries also sell unlimited mileage passes internally for use on their own railroads.

When and how does the pass become valid?

Within six months of the date of issue, it must be validated at any train information window before you board your first train. That's when the clock starts. It stops at midnight on the last day of validity, which means that you must arrive at your final destination by then.

Warning: Eurailpasses are not refundable if lost or stolen before validation or if you change your mind, say, after the first day of use and decide you have had enough. After validation, however, a missing pass can be replaced for the remainder of the valid period if you go to the nearest Eurail Aid Office with a copy of a police report on the loss plus your validation slip. Keep your validation slip separate from the pass itself.

How can I determine if a Eurailpass is for me?

If three or more people plan to travel together to many out-of-the-way places, it will probably be cheaper and easier to rent a car. If rail travel seems feasible but will be within one country, it will probably be cheaper to buy a pass sold by that country for internal use only. In addition to those one-country passes sold in the United States, similar tickets are offered internally for local currency by most European countries, with reduced fares for the elderly and students. Sometimes, however, you must be a resident of the country to qualify.

The Eurailpass Executive Committee calculates that for rail travel in at least two countries, a Eurailpass is usually cheaper than point-to-point tickets if you go at least 1,500 miles within fifteen days, 2,000 miles within twenty-one days, 2,400 miles within a month, 3,200 miles within two months or 3,400 miles within three months.

Looking at it another way, Dagobert M. Scher, assistant general manager for North America of the French National Railroads, noted that in the spring of 1984, one first-class round-trip cost $264 between Luxembourg and Rome, $266 between Hamburg, West Germany, and Vienna, and $320 between Paris and Copenhagen, compared with $260 for a fifteen-day Eurailpass.

Many Eurailpass fans say one of its best uses is not for long-distance travel but for one-day round trips from hub cities. In fact, some strongly advise the hub system so that you do not always have to seek new accommodations and carry luggage. Traveling overnight will save the cost of a room, but if you want a berth on the train you have to pay extra and you may miss some fine scenery.

Are there any other surcharges or pitfalls?

Yes. Most trains do not require reservations, but they are advisable in midsummer and are mandatory on the T.G.V. (*train à grande vitesse,* or high-speed train), which goes to forty-four destinations in France. You must pay a reservation fee on Trans Europ Express trains whether you book a seat or not, and you must buy either a boarding pass or have a seat reservation to ride an express in Spain. These surcharges tend to be nominal, but often you may encounter long lines unless you reserve at off hours sufficiently in advance. Seats usually can be reserved up to two months before departure and can be made through European railroad offices in the United States.

Baggage also can be a problem because checking often is time-consuming and porters and tote carts can be hard to find.

What literature can be helpful?

For a free Eurailpass brochure, map and condensed timetable, write to Trains, Post Office Box M, Staten Island, New York 10305. Two paperbacks that help you plan itineraries are the annually updated *Eurail Guide* by Kathryn Saltzman Turpin and Marvin L. Saltzman, which costs $10.95 at bookstores or $12 by mail from Eurail Guide, 27540 Pacific Coast Highway, Malibu, California 90265, and *Europe by Eurail,* by George Wright Ferguson, which costs $8.95 at bookstores or $9.85 from the publisher, Burt Franklin & Company, 235 East 44th Street, New York, New York 10017. Prices are subject to change. A useful companion to the Eurailpass is the Thomas Cook Continental Timetable, which is updated monthly and is available for $16.95 from bookstores that specialize in travel or by mail for the same price, including postage and handling, from the Forsyth Travel Library, Post Office Box 2975, 9154 West 57th Street, Shawnee Mission, Kansas 66201; phone (913) 384-0496.

10. Going by Bus

Some of the most extensive, least restricted, and most durable transportation bargains in the United States are to be found not on highly competitive air routes but in travel by bus.

For several years, competition has been extremely intense between the giants of the highways, Greyhound, a single company operating in all forty-eight contiguous states, and Trailways, a network of independently owned and operated bus lines dominated by Trailways Lines Inc. of Dallas. As each system strives to snatch business from the other and to develop new markets, the consumer is clearly the immediate gainer.

Cut-rate fares are being offered to dozens of destinations across the country. Many of them are effective for only brief periods and only between certain cities. All fares are subject to sudden change, and the special offers keep coming and going, so it behooves you to watch the advertising and to make sure at the ticket counter, before you part with your cash, that you have chosen the cheapest way possible to get from Point A to Point B.

Some reduced rates are for round-trips, others for one direction only. This means that occasionally it is cheaper to buy separate one-way tickets to your destination and back than a round-trip. Some reductions are restricted to students, some to the military, some to members of particular organizations, some to children, some to the elderly, and some to families traveling together. Sometimes there are unlimited-mileage passes good for a stipulated time in a stipulated state or region or throughout the country. Sometimes such passes are interchangeable between one bus network and the other.

Meanwhile, both networks are heavily promoting charter travel, with extra special rates and a variety of other incentives for groups. A typical bus holds thirty-nine to forty-six passengers, and your price advantage is greatest if you fill it. Your organization may prefer, however, to pay a bit more per person by carrying fewer passengers and having the bus company arrange more room between seats, tables between rows, and a bar for drinks and snacks while traveling.

Long-distance travel by scheduled bus in the United States is not everybody's delight. A crowded coach can be claustrophobic, especially when, as sometimes happens, your seatmate is jarringly short on deportment. Sightseeing on the interstate highway system can often be no more fascinating than peering into clouds at 35,000 feet. The food served at bus stops is often barely palatable. Rest rooms aboard buses sometimes lack water, soap, or towels—or all three; those in bus stations, and some of the people who frequent them, are often best left undescribed.

Because of its relatively low cost, however, bus travel can be distinctly advantageous for someone traveling up to five hundred miles who does not have to spend the night aboard and for whom a light lunch—possibly one brought along—will be sufficient. It can be an exciting, wholesome experience, meanwhile, for the vacation traveler who wants to see as much as possible within a week or a month and breaks the journey every night for the best dining, sightseeing, entertainment, and sleep available.

Bus lines in the United States do not normally take reservations for scheduled runs. If there are more passengers than seats for a particular departure, they will, if possible, add an extra bus or sometimes endorse your ticket for use on a competing carrier on the same route.

Touring

Touring by bus may not suit everyone's taste, but it could be an ideal way to cram a lot of sightseeing and relaxation into a short vacation at minimal expense.

Bus tours are available almost everywhere there are roads, whether in the United States or Europe or in remote areas of the third world. They range from a few hours to a month or more. For multiday tours you usually need advance reservations, but for those of a day or less, you can often just show up at the starting point and be assured of a seat.

Contrary to a popular impression, bus tours are not the preserve of solitary old people. Such tours do attract many widows and widowers, including some who are newly bereaved, because they provide an easy escape from depressing realities at home. But they also attract college students, young married couples, couples seeking temporary relief from the cares of home and children, and many foreign adults of all ages who want an easy way to see the United States.

Bus tours are ideal mixers. Perhaps it is the physical closeness of the passengers, the idea that this is a shared adventure, and the fact that everyone anticipates enjoyment. Perhaps it is the effort of the professional escort, frequently a teacher or graduate student on vacation from school, to bring people together.

Whatever the reason, it is hard not to establish a quick acquaintance with at least the person in the next seat. If he or she proves a dud, other contacts can easily be made at rest stops or group meals. Bus tours tend to have special appeal for introverts who would rather be extroverts and to vacationers who prefer to have everything arranged for them—transportation, meals, accommodations, admissions, and baggage handling. Tours usually guarantee admission to the sightseeing and amusement attractions, and arrangements are commonly made for passengers to avoid standing in line.

Almost every city in the United States has at least one company offering tours by bus. The New York area has dozens, and they go to virtually every part of the country plus Canada and Mexico. Some use buses all the way; others fly you to a takeoff point for bus travel in the region to be explored.

Bluebird, California Parlor Car Tours, Cartan, Casser, Maupintour, Olson, Parker, Percival, Talmage, Tauck—these are a few of the prominent names in the coach-tour trade. You may not have heard of them, but chances are your travel agent has and can give you detailed brochures and make your reservations.

Most of the above have nationwide reputations. Major cities, however, usually have high-quality local operators, many of whom sell directly to the public. You can probably find out about them by asking your convention and visitors bureau, if your city has one, or your Chamber of Commerce.

Some directories compiled for travel agents give comprehensive rundowns of what is available from where to where and at what price. For example, they tell an agent about excellent Rocky Mountain tours that begin and end in Denver and have arrangements for passengers from afar to fly to and from Denver at lower-than-normal fares. Many travelers fail to realize that when you vacation by bus, you do not necessarily have to take a tour that begins in your home town. There are, of course, tours of the West that take you all the way from New York and back by bus, but many travelers prefer to save the time that would be spent on interstate highways crossing the Midwest.

Some tours combine travel by motor coach with travel by air, rail, ship, or all three. A Tauck favorite has been a nine-day excursion to the Cariboo Mountains in British Columbia, including a helicopter flight to a remote lodge and high alpine meadows. Maupintour, meanwhile, has offered a fifteen-day tour of Alaska and Glacier Bay that begins in Anchorage and uses motor coaches, cruise ships, and narrow-gauge trains.

Coach tours vary widely, not only in where they go but also in what services they provide. Therefore, when making inquiries, these are some questions worth asking:

- If you are traveling alone, will single rooms be available, and if so, at what supplementary charge? If you are alone and prefer to share, will the tour operator permit it, and will he help you find a roommate?

- How many meals are included in the tour price? Many operators include only those that are specified in the published itinerary. When meals are included, will you have the entire menu to choose from, or will selections be restricted? Will you have to eat in a group, or can you sit alone or with whomever you wish?
- What type of hotels and motels will you stay at? If dinner is on your own, will evening transportation be readily available to take you to a choice of restaurants, or will logistical problems force you to eat where you spend the night?
- Does the tour price include sightseeing admissions?
- What is the policy on tipping? Usually travelers are expected to tip the tour escort and driver.
- On a typical day, how many hours will you be confined to the coach?
- Will seating be rotated so that everyone gets equal time in the choicest places?
- Will the coach have its own lavatory? How frequently will there be rest stops?
- What is the policy on smoking in the coach?
- Is there a choice of pick-up and drop-off points in the metropolitan area where the tour begins and ends?
- What is the free baggage allowance? Usually it is one suitcase on shorter tours and sometimes two on longer ones, with at least one of them stowed all day in a baggage compartment.

In general on vacations by bus, the more frills and the higher the quality, the higher the price. But one thing almost all of them guarantee is a friendly trip. With the escort as a talented catalyst— and many of them are—there is something about coach travel that helps strangers become friends and often to remain so long after the vacation ends.

If you have never taken a bus tour, however, and are wary, perhaps the best idea is to experiment on a one-day round-trip. Many such tours cost less than $25, and at that price you cannot go very wrong.

11. Chartering a Bus

Winter, spring, summer, or fall—whenever you want a brief adventure away from home, you can probably find a bus to take you on it. Often you will find a public tour to suit your taste, but it may prove a lot simpler and cheaper than you first think to charter a bus of your own. It could be easy to find forty or so people who work together, are members of the same church or synagogue, or belong to the same club and would gladly escape together.

A chartered coach, unlike an airplane or train or bus on scheduled service, can take you wherever and whenever you wish. Like your car, it can take you to and from historical picturesque sites, amusement parks, restaurants, and resorts that are reachable only by road. It can be a relatively inexpensive means of travel because costs are shared by all the passengers, and, in most places that you stop, you can take advantage of discounted group rates.

To illustrate the broadest range of possibilities, let's look at what is available by charter or public bus tour near New York.

Sightseeing? In all directions from New York City are museums, historic homesteads, wildlife refuges, and crafts centers that are open the year round. Those that are indoors have special appeal from January through March because they are free of the crowds that jam them much of the year.

Recreation? In the Poconos, Catskills, and Litchfield Hills of northwestern Connecticut, more than a dozen resorts offer entertainment, meals, and year-round sports for travelers who arrive during the morning and return home the same day.

Shopping? Several clusters of factory-outlet stores are within a day's round-trip ride of New York and almost always offer bigger bargains than you can find in the city. Prices are usually at their best shortly after Christmas.

Gambling? There are many opportunities in New York and elsewhere in the Northeast to charter buses or to join bus tours that take you—free—to and from Atlantic City. The hitch is that you usually must spend at least six hours there, on the assumption that you will spend most of those hours gambling at odds firmly in favor of the house. You pay the bus company for round-trip transportation, and upon arrival at the designated casino in Atlantic City, you get a combination of quarters, meal vouchers and credits for your next visit that usually totals more than your fare.

At sightseeing attractions, restaurants, and resorts, a busload of twenty to fifty people traveling together can generally command better rates than an individual, a couple, or a family traveling by private car. Some operators of one-day bus tours sell seats to individuals, although such offerings are much fewer in winter than the rest of the year. To find out about them, ask your local visitors' center, if there is one, or ask the Chamber of Commerce or the bell captain or concierge at a major hotel.

Many one-day bus tours for the public are small neighborhood operations. To find out about these, you will probably fare better with a travel agent in an outlying section of the city or in the suburbs than downtown. Often such tours are set up by smaller travel agencies in conjunction with operators of charter buses.

The biggest one-day group business is with organizations that charter buses for their own members. If you are not affiliated with such an organization but might consider joining one, check with your neighborhood community center, house of worship, or a municipal office for the elderly. Many organizations, particularly for the retired, have one-day tour programs.

To put together your own tour, the first thing that is needed is a human catalyst: the person who organizes the group, collects the money, and attends to the other details. Some may abhor such chores, but the common practice of providing free travel to the organizer can be a powerful attraction. And a group that is organized for one trip will often remain organized for many others.

Once the group is formed, the next step is to arrange the charter. There are two principal ways to do this.

One is to make all the arrangements yourself, which can be difficult and risky, especially for a novice. Another is to deal through a so-called tour broker, an individual or company with the professional expertise in arranging group bus tours. Although it may sound cheaper to do it yourself, you actually could be spared a lot of hassle, risk, and even cash by using a broker.

Some bus companies are also tour brokers in that they will

arrange everything you need, not just transportation. Some travel agents are brokers, as well. And there are many companies that are exclusively tour brokers; that is, they are middlemen who make arrangements for buses, hotels, restaurants, sightseeing, and anything else that a charter group needs.

Assuming that you provide a full load, one New York broker will take your group on a shopping tour of the factory outlets in Reading, Pennsylvania, for $35 a person or to West Point and Bear Mountain for $25, both trips including lunch. You can cancel up to forty-eight hours before departure with no penalty on the transportation but possibly one on the lunch.

Some tour brokers who deal in large volumes and have long-established reputations can guarantee a reliable and comfortable coach at almost any time, given at least two weeks' notice, and can, for everything else you need, frequently negotiate lower prices than you could. Even though brokers profit from your business, it may be cheaper to use them than to avoid them.

Legitimate tour brokers are licensed by the Interstate Commerce Commission, and many are also members of the National Tour Association, a trade group. You can get the names and addresses of member brokers in your area by writing to the association at Tudor Square, 120 Kentucky Avenue, Lexington, Kentucky 40502; phone (606) 253-1036.

If you are determined to handle everything, your first chore after forming the group is to charter a bus. A good starting point is to check the *Consumer Yellow Pages* under "Bus Lines" or "Buses— Charter & Rental." In most metropolitan areas, you will find the listings lengthy. Select perhaps half a dozen that seem closest to your neighborhood.

If you are planning a lot of charter travel, you might consider investing $25 in *Russell's Guides,* which list many of the major operators throughout the United States and in twenty-eight other countries. They also tell where the companies are licensed to operate. They are available postpaid from Russell's Guides, Post Office Box 78, Cedar Rapids, Iowa 52406.

When you call a charter operator, be prepared to state exactly when and where you want to go. The first question you should ask is whether the line is licensed by the I.C.C., if you are planning interstate travel, or by the appropriate state authority if you will not cross a state line. You should make sure that an I.C.C. license covers the area you want to visit. If the line does not have the appropriate license—and many so-called gypsy operators do not—avoid it. A license assures adequate insurance and bonding; lack of one can mean serious trouble if a mishap occurs, even if the operator has good intentions.

Among other details to ascertain from bus lines: whether they have or can borrow sufficient equipment to guarantee against breakdowns, the passenger capacity of available coaches, and whether there are rest rooms on board. Then discuss costs and methods of payment, and consider getting bids from several companies before you sign a contract. Rates can vary sharply.

In the New York area, a forty-six-passenger bus equipped with a rest room will probably cost $500 to $700 a day for transportation alone, depending on distance. Elsewhere the rates are probably cheaper. Some companies will allow you to cancel up to ten A.M. on the day before departure with no penalty; cancellation after that may cost $100 or so.

Besides arranging for the bus, consider what else you will need. Obviously, the more elaborate the lunch and any other frills, the more you pay. Many destinations, however, have special offerings to attract the charter bus trade. At the prices they advertise, which are subject to change, the meals are infrequently of top quality, and the portions are often minimal, but the main attraction is pleasant service in an atmosphere of fun.

Following are some illustrations of what you might have found not long ago at prices that are now out of date:

- The 180-year-old inn on Lake Waramaug in the Litchfield Hills of northwestern Connecticut offered a midweek "winter carnival party" at $11.95 a person, including tax and tips. Lunch entree choices were roast loin of pork, baked Boston scrod or Yankee pot roast. Between the suggested arrival time of 11:30 A.M. and the departure time of four P.M., travelers had free use of the inn's recreational facilities, including an indoor swimming pool, and were entertained by a pianist, a bingo contest, and a horse-drawn sleigh ride if there was snow. Bus fare, of course, was extra.
- The Interlaken Inn in Lakeville, Connecticut, offered a day package at $8.50 to $10 a person, depending on the entree: fillet of sole, seafood Newburg, beef Bourguignon, quiche Lorraine, or petit filet mignon.
- Grossinger's, at Liberty, New York, invited busloads to

arrive by ten A.M. and stay until five P.M., participating meanwhile in the regularly scheduled round of group activities and dining from the regular lunch menu. The tab: $14.14, including sales tax and tip.

- The Villa Roma in Callicoon, New York, near the Delaware River west of Liberty, charged $7 for a daytime outing in which lunch entrees included southern fried chicken, London broil, veal and peppers, and a fruit or tuna platter. For $19.50 a person, a bus group could have lunch and dinner at the resort (the evening meal featured Italian delicacies or prime ribs) and attend a show.
- At Pocmont, near Bushkill, Pennsylvania, in the Poconos, bus groups were offered full use of facilities plus lunch buffet at $8 a person, a table-service lunch at $8.75, or a dinner-nightclub package from $12.95 to $15.95, depending on entree. Tax and gratuities were included. On the dinner package, departure for home was 12:30 A.M.
- Buena Vista in Newfoundland, Pennsylvania, in the Poconos offered lunch packages at $8.47, including tax and tip, with a choice of breast of turkey, roast top round of beef, baked ham, or stuffed breast of chicken.

Of course, you do not have to accept rock-bottom offerings but can upgrade for a price. Or you can arrange to stop at virtually any restaurant or resort that handles groups; most will welcome your business heartily. Be sure to reserve far enough in advance, however, to assure the best service possible, and be prepared to pay a substantial deposit. Any establishment that does not require a deposit—particularly if you are a new customer—or that offers to serve you on no advance notice will probably prove more disappointing than fun.

12. Campers and Other RVs

After several lean years caused by soaring prices of gasoline, the recreational vehicle industry is thriving again. And it is striving to convince vacationers that its products offer the best and often the most economical way to roam leisurely about the countryside while taking along many comforts of home.

If the idea appeals to you, it is not necessary to commit yourself to a purchase that could reach tens of thousands of dollars. A growing number of businesses and individuals are offering rentals by the day, weekend, or, more often, the week. According to data compiled by Kampgrounds of America, a nationwide network of privately owned camping areas, a family of four, traveling with a tent that opens out from a trailer, could take a three-thousand-mile, twelve-day vacation in the Rockies for only $75 a day, including all expenses, or considerably less than traveling by car, eating in restaurants, and sleeping in motels.

The term *recreational vehicle*, or *RV*, embraces a broad and growing variety of camping trailers, house trailers, truck campers, converted vans, and motor homes from austere to opulent, from modestly priced to grossly expensive. The options are so numerous that before committing yourself to even a rental, it is important to understand exactly what you are getting, whether it will suit your needs and taste, and what it will cost. Prices, of course, are subject to change.

A good beginning might be to send for the pamphlet *Living in Style the RV Way*, available at this writing for $1.75, including postage, from the Recreational Vehicle Industry Association, Post Office Box 204, Chantilly, Virginia 22021. It gives clear, detailed, and illustrated descriptions of the different types of vehicles plus advice on how to choose one and where to get more information.

These are a few things you will want to know:

How much will a rental cost?

The basic cost will depend on the type of vehicle you rent, its size, and its furnishings and equipment. Rates also vary from season to season and from dealer to dealer, but you can get a good idea of going rates from the *RV Rental Directory*. It gives details of the offerings of about a hundred dealers in the United States and Canada and is available at this writing for $3.50, postpaid, from the Recreational Vehicle Dealers Association of North America, Suite 500, 3251 Old Lee Highway, Fairfax, Virginia 22030.

At the bottom of the scale is a camping trailer, a low, squat vehicle that can easily be towed by most cars and unfolds into a tent when stationary. To rent one, figure on spending $135 or so a week. At the top of the scale are motor homes, self-powered and mostly self-contained. Basic weekly rental rates for motor homes run from about $260 for the most modest, in low season, which varies according to where you rent, to $1,000 in high season for a thirty-five-foot air-conditioned luxury vehicle with a full bathroom, including tub, double-door refrigerator, a four-burner stove with oven plus a microwave oven, solid oak cabinetry, carpeting, and velvet upholstery.

One of the nation's largest rental companies, Altmans America Motorhome Rentals of Baldwin Park and Van Nuys, California, and forty franchise locations throughout the country, includes 100 free miles a day with a typical rental and charges eighteen to twenty-two cents for each additional mile, depending on the vehicle's size. The company also charges $6 to $8 a day for what is called a collision-damage waiver, without which the renter is responsible for the first $500 in accident repair costs. Gasoline costs extra, and Dave Altman, the owner, estimates that his biggest vehicles average about six miles a gallon and the smallest sixteen.

Another major operator, American Land Cruisers of Miami and Orlando, Florida, and Los Angeles, offers a sliding scale of charges to suit the amount of driving you intend to do. For example, in 1984 a small motor home cost $49 a day plus sixteen cents a mile with no free mileage, $62 a day with 100 free miles and sixteen cents a mile above that, or $81 a day with 250 free miles and sixteen cents for each additional mile.

For the same rates, the company was offering a new small diesel Winnebago, called the LeSharo, which is reported to average twenty-two to twenty-four miles a gallon. Housekeeping kits that include blankets, sheets, dishes, and utensils are provided at $20 per person extra for the entire rental period.

This company also sometimes has special promotional offers with airlines. One spring it offered Eastern Airlines passengers a twenty-foot motor home for $409 a week with 100 free miles a day and fourteen cents a mile above that. But added to those charges were $7 a day for a $500 collision-damage waiver, $12 a person for the week for linens, utensils, flatware, and dishes, and your round-trip air fare, at that time, at least $249 to Florida from New York.

What about one-way rentals?

One-way rentals are often discouraged, since rental companies say they have to "deadhead" employees—transport them empty-handed to the drop-off points to pick up the vehicles and return them to the point of rental. At this writing, American Land Cruisers was charging $50 for drop-offs in Florida but not in the same city as the pickup, and $250 if you drove between Florida and California.

Newton Kindlund, who owns Holiday Rental Vehicle Leasing Inc. in Orlando, said he would charge about $50 for a drop-off in Miami, about $250 in New York and $350 in Los Angeles.

Where can you rent?

If you deal with a major renting company, you are likely to get a new or nearly new vehicle that has been regularly serviced. Also, such companies often have arrangements for emergency repairs with workshops in places where their customers are likely to travel. Typically you will be reimbursed without prior approval for any repair costing up to $50. Usually, these vehicles are company owned. Sometimes you can get a better price by watching classified ads placed by individuals who own vehicles and rent them out for extra income, but you cannot always tell how well they have been cared for.

You can deal with most major renters directly or through travel agents. Chances are, an agent will steer you to a tour packager, such as Atpac Tours, a subsidiary of the Cortell Group of New York, or to a Vancouver-based dealer network called Motor Camping of North America. For European rentals, a travel agent can put you in touch with such companies as InterRent, Kemwel, Auto Europe, Europe by Car, Foremost Euro-Car, Europacar Tours, another Cortell subsidiary, for West Germany, and Maiellano Tours for Italy.

How many will a vehicle sleep comfortably?

The key word is *comfortably,* and to determine that, it's best to go beyond the manufacturer's or renter's claim and shop around personally. A lot will depend on the size and nature of your family; for example, the number, ages, and restlessness of your children.

Where can you park for the night?

Chances are you will use government or private campgrounds, and in midsummer you may have to reserve far in advance and arrive early in the day. Rates in private grounds average about $8 to $10 a night for two people and seventy-five cents to $1.50 for each additional person, depending on age. For details on the more than seven hundred affiliated grounds of Kampgrounds of America, send $1 to KOA Directory, Post Office Box 30162, Billings, Montana 59107. At this writing, sending $12 to the Good Sam Club at Post Office Box 500, Agoura, California 91301, will get you a year's membership in that organization of about 420 Good Sams, which is short for Good Samaritans. Membership, for which rates are subject to change, entitles you to a 10 percent discount at campgrounds displaying the Good Sam symbol.

Before taking to the road, check any bookstore that has a sizable travel section, and you will probably find the campground, trailer park, and recreational vehicle directories of such publishers as Rand McNally, Woodall's (distributed by Simon & Schuster), Wheeler's, and Trailer Life, the sponsor of the Good Sam Club. Also useful is the recently revised edition of *Free Campgrounds, U.S.A.*, edited by Mary VanMeer, but you may have to order it by mail. Send $9.95 plus $1.50 for postage and handling to East Woods Press, 429 East Boulevard, Charlotte, North Carolina 28203.

13. Sea Cruises

A Chicago businessman in his midfifties, tired of digging his family out of a late-winter blizzard, wanted to take his wife on a cruise. They could spare only a week away from their respective offices, so they decided to fly to Florida for a brief visit with relatives and friends before sailing on a four-night cruise out of Miami to the Bahamas.

Several companies were offering such cruises. After examining brochures and itineraries, the couple asked their travel agent to book space on the *Carnivale* of the Carnival Cruise Lines, sailing on a Monday in mid-March to Nassau and Freeport and returning to Miami on Friday. When told that the *Carnivale* was sold out, the agent tentatively reserved a cabin on the *Emerald Seas* of Eastern Steamship Lines, which made the same stops in reverse order.

This was marginally acceptable to the couple, but they really would have preferred the *Carnivale*. They wanted a newer ship, which it is, and they wanted to rendezvous briefly in Freeport with friends who would be there only on the day that the *Carnivale* called. So the businessman, who has influential connections in the cruise trade, tried to see what he could accomplish on his own— which is why he prefers to remain anonymous here.

He phoned a marketing officer of the Carnival Cruise Lines and asked if there was any way a cabin on *Carnivale* could be arranged. A few minutes later the officer phoned back and said a cabin could indeed be arranged if the businessman really wanted it. "I think you should know," the officer said, "that of the eight hundred passengers we expect to carry on that sailing, more than seven hundred will be college students."

The businessman blanched. "No thank you," he said. "My wife and I like to have fun, but I think we would find so many young people rather overwhelming."

The businessman then began to worry about the *Emerald Seas*. "Would you please try to find out," he asked his travel agent, "who our shipmates are likely to be?" Ten minutes later the agent phoned him. "College students," she said. "Almost a whole shipload of them." Further inquiries produced the information that between mid-March and mid-April, short cruises out of Florida are highly popular among students on spring break from school. Many students save all year to afford the $500 to $700 or so that it costs, including tips and incidental expenses, to cruise a few days in the sun.

With this knowledge, the businessman arranged to sail on the *Carnivale* a week earlier, just before the heavy student wave would begin. But suppose the Chicago couple—who, incidentally, are seasoned travelers—had not learned, in time to cancel their reservations, what was in store? Suppose they had flown to Miami and boarded the ship, to learn only there that instead of a "fun" vacation with a broad mix of outgoing people, they faced four days of misery amid what simply was not their sort of crowd?

At a hotel they probably could have left quickly, paying only for one day, and moved somewhere else. But on a cruise they would have been trapped unless they were prepared to forfeit their entire fare by leaving the ship before it sailed.

What this case illustrates is the need to ask questions, questions, questions, before you arrange a vacation on unfamiliar ground (or water). Perhaps the travel agent should have taken the initiative by asking the ship lines for profiles of potential passengers, and some agents who deal heavily in cruises probably do. But such a degree of protectiveness is really too much to expect, especially if the client stipulates when he wants to go and does not indicate any flexibility.

So if you, the traveler, are curious about your potential shipmates, you usually must ask your agent to ask, or directly ask the cruise line yourself. Cruises, like resorts, can differ sharply. The longer the sailing, the more affluent, older, and sedate the passengers are likely to be. Activities on some ships are more formal than on others. Some ships seek the patronage of young singles; others arrange activities and itineraries that attract primarily couples in late middle age. Still others accent special-interest programs, such as jazz festivals, lectures on the stock market, or lessons on playing bridge.

The crowd on most ships is likely to vary sharply from season to season, even sometimes from week to week. If you enjoy the company of lots of small children, cruise around Christmas; if you do not, Christmas on some ships is to be avoided.

Before you start even thinking about fellow passengers, however, these are some of the many other factors to consider in selecting a cruise:

- Where do you want to go? The Caribbean, the Mexican Riviera, through the Panama Canal, up the Inland Passage to Alaska, through the Mediterranean, to the South Pacific, to South America, around the world?
- Do you prefer ocean cruising, which can be rough at times, or would you consider a river, such as the Mississippi, the Danube, the Nile, the Amazon, or the Rhine?

- Do you have any special interests? For example, ancient history buffs might prefer the Greek islands or the Nile, adventurers might prefer the Antarctic or the South Seas, sun worshipers might prefer Mexico and bargain shoppers might prefer the Caribbean.
- Would you rather call at a lot of ports or visit fewer and spend more time at sea, enjoying shipboard activities? Ports of call tend to add to out-of-pocket expenses for meals, shopping, and optional sightseeing tours, although there is no compulsion to buy the tours.
- What sort of activities do you hope to find aboard ship: a bridge tournament, first-run movies, spectacular stage shows, big-name stars, lectures, a physical fitness program, full-scale gambling?
- What is the reputation of the ship's food? Can you have breakfast in your cabin, and is there room service all night long? For lunch, do you have a choice between a buffet on deck and a full meal in the dining room (or even both if you hurry—who will know)?
- How long can you afford to be away, and if time matters little, will a long voyage bore you? Do you prefer to sail from the port closest to home, or would you rather buy a package that flies you to the ship, which is already in the area where you are scheduled to sail?
- How much can you afford to pay? Of all the factors, this is perhaps the most important. Although bargains abounded in the cruise industry in 1984 and early 1985 because of overcapacity, in general you get what you pay for. The best key to quality is often the price per day for the cruise alone, stripped of any promotional incentive such as "free" round-trip air from and to home, the cost of which is usually built into the price. At this writing, minimum-rate cabins on good-quality cruises were running upward from about $185 a person a day, before any discounting.

Once you have answered these questions and have tentatively selected the cruise you want, it's time to go on to such questions as these:

- How should you select a cabin? Usually you have two choices: to pick a specific cabin at the going price or pick a price range. If you choose the former, you will be assured of that cabin, and if you have carefully studied the deck plan and are convinced that the size and location are best for your taste, you will probably be satisfied. If you select a price range, however, you run the risk of getting a cabin in that category that you do not like, but if the ship is not full, there is often a good chance of your happily being upgraded to a higher-priced cabin at no additional cost.

- Should you pay extra for an outside cabin? If a porthole and an opportunity to gaze at the sea from your cabin are all that important, perhaps you should. Remember, all cabins, whether outside or inside, have the same air-conditioning these days, and if your cruise is a short one with lots of activities and calls at two ports, how much time do you expect to spend in the cabin anyway?

- If you choose the least-expensive accommodations, will you get inferior service? On cruises, unlike transatlantic crossings of the *Queen Elizabeth 2,* absolutely not. The price affects only the type and location of your cabin, and sometimes where you dine, but on most cruises everyone is offered the same meals, entertainment, and service.

- How much will the cruise really cost? The prices in the brochure are for your cabin, meals, and most activities. But remember that tips are extra, usually an aggregate of 5 percent of the fare. Also drinks, albeit duty-free when you are in international waters, are also extra, as are purchases in ship shops and such services as hairdressing and massages. Optional shore excursions can also add substantially to your total tab, as can gambling in a ship's casino.

- If there are two sittings at meals, as there often are, should you choose the first or second? Essentially, this is a matter of taste. If you like to get up early, perhaps the first sitting is best, but it may mean eating dinner earlier than you like. However, if you choose the second sitting, you may finish dinner so late that you miss some of the evening activities and have no stomach for the midnight buffet.

Helpful to the novice cruise passenger is a brochure entitled *Answers to the Most Asked Questions About Cruising.* To an extent, it is a promotional instrument for the passenger shipping industry, but it has some very plain answers to some very valid questions. You can get a free copy, in English or French, by sending a self-addressed, stamped, business-size envelope to the Cruise Lines International Association, 17 Battery Place, Suite 631, New York, New York 10004.

Cruise Bargains

Nothing better illustrates the intense competition in the cruise industry than the many bargains offered when there is much more space than demand. Such was the case in the early-to-mid-1980s, when some new liners entered the market but demand for cruise travel remained relatively flat.

Secure your lifejackets, however, before you plunge into the sea of advertised promises and pay your fare. On careful examination, some offerings are laden with restrictions and are not as good a bargain as they first seem. Others portend a substantial sacrifice in passenger comfort.

For example, before you seize the bait that the third and fourth passengers in a cabin will sail free, it might be prudent to determine the size and sleeping arrangements of the accommodations and to ponder how much time you expect to spend there.

Late summer and fall are traditionally low season for cruising the Caribbean because of warm weather and the possibility of storms. In recent years, however, discounting and other lures have spread throughout the cruise industry and throughout the year.

Most hard-to-sell space has been in the medium-price range because minimum- and maximum-rate cabins typically sell out first. Some discounts theoretically apply to the run of the ship, but you may not be able to find a minimum- or maximum-rate cabin to which to apply it. Sometimes under a discount offer, however, you can get a medium- or higher-rate cabin for less than what was originally advertised as the cheapest space aboard ship.

What follows is a sampling of different types of price lures that have been available at various times; some, but not all, may be still around.

Air-Sea Packages—These are of two general types: "free" air transportation to and from many cities and the starting and ending points of the cruise or an air add-on to the cruise fare, depending roughly on how far you fly. "Free" air travel has come under substantial criticism on two grounds: that it isn't really free because thc cost is built into the cruise fare and that, in effect, it penalizes passengers who live where the ship is based and do not have to fly at all.

Some lines that offer free air travel reduce your basic cruise fare if you arrange your own flights. For example, the Royal Caribbean Cruise Line once offered a $50 allowance on seven- and eight-day cruises of its *Nordic Prince* out of Miami, $75 on ten-day sailings and $100 on those of fourteen days.

For a Far Eastern cruise of the *Sagafjord* that began in Los Angeles and could be joined en route, Norwegian American Cruises (which later was bought by the Cunard Line) offered to fly you free from anywhere in North America or give rebates of $500 for round-trips to and from Los Angeles, $1,100 if you joined the cruise in Los Angeles and debarked in Hong Kong, $1,300 if you boarded in Hong Kong and left in Honolulu, and so on.

Carnival Cruise Lines and Norwegian Caribbean Lines offered free air travel, and the cruise price was the same whether or not you took it, except that Carnival promised a $100 discount to southern California residents on its sailings out of Los Angeles.

Holland America Cruises offered round-trip air on Florida sailings for $50, $100 or $150 a person above the cruise price, depending on how far you flew. The Cunard Line said it would fly you free to and from San Juan for its sailings from there and for $99 to and from Mexican ports if you booked a higher-priced cabin; otherwise you paid $49 for San Juan and $149 for Mexico.

Reduced Prices on Unsold Space as Sailing Nears—Several companies and organizations have offered unsold cruise space at the last minute at discounts of up to 60 percent. At this writing, a leader among them is Spur of the Moment Tours and Cruises, 4315 Overland Avenue, Culver City, California 90230; phone (213) 839-2418 or, toll-free, (800) 343-1991. Other organizations require clients to pay annual fees. For example, for $45 a year per household (price subject to change), you can subscribe to the services of Stand-Buys Ltd., Post Office Box 2088, 26711 Northwestern Highway, Southfield, Michigan 48037; phone (800) 621-5839 outside Illinois, (800) 972-5858 in Illinois. Subscribers are given a confidential toll-free 800 number with a taped message that is updated daily and recites details on cruises and tours that have been reduced for quick sale. By calling a second toll-free number, you can make reservations.

Other membership organizations offering similar plans at this writing are Moment's Notice, 40 East 49th Street, New York, New

York 10017; (212) 486-0503; Discount Travel International, 7563 Haverford Avenue, Philadelphia, Pennsylvania 19151; (215) 878-8282; and Worldwide Discount Travel, 1674 Meridian Avenue, Miami Beach, Florida 33139; (305) 534-2082.

Third or Fourth Passenger in Cabin—On some ships, the third or fourth person pays sharply reduced rates; on others they go free in certain categories of cabins. The latter was once the case on the *Carla C* of the Costa Line out of San Juan, but they didn't get the free air travel offered the first and second passengers. On the *Cunard Countess* out of San Juan, for several months anyone forty years old or younger who paid the full price for a medium-rate cabin based on double occupancy could take along a companion free. Some lines give reductions for children up to age seventeen if they are accompanied by at least one adult or even if they occupy a separate cabin. Ask your agent for details.

Advance Purchase—To get a jump on the competition, cruise lines often offer substantial discounts, say $100 a person or more, if you reserve and pay for your cabin three or more months before the date of sailing. Sometimes you can get several hundred dollars off by booking this season for next. As long as cruise space in general is overabundant, however, it is debatable whether, if your vacation time is flexible, you will do better by accepting a preseason offer or waiting until the last moment, when some rates are cut drastically to fill unsold space.

Standby—A perennially popular standby program has been that of the Norwegian Caribbean Lines on its four ships—the *Starward, Southward, Skyward,* and *Norway*—that in the winter sail on seven-day cruises out of Miami every Saturday or Sunday. At least four weeks in advance, you select the weekend you would like to sail; when you make full payment, the line confirms the ship and accommodations that will carry you. At this writing the fare, subject to seasonal variation, is $659 for an inside stateroom based on double occupancy and $729 outside. Reductions are 30 percent or more from full fare, which sometimes brings them below minimum rate, although the cabins are usually of a higher category. The rate for a third or fourth adult in the same cabin is about $350, subject to seasonal variations.

From time to time, other cruise lines offer standby fares, too. Check your travel agent for what's available about the time you hope to go.

14. Car Rentals in the United States

Nothing seems to irk auto renters more than unexpected charges on the bill when they return a car. Business travelers who rent cars frequently learn to expect and understand the gaps between prominently advertised rates and what they ultimately pay. But the delight with which a vacation traveler picks up a subcompact advertised, say, at $69 a week with unlimited mileage can turn to angry shock when the cost at the end of the week proves to be almost twice that.

So many new policies, promotional offers, and restrictions keep arising in the car rental business that extra careful attention is needed to sort the worthwhile from the chaff. What appears to be an irresistible bargain may prove in the end to cost a bundle. This does not mean that you should shy away: For many city dwellers faced with sky-high garage rates and a paucity of onstreet parking places, it's much simpler and usually cheaper to rent a car for an occasional outing than to own one. And at many vacation destinations to which you fly, rental cars make it easy to get around.

Before you sign that contract, however, it is important to understand the options, limitations, and costs and to comparison-shop for the best possible deal. Bear in mind that what is cheapest may not be most suitable and that there are few true giveaways.

No auto rental bill is without what many customers call hidden charges, although they will be mentioned on the rental contract, often in fine print. Almost always, for example, you have to pay for at least as much gasoline as you use, if not for more. In most states, your rental is subject to sales tax, and you frequently have to pay a drop-off charge if you do not return the car to the same station, or at least the same area, where you picked it up.

You will have the option of paying extra for personal accident insurance and for full coverage for collision damage to the car. But if you do not choose the collision-damage option, you may have to put up a substantial deposit before the rental company will entrust the vehicle to your care.

If you reserve your car through a travel agent, as vacation drivers frequently do when they plan to fly or take a train to the pick-up point, be sure you understand exactly what you are contracting for. Don't hesitate to question your agent carefully about charges; the auto rental business is so competitive these days that the major companies have overwhelmed agents with detailed literature.

A popular device to entice travelers to fly certain airlines to some destinations is to offer them, once there, the "free" use of a rental car. That's what the now-defunct Air Florida did as part of its tenth anniversary—to offer its passengers to Florida "one day's free use" of a car from Alamo Rent A Car. A press release noted, however, that gasoline and collision-damage waiver were not included.

This meant, first, that under Alamo policy, you had to pay $7 up front for gasoline, with the company promising to provide at least six gallons. It meant that, for $5.95 a day, you would be relieved of any financial responsibility for damage to the car in a collision. This waiver, as it is called, is technically optional, but without it the driver is liable for the full cost of damages, regardless of who is responsible. This could run into thousands of dollars if the car is wrecked completely.

So your "free car" would probably cost at least $12.95, plus 5 percent Florida sales tax on the waiver. If you bought personal accident insurance to cover any emergency medical care on that day, that cost $2.50 more plus tax. If you picked up the car in Orlando and left it with Alamo at West Palm Beach there was a charge of $30 plus tax. The only expense you were spared was the basic rental: from $19 a day with unlimited mileage, depending on size of car. Of course, that alone was a bargain, but it hardly meant free rental.

If you reserve a car directly with the rental company, insist that the reservations clerk spell out all possible charges. And when you arrive at the pick-up point, read your contract carefully—even if it delays you a few minutes—and demand an explanation of anything you do not understand.

If you arrive at a peak hour and there are long lines and too few clerks at the pick-up counter, you may choose to compromise on this, but remember, you are doing so at your own risk. One alternative might be to ask a travel agent or rental agency to show you a standard contract before you leave home. Fine print may differ among companies and locations, but at least you will get an idea of what to look for.

Major rental companies commonly offer discounts to members of national organizations, such as auto clubs, religious and fraternal groups, and the American Association of Retired Persons. But such discounts are usually applicable only to basic daily rates, not to special offerings for weekends or the week. If, however, you or your spouse is employed by a large company that rents many cars, it may prove highly worth your while to check on whether it has negotiated a special corporate rate usable not just for company business but also for leisure travel by employees.

Ask your personnel department or corporate travel manager about this rate, and you may be entitled to a rental company identification card bearing the contract account number. When a rental car clerk types this number into the computer system, he or she is told what to charge you.

Here are some general points about car rentals to keep in mind.

Mode of Payment—Companies usually insist that you present a credit card, along with your driver's license, when you rent a car. This establishes your credibility as a person who pays his or her bills; it also suggests that you are likely to return the car in good condition rather than steal it or abandon it, because they can trace you through the card. You can, however, pay the bill with cash when you return the car. At some rental locations you may have difficulty getting change because the companies do not want to make their rental locations the target of robbers; in this case paying with your credit card is certainly simpler.

Some travelers are uneasy about being asked to sign a charge form on which no price has been written when they pick up the car. "It's like signing a blank check," a colleague of mine commented. Actually, it isn't. If you return the car to the same location, either the form is completed or it is returned to you and a new one is prepared. If you check out at a different location, a new form is prepared and the company ultimately destroys the old one.

If, by some error, you are charged twice, it should not be difficult to document to the credit card company that an error has been made. To do this, it is important to preserve your copy of the rental contract.

Gasoline—The days are long gone when most car rental rates were so much a day plus so much a mile, gasoline included. Today, virtually always, the renter pays at least for the gasoline. Sometimes, however, you are charged by the mile as well as the day. Usually the best deals include unlimited mileage, and many companies promote them as well as special rates for rentals by the weekend, week, or month.

Even some of the biggest companies, however, are unable to control the pricing policies of franchisees. If you plan to pick up the car from a franchisee, such as a neighborhood gasoline station, do not accept as gospel the rates and conditions quoted by the clerk at the 800 toll-free number who handles your reservation. Instead, reconfirm everything before you sign the rental agreement, and if you do not like what you are told then, look for possibilities to shop around.

The biggest rental companies promise to start you out with a full tank of gasoline and charge you to fill the tank when the car is returned. The price of gasoline at an automobile company pump is almost always significantly higher than it is at a filling station. You should fill the tank as inexpensively as you can.

Some companies promise you only half a tank at the outset and expect at least half a tank upon return. If you return with more than half a tank, you receive no credit for the surplus.

At this writing Alamo, an aggressively growing company based in Fort Lauderdale, Florida, charges customers $9.95 for gasoline and guarantees at least half a tank to start. "When the car is returned," a company spokesman said, "we don't check to see how much gas is left, and that eliminates delays at the check-in counter. In fact, we ask people to bring the car back as empty as possible." She said that if a car is returned after having been driven fifty miles or less, the customer receives a $5 gasoline credit; otherwise, no credit is given, even if, upon return, the tank is nearly full.

Liability Insurance—Major auto rental companies carry their own liability insurance and do not charge extra for it. This usually means you are covered for liability up to $100,000 a person or a total of $300,000 an accident for injuries or death, plus $25,000 in property damage. But some small local companies and some franchisees of larger companies do not carry this insurance. If a rental contract asks for the name of the company that insures your personal car, beware; this could be a tip-off that the rental company has little or no liability coverage.

Your personal auto insurance may or may not cover rental cars; ask your agent if in doubt. If you do not own a car, most major companies, upon request, will sell you what is called a named nonowner policy that provides $100,000/$300,000 liability coverage for any car you drive for nonbusiness purposes. Residents of New York City, for example, typically pay a premium of $70 to $80 for six months.

Collision Coverage—The collision-damage waiver that you have the option of buying for $7 or so a day when you rent a car is something else. Buying it covers you for the full cost of repairing accidental damage to the car while it is in your care. The amount you have to pay for damage if you do not buy this waiver has been soaring. At this writing Hertz and Avis require that without a waiver, which costs $6.95 a day (at that rate, $2,536.75 for a year), the driver pays the first $1,500. Budget, a franchise company that owns only a handful of the 1,800 rental agencies that bear its name, leaves most rental rules to its individual operators.

In some high-rental states, such as Florida, where there is also a high auto accident rate, it is growing increasingly common for companies to hold drivers responsible, as Alamo does, for the total value of the damage if the waiver is not bought.

With such high responsibility without the waiver, you have to be somewhat of a gambler to forgo one. This is especially true now that less and less collision insurance for auto owners covers short-term rentals as well as their own cars. So for many travelers, the waiver option is not really optional at all. Also, if you forgo the option, you often must put up a $200 to $400 deposit, to be refunded if you return the car undamaged.

If, however, your rental is being charged to a corporate account, the company may already have collision insurance and may even forbid your purchase of what would be redundant coverage. Check with your company before you go to pick up the car.

Personal Accident Insurance—At $2 to $2.50 a day at this writing, this option may seem cheap enough, but remember that medical coverage in accidents is typically limited to around $1,500 for the renter and $1,500 for each passenger. Check what health insurance you already have. John Britton, a Hertz spokesman, said, "If you have group medical insurance, ours is probably unnecessary."

Drop-Off Charges—You may be subject to these charges if you pick up the car in one place and return it to another, especially in another city. Company policies and methods of calculating such charges differ. If you rent from a major company, the charge may be minimal or may be waived if you leave the car in a city where rentals are as much in demand as in the city where you picked it up. If you drop off the car in a city where business is relatively slack, the charge may be steep to defray the cost of shipping the vehicle elsewhere.

If you rent from a smaller company, particularly one that operates only in one state, read your contract with extra care. You may be prohibited from taking the car outside that state. Some small companies permit you to drive out of state if you notify the company in advance, but you may forfeit the unlimited mileage or other advantages that usually go with the company's rates. You also may be subject to a whopping drop-off charge if you do not return the car to the state where you rented it.

The Bad News

Jerome Rebhun responded to an advertisement that seemed too good to be true. For just $79 a week, it said, Greyhound Rent-A-Car would, by advance reservation, provide him with a current model Ford Fairmont four-door sedan. The offer was limited to Florida, just where Mr. Rebhun, a certified public accountant in New York, was going.

So by phoning a toll-free 800 number late that April, he said, he obtained a confirmed reservation, No. 382477, for a Fairmont, a midsize car, for two weeks. But he said that on May 1, when he went to the Greyhound counter at the Orlando airport to pick up the car, he was first told that there was no record of his reservation, then told that no Fairmonts were available and that he would have to settle for a compact. Finally, when he agreed under protest to pay $40 extra, he was given a Fairmont, after all.

More than three months later, Mr. Rebhun was still awaiting responses to his complaint to the company and to a formal written complaint that he filed with the Orange County Consumer Fraud Unit in Orlando. A close study of the case, including extensive telephone interviews, indicated that he might have been a victim of a peculiar chain of circumstances.

To begin with, Mr. Rebhun thought he was dealing with a subsidiary of the Greyhound Corporation, the bus company, but he wasn't. Late that February, the corporation sold the rental company to Sidney H. Cohen of Baltimore and permitted him to continue to use the Greyhound name temporarily. It was Mr. Cohen's company that placed the ad that attracted Mr. Rebhun and that confirmed his Fairmont reservation.

In addition, Ralph Herz, director of marketing for the new operators, said there was no record that Mr. Rebhun ever picked up the car. It turns out that when he went to get the car he reserved, he wasn't even dealing with Greyhound Rent-A-Car, even though that was the name on the sign at the airport rental counter. Greyhound has a company-owned location near the airport and a connecting phone in the passenger terminal, but the counter office was run by a former franchisee who was permitted to use the Greyhound name and logo until May 31, a month after Mr. Rebhun's rental.

So on May 1 there were, in effect, two Greyhounds in Orlando, and Mr. Rebhun went to the wrong one. The former franchisee, Cloris Dale, who later operated as Payless Rent-A-Car, said that since late March, his office had received no Greyhound reservations. "In any event," he said, "we don't rent and we never did rent Fairmonts at the seventy-nine-dollar rate."

As Mr. Rebhun tells it, the clerk at the airport first said she had no record of his reservation, but when he gave his confirmation number, she seemed to find it on another list. After the dispute over the price, the contract was filled out on a Greyhound form. Asked why the clerk had not directed Mr. Rebhun to the proper Greyhound agent, Mr. Dale said the clerk had tried to do so, but the customer was adamant.

The Customer Fraud Unit forwarded Mr. Rebhun's complaint not to Mr. Dale but to Greyhound, against whom it had been lodged. According to Tim Hetz, public information officer for the State Attorney's office in Orlando, which helps the fraud unit, the complaint was forwarded to the company three times—on June 16, July 11 and August 1—before Greyhound acknowledged receipt. Months later, further action was pending.

"I'd like to accommodate the man," Mr. Herz of Greyhound said of Mr. Rebhun. "The forty dollars wouldn't kill me. But I don't want to seem to assume responsibility for something for which we have no legal obligation."

Shortly after Mr. Rebhun made his reservation, Greyhound changed its advertising so that the $79 offer in Florida was for "any car in the fleet." Mr. Herz said the chances were good that if you requested a Fairmont you would get one, but that the company would now guarantee only to provide you some car for $79, not a particular size or model.

The Weekend Car Renter

A perennial problem for many city dwellers is how best to get away for relaxing weekends at lakes, ski resorts, mountain hideouts, or whatever, within driving distance of home. Many people who live in such highly congested areas as Manhattan, central Philadelphia, or the near north side of Chicago simply do not own cars. So for those coveted escapes of a day, a weekend, or more, they turn to rentals, and that's where anxiety often starts.

As in many aspects of American life, nowhere does tension seem to build so fast as in New York, so I am using that as an example. If you live in another major city, your circumstances may be better and you need only pity the New Yorkers and be thankful you are not among them. For car renters in Manhattan, the situation is worst on Friday evenings and Saturday mornings in spring, summer, and early fall—especially at the outset of holiday weekends—when everybody seems eager to get away to somewhere. So if you are likely to become part of this pack, be prepared to face a miasma of complexities.

Despite efforts of rental agencies to make their peak-season operations more efficient, you may face long delays in picking up your car. You may end up with a car substantially different in size, features, and fuel consumption—an important consideration because you will be paying for the gas—from the one you reserved. You will certainly face rate structures that are confusing and subject to sudden change.

In some cases it may pay—in dollars and trouble saved—to pick up your car at an airport, where weekend rates tend to be cheaper than at Manhattan locations because that is where most cars are left at the end of one business week and needed at the beginning of the following one. Also, to save time and money, some weekend renters find it worthwhile to take the train part way, picking up their car at an office near the outlying station.

Rental rates can differ sharply from location to location in the metropolitan area, even within the same company, and can depend largely on whether a location is operated by the company or a franchisee. Because of this, don't depend solely on what you are quoted by the operator who answers a nationwide 800 number; it is worth the expense of a local or suburban phone call to seek rates directly from the site where you plan to get the car. Also, check out the smaller, independent rental agencies near your home; their rates are often—though not necessarily—cheaper than those of the big operators. Their emergency repair arrangements may be wanting, however, so a lot may depend on how far you plan to drive from home.

If you live on the West Side of Manhattan, it may seem logical to try first the Avis office at West 76th Street and Broadway or the Hertz office on West 77th Street, a block away. Those offices have tended to be exceptionally busy, however, on Friday evenings and Saturday mornings in the late spring and summer, so there could be advantages, even for residents of that neighborhood, to consider renting in Rego Park, Queens, for example, or White Plains, New York, or Stamford, Connecticut. But wherever you rent, if you are thinking of escaping the city for the weekend of Memorial Day, the Fourth of July or Labor Day, make your car reservations at least three weeks in advance. Even for other summer weekends, you should reserve two weeks in advance.

An Avis spokesman agreed that sometimes it might be easier to pick up a car in Rego Park than in Manhattan, but he was uneasy about steering potential customers to Queens. "Our office there is intended to serve the neighborhood market," he said, "and we have an obligation to do so. If the pattern changes, many people in that community won't be able to get a car."

The difficulty of moving large fleets through Friday rush-hour traffic from airports, where they are in heavy demand on weekdays, to Manhattan for the weekend is frequently cited by rental companies as the reason for delayed delivery to customers. Other reasons are the failure of midweek renters to return cars on time, and the failure of weekend renters to pick up cars on time.

"We ask a customer to come in no later than four P.M. Friday," the Avis spokesman said, "and he says O.K. But very often he comes in between five and eight P.M. anyway. We will never turn away a reserved customer because he's either a little too early or too late." The situation grows even more complicated, the spokesman said, because of "the very, very high percentage of double booking by customers on peak weekends, resulting in a very high percentage of no-shows."

Getting the size car you want can be important for both your convenience and your budget. Since October 1980 New York City has had a consumer protection regulation that says that a guaranteed car rental reservation for personal use must be honored by the company if you show up at the reserved location within half an hour of the time promised. If you reserve a four-cylinder subcompact at, say, $35 a day, the company must provide you with a car at that price, but not necessarily a four-cylinder model. Six- and even eight-cylinder ones may be substituted. But while you pay no more to the rental company, you pay substantially more for gasoline.

The consumer protection law permits the company to pay the cost of getting you a car from one of its competitors, if that is the only way it can meet its obligations to you. A spokesman for the New York licensee of Budget Rent-A-Car said her company sometimes did this and paid the rental difference if the competitor's rate was higher. Should the rate be lower, the difference goes to the client.

15. Car Rentals in Europe

In Europe as in the United States, if you are traveling widely, nothing provides so much flexibility as a drive-yourself car. But while such names as Avis and Hertz are as familiar in many European countries as at home, the car rental market is a lot different there. For example, the terms of a rental contract, your liability if something goes wrong, and how much you pay for a car can vary substantially from country to country. A lot can depend on whether you drive in only one country or cross borders.

To get the best and most reliable deal for your money, do not hesitate to ask questions and perhaps seek the help of a knowledgeable travel agent. It is sometimes cheaper to book through a travel agent than directly with the rental company, but either way you can often do best by reserving your car before leaving home because of inducements for advance bookings. But remember that if you do this and change your mind when you reach Europe, you may have to pay a much higher base rate.

Most tourist rates are based on unlimited mileage. Although the system can change abruptly, Avis has usually guaranteed its Western European rates in dollars for advance bookings, while Hertz, mindful of fluctuations in exchange rates, has guaranteed its rates in local European currencies. Hertz's guarantee in European currency is better if the dollar is rising; Avis's dollar guarantee is better if the dollar is falling in relation to European currencies. But whatever is happening, keep in mind that, as in the United States, advertised rental rates are only the beginning of a string of charges.

For example, in 1983 Avis advertised that you could rent a car in Britain with unlimited mileage for as little as $125 a week. But when Virginia Grimes of Levittown, New York, began asking questions, the lowest price quoted her was $275 for the type of car that she considered minimal for her needs. And that was before the cost of gasoline, insurance, and a 15 percent tax.

Of course, there was a reason for the higher cost. Miss Grimes—a freelance writer to whom I am not related and whom I did not know until she phoned me about her experience—had two particular needs: She wanted an automatic transmission and a trunk that could be locked and in which her baggage would be concealed.

Such needs are common among vacationers. Many of us are accustomed to the ease of automatic gear-shifting, and some people do not even know how to shift manually. And many of us will heartily agree with Michael Wellner, president of the Kemwel Group of Harrison, New York, which is prominent in the European auto rental market, who said in an interview: "I would personally not feel comfortable leaving my luggage exposed in the back of a car. I would not even do it here."

The problem is that to feel comfortable and secure while driving around Europe can be a costly affair. By all means, watch those attractive ads, but before you commit yourself, be sure that what you will get is what you want. Calculating the cost of a European car rental can be filled with distressing surprises. A study of Avis reservation rates for Britain at the time Miss Grimes was making her plans showed that to get a car with automatic transmission for a week, she would have had to pay a base price of at least $275—for a full-size Ford Sierra. Then would have come the extras.

Miss Grimes, like many drivers, says that she would have elected to buy what the rental trade calls a collision-damage waiver. Technically, it is not insurance, but waives a driver's obligation to pay a certain amount toward the cost of accidental damage. The company pays the rest. In Britain, based on exchange rates at the time, the waiver covered about $550 and cost the equivalent of about $28.88 a week. If Miss Grimes had bought insurance covering the death or medical care of anyone in the car at the time of an accident, she would have had to pay $13.12 a week more. So with all that, the cost of the week's rental would have been $317.

Western European countries typically apply what is called a value-added tax to most purchases. On auto rentals, such taxes varied at the time from zero in Switzerland to 25 percent in Belgium. In Britain it was 15 percent, so Miss Grimes's rental would have zoomed to $364.55. The rental would have come with unlimited mileage but would not have included gasoline, which in Britain was then running about $2.70 an imperial gallon (about a fifth more than an American gallon). And according to Jan Nyquist, then director of international sales for Avis, the rental car with automatic transmission would have averaged about twenty-three miles a gallon, compared with thirty to thirty-two for the company's least expensive vehicle.

It is obvious, therefore, that Miss Grimes's total auto rental bill for a week could easily have exceeded $450. In a sense, however, Avis insisted that it was offering her a bargain. The basic price quoted was among what the company called its "common rates Europe." This meant, Mr. Nyquist explained, that all rates for Avis rentals in Europe were guaranteed in United States dollars—the "common" currency for such arrangements—provided reservations were made in the United States before departure and the minimum rental period was three days. In most countries "common" rates were substantially below Avis's charges for reservations made locally. You did not have to prepay, however. If you preferred, Mr. Nyquist said, when you picked up the car two imprints would be made from your credit card: one on a form containing the dollar amount for the basic rental and the other to be calculated later in local currency for supplemental charges.

Hertz, meanwhile, had a program requiring reservations in the

United States at least seven days in advance but guaranteeing rates in local currencies. This meant that in a country like France, which had recently devalued the franc, Hertz had a price advantage.

The makes and models of cars available for rent in Europe vary from country to country, as do the rates. Almost all the cars are manufactured or assembled in Europe. Automatic transmission and air-conditioning are luxuries there.

So are locked trunks, because most small and medium-size European cars, and even some larger ones, have hatchbacks. More and more often, however, the rear hatchback door—the one that swings up—is attached to a shelf that conceals luggage when it is closed. You cannot always expect to find this in the smallest, cheapest rental cars, however, so be prepared to pay more if you want a guarantee of such a hatchback.

All such needs should be specified when you make your reservation. Also, be sure you consider carefully such factors as how much time you will spend in the car, how many people are in your party, and how much baggage there will be. As Mr. Nyquist put it:

"I've seen Americans who sign up here for a ninety-nine-dollar—or even a seventy-nine-dollar—a week deal, and then they get over there to pick up the car—maybe three or four people traveling together—and they get a vehicle that's slightly bigger than a bicycle. They simply can't use it. So we are saying this year, make sure you get what you need and remember that you get what you pay for."

When you reserve your car, either directly with the rental company or through a travel agent, be sure to get a confirmation number, especially if there isn't enough time to obtain a written confirmation by mail. This will give you some recourse if, as sometimes happens, the car that awaits you at your destination is not the type you ordered.

Avis, Hertz, the Godfrey Davis/Europcar network (represented by National Car Rental in the United States), and InterRent (represented by Dollar Rent a Car) are usually considered the giants in the Western European rental market, and Budget is represented through licensees in some countries. Some smaller American-based operators, such as Kemwel, Auto Europe, Europe by Car and Europacar Tours, try to undersell the giants, although they usually do not own their own cars but are agents for local entrepreneurs or even, by special arrangements, use the autos of a giant competitor.

A travel agent can steer you in the proper direction and explain the advantages and disadvantages of dealing with a giant or someone else. A lot will probably depend on the type of car you need, what country or countries you plan to drive in, and whether you are interested in a package that includes transatlantic air transportation and a car and possibly accommodations, too. Other options: Do you prefer to drop off the car somewhere other than where you pick it up, even in a different country, and is it important to have quick access to emergency repair facilities or even to a replacement vehicle?

If you have several choices of countries in which to rent, compare prices carefully. Factors such as whether the car is manufactured locally or imported and the rate of the value-added tax can affect prices substantially. Carefully investigate drop-off charges: They may be nonexistent, minimal, or a staggering $200 to $300. But one-way rentals are usually exempt from value-added taxes.

If you need a car for more than three weeks, ask a travel agent about leasing instead of renting. Leasing may be cheaper than renting because you usually get a factory-fresh car, it usually costs less than a long-term rental, and, in most countries, leases are tax-free.

Be sure you understand the appropriate driving laws. The car rental company or the American Automobile Association, if you are a member of an affiliated club, can help you with this. Even if you are not a member, a club can help you get an international driver's license, which some countries demand. If you plan to drive in Spain, ask about bail-bond coverage to avoid detention if you have an accident. When you pick up the car, make sure the rental company provides you with all the necessary insurance documents.

16. Renting "Wrecks"

They call themselves Ugly Duckling or Rent-A-Wreck or something similar to tempt the adventurous, but little is unsightly about what they offer. They are auto rental networks that specialize in well-worn cars, most several years old. Some are still quite attractive, mechanically sound, and rent for much less than most models of the current year.

Ugly Duckling is a chain of franchised auto rental agencies. It is one of two nationwide groups—Rent-A-Wreck is the other, larger one—that have found substantial profit in renting two-to-five-year-old vehicles, some with a number of scratches or dents but rarely battered enough to be shameful, at a fraction of the lowest rates of such industry giants as Hertz, Avis, Budget, and National.

In addition, there are dozens of unaffiliated operators across the country. They go by such names as Rent-A-Clunker, Rent-A-Junker, Rent-A-Jalopy, or Rent-A-Mess-For-Less.

Some drivers are turned off immediately by what they feel such names connote; others have tried "wrecks" but complain of windows that cannot be opened or closed, the absence of spare tires, and breakdowns far from home. But other renters are steadfastly loyal to such companies, insisting that they do not care about appearance as long as they can depend on the transportation.

The importance of a car's looks may ultimately depend on what you want the vehicle for. If you need it to attend a wedding, to go on a honeymoon or for an important business engagement where impressions count, a "wreck" probably is not for you. But for a day of metropolitan-area errands, to go fishing, or to pick up an offspring's belongings at college, it may be all right.

A few years ago in Westchester County, New York, one of the realities of life for Howard Slotnick, who has the Rent-A-Wreck franchise there, was that his Chevrolet agency was ailing, as was much of the American new-car business at that time. Mr. Slotnick also owns an auto-leasing business, which helps him profit from many of his new models. When he heard about Rent-A-Wreck, he decided that it offered just the sort of concept that could keep his cars in service—at a substantial profit—when their leases expired.

The prices quoted here are no longer valid, but they illustrate how rental rates for "wrecks" compare with those charged by major companies for current models. At one point you could rent an aging sedan from Mr. Slotnick's Rent-A-Wreck outlets in New Rochelle and White Plains for $16.95 a day with 100 free miles and ten cents a mile above that. At Hertz in the Westchester area at that time, you would have paid at least $39 a day, although with unlimited mileage.

Mr. Slotnick would have rented you a "wreck" for a three-day weekend for $45 with 350 free miles and for a week for $110 with 800 free miles. Hertz in Westchester, meanwhile, was charging $59.97 for a three-day weekend and $159 a week (the weekly rate contingent on your reserving at least twenty-four hours in advance) with unlimited mileage. Avis's rates were generally comparable to Hertz's.

In all these cases you would probably pay for the gas, and an economy-size model from Avis or Hertz would probably use much less than the bigger and/or older car you would probably get from Rent-A-Wreck. Therefore, if you wanted a car simply to run a few errands around town, you would probably save money by renting a wreck; if you planned a long-distance trip, you would probably do better otherwise. Keep in mind, incidentally, that a Hertz or Avis car, though of current model, may have been driven thousands of miles by the time you rent it.

In New York City, the gap between the "junk" agencies and the majors is usually greater than elsewhere. At one point in Manhattan, the Rent-A-Wreck franchisee (the same people who own Olins Rent-A-Car) was charging $17.95 a day from Monday through Thursday and $31.95 a day from Friday through Sunday, both with 100 free miles and ten cents a mile above that. The lowest Hertz and Avis weekday rates in Manhattan at that time were $55 from both companies. Rent-A-Wreck in Manhattan was charging $74.95 for a three-day weekend beginning as early as five P.M. Thursday and ending as late as noon Monday, with 400 free miles, compared with $119.85 at Avis and $139.97 at Hertz, both with unlimited mileage. In all cases, you paid for the gasoline you used, the company starting you out with a full tank.

After listening to what Rent-A-Wreck was offering, I decided to test for myself how the system worked. As a paying customer, using my own name but not identifying myself as a reporter, I rented three times from the outlet on West 76th Street in Manhattan, one of eight in New York City under franchise to the people who rent new cars under the name Olins.

All three cars I rented—two seven-year-old Pintos and a six-year-old A.M.C. Pacer—performed without fault. All had automatic transmission. Only on the first Pinto was there a defect that I believed to be potentially dangerous: The right front door could not be opened from the inside. (I reported this upon returning the car and was promised it would be fixed.)

No one had promised that the cars would be spotless, and they were not. The first Pinto had many scars, missing trim, and a highly conspicuous dent in the right front fender. No one had promised that the radio would have knobs for tuning, and it did not, so it was difficult to adjust the volume and change stations. But the car averaged twenty miles per gallon of gasoline, despite stop-and-go traffic.

The second car had no front license plate, a violation of the law in New York State, where it was registered. None of the cars contained registration papers. "When we supplied them, they were always being lost," Carl Feinstein, executive vice president of the New York operation, told me later. This also violated the law, but both Mr. Feinstein and state motor vehicle authorities agreed that most police officers would accept the driver's copy of the rental agreement as adequate evidence of ownership.

Cosmetically, the cars were no beauties, but Rent-A-Wreck had been open about that. On each occasion, I accepted without question the vehicle that the clerk assigned me, although Mr. Feinstein said later that I could have asked to choose among five to eight subcompacts and larger cars that are often available.

Because of the limited exit space at the company garage, I felt under pressure to drive away quickly, but each time I parked within half a block to test the lights, horn, turn signals, windows, and windshield wipers and to be sure that a spare tire and appropriate tools were in the trunk. I heard a fellow renter complain at the counter that the car he was returning—a red Ford with New York State license plate 680-ZBO—had no lug wrench, a shortcoming that, he said, delayed him substantially when he had a flat tire and had to wait for help.

On completing two of the rentals, I refilled the tank in New Jersey near the Lincoln Tunnel at $1.18 a gallon just before returning the car, and Rent-A-Wreck was satisfied; on the third trip, Rent-A-Wreck refilled the tank and charged me $1.50 a gallon. At Hertz or Avis, the biggest companies in the car rental industry, I also would have paid substantially more for their gasoline than for gasoline I could have bought myself.

The "junk" agencies are not always easy to find, especially since they are often on the fringes of major cities where overhead is relatively light, rather than at airports or downtown. The Los Angeles-based Bundy-American Corporation, which licenses the nearly 300 Rent-A-Wreck outlets in about forty states, maintains a nationwide toll-free telephone number, (800) 421-7253. In California call toll-free (800) 535-1391, or from Alaska or Hawaii call (213) 208-7712, a toll call. Operators will give you the address and phone number of the outlet closest to your desired pick-up point. Ugly Duckling headquarters in Tucson, Arizona, also has a toll-free locator number, (800) 843-3825.

To find a strictly independent agency, your best bet is to ask a used-car dealer in the neighborhood. He may rent cars himself. Also, you might ask the nearest auto club, a new-car dealer, or the police. Or check the *Yellow Pages*. Most agencies are open only during normal business hours and for a limited time on Saturday. Most are closed Sundays. You can pick up cars only during the agency's open hours, but often you can arrange to drop off a car at a nearby gasoline station if the agency is closed. Arrangements for drop-offs in a city other than the one where you picked the car up, even at a surcharge, are extremely rare.

Most agencies accept credit cards; some require them for payment. Those that accept cash usually demand a substantial deposit before you take a car. At some agencies reservations are mandatory; others are strictly first-come, first-served to avoid no-shows. At holiday times, reservations can be difficult to confirm.

Rarely will an agency deliver your car or provide pick-up service; instead, you have to go to its garage or lot yourself. Check carefully to see how far it is from the airport, rail or bus station, or hotel. Getting to the agency may entail a long or difficult trip by public transportation.

Jean Gerraughty of Rent-A-Mess-For-Less in Boston's Roslindale section said the agency was about ten miles from Logan International Airport, and that she would hold a car for about an hour if you called upon arrival by plane. She said the agency did a big business with college students in the Boston area. "We bought a lot of secondhand state police cars," Miss Gerraughty said in a telephone interview. "They are Ford LTDs, and everybody loves them. They no longer have any official markings on them, but people around here know what a police car looks like, and when they see one on the highway, they panic. Everybody slows down to the speed limit, and our drivers love it."

With many "junk" agencies you are required to buy a collision-damage waiver, which costs at least $4 a day if you are under twenty-five years old and $3 if you are older. The minimum rental age is twenty-one. This means that you are covered for damage to the vehicle in a collision, except for the first $200, which you must pay yourself. This is not liability insurance, so ask about liability before you rent: You may find that the car is not covered. If you already own a car, your liability coverage on that may cover a rental, too. If not, be certain that you understand the insurance implications.

Although your "heap" may be of the gas-guzzling variety, it will probably be roomy, although it could be an aging compact. It could be a Cadillac, however, or a station wagon or minibus, which are often in demand for family vacations or transporting offspring and possessions to or from college but which are frequently hard to get from the major national agencies.

Although the vehicle is supposed to be mechanically sound when you pick it up, everyone recognizes that older cars, like older humans, are more subject to sudden failure than younger ones. Therefore, wary of risking high repair bills, many "oldie" agencies will not let you drive very far from home base, say, beyond a radius of 150 to 200 miles, although you are permitted to drive as much as you want within that. Should your car break down within the permitted radius, the agency can usually get its own mechanic to you within a few hours or direct you to a service station where it has repair arrangements. In any event, you are usually required to call a special number, frequently available twenty-four hours a day, for authorization of any major repair and sometimes of minor ones. It may be wise to inquire in advance.

17. Airport Hotels

The jetliners whiz by as they land and take off—almost one a minute, it seems. Yet you hardly hear them. Instead, you enjoy the gentle melodies of a guitarist and chanteuse across the skytop lounge. Soon you will retire for the night and sleep soundly before leaving for Miami at 8:15 A.M.

Eight-fifteen? What an hour to have to be at Los Angeles International Airport, a time of so much rush-hour traffic on the freeways. You will avoid that traffic, however—in fact, you can sleep past seven A.M. and still check in for your flight with ease. That is why you have chosen to spend the night before departure at an airport hotel.

First-class and deluxe airport hotels and motels are a relatively new option for time- and quality-conscious travelers. Until a decade or so ago, they were few in number and modest in amenities. But according to a survey by *Frequent Flyer*, a monthly magazine aimed primarily at the business traveler, airport hotels have developed faster and made more money in one seven-year period than any other segment of the lodging industry.

Most of the new construction is not actually on airport property but within a fifteen-minute ride, usually less, by frequently sched-uled, free courtesy buses. A few hotels are actually within walking distance of ticket counters and departure gates, and some have enough on-premises recreational facilities—golf, tennis, indoor and outdoor swimming, jogging paths, and the like—to qualify as miniresorts.

From some, it is relatively easy and inexpensive to go downtown. So if you are spending the night in a city between connecting flights, you can have the best of two worlds: an evening on the town and a quick departure the next morning.

Airport hotels primarily court business travelers, who, according to *Frequent Flyer*, constitute 55 percent of their guests. In addition, 17 percent of the guests are there to attend meetings or conventions at the hotels, which have spent many millions of dollars to build appropriate on-site facilities. The remaining 28 percent of the guests are tourists.

Many of the newer airport hotels provide all the amenities of their most luxurious counterparts downtown yet often at rates 10 to 25 percent lower. Their prime attraction to corporate travelers is that they save money and time because it is not necessary to travel to and from downtown and to pay midcity hotel rates.

If a business traveler must see representatives of several widely separate companies in the same metropolitan area, it is often much cheaper to have them come to an airport hotel where meeting rooms are available than to call on them individually. Some airport hotels have mammoth convention halls that can accommodate thousands of people at trade shows and meetings for much less than such events could be held elsewhere.

A growing number of vacationers, however, are finding that airport hotels can have advantages for them as well. The typical image of an airport is of congestion, noise, unseemly surroundings, and little for a waiting traveler to do but get anxious. Few airports are known for quality food at competitive prices.

The newer airport hotels, however, whether on the premises or close by, are rapidly changing this image. They are proving that it can be not just convenient but also fun to stay there. Most offer free parking to guests, whereas it might cost $5 to $10 or even more to park at a hotel downtown. Many airport hotels permit guests who stay only one night to park their cars free for several days. This can be a decided plus for a New Yorker, for example, who must catch an early flight for a brief business trip or vacation and prefers to spend the night near the airport, rather than buck morning traffic.

The advantages of airport hotels can vary substantially, however, from city to city. A lot depends on the importance of the airport as a connection point, its location in relation to downtown, the quality and cost of public transportation, and the imagination, marketing talent, and financial investment that have gone into building and operating the hotel.

Like downtown hotels that earn their bread and butter from weekday business travelers, many airport hotels offer weekend packages at sharply reduced rates to keep occupancy as high as possible. Some beckon to newlyweds who go straight to the airport from their wedding reception or banquet, spend their first night of marriage there, then take off the next morning for their honeymoon site.

In one of its earliest promotions, the La Guardia Marriott in New York tried to entice residents of Brooklyn, Queens, and Long Island's Nassau County to spend Friday or Saturday night "vacationing" there. If you checked in either day the hotel offered, for $62.50 a person, a double room, dinner for two, breakfast in bed or in a restaurant on the premises, free parking, use of all recreational facilities, and a four P.M. checkout deadline.

The close-to-downtown, fourteen-story Logan Airport Hilton in Boston professes to have one of the best views of the skyline in the city. At off hours you can get to or from downtown in barely five minutes, but at busy periods it could take an hour and a half to get by car through the harbor tunnel—which is why many travelers prefer to spend the night before departure at an airport hotel. Once you have deposited your luggage, however, a subway trip becomes simple: The airport is only two stops from downtown.

The Ramada O'Hare Inn near Chicago's main airport has both outdoor and indoor swimming pools for year-round relaxation, two outdoor tennis courts, and a nine-hole golf course that is lighted for night play ($3.50 to rent clubs and balls). You can walk one block from the hotel to the Rosemont Horizon Arena to see college basketball (DePaul is the home team), the Ringling Brothers and Barnum & Bailey Circus in season, and occasional rock concerts, if you can get tickets on short notice.

Near Miami International Airport, the Sheraton River House does substantial business with passengers leaving on cruises and once offered a "stay and sail" package, including a room for one night, based on double occupancy, a drink, a Continental breakfast, and a limousine ride to the ship for $39.50 a person if you checked in on a Friday, Saturday, or Sunday. Most one-week cruises leave on Saturday or Sunday; many four-night cruises leave on Monday.

The Hyatt Hotel at Los Angeles International Airport has a rooftop lounge with music most nights and a view of planes taking off and landing. A shuttle bus ride takes only three minutes to airline departure areas, but, as with most municipal public transportation in Los Angeles, getting to places beyond the airport can be time-consuming and expensive. At the nearby TraveLodge International Hotel, guests who want to stray from the area are advised to rent cars.

If you are traveling in Europe, do not overlook the possibilities of staying at airport hotels there. In the Netherlands, for example, the Hilton International Schiphol Airport is linked by major highways and rail to all major Dutch cities. The capital, The Hague, is only eighteen minutes away and central Amsterdam is fifteen minutes.

For sightseers, the Aalsmeer flower auction, held every morning, is closer to the airport than to downtown Amsterdam, as are the Keukenhof Gardens and the area's flower fields. The Schiphol area is virtually a city in itself. For a price, you could live comfortably there indefinitely. But then, you might prefer to see a bit more of Holland.

18. Hotel Discount Plans

As hotel and motel rates have risen throughout the United States, clubs and discount cards have appeared that promise to save the traveler much money in exchange for nominal dues. Sometimes the promises are fulfilled, but often they prove empty or, at best, of questionable value. Some offerings have proved relatively durable, but others have been here today and gone tomorrow.

"The unbelievable card that gets you a free night's stay," said a full-page ad in *The Saturday Review* a few years ago. It referred to the International Travel Card, the creation of a Florida-based organization that promised that more than eight hundred "famous name" hotels and motels would lodge its subscribers for two nights for the price of one. The dues were $25 for one year or $40 for two.

"Make your reservations as usual," the advertisement said, "and show your Travel Card when you check in. You pay the hotel's regular published rate for the first night, and your second night is 'on the house'—absolutely FREE."

Similar discount programs—either twofers or reduced rates—have been promoted from time to time by such organizations as the Hotel Travel Card of Millburn, New Jersey; Discover Americard of Hartford, Connecticut; the Association of Informed Travelers of Salem, Virginia; the Airline Passengers Association of Dallas; Encore of Lanham, Maryland; and motor clubs. Some have offered discounts and travel-related services besides hotel plans; before you send in your first year's dues, however, it is prudent to find out exactly what you get.

In many of the hotel offerings, there are long blackout periods when no rooms are available because they have been booked or the hotel expects to book them at higher rates. In other cases one can get a cheaper rate without a card than with one. In major cities, the hotels that accept discount cards are sparse indeed and often are at the bottom fringe of respectability.

The bottom line in all this is that if a major hotel is willing to let rooms go cheap, it is because they otherwise would be vacant and thus lose revenue that could never be recovered. When better hotels get into such situations, they commonly discount rooms themselves through weekend packages or other gimmicks, such as distributing coupons that allow from one to four people to occupy, for $30 a night, a room that normally goes for $110.

At one time the nationwide Amoco Motor Club was unusual in that members, who paid $29.95 in annual dues, were entitled to buy coupons to stay at any Holiday Inn at 10 percent off. The hotel offerings of most other discount organizations are restricted to participating properties of the chains that offer them: Holiday Inns, Howard Johnson Motor Lodges, Quality Inns, or whatever. Among the many thousands of hotels and motels across the United States, few participate.

At one point a directory of the International Travel Card listed the Doral Inn at Lexington Avenue and 49th Street in Manhattan. But the listing warned, as do many of them, "Subject to room availability."

"I have very mixed emotions about getting publicity about our affiliation with the card," said Trudy Cohen, the Doral Inn's sales manager at the time. "We only accommodate cardholders if and when we project that we are going to have empty rooms. Recently that has been on weekends only."

When asked about an agreement of the Gotham Hotel at Fifth Avenue and 55th Street to honor the Hotel Travel Card, a two-nights-for-one plan, Anai Pakos, then assistant to the general manager, stated emphatically: "We do not want it publicized." The card is honored only if rooms are available, she said, and for several months, at least, there would be none.

Another New York outlet for the Hotel Travel Card was the Roosevelt Hotel at Madison Avenue and 45th Street. But a spokesman said the card would be honored only November 21 to 30 and December 12 to 31, when business was expected to be relatively slack.

A spot telephone check across the country of lodgings listed in discount directories produced similar restrictions almost everywhere. In Albuquerque, New Mexico, the owners or managers of four establishments that had been under current ownership for four months to two years said they had withdrawn from the International Travel Card. "Our rates are so low already that we cannot afford to give anything away," said Mohammed Nenshi, owner of the Tropicana Motel there, where rooms at the time began at $11.

Reached by telephone at his headquarters in Jacksonville, Florida, Thomas N. Kay, president of International Travel Card, insisted that his directories, which he said were published semiannually and brought up to date quarterly, listed only those establishments with which he had contracts. He acknowledged, however, that "there are going to be some changes in hotel ownership," and that this might present problems. In Mr. Kay's view, new owners inherited any contractual relationship with the International Travel Card. This view was disputed, however, by the operators in Albuquerque.

Big-city hotels customarily profit most on Sunday through Thursday nights, when they are patronized mostly by business travelers. So they often offer bargain rates to fill rooms on Friday and Saturday nights. Since two-for-one cards are often based on nondiscounted rates, a traveler can frequently get as much for his money or more without a discount card as with one.

At one time, the Hotel Travel Card listed only one establishment in all New York City: the Times Square Motor Hotel on West 43rd Street at Eighth Avenue. According to John Huber, the manager, the hotel also had agreements with the International Travel Card, Airline Passengers Association, Encore, the Association of Informed Travelers, and several other discount operations. Rooms for cardholders were generally available.

A spokesman for the New York City Human Resources Administration said department records showed that one-third of the hotel's guests were on welfare, one-third were pensioners, one-fifth were people who worked in the area, and the remainder were tourists. "We have a social service worker in there," the spokesman said.

You will not find the Times Square Motor Hotel or many other discount-plan hotels or motels in the *Official Hotel and Resort Guide*, a bible of the lodging trade. Nor will you find them in the *Red Book of the American Hotel and Motel Association*. Unfortunately, however, discount directories are usually available only after you have paid your dues in the organization, not before, so it may be difficult to find out in advance what you are likely to be offered.

If you are determined to conserve your hotel dollar, as most of us are, these are among the alternatives to discount programs to consider:

- If you have a choice, go off-season or on weekends to major cities or during the week to resorts.
- When you make your reservations, ask if any money-saving packages are available either then or, if your plans are flexible, at some other time a little earlier or later.
- Check your memberships in major national organizations, such as an affiliated club of the American Automobile Association, the American Association of Retired Persons, the National Council of Senior Citizens, or the American Society of Civil Engineers. Some memberships entitle you to discounts at some hotels and motels.
- If you are employed by a corporation that receives a business discount at major hotels, identify yourself as an employee when you make your reservations and ask if the discount applies to personal travel as well.
- If you and your spouse are traveling with your children—or with one or two other adults—ask about possible discounts if you all share one room.

Hotel discount cards are usually based on single or double occupancy only, so if three or four persons travel together, you often can do better without a card than with one. Also, twofer plans usually mean that only the second night is free, regardless of how much longer you stay. If you stay at a participating hotel a whole week, therefore, only one night could be free. Chances are you could do much better for a long stay by asking the reservations manager to suggest reduced-rate alternatives.

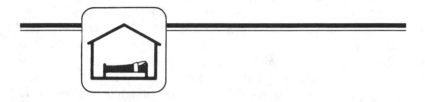

19. Europe's Small Hotels

A few years ago, making reservations at the small, charming, and often inexpensive hotels that can make Europe such a delight to tour was beyond reach unless you were on the spot or could reserve by mail. Getting a reply to a letter often took weeks, though, and letters frequently went unanswered.

Now, however, many of these small European hotels are accessible through centralized reservations offices in the United States. Many have also formed links with auto rental companies in plans that include guaranteed accommodations in most places in Europe that drive-yourself tourists are likely to visit. And some airlines have extended their hotel reservation services to embrace modestly priced accommodations, not just the very expensive.

The trick to obtaining relatively inexpensive lodging is to know, when you do your vacation planning, what sort of help is available. Here are some illustrations:

- A growing number of computerized reservation services available to travel agents in the United States can provide rapid if not immediate confirmation of lodging at small, relatively inexpensive hotels, usually at no charge.
- Many international airlines will confirm budget accommodations for their passengers, at least in the countries in

which the carriers are based. Not long ago, for example, KLM Royal Dutch Airlines said it could confirm rooms in the Netherlands for as little as $25 a night for two.

- Several companies that rent cars in Europe, such as the Cortell Group and the Kemwel Group, offer their customers—usually obtained through travel agents or airlines—packets of vouchers, each guaranteeing a night's accommodation at a participating hotel. Some plans require that you commit yourself to a specific itinerary in advance; under others, you commit yourself only for the first night initially, then at each stop book ahead for only the following night.

- Spain and Portugal have networks of picturesque, government-operated hotels and inns for motorists touring the countryside. Quick confirmation of accommodations is promised, but at popular places, especially in high season, you usually must commit yourself to a firm itinerary and pay for all your lodging before you leave home. Changes can be difficult and cancellations costly.

  Information and reservations for both the Spanish *paradors* and Portuguese *pousadas* can be obtained through Marketing Ahead, 515 Madison Avenue, Room 1206, New York, New York 10022; phone (212) 759-5170. Marketing Ahead levies a service charge, however, and some clients have reported that you can sometimes do better, both in price and in obtaining a room, by writing or having your travel agent write to each *parador* and *pousada* directly.

- In major European cities, and in some countries even in small towns, an increasing number of tourist offices, some government and some private, operate "space banks" for visitors who arrive without hotel reservations. Often without charge but sometimes for a small fee, they are equipped to get you a room in your price range by phone within minutes, although in peak summer periods it may not always be of the type and in the neighborhood you prefer.

Some experienced travelers advise that if you are interested in the European countryside rather than major historic cities or resorts, you simply get in your rental car or board a train, go wherever your fancy dictates, and assume you will find a place to stay when you get there—provided, of course, that you do not wait until evening. If the town of your first choice has no room, just get back in your car or, if you have determined in advance that service is frequent, get on the next train and go to another village.

The growing tendency of small, independently owned European hotels to affiliate themselves with international associations has forced up rates a bit. The hotels must share the cost of the central, increasingly computerized reservation services that such affiliations provide.

Central reservation networks are not completely reliable, however. If your travel agent requests a room at a particular hotel for specific dates, the reservations office will have a chart or computer terminal that lists those dates in one of three categories: "free sell," which means immediately confirmable, "sold out," or "available on request," which means that the United States office cannot be sure whether the room is available or not. Sometimes computers are not up to date. This happens when several agents, informed of a free-sell listing, try to make reservations almost simultaneously.

"If we confirm a reservation, we are very seldom wrong," said Hans Engel of American/Wolfe International of New York, which represents a wide range of European hotels, including many establishments in the budget category in Switzerland and Britain. "But sometimes," he added, "a traveler might have to be put up in some hotel other than the one where he had the reservation."

Put another way, "available on request" means "requested but not confirmed." It may mean that the representative will have to telephone or telex the hotel for confirmation, with the cost charged to the travel agent, who usually passes it on to the customer. With many smaller hotels, infallible confirmation can still be obtained only by mail, despite recent improvements.

Sometimes "sold out" means that the facility is fully booked at the time a reservation is requested but that the situation could change. Some experienced travelers advise, therefore, that if you are going to Europe at peak season, you should not necessarily be put off if a hotel of your choice rejects you six months in advance. Make alternate arrangements, but try the first hotel again a week or ten days before you leave; sometimes a group has canceled.

Because of the complications involved, many travel agents still do not try to book budget accommodations except for their best clients and for those who buy complete vacation packages, including transatlantic transportation, from them. Even then, many levy service charges for the time and out-of-pocket expenses involved in writing letters, sending telex messages or placing phone calls. Many agents complain of difficulty in collecting commissions from smaller properties in Europe. This problem seems to be easing, however, because when they book through representatives in the United States, they deduct their commissions from the advance payments.

Your travel agent should be able to determine easily whether a reservation can be confirmed quickly with no service charge. If the agent balks at helping you or asks a fee, you may prefer to write to the hotels yourself, allowing enough time for replies. With each letter, enclose two international postal reply coupons, which are available at post offices, to expedite a response, in which the hotel may request payment for the first night.

Better yet, if you have a friend in or near whatever European cities or villages you plan to visit, have the friend make reservations for you. It is often much easier on the spot than by mail.

If you choose a hotel-voucher plan from an auto rental agency, be sure to read the brochure carefully before committing yourself. Often a voucher represents payment in full at only some of the participating hotels; there is frequently a surcharge at others.

Also, whenever you have to pay more than a deposit in advance, be sure you understand how to obtain a refund if you change your plans and what penalties may be imposed.

In planning budget travel in Europe, a good place to start is by visiting or writing for literature from the appropriate foreign government tourist offices in New York. Another excellent source, available widely at bookstores, is the annually updated paperback *Let's Go: the Budget Guide to Europe*, prepared by the Harvard Student Agencies and published by St. Martin's Press.

20. Discounts for Older Travelers

Sometimes it pays to grow old. More and more Americans are discovering that a wide range of travel bargains are available exclusively to those who have reached the so-called golden years. To most people that age is sixty-five, but with the right credentials, which are easy to obtain, many bargains are available to those fifteen years younger.

For example, you do not have to be retired to join the American Association of Retired Persons. You simply have to be at least fifty and pay annual dues of $5, per person or per married couple. Just produce your membership card and claim discounts from several airlines, major auto rental companies, a broad selection of hotels and motels, and hundreds of sightseeing attractions across the country.

In many cities any sort of identification card that proves your age, such as a driver's license or Medicare card, entitles you to discounts on local transportation and a growing number of hotels, restaurants, theaters, sightseeing attractions, beauty salons, and shops. Lists are usually available from the local Chamber of Commerce or municipal office for the aging. The minimum age for senior discounts is usually sixty-five, but enough places have lowered the age to fifty-five or sixty to make it worthwhile to check before paying, and many will honor an A.A.R.P. membership card without asking how old you are.

The reason for such discounts is obvious. Life expectancy is rising in the United States; about 12 percent of the people are over sixty-five. Meanwhile, more and more people are aging in good health. Statistics show that older people, either retired or still employed but freed from many household burdens, have more time to vacation than the young. So the travel industry, seeking new sources of revenue, is eager to coax seniors to spend less time at home.

Airlines generally do not offer discounts on the basis of age, but exceptions are growing. For example, late in 1983 Eastern began offering people at least sixty-five a "Get Up and Go Passport," initially for $999, allowing a year of weekday travel to ninety-five cities. A second passport could be bought for a companion of any age, but both holders had to travel together. Passport holders also were entitled to 50 percent discounts from several major hotel chains.

Arrow Airways was offering discounts for older people between New York and Miami, and Delta had a reduced rate tie-in with the Days Inn chain. Many such offers are for limited periods, however, so when you inquire about reservations, it is worth asking what is available.

Amtrak sometimes offers discounts for the elderly, so ask what, if anything, is available when you are getting ready to go. The major bus networks usually reduce basic fares by about 10 percent for travelers who can prove they are at least sixty-five and sometimes younger.

As with all such discounts, they frequently apply only to basic rates and not to special promotional rates. So sometimes you may do better with a promotional rate than by seeking a discount on the basis of age. Also, discounts for the elderly are rarely volunteered; you usually have to ask about them when you buy your ticket, even if you are conspicuously at an advanced age.

Further, since the Trailways network is essentially made up of individually owned bus lines, some affiliated companies may not honor the offerings of Trailways Lines Inc. But even though the Greyhound Corporation owns all the lines bearing its name, travelers sometimes report difficulty obtaining even Greyhound discounts at small-town drugstores or other rural establishments that sell bus tickets on the side.

If you are convinced that you are not getting a discount to which you are entitled, immediately phone the public relations department of the company collect, if during business hours, or write to it later with a photocopy of identification that proves your age, and ask for a refund. Greyhound has its headquarters in Phoenix, Trailways in Dallas.

A growing number of hotel chains offer discounts at many if not all of their locations to anyone who can prove to be at least fifty-five or sixty or sixty-five—whatever company policy dictates. Be sure to ask about them when you make your reservation or at least when you check in—not when you check out, when it may be too late. Also, be aware that such discounts often do not apply to special group or corporate rates or to weekend packages.

Remember that restaurant discounts are often restricted to certain days, hours, or set menus; it may be necessary to tell the maître d'hôtel before he seats you that you will be dining under a discount plan.

For information on joining the A.A.R.P., write to it at 215 Long Beach Boulevard, Long Beach, California 90801. Its offerings include group life and health insurance, discount prescription medicines, investment opportunities, and travel programs, including tours of its own that alone can easily save you hundreds of dollars a year. If you are already a member, a brochure describing all discounts offered by the association is available by writing to Purchase Privilege Program Brochure, A.A.R.P., Post Office Box 2400, Long Beach, California 90801.

As an alternative, consider joining one of the four thousand or so local clubs affiliated with the National Council of Senior Citizens, which has a minimum age of fifty-five. Check your municipal office for the aging or write the council at 925 15th Street N.W., Washington, D.C. 20005, to locate the club that is most convenient. National dues at this writing are $7 a year for members of affiliated clubs or supporting labor unions, $8 for unaffiliated individuals, $9 for affiliated married couples, and $10 for unaffiliated couples.

The travel discounts available through the council are less extensive and sometimes smaller than those of the American Association of Retired Persons. The reason: The council has less than a third the membership of A.A.R.P., and in numbers there is strength.

Thus, members of A.A.R.P. usually get bigger discounts from car rental companies than do members of the council. But note that such discounts usually apply only to normal daily, weekly, and monthly rates, based on time and sometimes mileage as well. They rarely apply to the lowest priced promotional offerings.

In southern Florida, for example, an A.A.R.P. card could at one time have gotten you a subcompact car from Hertz for a week for $83.65, but you could have rented one at a promotional price of $79 without any affiliation at all. If you had chosen Avis, you could have rented a subcompact for $89.25 a week by producing an A.A.R.P. card, and the lowest weekly rate without one was $99. All these rates, incidentally, had restrictions and did not cover the cost of gasoline.

Those who do a lot of long-distance auto travel might also consider joining the September Days Club of the moderately priced Days Inn motel chain. Membership, available to anyone fifty-five or older, costs $10 a year for both husband and wife and offers a 10 percent discount on accommodations, food, and gift purchases at 95 percent of the chain's more than three hundred outlets across the country, plus discounts on auto rentals and at dozens of theme parks and sightseeing attractions. For membership information write to the September Days Club, 2751 Buford Highway N.E., Atlanta, Georgia 30324; phone (800) 241-5050.

A new organization for older Americans, with many programs besides travel, is Mature Outlook Inc., a subsidiary of Sears, Roebuck & Company. The address is Post Office Box 1205, Glenview, Illinois 60025; phone (312) 291-7800.

Travel discounts are also available for seniors going abroad. To learn about them write the nearest government tourist offices of the countries you plan to visit. Travel agents will know where the offices are. Ask particularly about discounts on railroads, which in most foreign countries are government-owned.

If travel plans in the United States include a stopover in a particular resort area, write to the local or regional Chamber of Commerce and ask if there are seasonal promotions offering discounts for seniors, which are increasingly common in the fall. Several popular tourist destinations have caught on to the idea that while younger Americans tend to think of September as back-to-work time, there are millions of people who have retired and do not think this way anymore. Here are some examples:

- The Williamsburg, Virginia, area often observes Senior Time in September. Your travel agent can tell you whether it is in effect this year.
- Throughout Tennessee, September has been Senior Class Month, a discount program involving private and public facilities that is one of the largest promotional campaigns ever assembled by a state tourist authority.
- Central Florida usually observes Senior Season from mid-

September to mid-December, with a host of discounts and special entertainment. For details write to Senior Season, Quality Inn West, 3330 West Colonial Drive, Orlando, Florida, 32808; (305) 299-6710. The area's premier attractions, Walt Disney World and Epcot, sometimes sponsor their own programs for part of the season.

A government leaflet with useful general advice is available free if you send a postcard to *Travel Tips for Senior Citizens,* Public Information Service, Room 4827-A, Department of State, Washington, D.C. 20520. For information on how you can get a Golden Age Passport, a free lifetime entrance permit for United States citizens sixty-two and over to all parks, monuments, and other recreational areas administered by the Federal Government, send a postcard to Public Inquiries, National Park Service, Washington, D.C. 20240.

21. The Fine Print on Tickets

Few travelers read the fine print on an air, rail, or bus ticket, even though the ticket is a contract between a carrier and a passenger. Most of us seem to care little about the fine print, and once we have used the ticket for a trip, we usually discard it.

Two major mistakes are implicit in this. First, it is simply not enough, these days, to *think* you know what you have bought. The sale is often veiled in disclaimers of responsibility, sharp restrictions on liability, and other conditions to protect the seller—not you—if something goes wrong. The carrier promises to transport you, but if its promise is not fulfilled in the way you expect it to be, there may be little it is obligated to do about it.

Second, experience has shown repeatedly that if, after your trip, you decide to lodge any sort of complaint, your chances of getting recourse are slim unless you can produce a ticket stub or coupon or photocopy of one as proof that you indeed made the trip at a particular date and time.

Let us examine the second point first. As a travel writer, I am frequently asked for help by people who complain about misinformation, overbooking, lateness, rude service, mishandled baggage, tainted food, and the like. Experience has taught me that a traveler's chances of winning recourse improve if he can produce specific information and proof. No evidence is stronger than a photocopy of a ticket—do not send originals, if you can avoid it.

On Amtrak, for example, if the extra-fare Metroliner is more than half an hour late on any segment of its run between New York and Washington, you are entitled to a refund of the difference between what you paid and the normal coach fare. You must turn over your ticket stub, however, to get the refund. In this case a photocopy is not sufficient.

A ticket receipt does not guarantee recourse to an aggrieved traveler, but at least it establishes what trip he is complaining about and that he was on it. It helps the carrier check operating records, trace missing baggage, or identify employees who might have been involved in misconduct.

An airline can turn a deaf ear to a broad-brush statement that it cancels flights at random and strands passengers in remote places. However, if a passenger produces a ticket receipt, the company cannot easily deny his complaint that Flight 123 was eight hours late on June 10, causing him to miss his Des Moines connection. There will be public records to prove his account.

Now for the other point: knowing what you have bought. A thorough early reading of a ticket, hotel reservation slip, or cruise contract can be revealing, indeed. Sometimes the information on tickets is scant, however, with an airline, for example, shielding its limitations of responsibility behind rules that it has on file in its offices. These rules are supposedly available at ticket offices for public inspection upon request, but they are often hard to find—and even harder for somebody who is not a specialist in transportation law to comprehend. As travel contracts now stand, you have few rights if something goes wrong. Here is a rundown on what some of the fine print says.

Airlines

Check any standard ticket of a major carrier, and you will discover that the company's liability is limited. A typical ticket states, for example, that liability for death or injury to a passenger is limited in most cases to $75,000, and liability for loss, delay, or damage to baggage is usually limited to $1,250 a passenger within the United States and to $20 a kilogram ($9.07 a pound) on most international flights. Sometimes the liability limit can be raised if you pay a fee, but in any event, liability should not be confused with insurance; to press a liability claim successfully, you must prove that the airline is responsible for what went wrong. Therefore, you should carry whatever insurance you deem necessary and not depend on liability alone.

The "conditions of contract" on the back of the ticket or on an accompanying slip outline the procedure for complaints regarding baggage. They also say that "times shown in the timetable or elsewhere are not guaranteed." The conditions include language such as this: "Carrier may without notice substitute alternate carriers or aircraft, and may alter or omit stopping places shown on the ticket in case of necessity. Carrier assumes no responsibility for making connections."

On the face of the ticket itself, there are several boxes to which you should pay special attention. One usually reads *restrictions* or *endorsements*. In airline code, which is explained in the airline's rules, these may denote special service that you need or have requested. Your ticket also states the period of its validity and what you paid and how. It may give codes denoting restrictions on stopovers, minimum length of stay at your destination, transferability of your ticket to another airline, refundability, and whether your reservation has been confirmed or simply requested.

It is in your interest to inspect all entries and ask that anything you do not understand be explained. It takes training and care to write an airline ticket properly, and even computerized tickets are only as accurate as the person who provided the system with the information.

Railroads and Buses

Ticket policies and carrier responsibility vary from country to country, and in many countries ground transportation is operated by the government. Often it is difficult to determine in advance what the conditions are, and much of this information will not prove useful anyway. It may be extremely hard to press a complaint once you have left the country unless your passage was arranged through a tour operator who does business in the United States and, if necessary, can be sued in an American court.

In the United States, tickets of Amtrak, the government-subsidized company that operates most of the long-distance passenger trains, tell little about conditions. But a detailed and surprisingly readable summary is in the system's nationwide timetable, available at many travel agencies and most Amtrak ticket offices.

For example, passengers are told that if they hold reservations in club or sleeping cars or in coaches on those trains that require reservations, such as Metroliners, a service charge will be levied on unused tickets or on cancellations made less than thirty minutes before the train's scheduled departure.

You have to ask questions, however, to determine that the service charge is usually about 5 percent of the cost of the ticket and that you may cancel by phone. If you do so, note on the ticket the phone agent's name and the cancellation code number he gives you. Then you must send Amtrak the original ticket, but make a photocopy for your own files.

The typical bus ticket in the United States merely says that the carrier's baggage liability is limited, that claims for baggage damage or loss must be supported by the original or a photocopy of the ticket stub, and that interstate seating "is without regard to race, color, creed or national origin." For further information, the ticket says, refer to the tariffs, or rules. The tariffs give details of any bargain fares, restrictions, or special services that apply either throughout the system or on specific routes.

Cruises

On request, Holland America Cruises supplied a sample of a typical two-and-a-half-page contract that bound the company and its passengers. Among other things, the company reserved the right to impose a fuel surcharge at any time before departure but also stated conditions under which an objecting passenger might cancel his passage and claim a refund.

The contract allowed the shipowner to change the time of sailing from or arrival at any port, to substitute a vessel, to change or cancel any sailing. It stated that refunds would be paid if an entire cruise was canceled, but usually not if a trip was interrupted, except because of the line's "negligence or willful fault." The ship could change course or itinerary, and the company had limited liability for injury to person or baggage. A passenger with a claim had to notify the company in writing within thirty days after a claim arose and had six months within which to file suit.

Such contractual conditions have been challenged in court many times, sometimes successfully. If you expect the recourse to be worth it, consider hiring a lawyer versed in travel and maritime law.

Hotels

The most important information you are likely to receive on a reservation confirmation slip—besides confirmation of the reservation itself and what it provides—is details of the company's policy regarding check-in time, cancellation, what rates include, and form of payment. Read these carefully and be sure to have the confirmation slip with you when you check in because many hotels, even those operated by some of the world's biggest chains, are noted for overbooking. They take a chance that the number of extra confirmations will be counterbalanced by the number of cancellations. Sometimes they win; sometimes they lose.

Rules regarding a hotel's liability to guests vary from state to state, according to law. Ask about them when you check in.

Auto Rentals

The back of a typical auto rental contract contains the conditions, but they are often in legalese that virtually defies comprehension by anyone but a lawyer. Avis, however, pioneered in simplifying contract language. The fact that you can understand such language is all the more reason to read it.

At best, many auto rental contracts are confusing, and you can often avoid spending extra dollars by knowing, before you sign, exactly what you will get and how much it is likely to cost. Usually, each rental company has one basic contract form; whether or not you get a discount or a special weekend or weekly rate depends not on the form itself but on how the blanks are filled in, so study the completed form as well as the contract language very carefully.

22. Travel Insurance

Little is more frightening than suddenly to lose all your money, identification, or baggage or to become injured or critically ill far from home. There is the initial shock and concern about how to recoup your losses. If health problems are involved, there is anxiety about your medical future and how to pay the bills. These bills can easily total thousands of dollars, with little if any part of it covered by insurance unless precautions are taken in advance.

I was relatively lucky. On a sunny midsummer Sunday morning, I suffered a heart attack at a flea market near Reading, Pennsylvania. The pain was mild and intermittent at first, so I shunned an offer to call an ambulance and, instead, had my wife drive me eight miles to the Reading Hospital, where I was sharply warned that any further move at that time might prove fatal.

Only eight days later did the doctor there let me be moved by ambulance, accompanied by two emergency medical technicians and a registered nurse, to a hospital in Philadelphia, where I could be close to my home, family, longtime personal physician, and friends. People in the ambulance business say the bill for the sixty-mile move was amazingly cheap: only $125, but I had to pay it all myself because none of my insurance covered it.

Not so lucky was an octogenarian social worker from Greenwich, Connecticut. She fell and broke a hip while sightseeing in Peking and was hospitalized there for a month. To her surprise, she was able to charge the hospital bill to her Visa card and was partly reimbursed later by Blue Cross. But there was no insurance to reimburse her the $1,800 that it cost to fly at the first permissible moment from Peking to New York—in first class to minimize discomfort—and go to Greenwich Hospital for further care.

Files of air ambulance companies show that many such moves cost much, much more: for example, $8,900 to transport a stroke victim from rural Texas, where he had been vacationing, to a hospital in Oakland, California, near his home; $13,232 to send a paralyzed traveler whose left lung had failed from India to California; $46,000 to fly two victims of severe heart disease from Montevideo, Uruguay, to Birmingham, Alabama, and $66,000 to fly a traveler with a broken neck—and accompanied by two physicians—from Saudi Arabia to Texas.

Mention of such horror stories is not to suggest that the prospect of enjoying travel should be clouded by anxiety over what could happen. For most people, the odds are overwhelming that it won't. But if you have an irregular medical history, are getting on in years, or enjoy vigorous sports or adventure travel in which accidents are common, it might behoove you to think a little about possible perils and to examine the options that could help defray enormous costs.

Many mishaps in travel are, of course, completely unpredictable. No one can foretell when an accident will occur or, even with the best of precautions, when baggage will go astray and never be seen again. And even the very cautious traveler can be vulnerable to the guile and expertise of professional pickpockets and other thieves who deftly make off with all your cash, traveler's checks, credit cards, and passport when given only a fleeting opportunity. Furthermore, in recent years there have been an alarming number of instances when airlines, tour operators, or travel agents left passengers stranded with worthless tickets when they suddenly went out of business before a trip began or while it was under way.

For all such perils, insurance is available these days. Some of the premiums are not cheap, and before you buy you should be sure you understand any restrictions and exclusions. Much of this insurance is sold through travel agents. The risks it covers have been broadened substantially in recent years, but the amount of coverage for each risk is sometimes quite limited. Such policies are often called "comprehensive," but they should be carefully scrutinized to determine, in each case, exactly what *comprehensive* means.

Comprehensive insurance is not the accident-only type of policy that is offered at airport counters or from credit card companies to cover particular flights or extended transportation. Rather, it offers many kinds of coverage, some of them packaged together and some sold separately. A typical policy may offer insurance covering accidents or illness while traveling, reimbursement for added expenses if you cancel or interrupt a trip, and compensation for the damage, loss, or theft of personal effects.

Among the principal packagers of comprehensive travel policies are the Travelers Insurance Companies, which call their program Travel Insurance PAK; ARM Coverage Inc., which uses the trade name Carefree; the Omaha Indemnity Company, an affiliate of Mutual of Omaha, which markets under the name Tele-Trip; and the Sentry Insurance Company of Stevens Point, Wisconsin, whose Travel Guard coverage has the endorsement of the American Society of Travel Agents, the biggest trade association in its field. All deal solely through travel agents except ARM, which can be reached directly at 9 East 37th Street, New York, New York 10016; phone (212) 683-2622.

These are some of the innovations in recent years, but not all policies offer them:

- Coverage against being stranded or sacrificing your prepayment if an airline or tour operator defaults.
- Coverage for extra expenses you incur if a plane is hijacked, a cruise line goes bankrupt, or airline employees strike unexpectedly.
- Reimbursement for emergency expenses if your baggage is misdirected or delayed.
- Evacuation assistance or reimbursement for it if doctors determine that you must be transported for emergency medical treatment that is not available where you are stricken.
- Personal liability insurance, should a claim be lodged against you for accidental injury of a third party or accidental loss or damage.

Rates vary among companies and according to state laws, but a complete package might cost about $60 to $80 a person for a ten-day trip. Such a package might include up to $500 in coverage for trip cancellation or interruption, $600 for baggage problems, $25,000 in accidental death benefits, $2,500 for medical expenses, $150,000 in personal liability coverage, $500 for trip contingencies such as strikes or an airline default, and $5,000 for emergency evacuation.

Some plans, such as Travel Guard, include coverage for what are described as unforeseen circumstances. As David J. Garber, manager of direct response and product development for Travel Guard's international travel products, explained it to my colleague Margot Slade, " 'Unforeseen circumstances' covers acts of God but not of governments." Thus, declared and undeclared wars, such as hostilities in Chad, are not covered. Nor are civil disorders of the kind recently seen in Sri Lanka.

"These are potentially catastrophic losses that would affect everyone," Mr. Garber explained, "and as insurers, we want to minimize risk." But an earthquake in Chile or a snowstorm in Denver? For these, he said, "travelers would be covered if their holiday is canceled and would recover from us the nonrefunded portion of their holiday money."

"What if the travelers do the canceling?" Miss Slade asked. "What if they hear of a hurricane headed toward Haiti and, being either nervous or prudent, decide not to hazard a holiday there?" Mr. Garber said claims investigators would decide these case by case.

Baggage coverage varies widely and sometimes is combined with other insurance, but in New York State you can expect to pay on a scale starting at $5.50 for $500 of coverage for three days. Before you buy, check your homeowner's or apartment renter's insurance: It may cover baggage lost away from home.

Since the default of the original Braniff International Airways in May 1982 and of several major tour operators, several insurance companies have been offering coverage to consumers who lose prepayments or are stranded. Claims may take long to process, however; the insurance companies usually insist on assurance that you cannot get any other compensation without protracted proceedings in bankruptcy court.

By far the greatest concern of many travelers, however, is to stay healthy—and to be prepared to pay what can be astronomical costs if they do not. Premiums for sickness and accident insurance depend on many factors, but through your place of employment you already may have ample coverage under Blue Cross/Blue Shield or another plan. But what about people who do not have private health insurance, such as people who are retired and covered only by Medicare, which is not usable outside the United States?

In recent years, special programs that cover travel outside the United States have been developed for such people and for those who are concerned—as more of us should be—about meeting exorbitant emergency travel expenses, both medical and otherwise. Each program is different; some cover most major emergency expenses while others provide only emergency deposits or cash advances to be repaid later. Fees, which are always subject to change, usually depend on the length of coverage. It is essential to study each program carefully before committing yourself to one. Here are some of the more prominent programs and their fees at this writing:

- International SOS Assistance Inc., Post Office Box 11568, Philadelphia, Pennsylvania 19116; phone (215) 244-1500 or, outside Pennsylvania, (800) 523-8930. Fees begin at $12 a person for one to seven days; long-term coverage is available.
- Assist-Card Corporation of America, 347 Fifth Avenue, Room 703, New York, New York 10016; (212) 686-1288 or, outside New York State, (800) 221-4564. Fees range from $30 a person for up to five days of coverage to $180 for ninety days. Available through travel agencies.
- Health Care Abroad, 923 Investment Building, 1511 K Street N.W., Washington, D.C. 20005; (202) 393-5500 or (703) 790-5655 or, outside Virginia, (800) 336-3310. Fees for this program, affiliated with Medex, a multilingual service that helps locate medical assistance and arrange evacuation if medically necessary, start at $2.50 a day with a $30 minimum.
- TravMed, Post Office Box 247, Frederick, Maryland 21701-0247; (301) 694-6588. This program, also affiliated with Medex, is operated by the International Travelers Assistance Association and is underwritten by the Monumental General Insurance Company of Baltimore. Basic dues are $3 a person a day.
- Europ Assistance Worldwide Services, 2100 Pennsylvania Avenue N.W., Suite 617, Washington, D.C. 20037; (202) 466-2919. This young American offshoot of a long-established Paris-based company provides a variety of emergency services, medical and otherwise. It costs $5 a person a year to subscribe to the program, and coverage is extra, depending on how long you will be away, for example, $30 a person for one to eight days. Some Europ Assistance services are also marketed through the Carefree program of ARM Coverage.
- International Medical Systems, 3 Waters Park Drive, Suite 217, San Mateo, California 94403; (415) 571-0611 or,

outside California, (800) 862-9900. Dues range from $45 for ninety days to $110 for a year.

- Near Inc., 1900 North MacArthur Boulevard, Suite 210, Oklahoma City, Oklahoma 73127; (405) 949-2500 or, outside Oklahoma, (800) 654-6700. Fees ranged from $45 a person for up to fifteen days to $120 a year, plus optional extras, such as for foreign hospitalization. A combination package plan was offered at $3.50 a day with a twelve-day minimum.
- Air-Evac International, 296 H Street, Suite 301, Chula Vista, California 92021; (619) 425-4400 or, outside California, (800) 854-2569.
- World Access Inc., Suite 200, 2115 Ward Court N.W., Washington, D.C. 20037; (202) 822-3978 or, outside the District of Columbia, (800) 482-0016. Initially this company handled only corporate accounts, but individual coverage was planned.

When you examine these programs, find out, for example, whether you are covered in the United States as well as abroad, whether the plan pays for a second move as well as for initial emergency transportation, whether the company arranges help for you or simply reimburses you later for expenses you must pay first, whether there are mileage limits and a ceiling on expenses, what sort of medical documentation and prior approval may be necessary, and how quickly you can expect help to be at hand.

One advantage of subscribing to a program that promises help, not just reimbursement, is that it probably provides expert aid in making choices you might find extremely difficult to make alone. Obviously, the companies are not in business to spend any more money than they must, but if you were left alone, you could easily be drawn into chartering a lavishly equipped air ambulance when emergency facilities on a commercial flight, at perhaps a third of the cost, might be ample. If it is left to you to choose, therefore, ask for guidance from a local hospital or police department. But be aware that without special protection, the cost could be a staggering burden for years.

Insurance for Skiers

Skiing is supposed to provide thrills and pleasure, and it usually does. It also involves risks, however, and when skiing far from home, it is wise to have insurance and other protection to cover them.

Accident insurance is widely available, not just for vacationers who plan to participate in rigorous sports but also for just about any sort of travel. Before buying, however, you should be sure that it meets all your possible contingencies and that you really need all the coverage you are paying for.

For example, many travel accident policies do not cover skiing or water sports because of risks; others do but only if you pay as much as 50 percent extra. Some policies cover only accidents on common carriers—multipassenger airplanes, trains, buses, and the like—which may be adequate for vacationers on escorted tours but not for those with a passion for adventure and physical exertion.

Some policies cover accidents anywhere away from home at any time; others apply at home as well. Some are restricted to travel accidents in the United States, others to travel abroad, and still others are global. Some are valid for only a specified number of days; others are good for all travel within a year and are renewable.

What all this indicates, of course, is the need to shop around. Your travel and insurance agents should be able to point you in the right direction. Do not wait until you get to the airport; policies sold at counters or in vending machines are often very limited in scope.

When winter is at hand, suppose a ski enthusiast from White Plains, New York, seeks out the slopes at Mount Mansfield, Vermont—to pick a destination strictly at random. Should he be so unlucky as to shatter the bones of a leg there, the ski patrol of the Mount Mansfield Company would take him to the Stowe Clinic, six miles from the base area, or, for more sophisticated care, to the Copley Hospital in Morrisville, Vermont, ten miles away. According to Polly Rollins, a company spokesman, there would be no transportation charge.

Gloria Wing, the nursing director at Copley, said that if the emergency could not adequately be dealt with there, she would call on Charles Hoag, who operates the Lamoille Ambulance Service in nearby Johnson, Vermont. Mr. Hoag said it would cost at least $184.25 to go by ground ambulance to the well-equipped Medical Center of Vermont at Burlington. If the victim insisted on going home, however, it would cost $800 to $950 from Morrisville to White Plains by surface or by air to La Guardia or Kennedy and by ground from there.

Basic Blue Cross/Blue Shield policies rarely cover ambulance service at all. Emergency transportation is commonly reimbursable, however, under major medical policies, such as those underwritten by Prudential, Metropolitan and New York Life. Based on interviews with spokesmen for those companies, however, it is likely that only the Morrisville-to-Burlington move would be covered, because a transfer to White Plains might be considered the patient's emotional preference not a medical necessity.

Whatever you buy, be sure you understand the section on exclusions, which will specify what is not covered. Ask about limitations on payments for specific types of fractures—"Some bones, such as the skull and thigh, are worth more than other bones," said John Cook, manager of ticket and travel plans for the Travelers Insurance group. Ask whether there is a deductible clause; frequently you must pay the first $50 to $250 yourself.

In winter, the focus of much travel accident insurance is on what could happen on the slopes. A lot seems to depend on where the slopes are.

"Basically, the farther one travels from home to ski, the more experienced the skier is, and the risk of accident is lessened," said Allan R. Morris of New York, a major initiator of travel-related insurance. "The problem comes from the weekend skiers. Here adverse losses do occur based upon the enthusiasm of learning and the inexperience."

Mr. Morris cited school ski outings by bus that, he said, are often arranged through travel agents. "I can almost assure you statistically," he said, "that out of one of these busloads of children there will be three accidents."

"We also have experienced severe losses," he added, "in the area of the swinging singles who participate in long weekend bus trips, participating in the joy of socializing and, in some instances, taking in liquid spirits in preparing themselves for the spirit of the festive weekend. Unfortunately, due to the night partying and the tiredness, it lowers their reflex actions on the slopes."

Mr. Morris's programs, packaged by ARM Coverage Inc. and underwritten by the Insurance Company of North America, are sold principally through travel agents. A particular agency usually sells only one brand of travel insurance, and sometimes—although not in the case of ARM—you must arrange your travel through that agency to buy the insurance it offers.

The coverage and rates vary substantially according to company, the extent and duration of coverage, and the state in which you live. A rough range, including at least minimal coverage for ski mishaps, is $8 to $10 a person for seven days. ARM does not charge extra for medical treatment of vacation skiers, but Omaha Indemnity levies a 50 percent surcharge on everyone who adds ski coverage to its basic travel accident coverage, and Travelers adds 50 percent or $5 a person, whichever is greater, to its accident/sickness policies.

"Virtually all insurance companies will exclude medical reimbursement for ski accidents if they result from athletic sports," Mr. Morris said. "There has always been a question in my mind as to what constitutes athletics. Obviously, a participant in the Winter Olympics would be excluded under this insurance. The same would be true with high school or college ski teams. However, when Mr. and Mrs. Public enter a ski competition at a private resort, this could conceivably be construed as athletic, even though it was done on a purely voluntary basis."

To plug loopholes, the hundred-thousand-member United States Ski Association offers supplementary insurance at $8 to $30 a year, depending on age. Howard Peterson, the executive director, said it covers "the more typical ski accidents," such as broken legs, by paying for evacuation, if necessary, to the nearest adequately equipped medical facility, and hospitalization up to thirty days. Only members, who pay $20 a year in dues, are eligible. For details, contact the United States Ski Association, United States Olympic Center, 1750 East Boulder, Colorado Springs, Colorado 80909; phone (303) 578-4600.

For travelers who must interrupt a prepaid vacation because of an accident, several trip-interruption policies—those that reimburse you for cancellation penalties and other extra costs—have recently been extended to cover emergency evacuation by stretcher. Travelers and ARM, for example, will reimburse you for the cost of the extra airline seats you must buy to accommodate a stretcher, but usually with a maximum limit that varies among companies. In all cases, if you are to collect, an attending physician must determine that evacuation is essential.

ARM covers transporting a traveler's physician and next of kin from home, if deemed necessary, to be with him in the accident area. Several insurance-related programs provide emergency evacuation services and various forms of on-the-scene medical, legal, and related assistance to stricken travelers abroad or worldwide. Check the list in the first part of this chapter.

Trip-Cancellation Insurance

Item. Sol Resch planned to take his wife to California. Six months in advance, he paid $388 to a travel agency near his home in Jackson Heights, Queens, for two round-trip tickets on charter flights between New York and Los Angeles. A week before they were to leave, Mrs. Resch hurt her back and was hospitalized. Her husband promptly canceled the trip and claimed a refund.

He had to go to court to get it—at a cost of $100 in nonreimbursable legal fees. The judge ruled in his favor only on the ground that Mr. Resch's travel agent had not warned him about cancellation penalties and about the availability of insurance to cover them.

Item. A nurse who knew about trip-cancellation insurance neglected to buy it because she did not think anything could go wrong with her plans. She paid $1,675 for one-way passage on the *Queen Elizabeth 2* to England, and a lot went wrong. Two days before her scheduled sailing, she fractured a foot. Her doctor insisted that she rest at home for a week and that in no event should she travel on an ocean liner until the foot healed. She canceled her passage, which normally would have meant a refund of half her fare. Because she was able to adjust her vacation to go on a later sailing, however, the Cunard Line gave her a full credit to be applied then.

Item. An Arkansas couple flew to Israel on Trans World Airlines to visit relatives. They had bargain excursion tickets that required them to stay in Israel from fourteen to twenty-one days. On the tenth day, the husband suffered an acute attack of hypertension—very nearly a stroke. Blood vessels in his eyes hemorrhaged, and he gasped for breath. An Israeli physician gave him emergency medication and advised him to return home at once.

The couple followed his advice. But it cost them $600 in additional air fares because they had to amend their tickets and pay the full economy rate. If they had had trip-cancellation insurance, they would have been reimbursed for the difference.

Cancellation insurance has become increasingly important in recent years. When Allan R. Morris, the New York insurance promoter, pioneered in the field in 1965, there were relatively few air trips that one could not cancel at the last minute and receive virtually a full refund. Today, however, more and more fares carry time restrictions or must be paid for in full by a specified time before departure, with penalties imposed for cancellation after that. On charter flights, the penalty is often 100 percent.

So the lesson is clear: If you are going on any sort of trip or portion of a trip where there could be a refund problem, cancellation insurance should be considered a must. It usually covers travel by air and sea and often by bus and rail as well as ground arrangements— hotels, meals, car rentals, escorted tours, and the like—that are paid for in advance.

The insured is covered for cancellation before departure, for having to leave a tour temporarily and catch up with it, and for early or late return home. But the reason must be medical and must be professionally documented—usually illness or death of the covered traveler or death or alarming illness of an immediate family member, whether also on the trip or at home. If at home, the relative must usually live in North America. The insurers feel the administrative problems of verifying illnesses abroad other than for the insured traveler would be too great.

A traveler who must interrupt a trip because of an accident or illness should get a letter from the doctor at the scene or it may be difficult to convince the insurance company later that there was really a medical emergency. Premiums vary slightly according to state regulations. You pay a rate for the state in which you live— probably at least $4 for $100 of insurance, depending on which company's policy you buy and what it covers. Generally one should buy enough to cover the penalty for cancellation or to cover the added cost of catching up with a tour or returning home at the full economy air fare. That is the most the company will pay you, incidentally, regardless of how much coverage you buy.

Cancellation insurance is generally sold through travel agencies, and the agent may require that you buy your trip from him, too, although the insurance company does not require this. A travel agency usually sells only one company's insurance and at commissions ranging up to 35 percent, so it may pay to shop around.

Every policy has its fine print, and it can be hard to understand. So it is incumbent on you, the purchaser, to know the limits of what you are buying and to be aware that there are many gray areas in which the company can bend for or against you, depending on its own assessment of your case.

Nowhere is the importance of this better illustrated than in the protection offered in case you cancel, interrupt, or cut short a trip because of illness or death. In most cases you must carefully document each claim with physicians' statements, copies of hospital bills and laboratory reports, and the like. In short, you must prove to the satisfaction of the company that you had no choice but to abruptly change your plans.

On your insurance application form and on the policy itself, you will find a section or sections headed *Exclusions*. To understand those sections is perhaps most important of all. Most policies will tell you that coverage pertaining to illness may not apply in case of a pre-existing condition.

For example, suppose you have high blood pressure but because of medication prescribed under the routine supervision of your physician, your condition has been stable for years. During a prepaid vacation in Europe, for which you have bought cancellation insurance, you suddenly develop severe dizzy spells and are advised by a hotel doctor in writing—this is important for the company—to return home, paying, say, $1,200 in plane and hotel penalties.

If the records of your doctor at home show that he noted no change in your condition and suggested no change in medication when you last visited her or him, chances are the insurance company will honor your claim for reimbursement. But if your doctor had, say, changed the prescription medication—even lightened the dose because you seemed to have improved—your claim may be disapproved on the ground that you had been medically treated within ninety days of the time your coverage took effect.

"Any change in medication would indicate an unstable condition and would be a cause for denial," said Ed Harrington of the Greifer Agency of Union, New Jersey, which markets Travelers Insurance in the New York area.

"It's one of those gray problem areas," Mr. Morris, the insurance promoter, said. "It's something I've got to play by ear when a claim comes in."

Suppose, however, that you are stricken by severe gastrointestinal upset—a condition totally unrelated to your high blood pressure. "The cause of the illness would be intake of food into the system," Mr. Morris said, "and chances are you'd be paid. But for dizziness, no."

With policies that cover cancellation because a close relative or even a business partner is stricken at home, the prevalent view is that a pre-existing condition of someone at home does not impair your coverage.

Here are other questions to ask about the fine print:

- If an insured person dies while traveling, does the company pay all or only part of the cost of shipping the body home?
- When does coverage begin and end?
- Does the policy cover all members of the immediate family who are traveling with the insured or must each have individual coverage? Does it cover adult children?

Cancellation insurance could add $100 or more to the cost of a trip, depending on the number of people traveling, but it can be well worth it. No one expects to cancel or interrupt a vacation, but the unexpected often happens and can prove costly, indeed.

23. Traveler's Checks

When I was seventeen and driving across the United States with a friend, I ate lunch at a drugstore in Zanesville, Ohio, paid with a $20 traveler's check and received $19.45 in change. Despite my obvious youth, casual dress, and an accent that clearly was not local, I bought gasoline with traveler's checks, paid rooming houses with them, and cashed them easily at small-town banks. I never was asked for any identification but had only to countersign each check in the presence of the person who accepted it.

Today, more than forty years later, the situation is far different. I usually wear a business suit, carry an attaché case, speak graduate-level English, and, I think, look respectable. Yet frequently I cannot cash a traveler's check without at least writing my address and phone number on the back and/or presenting one or two positive proofs of identification, such as a driver's license or passport. A few stores in which I have shopped will not accept traveler's checks at all, and some banks have refused to cash them because I had no account there. Such is a reality of the travel world today.

The traveler's check business is booming, with sales estimated at $50 billion in 1984 and growing 15 to 20 percent annually. But so is criminal activity in the field. American Express, which says it pays tens of millions of dollars a year in refunds for lost checks, once estimated that 48 percent of reported losses were because of theft. Widespread counterfeiting of checks has been reported in South America, and a major fencing operation for stolen traveler's checks, credit cards, and airline tickets was discovered a few years ago to be operating out of limousine services in Queens and Long Island.

The vendors of traveler's checks prefer not to publicize it, but, while their products provide travelers with one of the safest ways to carry large sums of money, complications increasingly arise in cashing them. A major reason is that merchants and the check companies are often at odds about what security measures are necessary and practical.

"All we require of merchants," an American Express spokesman said, "is to watch and compare. The cashier watches you sign the check and compares it with the way your name was signed when the check was purchased. If the two signatures are reasonably similar, we expect the merchant to accept it. We will not hold him responsible if the second signature is a forgery, providing it is a good one."

"Even if an outstanding forger comes in," the spokesman said, "and to the normal, reasonable eye his signature looks the same as the earlier one, we stand behind the check and honor it. We don't expect clerks to be handwriting experts." The company employs investigators to track down forgers and help prosecute them.

At the same time, the spokesman said, for establishments that want to be as cautious as possible, American Express provides a toll-free number to call when they feel uneasy about accepting checks for large amounts. The company tells them whether or not the checks have been reported lost or stolen.

A lot depends on where the check is being cashed. For example, if you buy $15 worth of gasoline at Bob's Downtown Conoco in Steamboat Springs, Colorado, and pay with a $50 traveler's check of any major brand, the attendant simply watches you sign, compares your name with the way you wrote it when buying the check, and, if convinced both signatures are yours, quickly hands over $35 in change. But if you try to cash a $50 traveler's check at some major banks in New York you may very well be turned away—even if you can document your identity thoroughly—simply because the bank does not sell that brand of checks or because you do not have an account there.

In the view of Eli D. Cohen, secretary-treasurer of the Duane Reade discount drug chain in New York, it is not always easy to watch and compare. This means, he said, that checks are sometimes bounced when his company submits them for payment.

"We have fifteen to twenty cashiers in each store," Mr. Cohen said. "They are often all very busy. It is very difficult for us to become detectives. We do our best, but we have a large transient trade—many out-of-towners and foreigners—and bingo, Duane Reade is considered an easy touch."

Winston Bowman, a credit executive in the Miami headquarters of Florida's Burdine department store group, said the stores' sales clerks are instructed to watch signatures carefully and to compare. Each check must be signed, dated, and made payable to Burdine's in the presence of the clerk. "We don't expect our salespeople to be handwriting experts," Mr. Bowman said, "but they must be sure that the original signature and the countersignature are reasonably similar." And if the check is of a large denomination, the customer may be required to go to a cashier's cage for authorization.

Darrell Bryant, an assistant vice president of the Dart discount drug chain in the Washington area, said his company not only followed the watch-and-compare procedure but also usually required that a driver's license or other positive identification be presented before a traveler's check would be accepted for a purchase.

Mary Moore, then director of consumer affairs for the D'Agostino supermarkets of New York, said her company had a problem with customers from the neighborhood who returned from trips with traveler's checks left over. "Sometimes the husband bought them and did the original signing," she said, "so he signs them again and takes off for his office, leaving his wife to try to cash them at the supermarket. That's a sticky one. We shouldn't accept checks that way, but sometimes a store manager will, if he knows the customer well and has her countersign it on the back."

Most hotels and restaurants in the United States, as they traditionally have, readily accept traveler's checks as payment, simply asking you to sign them, nothing more. But the wise traveler will carry the best possible identification anyway, because more and more banks and retail establishments require it. It is increasingly common to be asked for two pieces of identification, preferably one with your photograph, your address, phone number, and sometimes even those of your employer. Sometimes in banks it may be necessary to wait in two lines because an officer's endorsement is required before a teller cashes the check.

A cross-country spot check by telephone found these practices:

- To cash a traveler's check without making a purchase, you often have to go to a bank. After banking hours, your best bet is at the hotel or motel where you are staying. Merchants generally are uneasy about depleting their cash, but some supermarkets cash up to $75 in checks, even if you buy nothing.
- Big-city banks tend to be tougher than those in small towns, but there are always exceptions, and many large banks give branch managers a lot of leeway. Bankers in Steamboat Springs, Colorado, Spearfish, South Dakota, and Zanesville, Ohio, said they cash traveler's checks up to $1,000, but that an officer's endorsement is needed for more than $50. All said they ask for more than one piece of identification.
- Most retail establishments accept traveler's checks to pay for merchandise and give change according to the same rules they apply to the denomination of currency: If a $50 bill is accepted, so is a $50 traveler's check.
- Most establishments require at least one piece of identification bearing your name in print and your signature; more and more require two. A passport, valid or expired, is considered good identification because it has your picture; old New York State driver's licenses, which do not have pictures, are accepted with less enthusiasm. (In 1984 New York began a switchover to driver's licenses with photos.) Major credit cards are usually accepted as secondary identification.
- Although you receive your purchase and change instantly when you use a traveler's check, the establishment that accepts it must wait to use the money. Banks usually do not credit a business account for the value of a traveler's check until the check has passed through a clearing system, which may take several days.
- Gasoline stations tend to be relatively lenient in accepting

traveler's checks. Said Joe Monteleone, a transplant from Wilton, Connecticut, who was working for Bob's Downtown Conoco in Steamboat Springs, "I check the signature real close, and that's about all."

As the traveler's check sales volume grows, so does the intensity of competition among the suppliers. Once the field was dominated by American Express and Thomas Cook, to be joined later by the Bank of America and the First National City Bank of New York, now Citibank, and its parent company, Citicorp. More recently, Visa and then MasterCard, the credit card companies, entered the field in conjunction with banks that issue the checks and assume fiscal responsibility for them. The banks profit the most from the float—the money is in the bank's possession, for its own use, from the time you buy a check until you cash it.

Some suppliers issue traveler's checks in foreign currencies as well as United States dollars, the most common being the currencies of Britain, Canada, France, Japan, Switzerland, and West Germany. Deak-Perera, the foreign exchange dealer, also sells traveler's checks in local currencies issued by banks in Australia, Britain, Hong Kong, Italy, the Netherlands, Portugal, and Spain.

Deak-Perera contends that foreign-denomination checks save frequent air travelers from "the conversion hassle." It says that these checks are often easier to cash than dollar checks. Reports from travelers indicate, however, that this is often not true, and that the most important factor is the rate of exchange at the time either a foreign-currency check is bought or a dollar check is cashed. That can be a gamble.

The standard fee when buying traveler's checks is 1 percent of the amount bought. In most cases, the selling agent is allowed to keep the entire fee, so checks are often sold free, with the seller depending on the float to yield a profit. American Express checks are commonly sold free to members of clubs affiliated with the American Automobile Association; Thomas Cook or Visa checks are often free to account holders in the savings banks or savings and loan associations that issue or frequently deal in them.

American Express has a program under which holders of its charge cards can, by prearrangement, have access to twenty-four-hour traveler's check dispensers at major airports and many other locations. By inserting your charge card in the dispenser and punching in a code number, you get traveler's checks, and the amount plus a 1 percent fee is deducted from your designated bank account.

In many places traveler's checks can be bought with a Visa or MasterCard credit card or with a special card that a bank issues to its account holders to enable them to use automatic teller machines. Be careful, however: Such charge purchases are usually considered to be cash advances on which interest begins accruing immediately, not after the deadline for payment of your monthly bill, as with purchases of goods and services.

Also remember that there is a difference between cashing a dollar traveler's check in the United States and cashing it abroad. In the United States you are entitled to the face value; abroad your dollar checks will be worth what the dollar is worth on the retail exchange market at that moment in the local currency, minus a commission charged by the casher. The commission is not a charge for cashing the check but for exchanging the dollars represented by the check into the local currency.

Travelers to Britain once complained, however, that some banks there had been charging a fee for cashing traveler's checks above the usual exchange commission. Asked about this, Paul Feldman, a spokesman for American Express, confirmed that an "authorized encashment fee" for checks in dollars existed at that time in Britain, with the approval of the clearing-bank committee there. He said the fee varied from bank to bank.

Identification is almost always required to cash traveler's checks in foreign countries, but your passport provides that. Remember, however, that no matter where you are overseas, you will usually get more for your dollar checks from major banks than from commercial money changers, hotels, restaurants, or stores. It may cost you some extra time to stop at a bank, but the savings can be considerable.

Spurred by an American Express campaign, almost all the major traveler's check companies have relatively speedy procedures by which emergency funds can be obtained when checks are lost. American Express contends that in four cases out of five, refunds can be obtained within twenty-four hours.

The fifth case, however—the one that is not advertised—can be significant. It probably involves a traveler who does not keep a running record of the serial numbers of all the unused checks. Only if a traveler can provide such a record can a refund be made quickly.

Sometimes a record of the checks you bought, though not of what you spent, can be obtained from the bank, travel agency, or other organization that sold the checks to you. Usually, however, such information is available only during business hours and may cost you an international telephone call. If a record cannot be obtained easily, your refund could be subject to long delay.

The word to the wise, therefore, is to keep your serial number record up to date, no matter how much of a nuisance this may seem. Keep the record separate from your checks—perhaps one copy in a coat pocket and another in your suitcase at the hotel. Also, right after you buy the checks, leave a copy of all the serial numbers with a relative, friend, or business associate whom you can reach easily if you need the numbers.

Theft and Fraud

This section is based on an interview a few years ago. The gentleman has since retired, but the points he made are still valid.

Leonard B. Mountford keeps his traveler's checks and other valuables in an inside pocket of his suit jacket. It does not show, but the pocket is fastened with an oversize safety pin.

"I am a very experienced traveler," Mr. Mountford said recently, "and I've been ripped off."

But Mr. Mountford has a good record in keeping travelers from being robbed. He is based in London as a chief special agent of the American Express Company, and he travels widely in his mission to help curb fraudulent use of traveler's checks.

American Express is the biggest issuer of such checks in the world, although Thomas Cook, Visa, Citicorp, and the Bank of America are substantial competitors. As far as possible, their security officers work together to deter thievery and counterfeiting because the problems are common to all and are widespread.

Mr. Mountford spent twenty-five years with Scotland Yard before he joined American Express in 1963. He was interviewed in New York, where he was conferring at company headquarters. He said that fraudulent use of traveler's checks had risen sharply in relation to the value of checks sold. The exact figures are secret.

Apart from fraud, Mr. Mountford estimated that one out of every hundred purchasers lost at least some checks and that the main London office of American Express alone dealt with nearly seven thousand losses in a recent year.

Losses, not thefts. The number, Mr. Mountford said, is dramatic, and many lost checks are never seen again, although the company makes good to the loser. "Men on holiday," he said, "are by nature more careless than women, and they're the major victims."

Theft of traveler's checks, however, is another matter, and the expert said that in Europe, particularly, it is rampant. He insisted, however, that it had no relation to the indigenous security situation, because most people who steal checks go to Europe specifically for that purpose.

"They aren't professionals," he said, "because the double risk—in stealing the checks and in cashing them—keeps most professional criminals away. They are usually youths from Latin America—college youths who can't get jobs—and they hit Europe in waves, corresponding to the waves of tourists. They have been especially attracted by cheap air fares. They go from London to Paris to Rome to Madrid to Frankfurt and back, never farther than that."

As soon as they are settled in a country, he said, they get counterfeit passports and identification cards. He said they often carry blank identification cards and, after a theft, fill in a name corresponding to that on the checks.

He cited two principal methods of theft.

First, raiding hotel rooms early in the morning, during the dinner hour, or late in the evening. "Couples tend to be light sleepers," Mr. Mountford said, "but a single fellow usually sleeps heavily and is easy prey late at night. Or in the morning, when he's in the bathroom shaving, someone will enter the bedroom and call 'Room service,' whisk up whatever is lying on the dresser and be gone."

Second, theft by artifice. "They act in groups of two, three, or four," he said. "They know all sorts of tricks to distract the attention of a tourist who is checking into a hotel or shopping."

To prevent theft generally while traveling, Mr. Mountford offered this advice:

- Carry only sufficient cash for one day. Keep the rest in checks or traveler's checks.
- In a place other than where you keep traveler's checks, maintain a record of the numbers of all the checks you have not cashed.
- Travel slim. If you are a male, before you leave home, empty your wallet of all extraneous material, such as those credit

cards and membership cards that you cannot use while away. Put your traveler's checks in an inside coat pocket, fastened with a safety pin. Most of all, do not keep anything valuable in your rear pants pocket, where even a button can easily be ripped off without your knowledge.

- If you do not wear a jacket, put your money and checks in a plastic bag and put that inside another bag that you carry at your waist inside your shirt. The outer bag should be attached to a thong that goes around your neck.
- Never put valuables in a camera case—"It's like having a sign that says 'Steal me,' " Mr. Mountford said.
- When at a hotel, use its safe for your valuables, even if you are staying only one night. When taking money or traveler's checks from the safe, be wary of any passer-by who tries to distract you.
- If the door to your hotel room has a bolt and chain on the inside, use them. For rooms without bolts, consider carrying a small wedge of hard wood and kicking it under the door at the lock side. Maybe have another wedge for the window.
- If you're pushed or jostled in a crowd, drop your arms and turn around 180 degrees. This breaks contact with a thief. Look at the person who is doing the pushing. If he is a thief, he'll run, because he does not want to be recognized. If he is not, he probably will not mind.

Mr. Mountford and other American Express officials insist that the rise in fraudulent cashing of traveler's checks has nothing to do with the increasing difficulty in cashing them legitimately. Travelers have reported that even in highly sophisticated cities such as New York and the major capitals of Europe, more and more hotels and restaurants and shops will accept traveler's checks only from their patrons, only on presentation of indisputable identification, and only to the price limit of whatever product or service is purchased. A small but growing number of establishments will not accept them at all.

An American Express spokesman attributed this to "a greater general wariness in society as a whole."

"We are trying to counteract it," he said. "We tell merchants to 'watch and compare'; watch as the check is countersigned for cashing, and then compare that signature with the one put on it when the check was purchased. If the two signatures look reasonably alike, we will reimburse the merchant, even if one of them proves to have been forged."

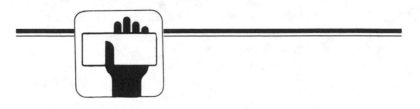

24. Credit Cards

For travelers, the value of credit cards is obvious. In effect, you are living off someone else's money—a bank's or a card company's, depending on what type of card you use—until your bills catch up with you, from several weeks to several months later.

In short, when you use a credit card to charge transportation, accommodations, meals, entertainment, or whatever, you can keep your money in the bank, where it earns interest, until the charges appear on your monthly credit-card bill.

With traveler's checks, however, it is the opposite: You lay out your money up front, plus in many cases a fee for the checks themselves, sometimes weeks or even months before you use the checks to pay bills. Meanwhile, the card company or bank uses your money and earns interest on it until you spend the checks and the hotels, restaurants, and shops deposit them in their own bank accounts for redemption.

Credit cards can also serve as identification to help you cash a personal check, and you can use them to buy traveler's checks up to a stipulated amount. They can also help you obtain a cash advance in an emergency in many parts of the world. Be careful, however: A cash advance is usually debited immediately to your credit-card account and interest charges begin at that moment.

Of course, credit cards are not uniformly accepted—and for that matter, neither are traveler's checks, although most established businesses will take them. Because businesses have to pay commissions to card companies, they are increasingly imposing minimum limits on the amount you can charge. Ten dollars is typical, although sometimes the limit is much higher.

When I travel in the United States or Canada, I try to use a credit card as much as I can. For each week I plan to be away, I carry $150 to $200 in traveler's checks for restaurants and other places that do not accept cards, and to cash in to pay for taxis, barbers, shoeshiners, tips, and the like. I also carry about $50 in cash for small payments when cashing a traveler's check is not feasible.

As soon as I return home, I cash in any remaining traveler's checks. Many people I know do not do this; they reason that it is comforting to have a safe traveler's check around the house just in case. I see no reason, however, why my actual money should not be back in my bank account, earning interest, as soon as possible.

There are two basic types of credit cards: One is the so-called travel and entertainment card, such as those of Citicorp, Diners Club and American Express. They permit you to charge as much as you like, providing you pay your monthly bills promptly. In some cases, such as in the purchase of airline tickets, payment may be extended over several months, but usually a bill must be paid in full at once, unless you have special credit privileges such as are offered with the American Express Gold Card.

The other type, such as Visa and MasterCard, is issued through participating banks and grants you a line of credit—often several thousand dollars but sometimes only a few hundred. With these cards you must keep track of each purchase to be sure it is within your credit limit; otherwise, your purchase is likely to be denied, or your elegant meal in that French restaurant may end with your washing the dishes—or, more probably, with your arrest.

With these cards you are encouraged to pay only part of your bill each month. In addition to charging you a fee for your card—sometimes a flat $18 a year or more, sometimes $1.50 or so for each month that you use it—the banks and card companies profit on the interest you pay on extended accounts, from 18 percent a year up.

Before going abroad, I determine as well as I can—usually from a bank or other major dealer in foreign exchange or from the latest edition of a guidebook that I trust—how widely credit cards are accepted in the countries I plan to visit. If I am going to a country in economic difficulty, such as Brazil, I try to determine whether there are parallel exchange rates: one set officially by the government and another, much more favorable to holders of dollars, that is widely used in the open marketplace with no potential legal problems for the traveler. In such countries, credit card charges are usually converted into dollars at the official exchange rate. In those countries, therefore, you can usually save a lot of money by using traveler's checks or cash.

When you use credit cards abroad, you enter a world of differing and often-confusing policies and practices on how charges in local currencies are converted into the dollar amounts that appear on your monthly bills.

"This past summer I toured Great Britain," Benjamin Rothfeld, an accountant who lives in West Hempstead, New York, said in late 1983, "and found it convenient to use credit cards. When statements came for payment, I was surprised to find that MasterCard charges were all converted at a rate that was six cents per British pound higher than Visa, American Express, or Avis."

So Mr. Rothfeld complained to the Bank of New York, which was handling his MasterCard account (his Visa account was with the Manufacturers Hanover Trust Company). "I stated that I didn't think the amount was significant; I thought the principle was significant," he recalled later. Lynn Matthews of the bank's credit-card administration department responded with a detailed chart showing how the conversions had been made. She said the bank had acted according to MasterCard regulations, but added apologetically: "Due to the confusion regarding this situation we have credited your account for $9.76."

Mr. Rothfeld and Bruce Glaser of Fairfield, Connecticut, who had a similar experience involving a trip to England, are among many travelers who have spoken out about apparent discrepancies in the way different organizations convert into dollars what Americans charge abroad. While no one seems to feel victimized in a major way, the implication is that in toto, some banks or charge-card companies are making large sums that rightfully belong to customers.

The banks and card companies vociferously deny this. They concede privately, however, that the conversion system can be extremely complicated and has flaws that they say they are striving to correct. Said a high bank executive who insisted that he not be quoted by name: "The entire subject of currency conversion is a can of worms."

Officials of the Bank of New York refused, as a matter of policy, to discuss the Rothfeld case or to suggest that if other customers had similar experiences, the bank would necessarily make adjustments. Responding to several of my questions, Peter T. Earle, then the bank's vice president for public affairs, said: "Currency conversion is a matter that is subject to the interpretation of constantly changing rules, regulations, and laws, which vary from one location to another and between one organization and another. Therefore, since we are a customer of the credit-card companies, we refer you to them for the appropriate answers."

A check with Visa International headquarters in San Francisco and MasterCard International headquarters in New York quickly produced the reason for Mr. Rothfeld's problem. Visa currency conversions were made at so-called wholesale exchange rates used for large transactions between major banks. MasterCard conversions, however, were at local retail buying rates, which meant higher dollar charges to the consumer. But Russell E. Hogg, president of MasterCard, said his company had recognized the inconsistency and since November 7, 1983, had been insisting that the banks that do its conversions use wholesale rates.

Mr. Hogg said, however, that MasterCard permitted a markup of up to 1 percent; Robert Miller, a senior vice president of Visa, said his company permitted only a quarter percent markup.

During four weeks of travel in Spain and Portugal in the fall of 1983, I used my personal charge cards of American Express, Diners Club, Visa and MasterCard. I kept records of each transaction and of the rate I received each time I cashed a dollar traveler's check for local currency in a Spanish or Portuguese bank. At home, after receiving my bills from American Express, Diners Club, and the Bank of New York, which controls my Visa and MasterCard accounts, I compared what had happened.

The Visa and MasterCard conversion rates appeared similar, especially for charges that had been billed to my account on or after November 7, 1983. American Express seemed competitive in Spain but billed me in Portugal at 117.65 to 119.06 escudos to the dollar when I could have gotten at least 123 by exchanging traveler's checks at banks there. Diners Club billed me at 120.19 to 120.81, Visa at 122.17 to 122.43 and MasterCard at 122.94 to 123.70.

On December 7, I sent a photocopy of my American Express bill to the company and asked about the discrepancy. On December 29, Nancy Muller of the public affairs department replied:

"We are presently conducting a thorough investigation of the conversion of the charges you incurred in Portugal, where conversion rates are determined by a Government-appointed entity. We will certainly let you know what our investigation turns up."

Eventually, American Express credited my account with $17.47.

Because of the way my bills flowed in, my cost was higher with American Express than with the others because it is faster and I had to part with my interest-bearing money earlier than I would have preferred. Some of my American Express transactions were on my October 5, 1983, bill and most of the remainder on my November 4 bill. Most of my Visa charges were not billed to me until November 10, however, and most MasterCard charges not until November 15. Most Diners Club charges were on a bill dated November 22, but one for a transaction in Spain on October 15 was not billed to me until December 22. In each case, I had close to a month to pay in full, free of interest.

I asked all four card companies how they did their conversions and billing. This is what they said.

American Express—The conversion rate depends on the country and its laws and is, the company says, "at least as favorable to you as an interbank rate, a tourist rate, or, where required by law, an official rate, which rate is in existence within twenty-four hours of the time that the charge is processed by us or by our authorized agents, plus 1 percent of the converted amount." After conversion, records of charges are sent to a regional overseas center where the rate is checked and a "summary of charges" is prepared for transmission to the United States and inclusion on the cardholder's bill.

Diners Club—Bills are collected in club offices overseas and sent to a central clearing house in Denver, which converts them according to the best interbank rate the club can get on that day. "We get three bids and take the lowest," Maureen O'Brien, a club spokesman, said. "Whatever we pay is the rate we give the customer, plus a one percent surcharge."

Visa and MasterCard—Conversions are made at interbank rates plus the appropriate markup by "merchant banks"—those in foreign countries that service the accounts of the businesses that charged you. Then the charges are put into the card company's computing system and transmitted to the American bank that controls your account.

Study your bills for each charge card, and you will find substantially different practices of providing or withholding information. For example, American Express itemizes each charge both in the foreign currency and in the dollar amount billed to your account. Enclosed with your monthly bill are copies of the original charge records that you signed abroad. The bill does not tell you the date money was converted, but if you look at the lefthand column headed *Reference No.*, the last three digits in each item tell you the day of the year the charge was processed at a regional center. For example, the digits 342 would represent December 8, the 342nd day in any year except a leap year.

Your Diners Club bill tells you the conversion rate and how much foreign currency was changed into how many dollars. The bill does not specify either your purchase or what foreign currency it was in; you have to refer to the slips enclosed with your bill to determine that.

Visa and MasterCard bills usually identify the transaction, the date it took place, the date it was charged to your bill, and the dollar amount. But they do not tell you the original charges in foreign currencies nor do they enclose copies of the original charge slips. So if you want to monitor conversion rates, keep the copy of each slip you receive when you pay for a meal or make a purchase.

25. The Best Way to Pay

For Sidney S. Rubin, it was a very special occasion—a birthday party for his wife at a posh hotel—and he wanted everything to be just right. Instead, because Mr. Rubin had counted on paying for the evening with a personal check, a lot went wrong.

Mr. Rubin's frustrations illustrate what can happen when consumers do not understand or are not adequately informed of what types of payment are acceptable by hotels and other providers of travel and hospitality services. It is a problem that recurs repeatedly, especially among travelers: In unfamiliar territory, particularly during nonbusiness hours when quick credit checks are impossible, your personal check may be useless, especially if you cannot produce a credit or charge card to prove that some large, reputable organization has investigated your financial background.

Nor are credit cards necessarily the entire answer. Several cruise ships and even a few hotels require payment by cash, traveler's check or—Mr. Rubin's preference—personal check.

Mr. Rubin invited more than thirty guests to a birthday reception one Saturday evening at the Plaza in New York. More than six weeks in advance, he paid a $200 deposit by personal check to reserve a deluxe suite.

The hotel's confirmation slip made no mention of how he should pay the balance. Nor was this subject mentioned when, about ten days before the party, Mr. Rubin committed himself to an extensive order of hot hors d'oeuvres, cold canapés, a birthday cake, French champagne, and premium liquors for a total price that he prefers to keep secret from his wife because, he said, "She might be shocked."

The afternoon of the party, the Rubins went to the Plaza, hoping to rest a few hours in their suite before the event. Asked by the receptionist how he intended to pay the balance of the bill, Mr. Rubin said by personal check. The hotel refused to let them check in. When he protested, the front desk referred him to the credit office, which referred him to an assistant manager, who referred him to an acting general manager. Still no luck.

Mr. Rubin, a lawyer for half a century, is by his own admission sort of old school. He does not carry credit or charge cards. According to a spokesman for the Westin chain, which operates the Plaza, any major credit card would have been accepted for payment, and a personal check might have been accepted if presented during business hours, when someone could have phoned the bank to verify its validity.

In desperation, Mr. Rubin phoned a friend whom he had invited for the evening. The friend, who did have a credit card, hurried to the hotel and authorized his host to use it. Finally, after waiting in the lobby more than two hours, the family checked in, and Mr. Rubin said the evening was a great success.

In a letter to Harry Mullikin, chairman and chief executive officer of Westin Hotels, Mr. Rubin acknowledged a company's right to make "any rule that it wants as to the mode of payment." But let people know in advance, he said, and do not expect that people generally will know the payment policy of the Plaza.

In a letter of apology, Mr. Mullikin replied that "you are absolutely correct." He said "it was the responsibility of our people to determine how you wanted to handle the financial arrangements." But he said it was company policy to request either a credit card or similar identification in cashing a personal check. In the future, Mr. Mullikin promised, "our people will be more sensitive in establishing credit procedures with our guests."

While Westin Hotels acknowledged that it should have told Mr. Rubin about its rules, the traveler should also ask for pertinent information that is not volunteered.

"Every company has a different policy," said Albert E. Kudrle Jr., former director of public relations for the American Hotel and Motel Association. "Most chains accept credit cards, but there are still some holdouts that don't. In fact, there are one or two hotels that accept personal checks but not credit cards. It is usually incumbent on you to ask about the form of payment."

Here is a rundown of how different segments of the travel industry deal with the different ways their customers might make payment.

Hotels—Directories of hotels and motels, either those published by individual chains and available free to any traveler or the comprehensive volumes bought by travel agencies for internal use, tell what charge and credit cards, if any, are accepted as payment. Many establishments that formerly accepted only charge cards, such as American Express and Diners Club, which expect the holder to pay the outstanding balance in full each month, now also accept credit cards, such as Visa and MasterCard, whose bills can be paid either in full once a month without interest or in installments with interest added.

Major hotels usually accept personal checks for deposits on advance reservations. They will commonly accept personal checks for the balance when you leave, provided you have arranged for this with the general manager or credit manager and allow him or her at least forty-eight hours to check your references. Some hotels will let you pay by personal check without prearrangement, provided it is during business hours at your bank, so that your account can be checked by long-distance telephone, usually at the hotel's expense.

"If you are not well known at the hotel," Mr. Kudrle said, "don't try checking out at two o'clock in the morning and giving a personal check. It just isn't going to work." You would probably have to leave at least your luggage behind.

If you have a Diners Club or American Express card to use as reference, many hotels, by arrangement with the card company, will give registered guests cash or traveler's checks in exchange for personal checks up to specified amounts. In some hotel chains, however, such privileges are available only at participating units or based on availability of cash.

As a rule of thumb, the smaller the hotel or motel, the less likely there will be large amounts of cash on the premises. Some hotels cash personal checks of noncardholding registered guests for small amounts but only upon presentation of indisputable identification and usually only with the manager's approval.

Airlines—Most scheduled airlines throughout the world accept major charge or credit cards as payment for tickets and excess-baggage charges. Full details are published in the *Official Airline Guides,* available at travel agencies and airline ticket counters. Typically you must produce a driver's license or passport or both and two valid credit cards as reference.

A few airlines will accept a credit card as reference for cashing a personal check, usually with a $50 limit. If you think you may need such facilities, ask the airline when you make your reservation if it offers them.

Amtrak—This government-supported company, which operates the nation's long-distance passenger trains, accepts all major credit cards as ticket-office payment for transportation as well as for food service in dining and cafe cars. It also accepts personal checks up to but not exceeding the Amtrak bill, including tip when you buy food and beverages, if accompanied by at least one form of current indisputable identification. Do not, however, expect a conductor to accept a credit card or check for your fare, although sometimes a conductor will, at his own discretion, take a check.

Bus Companies—Trailways and Greyhound, the nation's major long-distance bus networks, usually accept only Visa and Master-Card credit cards, and then only at regular bus stations. At such wayside bus stops as drugstores or gasoline stations, you will probably have to pay cash or by traveler's check unless the establishment accepts credit cards for the nonbus part of its business.

Greyhound and Trailways stations will accept personal checks for transportation if the local manager is willing and if you can identify yourself to his satisfaction, but do not count on this.

Auto Rentals—Peculiar to this business is that charge or credit cards are generally much better than cash or traveler's checks. "When we let somebody have a car," said a spokesman for Avis, "our major concerns are getting paid and security for the automobile. A charge card gives us the assurances we need."

John Britton, a spokesman for Hertz, put it this way: "A charge card positively indicates that the holder has been checked by its issuer—not only that he has a credit rating but also that he has a billing address. It establishes that that person really exists. It gives us assurance that a $10,000, highly mobile piece of equipment will be returned."

If you try to rent without a card, you usually have to fill out a credit application and allow enough time for your statements to be verified. Also, you will probably have to leave a cash deposit equivalent at least to the estimated cost of your rental and sometimes much more. At off-hours, an Avis station manager will sometimes, at your request, call your employer at home and ask for a reference, but do not expect to rent a car for cash or a personal check unless your reputation at the rental location has been established.

Cruises—Most cruise lines will not accept credit cards as payment for transportation and accommodations, although Cunard and Holland America are notable exceptions. Many, however, will accept them for purchases in gift shops on board. Check before you sail for the policy of the line you plan to use.

Travel Agencies—As a general rule, according to a spokesman for the American Society of Travel Agents, credit cards are accepted by an agent only if the provider of the travel services—air ticket, hotel room, etc.—you are buying accepts them and only for those services. The agent handles the billing to your credit-card account, noting exactly what you have bought and who provides it. Most agencies do not have their own accounts with credit-card companies, the spokesman said, because they do not want to pay the required commissions.

Most tour operators—the wholesalers who sell packages or complete tours through retail travel agents—do not accept cards, so you will have to pay with cash or traveler's checks or by personal check if the retail agent accepts it. Usually you make out your check to your travel agent, who in turn pays the tour operator. Unless you are well known to the agent or there is more than ample time for your check to clear the banking system, you will probably have to produce identification with the check.

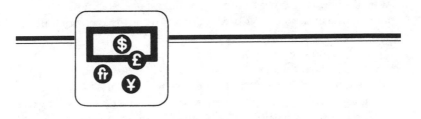

26. Foreign Exchange

This section was written by Margot Slade, assistant editor of The Living Section of The New York Times.

Travelers to Spain do it, to Bahrain do it; people barging on the Seine do it—they all deal in foreign exchange. The question is when to exchange American dollars for foreign currencies, where to exchange, how much, and into what: United States traveler's checks, foreign currency, foreign traveler's checks?

Experts are known to differ, and the experts on foreign currencies are no exception—except when it comes to playing the exchange rate markets. Everyone advises leaving that to the professionals.

Thomas F. Weiner, a senior vice president of Republic National Bank of New York, one of the leading wholesale dealers in foreign currencies, suggested that "prevailing exchange rates might determine where you take your vacation, such as, say, Mexico, where the rate might be comparatively good." Once that decision is made, he said, "keep abreast of foreign exchange rates." Exchange when it's convenient and do not play the waiting game.

Jacob Barak, assistant secretary in charge of foreign currency banknotes at Bank Leumi Trust Company of New York, which does a high-volume retail trade, echoed the sentiment: "People who travel for business or for pleasure don't care about foreign exchange rates for the same reasons that speculators do. American travelers want a reasonable rate of exchange for their dollars. Speculators want to make profits by wheeling and dealing in foreign currencies."

The problem with advising travelers regarding reasonable rates of exchange is that for every rule on currency exchanges there is an exception. The counsel offered by Mr. Barak was typical when he likened exchanging money to buying a pair of jeans: "In the end, you can always find it cheaper somewhere." So, shop around but do not waste a lot of time doing it. While you shop, however, here are some general rules to bear in mind.

Rule No. 1—On average, travelers do better exchanging over there than over here.

"Geography and the forces of supply and demand have a lot to do with the differences," Mr. Weiner said. Money is a commodity, and like any commodity its price is largely governed by the market forces of supply and demand. In most free-market countries, the exchange rate for tourists is a percentage point or two less favorable than the so-called interbank exchange rate, which is what banks charge other banks for transfers of enormous sums. The interbank exchange rate itself is governed by supply and demand.

"If a commodity is comparatively scarce, its price goes up," Mr. Weiner explained. "If a commodity is comparatively plentiful, its price goes down."

The exceptions are countries whose governments set official exchange rates. Where there is very high inflation, economic instability, or potential for political unrest—situations such as in much of South America, where sound currencies, such as the dollar, are particularly attractive—visitors will generally find both the official exchange rate and a more favorable unofficial rate set by supply and demand forces on the parallel or black market.

Money, like any commodity, must also be moved long distances, if it is needed in the United States for travelers going abroad. According to James B. Brew, a Citibank vice president and business manager for foreign currency exchange, "We've found that we can supply only thirty percent to thirty-five percent of our foreign currency from Europeans coming into the United States and Americans returning to the United States with foreign bills and coins. The remaining sixty-five to seventy percent must be imported." And that takes time and shipping expenses.

By contrast, Europeans may require several currencies within a few hours' travel from home. Thus, their currency outlets are many and deal with a wide variety and heavy volume of currencies supplied through tourist and business transactions or short-haul shipments. The lower overhead and greater volume of trade translate into better value for the United States dollar on exchange.

Rule No. 2—Travelers get more foreign currency for their dollars when their dollars are traveler's checks. Stephen D. Halliday, assistant vice president of sales and marketing for Thomas Cook Inc., spoke of disbursement costs. Edward O'Hare, a senior vice president of American Express, discussed processing expenses. Both were referring to the fact that traveler's checks move faster and easier through the banking system than cash, which must be counted, bundled, bagged, moved by guarded vehicles to the country of origin, and insured throughout transit. These costs are passed on to foreign currency customers.

Recent exceptions have been countries such as Greece: Not only has the dollar enjoyed a soaring value against the local currency—the drachma—but it has also been a much-sought-after commodity. Virtually anyone or any establishment has been prepared to deal in dollars but not with checks.

Rule No. 3—Travelers do not always do better at downtown banks than at airports, major hotels, or stores, mostly because banks may charge commissions that hotels and stores do not and because many major hotels and stores use the banks' own exchange rates. In Japan, for example, all currency outlets use the same rates on any given day when exchanging dollars into yen. According to recent visitors, some restaurants, such as Ten-Ichi, a well-known tempura restaurant in the Ginza, would not exchange money per se, but would accept dollars or dollar-denominated traveler's checks and return any change in yen.

Popular wisdom has it that hotels offer universally bad rates because they have captive audiences. Lis K. Brewer, manager of consumer affairs for Hilton International, acknowledged that "we would like to discourage the exchanging of money at hotels." But, she added, "Hiltons have a reputation for service to maintain, and this is something our guests want." Each Hilton, Mrs. Brewer said, uses the country's bank exchange rate as its standard.

What are travelers to do?

They should first check with the consulates of the countries they will be visiting—or with their travel agents—to learn about restrictions on the amount of United States dollars they can bring into a country or the amount of local currency they can take out and about the existence and legality of a parallel market. Before they leave the United States, travelers should determine how much foreign currency they will need for the first few days of their stay. On arrival, they should be alert to any bank holidays and should find out the central bank exchange rate as a basis for comparison.

After that, the best advice seems to be: Do what the experts do.

All foreign currency dealers surveyed advised travelers to exchange only as much as they expected to spend; use traveler's checks on which they might get better-than-cash rates overseas and that are insured if lost or stolen; have enough foreign currency on arriving in a country to cover immediate expenses, such as taxis, telephones, and food.

R. Leslie Deak, president of Deak-Perera U.S. Inc., a major dealer in foreign exchange and precious metals, offered a personal plan that experts in foreign exchange endorsed. Mr. Deak said he takes 25 to 50 percent of what he expects to spend in United States dollars, some in cash for immediate expenses on his return to the United States, and the bulk in dollar-denominated traveler's checks; 50 to 75 percent in foreign currency, mostly traveler's checks denominated in foreign currency, such as English pounds sterling or French francs, "because you can use them like cash when the banks are closed." His backups are his credit cards, which offer convenience but not always bargains, since they use official exchange rates and add a service charge.

Coping with Parallel Exchange Markets

A New Yorker who recently visited Brazil returned with a dozen tubes of Colgate toothpaste. She could not resist. At the Drogaria Popular in Rio de Janeiro she paid the equivalent of thirty-four cents for a 160-gram tube (5.6 ounces). At the Duane Reade discount chain in New York, a 7-ounce tube of Colgate cost $1.39 at the time.

It may seem eccentric for a tourist to stock up on toothpaste in Rio, but this experience illustrates how far the American dollar has gone there in recent years. Brazil, like some other countries with an official rate of exchange, has a so-called parallel rate that provides much more local currency for a dollar and therefore works strongly to the advantage of tourists. In Brazil, for example, at the official rate—the one banks use to buy and sell foreign currencies—you could get only a little more than half the cruzeiros for a dollar at this writing, minus a little for commission, that you could from unofficial money changers.

In dollar terms, this meant that when you spent your cruzeiros you could get toothpaste for thirty-four cents, a six-mile taxi ride for $2.70, a stein of beer for twenty cents or a steak dinner in a first-rate restaurant for $4.30, including tip.

Brazil is hardly alone with such bargains. Among other countries that in recent years (but not always) have had parallel rates that have been highly favorable to travelers from the United States are Argentina, Chile, the Dominican Republic, Ecuador, Egypt, Mexico, Trinidad and Tobago, and Venezuela. Before you rush off for a spree, however, some basic questions should be answered.

Under what conditions do favorable parallel exchange markets exist?

Generally you will find them in countries where the official rate, or, if there is none, the officially recognized rate, is far below what you can get for your dollar unofficially. This usually occurs in countries with very high inflation, economic instability, or a potential for political unrest—situations in which there is a great hunger for sound currencies, such as the United States dollar.

Are parallel markets legal?

In most countries, technically no, although in some they are officially tolerated and the only person considered to violate the law is the seller of local currency, not you, the buyer. Such is the case in several South American countries. But in other countries, such as Egypt and India, anyone who deals in a parallel market risks punishment if caught. Parallel markets exist in Soviet-bloc countries, but it is illegal and dangerous to deal in them. To be caught could mean arrest. So be sure to determine the local situation before you plunge.

Brazilians commonly refer to theirs as a black market, but it is hardly that. "Everybody uses it," said an official of the Brazilian Government Trade Bureau in New York. "If you go to Brazil and you sell some dollars on the black market, you are not doing anything illegal." Brazil restricts the amount of dollars that its residents may take abroad, but it is eager for as many to be brought into the country as possible. As a foreign tourist, as of this writing, you would not be questioned when you entered or left the country about the currency you had with you or about any transactions involving dollars and cruzeiros.

Economic and political conditions are always subject to change, so do not take what you read here as the foreign-exchange gospel for all time. But for one long period in the Dominican Republic, where one peso was officially worth one dollar, "on the street outside your hotel you could probably get one hundred forty to one hundred sixty pesos for one hundred dollars," said Nancy J. Friedman, then director of public relations for the Dominican Republic Tourist Information Center in New York. "It is not a black market," she said. "Dealing on the street is quite open and everyone does it. If tourists are nervous, they can get a policeman to watch the transaction."

If a parallel market is officially tolerated, where best should I change money?

Experienced travelers let common sense prevail. They ask around and will heed the recommendations of other travelers and residents of the country whom they trust. They will, obviously, avoid furtive dealings in hallways or on street corners, where they risk being cheated or receiving counterfeit bills. But they will probably find many established shopkeepers or hotel officials who readily change money on the side. Consider bargaining a bit, however, since parallel rates tend to fluctuate rapidly, and a lot can depend on how badly the seller of local currency wants your dollars.

How much money should I change?

Usually just enough to cover those anticipated expenses that can be paid in local currency. In some dollar-hungry countries, such as India, tourists' hotel bills must be paid in greenbacks or traveler's checks. In Jamaica, bills for hotels, auto rentals, and duty-free goods must all be paid in hard currency. If you still have local money when you leave a country, you may not be able to change it back into dollars at an airport bank unless you can produce a receipt showing that you bought at least that much money at the official rate. If you dealt in a parallel market, you obviously will not be able to do that, so your only recourse will be to take the money home and try to convert it at such foreign-exchange dealers as Deak-Perera or Manfra Tordella & Brookes or at a major bank that deals in relatively obscure moneys. You will sustain a loss.

If the parallel market is favorable, should I buy foreign money before I leave home?

It depends. Currency dealers in the United States and the foreign-exchange departments of major banks will readily sell you money at the parallel rate—if they have it. Citibank has branches at Kennedy International Airport in New York that largely do just that. Almost always, however, you can do better in the parallel market in your country of destination because a dealer in the United States has to pay for transporting the money, insuring the transfer, holding the currency for an uncertain period, and risking a decline in the exchange rate.

In any event, before you buy in the United States, be sure you are legally permitted to enter the destination country with its currency. Many countries prohibit the import or export of local currency or both, or limit the amount. India, for example, prohibits the import or export of rupees, but it is possible to buy rupees in New York. Some foreign-exchange dealers volunteer information on such restrictions, but often the burden is on you to ask. As an added precaution, check with a consulate or tourist information office of the country you plan to visit.

What about credit cards?

If you are going to a country where a parallel market is officially tolerated and highly favorable to you, you might as well leave your credit cards at home because transactions are usually converted into dollars and billed to you at the official rate, give or take a bit.

27. Getting Cash Away from Home

Nearly everyone who travels extensively has had the harrowing experience of running low on cash. While more and more expenditures these days can be charged on credit cards, many cannot, such as small purchases, taxi fares, tips to porters, and the like. A credit card may be accepted by Harrods in London, but it is rarely useful in the bazaars of India or North Africa, where not all bargains are inexpensive.

Because of computers and high-speed telex machines, it is much easier to get emergency money today than it was when you had to depend on money orders or when authorization from home to transfer money from a bank account had to be mailed from bank to bank or sent by telegram or cable. If you are stranded in a remote overseas town, it may still take a week or more to receive money, but increasingly money now reaches most travelers within minutes or a few hours except on weekends or holidays or, because of a time difference, after business hours at home.

Essentially there are two ways to get emergency money. One is to use a credit card. The other is to get money from the bank at home where you have an account. Here are some examples.

Charge Cards

Both American Express and Diners Club, the leaders in the so-called travel and entertainment charge card field, offer check-cashing privileges for their clients. Conditions often change, but at this writing holders of American Express green cards can cash personal checks up to $1,000 at offices of the company or its agents around the world. You can receive up to $200 in local currency and $800 in American Express traveler's checks, for which you have to pay the normal fee of $1 per $100.

In the United States you can make one such transaction every seven days; elsewhere, once in twenty-one days. The money cannot be charged to your American Express account; you must use a personal check and have it charged against your bank account, which must contain enough money to cover it if you want to avoid a lot of trouble later.

With an American Express Gold Card, you can cash a personal check up to $5,000 at the same offices during any seven-day period and receive $500 in local currency and $4,500 in traveler's checks. Or you can get cash for personal checks up to $1,000 a week at any branch in the United States of the more than 2,000 banks that issue Gold Cards in behalf of American Express.

With either a green card or a Gold Card, you can cash a personal check for up to $250 in the United States or Canada at any hotel where you are a registered guest and plan to charge your bill to your card—providing the hotel says it has enough cash on hand, which can be a problem late at night or on weekends. Elsewhere, at participating hotels—which means not everywhere that accepts an American Express card for payment of bills—the check-cashing limit is $100. You can also cash a check for up to $50 at ticket counters in the United States of certain airlines, providing you hold an air ticket that you used or plan to use within forty-eight hours.

At this writing, American Express has seventy-five machines, most of them at airports and most of them in the United States, that dispense traveler's checks to people with a green card or Gold Card. To use a machine, however, you must be enrolled in the company's express cash program, which provides you with a personal identification number, different from the number on your charge card. With a green card you can get up to $500 in traveler's checks from a machine and with a Gold Card up to $2,000. The money is debited not to your American Express account but to the personal bank account that you specify upon enrolling.

Also, with the same identification number you can get up to $500 in cash from any of more than 1,200 automated teller machines at banks, shopping centers, and elsewhere in the United States; the money is debited to your account at your home bank. To locate the closest usable automated teller machine or the closest bank that will cash a check for a person with a Gold Card, phone toll-free (800) CASH NOW, which is (800) 227-4669.

At this writing, Diners Club has more restricted check-cashing facilities. You can cash a personal check for up to $250 at a participating hotel in the United States or Canada ($100 elsewhere) where you are a guest; the company says outlets of about fifty hotel groups are taking part. Or you can cash a check for a minimum of $250 to a maximum of $1,000 once every fourteen days at any branch of the New York-based Citibank, which has offices in more than fifty countries. If abroad, your Diners Club card entitles you to exchange currency at no commission charge.

In foreign countries, your Diners Club card entitles you to a cash advance of $250 to $1,000 from participating banks and hotels, with the money debited to your club account. Some countries limit the maximum amount, however. In China, the maximum is $800 and other countries permit a service charge of up to 4 percent. To get such cash, you have to show both your club card and your passport.

Bank Credit Cards

Visa and MasterCard allow you to get cash advances at participating banks and some other places. These advances are regarded as loans, and interest accrues from the moment you receive the money. You cannot get an advance for more than is available in your line of credit, sometimes only a few hundred dollars.

To determine whether the amount you seek is within your credit limit requires communication with the bank that services your account. Both card companies, however, use sophisticated computerized equipment that, they say, can in most cases approve a charge—or deny it—within six or seven seconds, twenty-four hours a day, seven days a week, including holidays. Where this equipment is not in place, however, it can take much longer, and Richard Rossi, manager of public relations for Visa International, conceded that while all advances are supposed to have authorization, in practice, especially overseas, "that doesn't always happen" for small amounts.

Eileen Naughton, a spokesman for MasterCard International, said some overseas banks limit the size of a cash advance but that company policy requires that the maximum be at least $250 in twenty-four hours, payable in local currency and providing it is within your credit limit. Domestic banks, she said, must advance up to $5,000 if your credit limit allows it.

If your Visa or MasterCard was issued by a bank that participates in an automated teller network, such as Plus or Cirrus, you can use the card in the teller machines of any other bank in the network. MasterCard, incidentally, issues some customers a preferred gold card that generally increases your credit limit but does not provide extra benefits in getting cash. Visa's Premier card, however, allows you to cash checks up to $250 at participating hotels.

Other Resources

If you do not have a charge or credit card, you are probably in trouble unless you are in a city where your bank has an office. Rarely can you cash a personal check at a bank other than your own. Overseas, your best bet is to go to the nearest United States consulate. The State Department does not like to advertise it, but consular officers are empowered, in return for your promissory note, to lend you a small amount—up to about $50, say—in an emergency to tide you over until you can get money from home. Consulates will help you reach the folks at home by cable, telex, or phone, but you must reimburse the consulate for the cost.

If you have to send home for money, be sure to specify the address where you will pick it up: a United States consulate, a bank, an American Express office, your hotel, or wherever else seems both practical and appropriate. The following organizations can help the person at home to whom you have appealed for help.

State Department—If you are trying to help someone overseas, you can wire a Western Union money order or mail a certified personal check, made out to the Department of State, to the Citizens Emergency Center, Department of State, Washington, D.C. 20520. You should specify to whom the money is to be sent and at which United States consular office. The department will telegraph the money accordingly, but you have to notify the recipient where to pick it up.

For information and advice, you can call the emergency center at (202) 632-5225. In bona fide emergencies, you can also try (202) 655-4000 and ask for the State Department duty officer who can deal with your problem.

Western Union Telegraph Company—This company, not to be confused with Western Union International Inc., which is not in the personal money transfer business, has several ways of transmitting money. Domestically the most common is a money order, which can be bought at most of the company's 140-odd own offices and 7,100 agencies, such as neighborhood pharmacies, throughout the country. Check your local white pages under Western Union. Within minutes, word to pay the money is relayed to the designated office or agency close to the intended recipient.

Hours of Western Union outlets vary, and agencies sometimes run short of cash. When this happens, there are usually alternate arrangements with a local bank, but the process can take time. Also, Western Union charges according to the amount transferred: To send $1,000 costs at least $21 and could be substantially more.

Western Union has another system under which a holder of a MasterCard or Visa card can phone toll-free to (800) 648-4920 and send or receive up to $1,000 within hours, provided the appropriate agency at the receiving end is open and has the cash and provided you are within your credit limit.

Bank Transfers

For its international money orders, Western Union goes through the Chase Manhattan Bank, but it is usually much cheaper if you go through a bank yourself. Which bank you choose should be largely a matter of convenience. The major big-city banks have extensive international money-transfer operations by telex, and any of their branches can steer you correctly and explain the alternatives. Charges tend to be nominal; Citibank's is a flat $10 for each transaction. You should normally allow five to seven business days for the money to reach the recipient. Occasionally, however, something delays the procedure, and it is necessary to keep after the banks at both ends.

Sometimes you can save substantial time by working through the American office of a foreign bank. A New Yorker who wants to rush money to someone in Sorrento, Italy, for example, might do better to go through the Banco di Napoli at 277 Park Avenue, which has five hundred branches in Italy and can telex the money directly to the appropriate one.

If you are a suburbanite, you might consider dealing through your local bank, even though it is not a leader in the international field. The Fidelity Union-First National State Bank of New Jersey, for example, does what the major New York banks usually will not: It telephones a correspondent bank overseas and has emergency money delivered hours quicker than by telex. Of course, the customer pays for the phone call and a bank commission.

Foreign-exchange dealers—companies such as Deak-Perera—can be particularly useful with telephone transfers provided they have a sufficient balance in a bank in the country where the money is to be paid. Deak-Perera says it is able to deliver money quickly, right to a recipient's hotel rather than a pick-up point, a service that is relatively uncommon. Sometimes there is a delivery charge, and Deak-Perera also usually gets a commission from the process of converting dollars into local currency. One thing to keep in mind: The amount of money you receive may be less than the amount sent, especially if it is transmitted in dollars and converted to local currency. A commission is likely to be taken out for the transaction.

An organization that issues traveler's checks, such as American Express, Thomas Cook, or the Bank of America, will telex funds overseas for their purchase. A person wanting them should notify the home bank to transfer appropriate money to the nearest issuing office for relay of authorization to the destination.

A relative or friend at home can also take up to $500 in cash to a domestic American Express office and have authorization to issue an equivalent amount of cash telexed to one of the company's overseas offices at a cost of $25. If the money is not picked up within fourteen days, it is returned to the person who provided it.

If you are planning extended overseas travel, here are some tips:

- Find out before you leave home who your bank's representatives are in the countries you plan to visit. Also find out how much money you can get in that country; the limit can vary according to bank and government regulations. Your bank should be able to advise you on this.

- If your checking account is in a small bank, let one of the officers know your travel plans. This can facilitate approval of emergency transfers because the officer will be less likely to doubt that a telex from you in, say, Bangkok, is legitimate.
- Ask Diners Club, American Express, or your bank in the case of Visa or MasterCard for a list of banks in the countries you intend to visit that can provide emergency money against your card or with your card as reference for cashing a personal check. The acceptance of cards is expanding abroad, but it is far from universal.
- Find out whether you can get cash in dollars as well as local currency. If in local currency, will you be able to convert any excess into dollars when you leave that country?
- When you leave home, take your checkbook and be sure your checks or some other bank identification show your account number and home branch. If possible, also take a letter of introduction from the branch manager of your bank attesting to the fact that you have an account there.

28. Passports

With the Federal offices that issue passports deluged by applications most springs, a colleague of mine thought of a way to avoid a major delay. When she first applied in New York—and stood in line two hours to do so—a passport was promised her by mail in about a month. Much too late, she thought, because she planned to fly standby to Europe within a week, which meant she would buy her ticket on the day of departure, if space was available. The passport officer told her there was no way his procedure could be speeded unless she could produce an airline ticket with a confirmed reservation on a specific date.

So my colleague hurried to the nearest transatlantic airline office and, with a credit card, bought a $700 one-way ticket from New York to London, with a confirmed seat on a flight two days later. She showed this ticket at the passport office and picked up her passport later the same day. Then she turned in the airline ticket, and a voucher was submitted to her credit-card account for a full refund.

Even this shortcut exacted a toll, however, in the time she stood in line and in nervous energy. It underscored a reality for those of us who plan to travel abroad: You need a passport for most such travel, and if you do not have a valid one, allow more than ample time to get it. It is usually mailed.

In the so-called off-season, which the State Department describes as September through February, two to three weeks should be sufficient. In late April, at the height of the peak season, the United States Passport Agency advises allowing at least three weeks, and sometimes it has taken twice that or more.

Under the rules, those seeking passports for the first time are required to apply in person. At peak season in New York that has commonly meant a delay of at least half an hour at the Passport Agency's office at 630 Fifth Avenue in Rockefeller Center simply to get information, plus at least several hours' wait in line to submit your application. Sometimes around midday, a line has extended down a staircase to the floor below, out the door to Fifth Avenue, south to 50th Street and west on 50th, halfway to the Avenue of the Americas.

Here are facts you should know about United States passports and ways to help make the application process as painless as possible:

When a Passport Is Needed—Except for travel to Canada, Mexico, and some places in Central and South America and the Caribbean, all American citizens need a valid passport to leave and return to the United States and to enter foreign countries. Each individual must have a passport; family passports are no longer issued. Even if a valid passport is not required for your destination, you will usually need proof of United States citizenship or permanent residence. No proof is better than a passport—even if out of date—or your birth certificate, naturalization papers, or the like. A driver's license is widely accepted as positive identification but not as proof of citizenship.

When to Apply—The wise traveler does not wait until a trip abroad is imminent but starts making plans six months to a year in advance. If you are likely to go abroad at least once a year—and sometimes on short notice—it is wise to have a valid passport at all times. It is good for ten years from date of issue for adults, five years for those younger than eighteen. Passport applications ask about proposed travel plans, but replies are not mandatory.

You can update your passport at any time, even if it still has years of validity. A spokesman for the State Department's Bureau of Consular Affairs suggests that if you expect to go abroad in the last year of validity, you get a new one three to six months before departure.

Should your passport expire while you are away, you can quickly get a new one at any of the 240-odd United States consular offices abroad. But, if you plan to go to countries that require visas—that is, permission, stamped in your passport, to visit countries for a specified purpose and limited time—you should get a new passport far ahead. Foreign countries will usually not issue visas that are valid longer than a passport, and visas are not transferable from an expired to a new passport.

Where to Apply—If with your application you can submit a passport issued to you within the last eight years and you were eighteen or older when it was issued, you may apply by mail, and forms for this purpose are available at any of the regional offices of the United States Passport Agency: in Boston, Stamford, Connecticut, New York City, Philadelphia, Washington, Miami, Chicago, New Orleans, Houston, Seattle, San Francisco, Los Angeles, or Honolulu. Check the appropriate telephone directory—under United States Government, Department of State—for the address. Additional offices are planned, and the forms can also be obtained from clerks of Federal or state courts of record and at many post offices. Ask at your nearest post office for the most convenient one.

If you have never had a United States passport or if yours is more than eight years old, you must complete an application and appear in person at the Passport Agency or appropriate court or post office. You can frequently get instant service at courts or post offices, even in high season, but allow at least two weeks for handling. You must submit proof of citizenship: Any out-of-date passport, regardless of how old, will do; otherwise a certified copy of a birth certificate or naturalization papers is preferred. If neither is available, a baptismal certificate or record of elementary school enrollment is commonly accepted. You also need additional proof of identity; credit cards and Social Security cards are not acceptable. Any applicant at least thirteen years old must appear; a parent or guardian may appear in behalf of a younger child.

For both initial and subsequent passports, you have to submit two identical two-by-two-inch photographs, normally taken within the last six months in either color or black and white. Polaroid photos are acceptable; vending machine products are not. Submit your expiring passport if you are applying for a subsequent one.

What Does a Passport Cost—A first passport costs $35 for adults, $20 for those younger than eighteen, plus $7 for processing if you appear in person. The processing fee is waived if you apply by mail. Personal checks are accepted.

Coping With Emergencies—In an emergency, the Passport Agency can usually get you a passport within one business day, provided you present an airline ticket with confirmed reservation. You still may have to stand in line for hours, but in the estimate of a spokesman for the New York office, if you reach the head of the line by 1:30 P.M., you will get your passport later that afternoon. The office is open from 8:30 A.M. to four P.M. Monday through Friday.

In an off-hours, weekend, or holiday emergency, call (202) 632-5225, (202) 632-1512, or (202) 655-4000 and ask for the State Department emergency duty officer. He or she will determine whether a genuine emergency exists and, if so, will arrange for you to get a passport quickly at the office most convenient for you. The off-hours number of the New York office is not available to the public.

In rare extreme emergencies, even these requirements can be waived, and the State Department will instruct an airline to carry you without a passport. Through diplomatic channels while you are in flight, the country of destination will be asked to admit you on the condition that you go to the nearest United States consular office there as soon as possible and obtain a passport. If a visa is required, you will then have to arrange for one with the appropriate authorities.

For virtually everything you need to know about passports, send a postcard with your name and address to the Department of State,

Room 6811, Washington, D.C. 20520, and ask for the free leaflet *Your Trip Abroad*. Allow at least a month for delivery.

These leaflets are also usually available at regional offices of the Passport Agency.

29. Visas

Many foreign countries admit Americans freely; getting permission to visit others can be tedious and time-consuming, requiring careful planning far in advance.

The key requirement is a visa, the stamp placed in your passport by an official representative of a foreign country to permit you to visit that country for a specific purpose and for a limited time. For travel to Western Europe and most of the Western Hemisphere, Americans usually do not need visas. But they do need them to go to Argentina, Brazil, Japan, most of Africa, Eastern Europe, and the Soviet Union.

Because the rules of entry vary so much and are subject to sudden change, you should check on each country you plan to visit. Suppose you want to go to Nigeria and have a confirmed reservation on Pan American from New York. If you show up at Kennedy Airport without a Nigerian visa in your passport, the airline will probably turn you away until you obtain one. And because Nigeria commonly does not issue visas quickly, even to bona fide tourists, this could easily set back your departure by ten days and upset hotel reservations and other plans.

Unfortunately, there is no one agency to which travelers can go for information on what they need for what countries. There are, however, some annual lists that can help, although some of the details in them may quickly become outdated. Ask at the nearest United States Passport Agency for a free copy of the State Department's leaflet *Visa Requirements of Foreign Governments*. Or write for a copy by sending a postcard to the Department of State, Passport Services Correspondence Branch, Room 386, 1425 K Street N.W., Washington, D.C. 20524.

Travelers who are interested in Latin America can glean a wealth of information on visas, health requirements, locations of government tourist offices, and other travel matters from a twenty-page booklet called *Requirements for the Entry of United States Tourists Into the O.A.S. Member States*. It is available for $2.25 from the Department of Publications, General Secretariat, Organization of American States, Washington, D.C. 20006. Make your check or money order payable to the Organization of American States.

Visas are usually issued by consulates of the countries that require them. To locate the appropriate consulates, check the latest Congressional Directory, which is available in most public libraries. The directory lists the cities that have them; for the exact address, check the appropriate telephone book. Some governments maintain consular sections only in their embassies in Washington. A few issue visas through their missions to the United Nations. Those that have separate consulates in New York are listed in the Manhattan Yellow Pages under "Governments—Foreign Representatives" and in the white pages under the name of the country.

If you plan to visit only a few countries where visas are required and you have the time, it may be easiest to visit the appropriate consulates and get them yourself. Some visas are free and are issued within a few minutes, but check first by phone about office hours; some consulates deal with the public for only a few hours in the morning. If you apply for a visa by mail, be sure to send your passport registered. If you plan your trip through a travel agent, he or she can probably get visas for you, although he may charge a service fee above any set by the consulates.

For extensive travel requiring visas, you or your agent may find that it pays to use a professional visa service. A list is at the end of this chapter, and some services will send you a free brochure by mail.

Agency fees usually begin at about $8.50 a visa, depending on the amount of work involved, plus charges by the consulate, which range from nothing to several dollars or more. Special services by an agency, such as arranging to translate portions of your passport into Arabic, as is sometimes required by some Arab countries, cost extra.

Allow the agency whatever time it advises is necessary because it can send your passport to only one consulate at a time. Rarely, however, should you apply for a visa more than three months in advance; in fact, some visas become invalid if not used within ninety days of date of issue.

Some governments ask that you apply for a visa only at the consulate closest to your home. In many cases this rule is waived if you are already abroad; if you are in France, say, you can apply for a visa to Japan by visiting the Japanese Consulate in Paris.

Sometimes you can fly to a country without a visa and be issued one upon arrival. Some visa applications, however, take weeks to process. Some require that they be accompanied by several photographs and, if your intention is to study or do business or anything else but visit as a tourist, that you submit letters of reference. Many governments ask you to produce a ticket to prove that you have confirmed transportation into and out of the country.

Some visas allow travelers to enter and leave a country repeatedly within a specified period, which can embrace several years. At the other extreme for many years was Burma, which would grant American tourists only a one-time, twenty-four-hour transit visa, providing they could present evidence of guaranteed onward transportation in the same direction in which they entered the country. A round-trip ticket was unacceptable. In recent years, however, Burma has been granting tourist visas valid for stays of up to seven days.

In applying for entry to the Soviet Union, you must specify in your application exactly what places you want to visit, and your visa will limit you to them.

Some black African countries, meanwhile, exclude you if your passport bears a visa for South Africa. Israel does not require visas of American tourists but some Arab countries will sometimes, depending on the political climate, bar you if you have an Israeli stamp in your passport—such as an entry or exit stamp. If such an Arab country has already granted you a visa, it will be considered void when you try to use it.

For this reason, the Israeli authorities will usually accede to an American's request to have entry and exit stamps put on a separate piece of paper, instead of in your passport. As an alternative if you plan to visit Israel and Arab countries or black Africa and South Africa, the State Department can issue you two passports, one valid for the usual ten years and usable almost everywhere and the other specifically for Israel or South Africa and valid for perhaps six months.

To visit some countries, however, an American citizen does not need even a passport. Some, such as Mexico, require that you carry only a tourist card, which is available from the appropriate country's official tourist office in the United States, from the airline that carries you to your destination or even upon arrival at the destination itself. Some countries require no special documentation at all.

In fact, visitors to Canada need only board a bus, train, or plane or climb into a car and go. Just be prepared to establish your identity with border officials—a driver's license will usually do. If any doubt may arise about your citizenship, carry a voter registration card, a copy of your birth certificate, or a passport, even an expired one, to prove it.

But wherever you go, even to the closest and presumably friendliest of countries, check out in advance the rules on length of stay. If you have a summer job arranged in Canada or plan to live there indefinitely, you will probably have to get a visa before you go or you may risk being expelled when the purpose of your journey becomes known to officials there. Some Western European countries require a visa if you plan to stay more than ninety days, regardless of how you intend to spend your time. Many visas can be extended in the country itself if you want to stay on; some cannot, which means that you must leave when the visa expires and apply outside the country for readmission.

For typical vacation travel, United States citizens are welcome without visas to most countries they are likeliest to visit. This absence of red tape began in the post-World War II years, when devastated European countries were eager to attract American travelers to stimulate their economies. In contrast, the United States requires entry visas of citizens of most other nations, even those to whom we profess especially close relations.

Some Latin American countries, led by Argentina and Brazil, have rebelled against what they consider to be a lack of United States reciprocity. As a result, American citizens, even short-time vacationers, now must have visas to visit these countries. Moves have been made in Congress to waive American visa requirements for vacationing foreigners, but unless appropriate legislation is passed, restrictions on Americans could grow.

If you are not a United States citizen, even if you have lived and worked here for decades, you are nonetheless probably subject to the travel regulations imposed on citizens of your country of origin. Foreign residents of the United States should check carefully, therefore, before even crossing to the Canadian side of Niagara Falls for a half-hour excursion; they could have difficulty returning home.

Here are some of the services that specialize in obtaining foreign visas. Prices are subject to change.

In New York

Foreign Visa Service, 18 East 93rd Street, New York, New York 10028; phone (212) 876-5890. Charges: $10 per visa plus consulate fee.

Global Visa Service, 211 East 43rd Street, New York, New York 10017; (212) 682-3895. Charges: $20 per visa plus consulate fee and cost of postage or hand delivery, if preferred.

Travel Agenda Inc., 119 West 57th Street, Suite 1008, New York, New York 10019; (212) 265-7887. Charges: $8.50 per tourist visa and $15 per business visa plus consulate fee.

Visa Center Inc., 507 Fifth Avenue, New York, New York 10017; (212) 986-0924. Charges: $9 to $30 per visa plus consulate fee.

Visa Pioneers Ltd., 245 East 40th Street, New York, New York 10016; (212) 687-9477. Charges: $18 per visa plus consulate fee.

In Washington

Travisa, 2121 P Street N.W., Washington, D.C. 20037; (202) 328-1977. Charges: $25 per visa plus consulate fee, but rate decreases if more than one visa is needed. Claims to be able to get almost any visa within twenty-four hours. Travisa has branches at 127 Peachtree Street N.E., Atlanta, Georgia 30303; (404) 522-5132, and 1101 Washington Boulevard, Detroit, Michigan 48226; (313) 363-0119.

Visa Expediters, Box 19444, Washington, D.C. 20036; (202) 387-4789. Charges: $15 per visa plus consulate fee for individuals, $7.50 for members of groups.

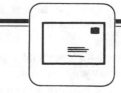

30. Getting Mail from Home

One of the most important needs of a traveler is to maintain a link with home. Few people who are far from home want to be cut off to the extent that they cannot at least receive occasional letters. And when emergencies occur, travelers should know where and how to get money quickly.

In many circumstances and in many places, it is not as easy to receive mail while traveling as it was thirty years ago. In the major capitals of Europe, picking up mail at an American Express office was once almost a ritual. Receiving, sorting, and dispensing letters to travelers was a major service offered by the company. For young Americans traveling in the early post-World War II years, when cheap hotel rooms were plentiful and reservations for them were rarely necessary, all a visitor to Paris had to tell the folks at home was to "write to me care of American Express." Every business day, when tourists gathered in the basement of the company's big office at 11 rue Scribe for the latest delivery, it was a social happening—a time to touch base with old friends who also happened to be in Paris, to make new friends, and to devise all kinds of impromptu and long-range adventures.

Now, however, the company's mail services are being cut back. In his no-nonsense bimonthly newsletter called *Economy Traveler*, the publisher, Edward L. Perkins, said that in peak season, "waiting lines at understaffed client mail counters in London and (particularly) Paris can sometimes be so long as to detract seriously from the convenience of the service."

In response to a question, an American Express spokesman said that because of the expense, the mail program was in flux. "We are trying not to do it anymore," she said. She said the program was confined to participating offices, primarily those in major cities in Western Europe, and was free only to clients of the company, which means holders of an American Express card or buyers of the company's traveler's checks or tours. A handling fee, usually 75 cents a letter, is charged to others.

A State Department spokesman said mail for unofficial travelers, if addressed in care of a United States embassy or consulate, would probably be returned to the sender. "We are equipped normally to deal only with official mail," he said, "and we have a problem of what to do with mail that is not picked up."

If you have a firm itinerary before leaving home, it is usually safe to have mail sent to the hotels where you have reservations. The envelope should bear the notation: "Please hold for arrival about (whatever the date)." When you reach the hotel, do not assume that waiting mail will automatically be given to you. Instead, even at the highest-priced establishments, insist that the desk clerk check his held letters thoroughly. Many hotels promise to forward letters after you check out if you leave an address, but do not count on it.

If you lack a firm itinerary, there is always the post office. Every post office in the United States has what is called general delivery, where mail is held for transients or others with no local address. The envelope must specify the particular branch where the mail is to be picked up, and for this your correspondents must know the ZIP code. For example: Miss Flora Jones, c/o General Delivery, Ansonia Station, New York, New York 10023.

Post offices and most public libraries have ZIP code directories. You can also get the information you need by phoning the ZIP code information number listed in your local telephone directory under "Postal Service" in the United States Government section.

Letters are usually held ten days, then returned to sender. To pick up your mail, you usually have to identify yourself; a valid driver's license or voter registration card is generally sufficient.

Outside the United States, the universally accepted term for general delivery is the French phrase *poste restante*. Under the rules of the Universal Postal Union, which embraces virtually all countries, personal mail sent care of *poste restante* and marked "to be called for" will be accepted and held for pickup at the main post office in the specified community. To be turned over to you, however, it must bear your name just the way it is in your passport—no aliases or nicknames.

The length of holding time varies: In Ghana it used to be two months, a spokesman for the United States Postal Service said, in

Finland one month, and in the Ivory Coast "until a fortnight following the fortnight of the letter's arrival." Some countries, among them Argentina, Brazil, and France, levy a nominal *poste restante* fee.

31. Travel Newsletters

Many travelers have special interests that demand more information than newspapers and magazines can usually provide. To meet this need, specialized newsletters have been developed in recent years. Some have grown quickly and have proved highly durable, although the mortality rate is high.

Quality varies widely. Some promise much more than they provide and are little more than excerpts of press releases from the travel industry. Some reflect the highly personal—and sometimes thinly documented—impressions and opinions of the publisher.

Others are well researched and well documented and represent a lot of diligent, unbiased reporting. Some of these are also attractively packaged, others are essentially typewritten pages with no illustrations.

The publications mentioned here are a sampling of what is available. In selecting them, the term *newsletter* was applied rather loosely. Some indeed meet the popular image of newsletters: four to sixteen pages crammed with text but with few if any illustrations. Others are really travel newspapers or magazines but are included here because they clearly cater to people with more specialized interests than most vacationers have.

Most publishers will send a sample copy on request. Usually they charge for this. Some publishers promise refunds to dissatisfied subscribers. The prices quoted were valid in 1984 and are subject to change.

Passport, 20 North Wacker Drive, Chicago, Illinois 60606; (312) 332-3571. Monthly. $40 a year. Samples unavailable.

In existence for nineteen years, *Passport* is for the sophisticated, experienced traveler who cares more about comfort and cultural attractions than expense. Each month subscribers get the eight-page *Passport* newsletter plus an extra—sometimes a two-to-four-page special report called *Visa;* sometimes a booklet such as the recent one on 132 unusual museums in Europe.

Passport's publisher, Moris T. Hoversten, believes in brevity and frankness, whether laudatory or critical. For example, a *Visa* report in March on a new Caribbean resort said: "We recently spent four days there. Glad to leave in spite of the fact that it's one of the most beautiful settings in the Caribbean. Several other people also glad to leave. Felt they were being gouged and treated like second-class citizens."

International Travel News, 2120 28th Street, Sacramento, California 95818; (916) 457-3643. Monthly. $11 a year. Sample copy free.

The April 1984 issue of this tabloid-size paper ran forty-eight pages, including advertising. The paper consists largely of first-person accounts of readers' adventures, ranging from wonderful to horrifying. Most accounts appear to be from highly experienced, frequent travelers. These contributions, plus staff articles, surveys, and ads, provide a lot of information about offbeat travel, particularly specialized tours, such as cultural programs, backwater cruises, and escorted vacations by minibus or private car.

Travel Smart, Communications House, Dobbs Ferry, New York 10522; (914) 693-8300. Monthly. $37 a year; $29 for new subscribers only. Sample $1.

Herbert J. Teison, the editor and publisher, and Mary Hunt, the able managing editor, consistently offer an authoritative, comprehensive newsletter for the budget-conscious traveler who wants quality at bargain prices. For example, a recent issue carefully studied car rental rates in Europe and advised travelers on questions to ask before signing a contract. Another issue told of bargains in the Laurentians, in Switzerland, on the Riviera, and elsewhere.

Travel Smart says it carries no ads, yet it does contain a column of travel notices, which closely resemble classified ads and promote specific destinations, tours, and travel products. Also, subscribers are offered discounts on some travel if they book through the publication.

Travel Smart for Business. Monthly. $125 a year; but $96 for new subscribers only. Sample $10.

This, too, is published by the Teison-Hunt team (same address and phone number as *Travel Smart*) and is aimed at the frequent business traveler. Some recent topics: saving money by buying intra-European air transportation in European currencies instead of dollars, new hotels in Atlanta, getting to and from airports, and studies of bonus programs for frequent air travelers. Each issue also contains listings of what are called the best daytime coach fares between certain American cities for travelers who cannot buy tickets in advance.

Frequent Flyer, c/o *Official Airline Guides,* 2000 Clearwater Drive, Oak Brook, Illinois 60521; (800) 323-3537 outside Illinois, (800) 942-1888 in Illinois. Monthly. $24 a year. No samples.

A slick magazine that improves with each issue, *Frequent Flyer* is aimed specifically at the audience from which it takes its name. It is provocative and perceptive and eager to look toward what travelers can expect tomorrow. The editor and publisher, Martin B. Deutsch, is involved in several travel publishing enterprises, and the managing editor, Coleman A. Lollar, has earned wide respect among readers and colleagues. The magazine covers not only air travel but also such related matters as beating the potentially high cost of telephoning from afar, hotel security, and where to find tournament golf.

The Hideaway Report, Harper Associates Inc., Post Office Box 300, Fairfax Station, Virginia 22039. No phone queries. Monthly. $65 a year. Sample $5.

This newsletter lives up admirably to what it professes to be: "a connoisseur's guide to peaceful and unspoiled places." Each issue contains frank descriptions and assessments of resorts, hotels, and inns that have been visited by the anonymous editor and publisher, who uses the pseudonym Andrew Harper.

Very Special Places, Post Office Box 3885, New York, New York 10185. No phone. Eight times a year in two editions: four on the Americas and four on the rest of the world. $24 a year for one edition, $40 for both. Sample $5.

This is a new effort by Ian Keown, the author of the guidebooks *Very Special Places, Caribbean Hideaways* and *European Hideaways.* The newsletter promises "independent, confidential reports on inns, resorts, hotels, and hideaways of exceptional character," but not all the research is done by Mr. Keown. "I have very trustworthy people," he said, "people who have worked ten years or so on my guidebooks."

Entree, Post Office Box 5148, Santa Barbara, California 93108; (805) 969-5848. Monthly. $30 a year. Sample free.

William T. Tomicki, the publisher, says he is uncompromising in his assessments of hotels, restaurants, tours, and shops, and a glance at his two-year-old newsletter supports this. A recent review of a new Los Angeles restaurant said: "Why Angelenos keep the reservations phones here ringing off the hook is a mystery as profound as the Bermuda Triangle" because "the food fails miserably."

"I don't write about anything I don't personally experience," Mr. Tomicki said. "I just don't trust anybody else's opinion." But he said that while he prefers to pay his own way and incurred $100,000 in charge-card bills in 1983, "sometimes in a small operation like this we fall prey to invitations."

Economy Traveler, Box 27337, San Francisco, California 94127; phone (415) 753-0140. Every other month. $20 a year. Sample copy $1.

This twelve-page newsletter contains the meticulous research of its editor and publisher, Edward L. Perkins. Each issue focuses authoritatively on several timely subjects, such as how to evaluate a package tour, a comparative study of car rental costs in Western Europe, and how to shop for discounted air tickets from the United States to Asia. Mr. Perkins can be blunt and outspoken, and his critical surveys are uncompromising. He accepts no advertising, and he exhaustively documents what he says. At this writing, however, it seems likely that the newsletter will be absorbed by a new enterprise of the Consumers Union, so check before sending money.

32. Basic Guidebooks

Shortly before the Christmas and Hanukkah holidays, the next year's editions of the major guidebooks begin to appear as publishers and stores promote them as gifts. If a traveler is on your holiday list, however, he or she may prefer not a book that concentrates on the latest hotel and restaurant listings but a less timely volume that stresses culture, history, and detailed descriptions of prominent sights. Some such guidebooks take years to become outdated, and even then they make excellent reading at home as well as useful companions during a trip.

For example, ponder this: "Men raise their hats to each other, and do not wait for a lady to bow to them before uncovering. A man kisses a married woman's hand, but not that of an unmarried girl. Newcomers to a district are not called upon in France and have to rely on letters of introduction to make themselves known."

Outdated stuffiness? Perhaps. But such is the sort of carefully researched advice, appropriate for its time, that was typical of perhaps the greatest guidebooks ever published, those that Karl Baedeker introduced in Germany and then to much of the world more than a century ago. Baedeker believed that a guidebook should not only describe tourist attractions but also instruct, so that the traveler in Rome can do as the Romans do and understand how and why they do it.

The quotation is from the 19th revised edition of Baedeker's *Paris and Its Environs,* published in English in 1924. Buy a copy and be reminded, delightfully, of a bygone age. Galleries in the Louvre have been substantially rearranged, you can no longer get to Versailles by streetcar, and it no longer takes two hours or more to fly to Paris from London. But from Baedeker's *Paris* you can comprehend the magnificence of the museums, palaces, public gardens, and boulevards in a way that is impossible with most guidebooks published today.

Although the original Baedeker publishing house in Leipzig disappeared with prewar Germany, many of its clothbound guidebooks are still available from about $25 upward a copy, depending on their condition. You can find a selection at many bookstores or mail-order houses that specialize in travel books. It is best to write or phone first to be sure you can get what you want.

Some excellent cultural series are in print and go far to fill the gap that the demise of the original Baedeker series left. Their sometimes exhaustive material on museums, medieval cathedrals, and 18th-century palaces is much more durable than the symbols that meat-and-potatoes guidebooks, those that merely direct you to the sights, often use to denote price and quality. In addition, one good guidebook, rather than an unwieldy assortment of booklets and folders on individual sights, is usually sufficient.

For example, the typical tourist can effectively do all of London with the Blue Guide to that city, part of a growing series published by Ernest Benn Ltd. of London and distributed in the United States by W. W. Norton, or all of Paris with a Michelin Green, which with a little nudging can probably be squeezed into an inner pocket of a man's jacket. The Blue Guide to London, for example, provides most of us with more than ample assistance in seeing the British Museum, the Victoria and Albert Museum, Westminster Abbey, and much more.

A problem with cultural guidebooks is that they are often relatively expensive. The Cadillacs of those currently in print are Nagel's Encyclopedia-Guides, of which about forty volumes are published in English at company headquarters in Geneva, and the most comprehensive of which are in the $45 to $65 price range for hardcovers. The company justifies the $65 tab on its China book, for example, on the ground that it has 1,504 pages, ninety-two black-and-white diagrams, and twenty-five diagrams and fifteen maps in color.

Because of their prices and retailer complaints of slow turnover, Nagel guidebooks are usually found only in top-of-the-line bookstores with extensive travel sections. I know of no store that has them all, so your dealer may have to order them specially. In New York, try the Complete Traveller, 199 Madison Avenue; the Traveller's Bookstore, in the lobby of 22 West 52nd Street; or the main outlets of B. Dalton, Doubleday, Rizzoli International, or Scribner, but call before you make a special visit.

Nagels come in hardcover only; Blue Guides, however, come in both cloth and paper, and Michelin Greens in paper only. The Greens are the cultural versions of the Michelin publishing effort; the better known Red Guides are meat-and-potatoes offerings. Because clothbound Blue Guides average about $10 more than paperback versions, many bookstores do not handle them on the ground that they are hard to sell, so they may have to be specially ordered. As a gift intended to be durable, the hardcover book's extra cost may be worthwhile.

In studying in-print cultural guidebooks that I consider among the best, I eliminated the new Baedeker guidebooks, which appeared around 1983 under the imprint of Baedeker Stuttgart. English editions are published in Britain and distributed in the United States by Prentice-Hall in paperback. I found the volumes for France and Spain to be much too once-over-lightly, especially in the A-to-Z section that forms the main part of each. There are many street plans and brief descriptions of villages but no real guidance in helping a traveler select what to see in an orderly manner or determine how much time to devote to it. The 316-page book on France devotes only one page to the Louvre, compared with eighty-six pages in the original Baedeker's *Paris,* and the 304-page volume on Spain devotes only twenty pages to Madrid.

In contrast, the Michelin Green guidebook to Paris is divided into thirty-five walking tours, each with a map with arrows. Sometimes, however, the maps are complicated and relatively hard to follow. Each sight is rated by stars and type of display in the book, so you can quickly determine what Michelin highly recommends you see, simply recommends, says is interesting, or suggests you see "if you have time." Thirteen pages are devoted to the Louvre.

Less emphasis on directional maps but much more descriptive detail is to be found in the Blue Guides, each of which has an atlas in the back. The book on London blends one walking tour into the next and also tells you how to get to the start of each tour separately. Meanwhile, the Blue Guide to the Loire Valley, Normandy, and Brittany is laid out in the form of routes that are easy to drive in a day or less, with detailed descriptions of what to see along the way.

Many guidebooks devoted exclusively to walking tours have appeared in recent years, and one of the best is the periodically revised *Turn Right at the Fountain* (Holt, Rinehart & Winston, 336 pages). The book, first published in 1965, developed from a series of articles that its creator, George W. Oakes, wrote for *The New York Times* in the early 1960s. Since Mr. Oakes's death, new material has been provided by Alexandra Chapman to guide the stroller through the twenty-one European cities with directional maps.

33. Offbeat Guidebooks

The title—*India: A Travel Survival Kit*—bothered me at first. It seemed to suggest that without this guidebook a visitor might face all sorts of dangers. This was not the way I preferred to think of a nation that had been my home for nearly seven years, in which I had traveled widely, and that I still regard with respect.

Then I skimmed the 696-page paperback and found it to be one of the best guidebooks to India—or any country, for that matter— that I have seen. It is a meat-and-potatoes book, crammed with practical advice from writers who have studied the country thoroughly. While not emphasizing history and the arts, it covers these subjects amply for most travelers. It suggests what to see and where to stay and eat, not just in the major cities and other places that tourists frequent but also in some remote towns where a foreigner might justifiably feel anxiety about prospects for survival.

Its three writer-researchers—two Britons named Geoffrey Crowther and Tony Wheeler and a Nepalese named Prakash A. Raj—drew not only on the results of their own extensive travels in India but also on additional information, suggestions, advice, and assistance from other travelers who knew their work. Mr. Wheeler and his wife, Maureen, have collected many fans since they started Lonely Planet Publications in the early 1970s.

Lonely Planet, with an office in Berkeley, California, is one of a growing number of small publishing companies that are putting out some of the best guidebooks on the market today. An unfortunate fact of travel publishing is that the volumes most prominently displayed and widely available in bookstores may not be the best; in fact, many of the best cannot be found in bookstores at all.

The question is: Where do you find these useful books? If you live in a major city, some of them may be carried by the largest bookstores or more probably by those that specialize in travel. New York, for example, has two of these stores: the Traveller's Bookstore, 22 West 52nd Street, New York, New York 10019; phone (212) 664-0995; and the Complete Traveller, 199 Madison Avenue, New York, New York 10016; (212) 685-9007. Both also sell by mail and have catalogues. Or you can try a mail-order house that specializes in travel books, such as Wayfarer Books, Post Office Box 1121, Davenport, Iowa 52805; phone (319) 355-3902; Book Passage, 57 Post Street, Suite 401, San Francisco, California 94104; (415) 982-7866 or toll-free (800) 321-9785, or the Forsyth Travel Library, Post Office Box 2975, 9154 West 57th Street, Shawnee Mission, Kansas 66201; (913) 384-0496.

Following is a sampling of what a few of the smaller publishers have available, in paperback unless otherwise noted. It is not a comprehensive list but is intended to give some idea of their output. In most cases you can order directly from the publisher, which often will absorb the cost of shipping, a service for which mail-order houses usually charge extra. Some publishers accept mail-order payment by credit card. Most send a catalogue without charge upon request.

Lonely Planet Publications, Post Office Box 2001A, Berkeley, California 94702; (415) 428-2211. Besides the one on India, Survival Kit guidebooks are also in print for most countries of South and Southeast Asia and the Far East as well as for Australia, Canada, Mexico, and Turkey. Prices range from $6.95 for Burma, Pakistan, Sri Lanka, and others to $14.95 for India.

In addition, Tony Wheeler's *South-East Asia on a Shoestring* ($8.95), now in its fourth edition, has a strong following among younger travelers, many of whose suggestions are incorporated as the book is revised and expanded. Lonely Planet started, incidentally, with *Across Asia on the Cheap,* the product of a long, mostly overland trip that the Wheelers made from London to Australia. It is still in print under the title *West Asia on a Shoestring* ($7.95), concentrating on travel from Turkey to Bangladesh.

There are also Shoestring books on Africa and South America and a relatively new Phrasebook series to help travelers cope with common linguistic obstacles. Though Lonely Planet aims many of its books at the thrifty traveler, the focus is not simply on saving money. Rather, they are written on the assumption that you need not be rich to have extremely rich travel experiences.

Pelican Publishing Company, 1101 Monroe Street, Post Office Box 189, Gretna, Louisiana 70053; (504) 368-1175. Among the best of this company's books are the Maverick Guides to Australia ($10.95), New Zealand ($10.95), and Hawaii ($9.95) by Robert W. Bone, a feature writer for *The Honolulu Advertiser* who has traveled widely and worked as an editor and reporter in the United States, Europe, South America, and the Caribbean. They give the necessary practical information but are also strong on local history, geography, and lore. For example, in a section on picturesque patterns of speech, the 1984-85 edition of the *Maverick Guide to Australia* tells us that a bicyclist there is called a *bikey,* that to *grizzle* means to complain and that a *ratbag* is an eccentric character.

Mr. Bone says in his introduction that his Australia book was partly subsidized by the government-owned Australian Tourist Commission, but he insists that he had complete editorial freedom.

The Pelican list also includes unusual regional American guidebooks, including the two-volume *Pelican Guide to Old Homes of Mississippi* ($4.95 for Natchez and the southern part of the state and $3.95 for Columbus and the northern part), *Pelican Guide to Plantation Homes of Louisiana* ($4.95), and *Pelican Guide to the Ozarks* ($4.95).

East Woods Press, 429 East Boulevard, Charlotte, North Carolina 28203; (704) 334-0897. East Woods, an imprint of Fast & McMillan Publishers Inc., offers a number of bed-and-breakfast guidebooks, a field in which output is growing in direct proportion to the mushrooming number of private homes that offer overnight stays for a not-always-economical price. In the company's catalogue are bed-and-breakfast or guesthouse guides to California, New England, the mid-Atlantic states, and the South ($7.95 each, paperback), and a revised and updated edition of *The Best Bed & Breakfast in the World* ($10.95), which actually means only England, Scotland, Ireland, and Wales, although it includes more than 800 establishments.

For nature enthusiasts, East Woods titles include regional hiking, fishing, backpacking, and white-water rafting guidebooks, including Elliot Katz's *Complete Guide to Backpacking in Canada* ($13.95 cloth; $7.95 paper).

Globe Pequot Press, Old Chester Road, Box Q, Chester, Connecticut 06412; (203) 526-9571 or (800) 243-0495 in Eastern states outside Connecticut or (800) 962-0973 inside Connecticut. One of the better guidebooks of this company, an affiliate of *The Boston Globe*, is Frederick Pratson's *Guide to Eastern Canada* ($10.95). Its 480 pages and twenty maps include just about all you need to know to tour Ontario, Quebec, the Maritime Provinces, Labrador, and Newfoundland.

The press's strongest offerings cover New England. They include guidebooks to thrift shops and factory outlet stores, to Nantucket, Martha's Vineyard, New Bedford, and other popular vacation spots and the excellent *Boston Globe's Historic Walks in Old Boston* ($9.95) by John Harris, former editor of the newspaper's Sunday edition.

Also notable are the regional hiking, bicycling, canoeing, fishing, walking, and skiing guidebooks of the Countryman Press and Backcountry Publications, Post Office Box 175, Woodstock, Vermont 05091; (802) 457-1049; Earl Steinbicker's *Daytrips in Germany* ($9.95) and *Daytrips From London* ($8.95), published by Hastings House, 10 East 40th Street, New York, New York 10016; (212) 689-5400; *Weekending in New England* ($8.95 in stores; $10.25 by mail) by Betsy Wittemann and Nancy Webster and published by the Wood Pond Press, 365 Ridgewood Road, West Hartford, Connecticut 06107; (203) 521-0389; and the American distribution by Hippocrene Books Inc., 171 Madison Avenue, New York, New York 10016; (212) 685-4371, of a British series of reissued travel classics by such authors as Hilaire Belloc, Edith Wharton, Martha Gellhorn, and Fitzroy Maclean.

34. The Road Map

Although rarely available free in gasoline stations anymore, road maps have improved greatly in variety and quality in recent years. They are available from many sources, sometimes still without charge.

To get exactly what you want, however, you may have to visit a book or map store or order by mail. Store prices range from about $1.50 for the least expensive maps of states and cities in the United States to $10 or more for the costliest covering countries and cities overseas. But many of the best maps—offered by state governments in the United States, provincial authorities in Canada, and some overseas tourist bureaus—are free.

Many state government maps are updated annually and contain much more cartographic detail, such as back roads, hiking trails, and the location of the smallest hamlets, than can be found elsewhere. Often on the reverse side are brief descriptions of leading sightseeing attractions and such useful travel information as the addresses and phone numbers of state police barracks and hospital emergency rooms, hunting and fishing regulations, and directories of state parks and campgrounds.

Of maps for sale, Edith Snizek, manager of the Rand McNally Map Store in New York, reserves her highest praise for those of private European publishers, many of whose work she stocks. "In the United States we're just really interested in showing superhighways and the names of towns," she said. "We don't even attempt to show terrain, and we don't place our dots so carefully to show where the center of town is and what's off the road."

Miss Snizek's principal longtime competitor, Samuel B. Whinery, former president of the Hammond Map Store in New York, gave top marks for foreign maps to the Bartholomew series published in Britain. "They are notable for accuracy and quality of cartography," he said, "and are very complete."

Here are some of the prime current sources of road maps and how you can best tap them.

Government Tourist Offices—Each state government in the United States issues its own detailed road map. All are free, but there is no central national office that distributes them. Generally, this means that you must write or call each state tourist information office individually and wait several weeks for a reply because maps are usually sent by the slowest mail service to save public money.

In the New York area, the only government office where you can pick up several free state maps in one trip (but supplies are limited) is the New England Vacation Center, in the downstairs concourse of 630 Fifth Avenue in Manhattan, which stocks maps of the six states in its region. It is open nine A.M. to five P.M., Mondays to Fridays.

If you address a postcard to the Government Tourist Information Office in the capital of whatever state interests you, it should eventually reach the proper department, even if its official title is different. Use the ZIP code that your post office provides for the state capitol building. Some state tourist offices have toll-free— 800—telephone numbers. Ask directory assistance at (800) 555-1212 if there is one usable in your area for the state in which you are interested.

Free individual maps of Canada's ten provinces and two territories, plus a national Canadian map, are easier to obtain. All are stocked by the Canadian Consulate General, Tourism, 1251 Avenue of the Americas, New York, New York 10020; phone (212) 757-4917. Office hours are nine A.M. to four P.M. on business days, but the telephone is answered until five P.M.

For maps of other foreign countries, write or call the appropriate government tourist office in New York. Look in the Manhattan white pages under the country name or in the Yellow Pages under "Tourist Information."

Gasoline Companies—Several major American gasoline companies still issue domestic road maps and sell them to service stations, which sell them to the public, sometimes in vending machines. Only Exxon gives maps to retailers free, but often these retailers charge the public for them. Service station prices, whatever the brand of products sold, range from twenty-five cents to $1.50 a map—more often toward the high end. Expect to find maps of only the state you are in and those states nearby.

Exxon still maintains walk-in touring centers during business hours at 1251 Avenue of the Americas in New York's Rockefeller Center and at 800 Vell Street in Houston. They provide free maps of states and major metropolitan areas across the country, marked with routing advice if you wish. Mobil Oil also provides free maps and customized route markings, but only by mail. John Flynn, a spokesman, said it could deliver in two weeks. Write to the Mobil Travel Bureau, Box 25, Versailles, Kentucky 40383.

Auto Clubs—Some auto clubs, including some sponsored by gasoline companies, provide free maps to dues-paying members. The biggest of them is the American Automobile Association, which has affiliates across the country. Regardless of which affiliated club you have joined, you can walk into any one that displays the A.A.A. symbol and get free maps, detailed Triptiks with marked routes, state or regional tour guides, and other travel material. (Check the telephone directory under "AAA.")

Retail Stores—Many larger bookstores, such as the main B. Dalton and Doubleday outlets on Fifth Avenue in Manhattan, carry both domestic and foreign road maps, and Rizzoli, at 31 West 57th Street, sells European maps, but stocks at all these shops are not extensive.

A wide selection of road maps is offered at the Complete Traveller, 199 Madison Avenue. But overall, no retail walk-in selection comes close to the comprehensive domestic and foreign stocks at New York City's two contemporary map stores: Rand McNally, 10 East 53rd Street; (212) 751-6300 and Hammond, 57 West 43rd Street; (212) 398-1222. These two shops have virtually every sort of contemporary map imaginable—not just for motorists but also for hikers, bicyclists, and aerial and nautical navigators. Both carry the Rand McNally line of domestic road maps and augment it with city, suburban, and metropolitan area street maps, guides, and atlases from virtually every cartographic publisher. Domestic maps usually range from about $1.50, atlases from $5.50.

They also carry a variety of Australian, New Zealand, Asian, and African maps, but their biggest foreign stocks are the European national, regional, and city maps from such highly regarded publishers as Bartholomew (Britain), Michelin (France), Hallwag (Switzerland), and Falk (West Germany). The Rand McNally store, but not Hammond, also carries the maps of Kummerly & Frey (Switzerland) and Geographia (Britain). Prices range from about $2.50 to $7.

Both map stores accept telephone orders: Hammond's will charge any purchase exceeding $20 to a major credit card; Rand McNally's minimum for credit cards is $30, but it will ship collect by United Parcel Service. Both stores charge for shipping, so ask about this when you order.

Retailers by Mail—Take your pick of the following, but write or phone first for a current catalogue: Forsyth Travel Library, Post Office Box 2975, 9154 West 57th Street, Shawnee Mission, Kansas 66201; (913) 384-0496; Bradt Enterprises Inc. (the country's principal source of Latin American maps), 95 Harvey Street, Cambridge, Massachusetts 02140; (617) 492-8776 (send $1 for catalogue); the Complete Traveller, 199 Madison Avenue, New York, New York 10016; (212) 685-9007.

35. The Right Luggage

"No one set of luggage will do everything well," in the view of R. Michael Meek, whose family has been in the retail luggage business in Denver for more than 110 years. "It's like with cars," said Mr. Meek, president of the A. E. Meek Trunk and Baggage Company. "A four-door sedan will do everything reasonably well, but it won't do special things. Sometimes a two-door subcompact or a station wagon will do much better."

Harvey Maltz, owner of the Edward Harvey Company, which has two retail luggage stores in Boston, put it slightly differently. "There is no such thing as a perfect suitcase," he said. "You never take the same trip twice. You never go to the same place at the same time for the same purpose for the same length of time. So you reach out and you have all this luggage available at home, but you never have quite the right piece."

Mr. Meek and Mr. Maltz are not suggesting that you buy new bags each time you travel. Rather, they are making the point that thirty or so years ago the options were few—perhaps a wooden box-type suitcase, a matching set of several sizes, or a two- or three-suiter. Today, however, the choices are extremely diverse. Go into a luggage shop and chances are you will be faced with a wide array of brands, shapes, construction, types of covering materials, hardware, and, of course, prices.

To help you make a decision, several experts were asked what factors to consider. Besides Mr. Meek and Mr. Maltz, they included three other major retailers: Leo Gleicher, president of Gwin Inc. of River Edge, New Jersey, which operates the Innovation luggage stores in the New York area; Jack Rubin, owner of Rubin's Luggage of Huntington and Smithtown, New York, and Willy van Dooije-weert (pronounced DOY-uh-vyert), president of the five Great Luggage! stores, as they are known, in Minneapolis and Saint Paul. Also interviewed were Howard Kaplan of New York, executive director of the National Luggage Dealers Association, and Charles Harband of San Francisco, executive secretary of the International Luggage Repairmen's Association, who has nearly fifty years in the trunk manufacturing and luggage repair business. Here is what they said.

Determining Needs—Before setting foot in a luggage store, consider what sort of trip you plan to take and what you are likely to take along. While it is hard to predict what sort of purchases you will make on the way, you probably can foretell whether you are likely to do much shopping and whether you will be able to ship purchases home rather than carry them with you.

The principal factors to be considered are these: How do you plan to travel? If by plane, for example, your luggage needs will probably be different from a trip by car. How long do you plan to be away? What is the reason for your trip—business, pleasure or both—and how formal will it be where you are going, a consideration that determines what you wear? Are you going alone or with a companion of the same or opposite sex or with your spouse and several children? How are you going to get to and from the airport or rail or bus station—by public transportation or in a relative's or friend's car? And will you have to carry your bags yourself at connecting points or through customs? What is the climate where you are going, and will you be going from one type to another—hot to cold, rainy to arid—on the same trip?

Type of Construction—As outlined by Mr. Meek, there are three basic categories of luggage today. One is the hard box, such as the molded luggage of Samsonite or American Tourister and the aluminum alloy cases of Zero Halliburton, which usually retail from about $325 to $550. These are especially durable and watertight, and can usually be handled roughly without disturbing the contents. But they are relatively heavy; the twenty-nine-inch, four-suiter Halliburton, probably the heaviest, weighs nineteen pounds.

A second category is semistructured, which means that there is a basic frame but soft or semisoft sides, usually with zippers, allowing room for expansion. "If you put an extra sweater in, it's going to bulge a bit." Mr. Meek said, "but you won't wrinkle anything." Most of the people interviewed agreed that among the better brands are French, Ventura, Skyway, and Hartman. For the traveler who simply must travel heavily laden, such as a professional entertainer, several retailers spoke admiringly of the French jumbo garment bag, which can carry up to eight men's suits or fifteen to eighteen lightweight dresses and has suggested retail prices from $505 up, depending on the length of the bag and type of covering.

The third category is totally unstructured, soft, casual luggage— the most prevalent on the market today. It can be in the form of a duffel bag, a backpack, or a suit or dress bag to carry aboard a plane and hang up or fold over and stow beneath a seat. It usually lies perfectly flat for storage, will carry as much as anything on the market, and weighs practically nothing. If the material used is of superior quality, such as Cordura or ballistic nylon, it is virtually indestructible. Those interviewed mentioned that among the leading brand names are Bill Bayley, Pegasus, and Andiamo.

Most of those interviewed discounted the suggestion that belongings might be more vulnerable to damage or theft in soft luggage than hard. They suggested that soft bags be packed to the limit, with clothing used as an outer buffer to protect anything fragile. As for theft, they reasoned that someone with a sharp and strong enough tool to rip Cordura nylon would probably find it easier to take the whole bag, so that soft or hard construction would not matter. "Anything that looks very expensive is vulnerable to a rip-off," said Mr. Kaplan.

Most major luggage manufacturers make a variety of tote bags—from purse-size to full-size carryons—for items you may need while aboard a plane. Some also make collapsible bags that can be folded to take up virtually no room in a larger bag, then be unfolded and used for purchases you make while traveling. Bear in mind, however, that pressure is growing in the airline industry to confine hard or sharp objects to bags that can be stowed beneath seats and to ban them from overhead storage bins.

Shopping Around—Because of the wide variety of luggage, do not hesitate to ask questions about each type you are shown. Ask about the hardware (are the handles screwed in or simply riveted so that if they break off they cannot be screwed back in?), the type of stitching and the quality of the thread, the strength of any straps, the locks (combination locks are usually the most secure), the quality of any attached wheels, and the terms of the manufacturer's warranty. Be sure that a sale is a sale, not merely the reduction of an artificially high price.

Accessories—Because porters and baggage carts are increasingly rare at airports and stations, you may want a suitcase with wheels, attached or detachable, or even a carrying cart. If you decide on a cart, don't overeconomize; anything that retails for less than about $18 is probably worth little or nothing. A typical price is about $30, but sizes vary. Among the leading cart manufacturers are the Products Finishing Corporation of Brooklyn and Remin Laboratories of Joliet, Illinois; most luggage stores stock the products of one or both.

Other Guidance—Besides making luggage and promoting it, the Samsonite Corporation publishes an excellent thirty-two-page leaflet titled *Getting a Handle on Luggage* that includes advice on selecting, packing, and safeguarding luggage. For a free copy, send your request with a self-addressed No. 10, or long business, envelope bearing first-class postage to the Samsonite Traveler Advisory Service, Post Office Box 38300, Department 20, Denver, Colorado 80238.

36. Travel Gadgets

At TravelMarket in San Francisco you can buy a packet of fourteen ear plugs for $3.50. "Silence, please," the store's literature says. "These imported beeswax ear plugs are the B's knees when foreign noises come between you and your sweet dreams."

Ear plugs are among the growing number and variety of travel accessories on the market these days. If you listen to their promoters, plugs are important to the well-being of virtually every kind of traveler, from the subway straphanger in New York to the pampered cosmopolitan aboard a Concorde jet. But are they essential for you? Might you do just as well by simply stuffing a couple of wads of absorbent cotton in your ears or listening to music on a tape recorder or perhaps doing nothing at all but absorbing the myriad noises of the real world?

Different people have different conceptions of what they simply must take with them when traveling. My wife, Mimi, for example, will not leave home without a Swiss Army pocket knife with at least a bottle opener and preferably a screwdriver attachment, too. She carries a travel lock, a small sewing kit with safety pins, and a French net bag that rolls up into virtually nothing until she needs it.

I must carry a small spiral notebook—the kind you can buy in a discount drugstore for about fifty cents. Starting from the front, I take notes on what I see and hear; from the back I record my expenses and keep a log of photographs I have taken. Because I must carry a number of medicines for high blood pressure and glaucoma, I bought a hanging kit to organize toiletries—like the one that Le Travel Store in San Diego sells for $17.50. A close friend of ours always carries a portable smoke alarm with detachable flashlight ($30 from Le Travel Store). He also carries several medicines, but he prefers to lump all the containers in a disposable plastic food-storage bag.

Whatever you can possibly imagine in travel accessories, there is probably somebody, somewhere in the world, who makes it. For the many that are manufactured abroad, there are at least a dozen importers in the United States, some of them wholesaling to other entrepreneurs and some selling directly to the public in stores or by mail order. Many accessories, especially of the gadget type, make excellent gifts, particularly for the man or woman who seems to have everything. While some mail-order services promise shipment within a day or two after an order is received, deliveries can sometimes take weeks.

These were among the diverse products that were recently available, with prices subject to change:

- A variety of travel alarm clocks with a variety of features at a variety of prices. For example, a shirt-pocket-size clock that shows two time zones at your command was offered for $13.95 by Cognito, 1280 Saw Mill Road, Yonkers, New York, 10710; phone (914) 423-6000 or, outside New York State, (800) 431-2797. Meanwhile, a dual-time clock with luminous hands and a thin gold trim case was offered for $55 by the Travel Store (not to be confused with Le Travel Store), 56-1/2 North Santa Cruz Avenue, Los Gatos, California 95030; (408) 354-9909.

- A wide variety of belts, pouches, holsters, and under-the-shirt vests to stash such valuables as passports, traveler's checks, credit cards, and substantial amounts of cash. Some are easy to reach while you are fully dressed; others require that you retire to a private area to get at them. Toward the bottom of the spectrum, Hudson's, an army-navy-type store at 97 Third Avenue, New York, New York 10003, offered a nylon-and-cotton money belt for $3.98; at the high end, a lightweight, four-pocket, machine-washable security garment to be worn under shirt, dress, sweater, or blouse was offered for $19.95 plus $2 shipping and 5 percent sales tax for New Jersey residents from Travel Safvest, Box 576, Cranbury, New Jersey 08512; (609) 655-4777. While acknowledging the utility of a money belt, my wife prefers to stitch her own from a scrap of cloth and pin it inside her lingerie.

- Credit-card-size calculators to help you deal with fluctuating

206 • Before You Go

currency-exchange rates. You enter the current exchange rate of the local currency, and it is held in memory until you change it. You can then enter an amount in local currency and quickly convert it to dollars, so that you can get a better grasp of whether or not a potential purchase is a bargain. One model cost $18 at Le Travel Store, 1050 Garnet Avenue, San Diego, California 92109-2875; (619) 270-0642 or, outside California, (800) 854-6677. Another model cost $20 at the Travel Store in Los Gatos. Still another cost $21.45 from the Traveler's Checklist, Cornwall Bridge Road, Sharon, Connecticut 06069; (203) 364-0144.

• Voltage converters and plug sets that allow your American-made electrical appliances, such as hair dryers, shavers, curlers, and contact-lens sterilizers to be used anywhere in the world. Converters alone cost about $17.50 to $18 in travel stores; perhaps cheaper in discount appliance stores that cater to recent immigrants with families abroad. Converters plus plug kits run from about $24 to $26.50 in such places as the Travel Store, Le Travel Store, Traveler's Checklist, and the Complete Traveller bookstore, 199 Madison Avenue, New York, New York 10016; (212) 685-9007.

• Double-voltage steam irons with fold-down handles. The Travel Store in Los Gatos offered one by Franzus for $46 and a General Electric for $43. A Sunbeam was offered for $39 plus $3.50 for shipping from the Sharper Image, 680 Davis Street, San Francisco, California 94111; (415) 344-4444 or, outside California (800) 344-4444.

• Imitation jewels—the company calls them "fabulous fakes"—that permit you to look dazzling while your genuine treasures remain at home. The fakes are not necessarily cheap—for example, a canary diamond eight-karat cubic zirconia ring cost $525—so Camalier & Buckley, one company that offered them, sold for $25 more a burgundy velvet jewel case that is designed to fit into a hotel safe-deposit box. The company's main store and mail-order address is 1141 Connecticut Avenue N.W., Washington, D.C. 20036; (202) 783-1431.

• Various security devices for hotel rooms, such as the Kee-Blok, a portable gadget that can be attached quickly to any key-in-knob door lock. It prevents anyone from entering until you return, although in some hotels you may be required to leave the Kee-Blok key with the manager for emergency use. The device was sold for $21.95 plus $2 postage by Christopher's Travel Discoveries, 10 Fenway North, Milford, Connecticut 06460; (203) 874-5086.

- Wheels and straps to be attached to your luggage to make it mobile. Many luggage stores sell them, but if you have difficulty finding any, try Traveler's Checklist (mail orders only), the Travel Store in Los Gatos (mail or in person) or TravelMarket, a shop that recently moved to Golden Gateway Commons, 130 Pacific Avenue Mall, San Francisco, California 94111; (415) 421-4080.

Luggage shops, department stores, gift shops and even drugstores usually carry a limited range of travel accessories, but in recent years stores that are almost exclusively devoted to travel have opened around the country. Some primarily sell books and maps, but others sell books as a sideline and stress accessories. These are among the very new travel shops:

- Passenger Stop Inc., 732 Dulaney Valley Court, Towson, Maryland 21204; (301) 821-5888.
- La Valise, 30 East First Street, Hinsdale, Illinois 60521; (312) 323-9699.
- Entourage, 438 Park Place Center, Kirkland, Washington 98033; (206) 827-2924.
- Le Bon Voyage, 6 Faneuil Hall Marketplace, Boston, Massachusetts 02109; (617) 523-6640 and 52 John F. Kennedy Street, Cambridge, Massachusetts 02138; (617) 864-2060.

Among the more unusual items you could find in travel shops or recent mail-order catalogues were the three-in-one Catastrophie kit, including a no-sew button kit, an eyeglass repair kit, and a minisewing kit, $5.50; the Travel Rescue Kit for Montezuma's Revenge (diarrhea), $25, and the Tinkle Cup for the Discriminating Lady Traveler, $7, all Travel Store, Los Gatos; Secret Space, authentically labeled cans of shaving cream, deodorant, tennis balls, beer, etc., with false bottoms for hiding valuables, $31.95, Complete Traveller; a Pocket Survival Tool, four screwdrivers, file, pliers, leather punch, can and bottle opener, razor-sharp blade, all in one, $45 plus $2.50 shipping, Sharper Image; Dent-Aid dental emergency kit, $21.95 plus $1.75 shipping, Traveler's Checklist; a battery-operated portable blender, $65, Camalier & Buckley; and the Itty Bitty Booklite, which clips onto your reading material, $30 at the Travel Store, Los Gatos, and $19.95 at Complete Traveller.

With such travel accessories, as with most unfamiliar items, it is preferable to see them before you buy. Quality can vary substantially, depending on the manufacturer, and prices for the same quality can vary considerably from store to store. Also, some items that sound practical may not seem so useful when at hand.

Some stores that also sell by mail do not include their entire stock in their catalogues. Some charge for their catalogues, others send them free, and still others refund the catalogue price if you place an order. Delivery of most items costs extra; when you order, be sure to ask how delivery will be made because that could affect both the speed and the charge. Most companies will accept credit cards to pay for mail or phone orders; all will accept money orders or cashier's checks, but some will not accept personal checks.

If you plan to order or make inquiries by phone, be aware that most accessories businesses on the West Coast do not open before eight or nine A.M. Pacific time, which is three hours behind Eastern time. A notable exception is the Sharper Image, which accepts phone orders at any time.

Be sure to ask about refund policies in case you do not like what you receive. This can be extremely important if you buy sight-unseen.

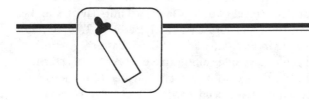

37. Children on the Road

Every once in a while, the airlines, railroads, bus companies, and hotels seem to discover children. You cannot count on it, but more often than not the "discoveries" occur when the market is soft and there is more space than demand. Suddenly one major company bursts forth with advertising that coaxes you, the adult traveler, to take along not just your spouse but the youngsters as well for a greatly reduced price or even free. Very quickly the competition joins in, and it almost seems from the ads that you cannot afford to leave the children at home.

Close examination often reveals, however, that it can be extremely difficult to determine which "bargain" is best—or whether it is a bargain at all or simply a gimmick to generate business. Sometimes you will even discover that there are cheaper ways to take the children to the same place than those that are heavily advertised.

For example, in a campaign a couple of years ago, newspaper ads in New York announced in large type that "Eastern gives kids a free ride." Smaller type said, however, that the offer, for travelers under eighteen, was available for only two months, only to five destinations in Florida (Miami, Fort Lauderdale, Orlando, Tampa, and West Palm Beach) and only on Tuesday, Wednesday, and Thursday. It pointed out that each youngster had to be accompanied by an adult—one child per adult. Further, the ad said, "Seats are limited"—a signal that only a certain number were allocated for the offer, and airlines usually keep such numbers secret.

Pan American World Airways and Trans World Airlines announced similar offerings. But when you began comparing fares, you quickly found that airline pricing had become so zany under Federal deregulation that children were extremely lucky to have adults to shop for their tickets.

One morning during that period, I asked a travel agent for the fares I might have to pay for one confirmed adult coach ticket from New York to Miami for travel two days later, a Thursday. Using her computer terminal, the agent replied quickly: $89 on T.W.A., $99 on the now-defunct Air Florida, and $180 on Eastern Airlines or Pan Am. A child could have gone along free on T.W.A., Eastern, or Pan Am, but the difference in adult fares made it obvious that choosing T.W.A. would have been thriftiest. On Air Florida, the child would have been charged $84, and the total for the two of us would have been $3 more than on Eastern or Pan Am.

No one was carrying children free to Florida on weekends. Some airlines at that time were offering a special weekend child's fare from New York to Miami of $79 one way, however, and T.W.A., in fact, dropped its adult fare to $79, too, on Saturdays and Sundays.

The lesson in all this is that if you treasure your dollars, it is important to ask about different fares on different days and about other restrictions. At the time of the campaign discussed above, Eastern was allowing a child to fly free midweek to Florida if the accompanying adult was traveling on a seven-day advance-purchase discount fare, which then was as low as $82 one way. If the adult was flying first class (at $220), the "free" child went first class, too. On Pan Am, however, the fly-free offer did not apply if the adult had paid a discount fare. Also, if the adult flew first class or Clipper class (Pan Am's name for its extra-frills business class), the free child had to sit in the rear cabin amid adults who had paid less.

On flights within the United States, children from two through eleven years old usually pay half the applicable adult fare. Infants under two go free, on the assumption that they will not occupy seats. Children twelve and over usually pay adult fares. So the inclusion of youngsters as old as seventeen in the fly-free program to Florida meant that because of the one-adult-per-child rule, if a couple traveled with more than two children in midweek, any extra teen-agers had to pay the adult fare. But any teen-ager paying adult fare was entitled to be accompanied free by a younger sibling.

So if you are planning a family excursion by public transportation, be sure to keep a calculator at hand. Ask about concessions for children and about family plans. Special promotions come and go, and it is often impossible to predict where and when you will find one and how long it will be available and with what restrictions. Some are widely advertised, but you learn about others only if you ask.

As a general rule, wherever you fly with children, be sure that when your reservations are made, the airline is told if you all expect seats together. Try to check in early at the airport and ask to be boarded first. Usually, requests to be seated together are honored; if you do not ask, however, you may find your family distributed all over the aircraft with no one to look after the little ones.

On international flights, different rules may apply. For example, an infant under two, held in arms and not occupying a separate seat, is usually assessed 10 percent of the adult fare. But each additional infant accompanied only by the same adult is charged 50 percent. Children over twelve usually pay adult fares. But youngsters between two and eleven customarily pay either half or two-thirds of the adult fare, depending on the country of destination. The percentage is sometimes much higher on restricted, discounted economy fares, and usually there is no children's reduction for cut-rate standby transatlantic flights.

If you are going to Europe with children, think twice before signing up for a low-cost charter flight. They usually give no discount or very slim discounts for children, so a family's total cost may be higher than by scheduled service.

Bargains for children grow at many destinations if you buy a land package (accommodations, car rentals, meal plans, sightseeing, etc.) with your air fare. Such a combined purchase often entitles you to cheaper transportation than if you buy an air ticket alone. But before committing yourself to a package, study all its elements and be sure you want enough of them to justify the cost, whatever it may be, and the strings that are often attached.

The hotel "bargain" may require that everyone sleep in the same room. Are you and your spouse so eager to save money that you will not mind sharing your bedroom and bathroom with, say, a sixteen-year-old daughter and seventeen-year-old son and perhaps a younger child as well? On the other hand, most large hotels in major American cities offer such drastically reduced weekend packages that it may not strain your budget to take two rooms instead of one. Most hotels do not advertise discounts specifically for renting two rooms, but if the house is not full, a reduced rate can often be negotiated on the spot with the manager.

Like the airlines, Amtrak and the nation's two major bus networks, Greyhound and Trailways, offer reduced children's fares. Ask about the reductions before you buy your tickets: Some are linked to family plans or have other restrictions.

Some cruise lines offer inducements to take your youngsters with you when you sail. Commonly, a child's fare is 50 percent of the lowest adult rate on the ship. On some lines, children travel free. The hitch, though, is that they usually must share a cabin with their parents—which, as with a hotel room, is not everyone's concept of an ideal vacation. Sometimes, to travel free, a child must be the third or fourth person in a cabin normally occupied by two adults. Some lines will carry third and fourth adults free, too.

There is a drastically different side, however, to the matter of travel by children, and that concerns the growing number who do not have an adult to accompany them. They not only do not travel free, but they are also often charged more than other children because they are alone. And significant questions arise about their safety and who is responsible for providing it.

If the child is going by air, safeguards abound, although sometimes there are lapses. Major airlines have intricate regulations intended to make sure that in flight and while making connections, a young traveler is under the care of a responsible employee. A parent or guardian, meanwhile, must usually guarantee to the airline in writing to provide an adult to take the youngster to the airport of origin and remain there until the plane departs, and for another adult to await the child at the destination airport.

If you are planning to send your child by bus, however, expect little from the company besides transportation. If you are a New Yorker, chances are you will be at the Port Authority Bus Terminal when your eight-year-old son returns from a week with Grandpa in Vermont. But should a subway breakdown prevent you from getting there on time, your son could be on his own at the terminal—a prominent hangout of derelicts, the deranged, and the depraved—until and if he is spotted by a roving youth-services patrol.

A prominent reason that travel by unaccompanied minors is increasing is the growing rate of divorce. After a marriage breaks down, the mother may remain in White Plains, say, while the father may get his company to transfer him to Denver. They may share custody rights, however, with the child or children spending part of the year with each parent. Very likely, no adult relative or friend is available to travel with the child. Even if one was, it would probably be too expensive, so the child goes alone.

According to Charles Novak, manager of corporate communications for United Airlines, such situations took an unusual twist a few years ago when his company, to spur business after a long strike, gave every passenger for a limited period a coupon allowing half-fare travel on a future flight. The coupons were transferable. "We had quite a problem," Mr. Novak recalled, "with divorced parents arguing over which one should get the child's coupon."

Also traveling alone may be children on the way to or from boarding schools, summer camps, or visits with relatives or friends. Sometimes on international flights an unaccompanied traveler is only a few months old. For example, perhaps a husband and wife immigrate to the United States from India, and the wife, observing Hindu custom, goes home to her parents in Bombay to give birth. As soon as she is able to travel, she rejoins her husband in the United States, leaving the infant with its grandparents. As soon as the baby is three months old—the minimum age for solo travel on Air-India—the grandparents send the child to the parents. Such a situation may occur relatively infrequently, but it happens often enough for special regulations to be published to cover it.

Such infants are considered unaccompanied only in the sense that no parent or guardian is with them. They are commonly charged the adult fare so that a professional attendant, assigned by the airline to serve the infant exclusively, can occupy a seat and hold the baby.

For most travel by public transportation, a person at least twelve years old is considered an adult. Such a child usually pays the applicable adult fare and gets little if any special attention unless it is requested. For unaccompanied children under twelve, however, regulations, conditions, and facilities vary widely, so it is important to check carefully in advance.

Here are some rules that are common but not universal on flights within the Western Hemisphere, so check first with the airline you plan to use.

Unaccompanied children under five are not carried. Those five to seven years old are carried only on direct, although not necessarily nonstop, flights on which there is no change of planes or on connecting flights that involve only the same airline, not transfers to other carriers. Unaccompanied youngsters eight to eleven, however, are permitted to make interline connections.

Half-fare offerings for children under twelve or "kids fly free" promotions on highly competitive routes usually do not apply to unaccompanied youngsters; instead, they usually pay adult fares.

More or less typical are the procedures of Eastern Airlines, which were explained by a team of senior officials of the company in an interview by telephone conference call. An adult who plans to send an unaccompanied child must say so when making the reservation. A record, including details on who will meet the child, is immediately set up in the computer system, and a printout is given to a flight attendant upon takeoff.

At the airport on the day of departure, a form is completed with specifics on the flight or flights, including seat numbers. The form includes the name, address, telephone number, and relationship of the person who will meet the child on arrival. The form is signed by the adult who takes the child to the airport and by the accepting agent. A button is pinned on the child, identifying him or her as unaccompanied.

If the flight leaves on time, the process is usually smooth. At the departure gate, the airline takes over. If a connecting flight is involved, the child is the airline's responsibility at the intermediate airport and is supposed to be kept under close escort. At the destination, the child is escorted off the plane by an attendant and is turned over to the specified "accepting parent or guardian," who signs for him.

Should the adult not be there, however, the youngster is supposed to remain in the airline's care. Attempts are made to locate the adult, but the airline reserves the right to return the child to the airport of departure, at the family's expense.

Quite often for weather or mechanical reasons, things do not go smoothly. If an originating flight is delayed, the airline will probably insist that the accompanying adult stay around.

"In one case recently," said Mr. Novak of United, "a heavy fog suddenly closed in and the plane couldn't take off. But the parents didn't know that, because they left the airport as soon as they saw the child go through the departure gate. It was the last flight of the day to the child's destination, and we were stuck with him. One of our people took him home overnight—which, incidentally, happens many times."

Major airlines usually take pains to keep unaccompanied minors content, and thereby, among other things, keep peace in the plane. They often seat them near each other, feed them before adults, and provide games and trinkets to hold their attention.

Airlines encourage parents to send along a small bag with items that the youngster might want in flight and to specify in advance any special dietary, medical, or other needs.

In surface travel, however, provisions are quite different in the United States. Subject to change, Greyhound and Trailways accept unaccompanied children as young as five providing a responsible adult accompanies them to the departure gate and, in the bus driver's opinion, the youngster seems capable of traveling alone. Children five through eleven are accepted by Greyhound only for trips scheduled for five hours or less and on one bus. Trailways asks parents to have solo children travel only in daylight, and an itinerary, including any scheduled connections, is stapled to the ticket. A solo child is usually seated near the driver. If a connection is missed or the child is not met at the destination, the driver is supposed to get help from a supervisor. On both bus systems, children under twelve pay half the adult fare.

"We are liable as long as the child is in our safekeeping," a

Greyhound spokesman said. He said this included depositing the youngster "at a safe place" and helping him change buses, if necessary. If there is no adult at the destination to pick up the child, he said, the line usually takes a common-sense approach and often enlists the help of a security guard or Traveler's Aid.

"It is the responsibility of the parent or guardian, however," the spokesman said, "to see that minors are met at the destination."

Robert Forman, vice president for safety and security of Trailways Lines Inc., insisted that because "most bus drivers are parents themselves, they take children under their wing." But Roger P. Rydell, the company's vice president for public relations, acknowledged that airlines were better equipped than bus systems for the job. "They have stewardesses available where we do not," he said, "and they have massive ground crews. We have to rely very much on our drivers and ticketing personnel."

When asked about facilities at the Port Authority Bus Terminal in midtown Manhattan, Bob Walters, patron services coordinator for the authority's terminals, tunnels, and bridges, said the bus companies "really have no one there to take care of kids."

"We have a youth services unit," he said, "with social workers and plainclothes officers who constantly patrol the terminal sixteen hours a day. If they spot a lone kid, they approach him and ask what the problem is. If he says that Aunt Minnie didn't show up, the patrol takes him to the office and makes a phone call to straighten things out." Between eleven P.M. and seven A.M., Mr. Walters said, the responsibility is left to the terminal police.

Amtrak does not accept unaccompanied children under eight "under any circumstances," said John McLeod, an Amtrak spokesman. In fact, he said, anyone under twelve must normally be accompanied by someone over eighteen. But he said that children eight to eleven are often accepted, providing a parent or guardian signs a release form and guarantees that the youngster will be met at the destination. The child is charged the adult fare.

"Such travel is permitted," Mr. McLeod said, "only upon the specific approval of the person in charge of the station of departure. Travel must be in daylight, no transfers may be involved, and a personal interview must indicate the youngster's capability of making the trip alone."

"We can't be as easy as an airline," he said, "because of the nature of our beast. Aircraft have only one or two entrances, but on a train you can go in and out all sorts of doors."

216 • Before You Go

Help at Airports and in Flight

Emile A. Okal, a teacher at Yale, was waiting with his wife and their four-month-old daughter at Logan International Airport in Boston for a flight to Paris. Shortly before boarding time, Mr. Okal wrote later to airport authorities, his wife wanted to change the baby and nurse her.

"Changing a baby requires nothing but a table," he said. "Nursing merely requires the mother to be seated on a chair or couch. None of the several ladies' rooms my wife visited provided either of these very basic facilities: a chair and a table. After a long argument with airline officials and airport personnel (each bouncing responsibility in this matter at the other in the most unpleasant way), the airline finally agreed to let my wife use their employees' ladies' room, which has a couch."

Logan is among the busiest airports in the world. According to *Hickman's World Air Travel Guide*, an authoritative reference source published by Hammond, it handles 13.5 million passengers a year and 250,000 planes. It has a duty-free shop, a bar, a restaurant, a barber shop, several lounges for dignitaries, and a variety of stores. But except in the Eastern Airlines terminal, used mainly by shuttle passengers to and from New York, it had, when the Okals were there, no convenient place to attend to the common needs of infants.

Shortly after Mr. Okal complained, conditions at Logan improved. Said Jo Ryan, who was public relations manager at the airport at the time: "In the past when we put chairs in the ladies' room, they would disappear. But we have just installed specially designed and constructed chairs for all ladies' rooms. We also have counters that we think are adequate for changing diapers."

That was a few years ago, but a recent spot check with officials of a dozen major American airports indicated that while most offer more than Logan used to, facilities are limited, at best. Few airports have nurseries or other special areas for children that are accessible to fathers as well as mothers. If an infant is accompanied by one parent, it is usually the mother, but in more and more cases it is the father. Men's rest rooms with tables or shelves or other fixtures on which diapers can be changed are rare.

If a flight is delayed several hours, passengers usually have no choice but to carry their infants—in their arms or in back carriers or slings—the entire time. Sometimes an empty seat can be found in which a baby can sleep, but when delays occur, airports are likely to become extraordinarily crowded. Some airlines keep a few strollers around or provide baby seats for use in departure lounges, but bassinets are rarely to be found.

Once in the air, traveling with a baby usually becomes easier, although facilities and services vary. Common Sense Rule No. 1, however, for anyone who plans to fly with an infant is to tell the airline about it when you make your reservations. On most international flights you are required to do so because the child is charged part of the adult fare. Within the United States, however, infants under two who do not occupy seats usually fly free, so the airline may not know you plan to take baby along unless you say so.

When told about baby, a reservations agent can put notations into the computer system. If baby is not solely on formula that you bring along but needs a special diet, such as strained or finely chopped fruit, meat, and vegetables, these foods usually can be arranged with at least twenty-four hours' notice. If you request it when you make reservations, you can probably be assigned a bulkhead seat. On many planes this means there is room for a bassinet, provided by the airline on request, in front of you. Then only during takeoff and landing will you have to hold the baby in your arms—with your seat belt around you but not around the baby.

Some airlines do not provide bassinets or other in-flight carriers because they contend that none are suitable. They will, however, try to place a passenger with an infant beside an empty seat, if there is one, so that the baby can be put there after takeoff.

Spokesmen for just about every airline insist that flight attendants are told to give parents whatever personal assistance they can. "Many flight attendants have kids of their own," a spokesman for Eastern said. "Twenty-five to thirty percent of our female attendants have them. They know what it's like when they go on pass and ride with their own kids. So their hearts go out to travelers with infants. Whenever possible, they try to give parents a break, especially if one parent is saddled with two or three children. A mother should be able to eat her own meal in peace and go to the toilet."

Because of cutbacks in flights in recent years and high labor costs, however, long-haul aircraft tend to be crowded and to operate with minimal staffs. Considering that attendants serve drinks and meals, rent headsets for stereo and in-flight movies, and attend to diverse passenger demands, empathy and good intentions may not result in much help for those with infants if there is little time.

Like the handicapped, parents with infants can be boarded before other passengers, but on board they may be largely on their own. Most aircraft carry milk but not baby formula. Attendants are usually not allowed to mix formula anyway, although they will usually warm bottles. Planes do not usually stock baby food unless a passenger requests it in advance. Some aircraft stock diapers; others do not.

With the notable exception of the European-built A-300 Airbus, the lavatories on most planes have no facilities for changing diapers, so this must be done at the seat, as must any breastfeeding. Some planes in the new generation of aircraft, such as Boeing 757s and 767s, may have changing tables, but it depends on what the airline orders. Don't count on it. On long-distance buses and trains, there are no special services for babies, although some new Amtrak coaches have large restrooms where diapers can be changed and babies can be nursed in privacy. An Amtrak spokesman said diaper-changing tables were available in women's rooms in new or rebuilt stations, such as those in Jacksonville, Florida; Miami; Minneapolis-Saint Paul; Rochester, New York; and Washington.

At many bus depots around the country, sanitary facilities for adults, let alone infants, are primitive if they exist at all.

38. Traveling with Pets

Each year it gets easier to have a pet dog or cat accompany you on a vacation or to make arrangements to leave it comfortably and safely near home. Excellent information is available on such things as whether hotels have special arrangements for pets or will accept them at all, but you have to know where to find it.

Because it does not occur to them to ask, many people do not learn about facilities for pets until it is too late. Such was the case with Robert Berger, a lawyer, and his wife, Ruth Lepson-Berger, a poet, of Watertown, Massachusetts. They are deeply attached to their golden retriever, Jazz. Except in the most unusual circumstances, they would not go away overnight without taking Jazz with them. So when they drove to Pittsburgh to attend a cousin's wedding, Jazz went, too. The Bergers, eager that their pet be comfortable while they attended the wedding festivities, carefully selected a motel—the Holiday Inn in Monroeville, Pennsylvania, just east of Pittsburgh—because it was close to the wedding site and they were told it welcomed pets.

When they arrived, however, they discovered that the air-conditioning in their room would operate only when they were inside, with the door chain-locked. They could not affix the chain from outside. Their only choice, they reasoned, was either to leave Jazz in an unventilated room or to take him wherever they went. So along he went to a rehearsal supper that evening and the wedding and luncheon the next day—waiting in the car each time while his owners, somewhat guiltily, joined in the revelry.

Only after the Bergers returned home and described the incident to me did they learn that the Holiday Inn might have offered them satisfactory alternatives if they had explained their problem to an employee there. I telephoned George Hollander, then general manager of the inn, who said the motel had two outdoor kennels, available to any guest. And he said Jazz could have been left in the room anyway, because although the inn's Lock-A-Watt energy-saving system controls operation of the cooling mechanism in the air-conditioner, the fan that brings in air from the outside and circulates it operates even if the chain is not affixed. This usually keeps a room comfortable enough for a pet, he said.

One might expect a hotel to volunteer information about care of guests' pets. In the Bergers' case, however, the staff members apparently did not know that the couple had brought a dog with them because Jazz was never taken through an indoor public area where they might have seen him.

The lesson in this saga is obvious: If you plan to travel with a pet, do not hesitate to ask questions when you make your plans and as your trip progresses. Or if you prefer to travel without your pets but also do not want to worry about what might be happening to them at home, examine all those possible alternatives, as well.

A lot of sound professional advice is available these days for both types of pet owners—much more than was the case a few years ago.

Hal E. Gieseking, who has extensively researched both types and whose writing on travelers and their pets has been widely published, strongly advises that if you leave your pet behind, the surroundings be as familiar to it as possible—preferably your own home. He suggests "sitter exchange" arrangements with neighbors, or hiring a sitter, such as a college student or retired person. Some travelers provide free room and board in their homes in exchange for pet-sitting.

If you, like many travelers, prefer to leave your cat or dog in a professionally run kennel, choose carefully. Your local Humane Society or the American Society for the Prevention of Cruelty to Animals may refuse to recommend any, but the Humane Society will probably at least tell you if any that you ask about have a bad record. A directory of kennels, designating those that are members of the American Boarding Kennels Association, a nationwide non-profit organization established to promote high standards in the pet-boarding industry, is included in the booklet *Where to Buy, Board or Train a Dog*, available free from the people who make Gaines dog food. Write to Gaines Booklets, Post Office Box 8177, Kankakee, Illinois 60902.

Contrary to a common impression, the A.S.P.C.A. says that cats, too, can learn to travel well by car if you start with short trips near home.

"The most important thing, if you are traveling more than a mile away from home," said Dr. Gordon Robinson, an A.S.P.C.A. veterinarian in New York, "is that a cat should be in a ventilated carrier, not loose in the car. If loose, it could jump out of a window quickly when you stopped for gas. A cat doesn't come back when you call; instead, it could quickly disappear and you would never see it again."

Dr. Robinson and other experts strongly recommend that whether your traveling pet be a cat or dog, it wear a collar with a plate giving your name, address and telephone number. In an interview with my colleague Sarah Ferrell, Dr. M. L. Keating, senior staff clinician at the Henry Bergh Memorial Animal Hospital in New York, stressed the importance, when traveling by car with animals, of keeping their temperatures normal. In summer, temperature control is of utmost importance. "Dogs' and cats' body temperatures rise rapidly in warm weather since they don't perspire—much faster than human temperatures rise," Dr. Keating said. It is imperative, in hot weather, to exercise the animal in the early morning, to travel in the cooler hours of the day, and to keep the air-conditioning on or the window rolled down a few inches. When cooler weather comes, heat prostration is less of a threat.

The A.S.P.C.A. has free, single-sheet information bulletins, in English and Spanish, on the care and handling of pets. Among them is a blue sheet entitled *10 Easy Steps to Remember When Traveling With Your Pet by Car*. The society also offers *Traveling With Your Pet*, a booklet primarily for air travelers. For details on how to get a copy, contact the A.S.P.C.A., Education Department, 441 East 92nd Street, New York, New York 10028; phone (212) 876-7711.

A principal value of the booklet is its directories of health requirements for traveling with cats or dogs both within and outside the United States. If the dog is traveling in your car, chances are you will never be asked to produce a health certificate or evidence that it has been inoculated against rabies within the last six months or year. But if you are shipping the pet by air, you will have to produce such evidence before the carrier will accept it.

Most American states require health certificates and rabies inoculation. Hawaii is notable for its requirement that pets be placed in quarantine for 120 days at the owner's expense, so if you plan to vacation there briefly, forget about taking Towser with you. Britain requires six months' quarantine, and Australia bars dogs or cats except those that have been quarantined a year in Britain or nine months in Hawaii. At this writing, the Soviet Union does not admit animals at all.

Most hotel and motel directories and many guidebooks in the United States tell which of the listed places accommodate pets. An excellent source of such information is the periodically updated *Touring With Towser*, a directory devoted to the subject. It is available for $1.25 by writing to Gaines Booklets, Post Office Box 8177, Kankakee, Illinois 60902.

Among other things, *Touring With Towser* tells, with each listing, whether you may leave a dog in a room alone, whether there is an extra charge to accommodate the pet, whether the owner must assume responsibility for damage, whether there is a special area for walking dogs, and whether, at your request, the motel will arrange for boarding at the nearby kennel.

The directory also notes pointedly those states—such as North Carolina and Hawaii—where, by law, dogs are barred from bedrooms in any inn or hotel. It says that kennel facilities are available in many hostelries in those states, but advance reservations are often necessary.

If you leave a dog unattended in a hotel room, keep it caged, put a "do not disturb" sign outside the door or leave word for the maid on whether or not it is safe for her to enter.

Much of the professional advice on traveling with pets is based on the premise that you will probably be going by auto, because Amtrak, Greyhound, and Trailways do not accept pets except for guide dogs accompanying the deaf or blind.

On the French National Railroads, however, any pet can, if other passengers do not object, ride in a seating compartment for 50 percent of the second-class fare; small animals should be kept in containers or muzzled if they are let out; large dogs must be muzzled. Pets can also travel in sleeping compartments. There is a limit of one animal to each compartment.

Pets are not allowed in sleeping compartments on the railroads of West Germany, but leashed and muzzled dogs, if they do not annoy other passengers, can travel in seating compartments for 50 percent of the second-class fare, and cats and birds are free. Cruises and tours are another question. Although operators' policies differ, most travel agents do not encourage their clients to sign up for themselves and a pet. Charles Woodhull of Destination Travel in Manhattan told Sarah Ferrell: "I would strongly discourage people from taking pets on a tour. Tour operators have to think of the other people. Someone might have an allergy or something."

Mrs. Ferrell reports that in Europe there is no real need for a *Touring With Towser* because the Michelin Red Guides indicate the hotels and dining rooms in which dogs are not welcome. More often than not, when dogs are prohibited from a restaurant in France, it is because there is a resident and territorial dog attached to the premises. At this writing, dogs can stay at the Gritti Palace in Venice, although they cannot enter the restaurant, but cannot stay at the Hassler-Villa Medici in Rome; they can dine in Paris at the three-star Tour d'Argent but are turned away from the three-star Lasserre or the three-star Taillevent.

In the United States there are several ways to send pets by air. At this writing, some airlines, such as American and United, permit a pet to accompany you free in coach class (but not at all in first class) if it is small enough to travel in a container that fits under the seat ahead of you. Other airlines levy a fee for pets, typically $21 regardless of destination on domestic flights, again only in coach class. Some airlines sell a small, reusable plastic container for pets for $20 and up depending on the airline and the size of the animal, but others provide a cardboard container free.

On international flights, in-cabin pets are charged at the excess-baggage rate that applies to that trip. From New York to Paris at this writing—but almost certainly changed by the time you read this—it is $53 on T.W.A. for a pet plus portable kennel with a combined weight of up to a hundred pounds. International flights can be even more complicated, however. Merle Richman, a spokes-man for Pan American World Airways, told Sarah Ferrell: "You have to check all the regulations. For Buenos Aires, for example, we allow you to take a pet under the seat, but we can't allow you to bring it back that way. Argentine regulations prohibit carrying a pet in the cabin."

Airline procedures for shipping pets as checked baggage on your flight or as freight, usually not on the same plane you take, can be cumbersome and expensive—and risky regarding climate control and provision for meals and exercise. While such forms of shipment may be practical if you are making a permanent move or plan to be away a long time, they may cause too much anxiety or discomfort to justify taking a four-legged friend on a week's trip to Hawaii, a winter ski jaunt, or a brief escape to the Caribbean.

With several days' notice you can probably arrange to have your dog go as excess baggage in the pressurized cargo hold of the flight you are on. On domestic flights at this writing, the charge is typically $21—the same as in the cabin. To go this way, however, the total weight of the dog plus its kennel usually must not exceed a hundred pounds and the combined length, width and height of the kennel must not exceed one hundred inches.

Airline personnel usually do not check animals through on connecting flights, so if you are flying from, say, New York to Sacramento, California, with a change of planes in Chicago, you not only can visit your pet in Chicago to make sure it is all right, you may have to, to recheck it to the final destination. Some airlines will allow you to check animals through on connecting flights of their own company, but never when a connection is to another carrier.

An alternative is to send the animal by air freight, which is usually much costlier than sending it as baggage. From New York to Los Angeles, according to a T.W.A. estimate at this writing, it is about $145 for a dog and kennel up to a total of 100 pounds and rises in proportion to extra weight; from New York to Paris, $3.05 a pound up to 100 pounds and $2.35 for each additional pound up to 220.

In his book *Protecting Your Pets,* which was published in 1979, Hal E. Gieseking noted that at that time it could be quite expensive—$294—to send a Great Dane in a portable kennel from Amsterdam to New York. He strongly advised having the owner's Social Security number tattooed on a dog's inside flank.

Examining various transport alternatives—for example, retaining a commercial shipper who specializes in pets—Mr. Gieseking is especially wary of sending animals as air cargo. "Airlines frequently 'bump' pet shipments," he says. "The reason is that kennels require a greater amount of space than the size of the box itself. There must be space around the kennel to permit ventilation and to give the animal air to breathe. During busy periods, the airlines could leave kennels sitting overnight while they load the cargo holds with more profitable freight. That is one reason you should never ship your pet during holiday periods."

By sending $1 to the American Boarding Kennels Association, 311 North Union Boulevard, Colorado Springs, Colorado 80909, you can get a booklet called *How to Select a Boarding Kennel.* It contains a roster of association members, many of whom arrange pet shipment by air and attend to all the details. You drop your pet at the kennel a couple of days before you leave and pick it up at the destination airport.

For arrivals at Kennedy Airport in New York, cats receive tender loving care for $8 a day at this writing and dogs for $12 at the A.S.P.C.A. Animalport until you pick them up, but the service is not for long-term boarding. Phone (718) 656-6042 for details, including current rates.

Rates and shipping practices vary among kennels, so check before you commit yourself. Also, you will probably prefer to choose one relatively close to your home. Two selected at random and questioned about their services and charges (subject to change) are the Willow Pet Hotel of Deer Park, New York, which draws customers from New York City as well as Long Island, and the Hillsborough Boarding and Grooming Kennels of Somerville, New Jersey, most of whose customers live in central New Jersey. Both serve all three major airports in the New York area. The only Boarding Kennels Association member that is actually in New York City is World Wide Pet Transport, 13-14 College Park Boulevard, College Park, New York, 11356; (718) 539-5543.

According to Marquetta and Fred Wheeler, who own Hillsborough, the New Jersey kennel would charge you $65 to prepare and deliver your dog to Newark Airport ($75 to La Guardia or Kennedy) plus $16 for a health certificate and rabies inoculation, plus $30 to $65 for a very hard plastic kennel, plus the cost of shipment as excess baggage or air freight.

The charges at the Willow Pet Hotel, according to Jack Rosenzweig, the owner, are similar: $55 to prepare and deliver your first animal for shipment anywhere in the United States plus $5 for each additional one, and $75 for international shipment of the first pet and $5 for each additional one. Mr. Rosenzweig said his charges included a phone call to the owner or agent to tell him when the plane carrying his pet has taken off.

Staff members of kennels shipping pets are required by government regulations to check the air temperature at the airport of embarkation and what it is expected to be at the destination when your pet arrives. Under Federal regulations, shipment is usually forbidden if it is hotter than 80 degrees or colder than 45, although there are exceptions. "If you're sending a Siberian husky who spends most of his time outdoors and you have a government-recognized acclimatization certificate," Mr. Rosenzweig said, "you can send him if it's colder."

PART II
ON THE ROAD

At last you are on your way! Your hope, obviously, is to have as carefree a journey as possible, and after all the planning, all the preparation, you certainly deserve it. It seems at this point as if nothing can go wrong.

Chances are, very little will. There are, however, many pitfalls in travel today, and the more you know about them, the better equipped you will be to cope with them if they come your way. Much of what happens in travel is unpredictable—and that is where a lot of the fun lies. But sometimes the unpredictable can cause great anxiety, even fright. So you can benefit greatly by knowing and understanding your rights, how to protect yourself and your possessions, how to deal with emergencies, and where to seek different types of help.

For a taste of how some travel problems can be dealt with, read on!

39. Air Travelers' Rights

What should you do if you are flying at 35,000 feet and you think the airline is treating you badly?

The Civil Aeronautics Board will no longer be able to help you. Under airline deregulation, it went out of business at the end of 1984, and at this writing there is considerable doubt about how the Department of Transportation will assume the responsibilities inherited from the C.A.B. for protecting consumer rights. A lot of discretion has been left to the airlines, so if you feel aggrieved, a lot may depend on how and when you complain.

Perhaps, as sometimes happens on crowded planes, the economy-class washrooms become unsanitary or run out of supplies. Perhaps you dislike a meal. Perhaps cigarette smoke is bothering you, but no effort is made to find you a different seat. Perhaps an attendant is rude.

"Be insistent but be professional," advised Carmen Cappadona, who used to be a C.A.B. field representative in New York. "If you are complaining on board an aircraft, try to get the matter resolved as discreetly as possible, because you may wind up with a hothead as a pilot or cabin attendant. The pilot may put down the plane at the next possible stop and have the F.B.I. meet you."

In one such incident, a pilot landed the plane short of its destination when a dispute arose among passengers over smoking. But sometimes it works the other way. Once, just before takeoff, another pilot apologized profusely to the passengers because there were cockroaches aboard. After making some unkind remarks about his airline, he politely asked everyone to disembark so that the plane could be fumigated.

Among passengers who have felt compelled to complain in flight was Ida M. Glasberg of Weston, Connecticut, who was flying with her husband, Oscar, on an Aer Lingus jetliner from New York to Dublin. She said that within an hour after takeoff, the washrooms in the economy-class area were flooded with water, apparently from a leak, and lacked toilet paper and towels. Only after persistent pleading, she said, were she, her husband, and a few other passengers permitted by the chief flight attendant to use first-class facilities. Mrs. Glasberg said that at the request of the chief flight attendant, she gave her a two-page report, addressed to the director of customer services, describing the incident and commenting that the flight attendant had been "most courteous."

Ethna Hess, a customer relations executive for Aer Lingus in Dublin, said in reply, "I could not agree with you more that in the face of this most unusual situation, discretion should have been exercised and all female passengers allowed to utilize the first class facility."

"When aircraft are full, our stewardesses are faced with two problems," said an Aer Lingus customer services representative in New York. "They must cope with limited facilities for economy-class passengers yet must try to maintain some kind of privacy for those in first class. In the case of Mrs. Glasberg, we kind of feel that they did not react as quickly as they might have done."

It is no secret that most major airlines do not give the service they once did—at least not in economy class. Many carriers are in economic difficulty, and they have cut flight and ground staffs to the minimum that their consciences and union contracts allow. They are nibbling at amenities that passengers have long taken for granted.

If you are stranded at an airport because of a storm or other act of God, the airlines are less likely to provide you with free meals and lodging or even to help you fend for yourself than they used to be. "We do not create snowstorms, so we will not pay for them," Charles Novak, a spokesman at United Airlines headquarters in Chicago, said. He added, however, that for severe hardship, policies were flexible: "It's up to the local station to decide what they want to do. We're not insensitive to this."

Safety standards are being maintained, however—the law requires it—but gone are the days when minimum-rate passengers on competitive routes were routinely served prime steak and complimentary champagne. They have also lost much personal attention from cabin attendants, well-stocked rest rooms that were invariably tidy, and uncrowded seating arrangements.

On some routes where promotional fares have failed to generate much new business, you may still be able to stretch out across several empty seats. But don't count on it; airlines cannot tolerate slack loads for long.

Although C.A.B. rules did not generally cover airline amenities, until a few years ago it was customary for major airlines to provide complimentary meals, accommodations, ground transportation, and long-distance phone calls for passengers who had checked in or were in transit and whose flights were badly delayed or unable to operate because of inclement weather or other acts of God. Unless the airline is clearly responsible for the delay, such amenities are now rare for passengers beginning their journeys. Some airlines have even dropped them for connecting travelers as well.

But a senior official of American Airlines qualified this. "We do not intend to penalize the traveler if it's the last trip of the day and it's snowing outside," he said. "We won't say we'll never do this or that. The local manager has prerogatives. If someone is elderly, indigent, or disabled, obviously we're not going to tell him to sleep on a bench somewhere."

In flight, sometimes even first-class passengers complain of being shortchanged. Among them was Tom Bleasdale, an executive of a major multinational corporation with headquarters near Boston. A frequent traveler, he said that on two Trans World Airlines flights that he took from Boston to London, passengers with economy-class tickets were seated for the full flight in the first-class compartment, where he had a seat at the first-class fare.

In a letter to C. E. Meyer Jr., president of T.W.A., Mr. Bleasdale said that on the second flight there were more economy passengers in the compartment than first-class passengers. The economy travelers received all the first-class privileges, he said, and the compartment was so full that he did not get the service to which he felt entitled.

Asking for a refund of the difference between the economy and first-class fares, Mr. Bleasdale wrote: "In view of this situation, and as a regular customer, I feel entitled to enjoy the privilege of the first-class cabin at the same fare paid by less frequent and, possibly, less loyal customers."

Replying in the president's behalf, Rosemary Aurichio, director of customer relations for T.W.A., apologized to Mr. Bleasdale for "your disappointing experiences," but said that "under no circumstances" could the airline consider his request for a refund. "In those rare situations when more passengers with valid tickets and confirmed reservations than we can accommodate present themselves for a flight," she wrote, "we have an obligation to provide them with the first available transportation to their destination, and this

includes first-class accommodations on the same flight, if available."
"Those passengers who paid for first-class transportation," she
added, "received the service to which they were entitled."

The degree to which Mr. Bleasdale and other first-class travelers
sometimes get less than their money's worth is debatable. As far as
could be determined from a spot check with major airlines, many
frequent long-distance travelers in first class and the slightly-less-
posh business class grew accustomed to receiving extra attention
when their compartments were not full. As airline operating costs
have risen, however, and less-economical flights have been
discontinued, planes have generally been fuller. Sometimes as a
result of overbooking and sometimes because other flights have been
canceled, economy passengers are upgraded to business or first class.

Once in a first-class compartment, they get the works: a spacious
seat, often a stretch-out "sleeperette"; free cocktails, sometimes even
before takeoff; free wine with lunch or dinner; the fanciest cuisine
the airline offers; and free headsets for the movie or music. On some
airlines they even get a gift, such as a toilet kit.

A principal source of complaint among full-paying first-class
passengers seems to be not so much that they must share the goodies
as about the upgraded companions with whom they must share
them. In a telephone interview, Mr. Bleasdale spoke ruefully of
"these guys with banjos and fancy outfits in the next seats, crowing
about how they got a bargain."

Airline spokesmen appear sensitive to this; in fact, Morris G.
Simoncelli of the New York office of Japan Air Lines said: "If we
have to upgrade, we're pretty careful about whom we put up there.
No blue jeans, no noisy ones, that sort of thing. We don't want
anyone whooping it up about how they made it and got into first
class."

On J.A.L., however, the need to upgrade on its Tokyo-New York
route is infrequent because it has only one flight a day in each
direction. Airlines commonly overbook in economy class to compensate for anticipated no-shows. J.A.L. virtually eliminates no-
shows on this route, however, because it has the clerical capacity to
telephone all its confirmed passengers shortly before departure and
verify that they plan to use their reservations. Thus, it has little
reason to overbook.

But on airlines with several wide-body flights a day on the same
route, it is difficult if not impossible to keep so closely in touch,
especially with economy-class passengers. Some routes, such as New

York-Miami, are notable for no-shows, so there is often a strong tendency to overbook. Under Federal rules, however, passengers with confirmed reservations who are bumped from domestic or international flights of United States carriers may qualify for a compensation up to double the cost of their ticket or $400, whichever is less, plus alternate transportation to their destination.

Obviously, airlines try to avoid paying such compensation. One way is to upgrade. Another is to ask for volunteers who are willing to give up their seats in return for guaranteed transportation within two or three hours on the same airline plus a bonus, sometimes $100 or so in cash, sometimes a free trip later at no cost. In early 1984, for example, United Airlines was offering volunteers on its New York-Chicago route free round-trip transportation anywhere the carrier flies, such as between the East and West Coasts, subject to seat availability, which meant probably not around holidays.

Sometimes first-class passengers are downgraded to economy class. First class is rarely overbooked, but downgrading can occur when, for example, seats in that section must be given at the last minute to airline personnel who are deadheading to a destination to operate an unexpected flight. Some union contracts stipulate that in such situations, certain employees must go first class. The only obligation to a downgraded passenger, meanwhile, is to refund the difference in fares.

If you have any reason to believe you are being treated unfairly by an airline, insist on seeing the company's "conditions of contract"— its rules that govern your passage. The law requires that copies of such rules be available for public inspection at all airline ticket offices and airport check-in counters.

If the problem arises at an airport, the first person to approach is the airline's customer service representative on the scene. If there is none, however, or if there is but he or she leaves you dissatisfied, the airline's top official on duty at the airport usually has the last word—for the moment, at least. It does not matter what the reservations clerk told you on the phone when you booked your ticket, if the senior official at the airport thinks you have been undercharged, he can insist that you pay more. Your best bet in such a situation is to swallow the problem temporarily, then complain in writing as soon as you can to the customer relations department at carrier headquarters. The more details you can include, such as dates, times, and names, the better your chances of recourse.

Often all you will get in return is a defensive letter that may make you feel worse, but Federal laws permit many rules to be bent in your favor if the airline agrees that while its action may have been legal, you were not at fault.

If a grievance arises once you are airborne, you should complain to the senior cabin attendant. Most will help if they can. But if you do not receive satisfaction, you have no recourse until you are safely on the ground again. You have no right to demand to see the captain to appeal the senior attendant's decision.

Some airlines provide on-board complaint forms that can be left with the attendants or mailed to company headquarters. If there are no such forms, do not hesitate to write to the airline as soon as possible after the flight. All the major companies maintain customer relations departments that at least will pay attention. If you remain dissatisfied, write to the Department of Transportation in Washington and ask that your complaint be directed to the office that handles consumer protection.

Getting What You Pay For

A few years ago, before there was much deregulation and before airline economics turned sour, five carriers were operating more than thirty nonstop flights a day in each direction between Miami and New York. But only three airlines made a total of six nonstop round-trips between Miami and Philadelphia. Let's examine the impact of this disparity in competition on in-flight amenities for the traveler.

Delta Air Lines, for one, was advertising heavily in both New York and Philadelphia that "Delta puts on the ritz." Its New York advertising said this meant that, even in economy class, "the entree is filet mignon, charcoal broiled, on brunch, lunch, and dinner nonstops." Its Philadelphia advertising, however, said that "the entree is beef en brochette, chicken Hawaiian, or another deluxe dish"—not quite the same.

Asked about this, Al Kolakowski, district director of marketing for Delta in New York, said that tests had shown that New Yorkers in particular love steak, but "a Philadelphian is a different breed of cat." Thus, menus out of Philadelphia were rotated—presumably saving Philadelphians the boredom of steak on every flight and certainly saving the airline considerable money.

40. Political Hot Spots

Shortly after two o'clock one April afternoon, telex machines began to clatter in about a dozen major newspaper offices around the country. They transmitted a forty-five-word message, an official travel advisory from Washington. "In view of the current labor dispute in Bermuda," it said, "which now involves strikes by hotel workers, bus operators, taxi drivers, and airport services, the Department of State recommends that U.S. citizens planning to vacation in Bermuda defer plans to visit there until the situation improves."

Unfortunately, the advice was a little late for Blanche and Leonard D. Lewis of Great Neck, New York. They had flown from New York to Bermuda—and back because of the strikes—on American Airlines the previous day. But even if the warning had come in time, it is doubtful that they would have received it. Despite various channels that have been set up to tell vacationers of potential difficulty—from strikes to political terrorism to outbreaks of disease to scarcities of available hotel rooms because of fairs—the word often does not filter down unless you go after it.

It behooves you, the traveler, therefore, to find out what complications lurk in the country you plan to visit before you have sacrificed hundreds or even thousands of dollars and exposed yourself to a host of inconveniences. Jam-packed hotels may not dissuade you if you plan to stay with friends. But you have a right to know what to expect, and often a State Department advisory will tell the travel industry, which can tell you.

Based primarily on reports it receives from United States embassies and consulates throughout the world, the State Department issues a travel advisory whenever officials feel one is warranted. Some are valid for a specified period, others indefinitely. When a situation that had been covered by an open-ended advisory eases, a new advisory is issued.

At one time not long ago, United States citizens were under advice, because of political conditions, not to visit El Salvador at all and to make only essential visits to Bolivia, Chad, Guatemala, Iran, Iraq, Lebanon, Libya, Sierra Leone, Syria (except Damascus), and Uganda.

The advisories are sent by telex, on request but without charge, to bona fide travel-related companies or trade organizations, as well as to newspapers and wire services, which have the capacity to make the information widely available. "Everybody on the list now, except for U.S. Government agencies, asked to be put there," a State Department official said.

Thus, your travel agency, which should be a prime source of guidance on anything to do with your travel, could be on the list, as could the operators of package tours. The information in the advisories is widely disseminated through the travel trade press, however, as well as through the publication of the American Society of Travel Agents, *ASTA Notes*, which goes to all members of that association.

If you are at all uneasy about conditions at your destination, there are several sources you can consult for current information. Although the State Department will not place a private individual on the advisory list, you can get the latest word on any country or area by calling the department's Citizens Emergency Center in Washington, (202) 632-5225, between 8:15 A.M. and five P.M. Mondays through Fridays.

In addition, try the consulate or government tourist office of your destination country in New York or other large cities around the United States or its embassy in Washington. Obviously, government representatives can be expected to put the best possible face on problems in their countries, but they also usually realize that candor is in their long-range interest.

"More and more today," said W. D'Arcey Crooks, former marketing and public relations manager of the Caribbean Tourism Association, "governments are recognizing that true statements are the best way to deal with situations, rather than to try and cover up."

The Caribbean Tourism Association, 20 East 46th Street, New York, New York 10017; phone (212) 682-0435, can advise you of travel conditions in its area, as can the Pacific Area Travel Association, 228 Grant Avenue, San Francisco, California 94108; (415) 986-4646. Or you might try the American Society of Travel Agents, 4400 MacArthur Boulevard N.W., Washington, D.C. 20007; (202) 965-7520.

Another source of advice is an airline that flies to where you are going: If the one on which you have reservations does not sound convincing, call the others as well. United States airlines with international routes usually get the State Department advisories and have their own direct communications with embassies and consulates as well as with their own representatives overseas. When they think it is warranted, they cancel flights, but if they do operate in an iffy situation, they are unlikely to encourage passengers to cancel bookings.

Perhaps if Blanche and Leonard Lewis had asked American Airlines for advice instead of waiting to be told, things might have turned out different. But they had not been uneasy. "We had no idea of conditions in Bermuda," Mrs. Lewis recalled later, "but while in flight the stewardesses informed us of the strike and how it was spreading."

"When we landed the ground crews would not remove our luggage," she continued. "We were then told, by an American Airlines local representative who had boarded the plane, that we would have to disembark and go through customs. He told us that the airport was surrounded by pickets and that there was no way of getting in and out of the airport. He thought it would be in our best interest to return to New York."

Not only were the Lewises deprived of a long-awaited vacation, but they had to pay their full air fare. When they wrote to American asking for a refund, C. A. Smith, a staff assistant in the executive office, replied that only after the flight had left New York did the company become aware of the seriousness of the strikes and that beginning the next day it began telling passengers before flights took off. The unrest ended a week later.

"While I can certainly sympathize with the unfortunate situation you encountered," Miss Smith wrote to Mr. Lewis, "and understand your reasonable request for a refund, I must respectfully decline to do so. You did use the transportation, and we do collect the proper fares for such transportation."

Asked for further comment, Eugene Dieringer, director of customer relations for American, said the airline had no knowledge until after the Lewises' plane had taken off that the situation in Bermuda had deteriorated. "Hindsight is always clearer than foresight," he said about their complaint.

According to Paul M. Bessel, former general counsel of the American Society of Travel Agents, when the best-laid plans of travelers go awry, they must depend on the good will of airlines, travel agents, and the tour operators who supply the travel agents with tour packages.

"I have to admit it," Mr. Bessel told my colleague Margot Slade, "some travel agents or tour operators will look at a hurricane-devastated Dominican Republic or a flooded Florence and tell clients, 'The country is still there, though the Red Cross is providing disaster relief; and the hotel is still there, though there's no running water. So, we're going. If you want to cancel your trip, that's your business.'"

As reconstructed by Kathryn P. Wright, then manager for the United States of the government-operated Bermuda News Bureau, the labor strife on the island began in mid-April 1981 with a walkout by government employees in hospital and blue-collar jobs. It began to disrupt tourism when taxi drivers struck in sympathy on April 25 and hotel workers joined them April 28.

On the twenty-eighth, strikers picketed the entrance to the airport and passengers had to carry their own baggage from the claims area to the departure gate, where volunteer drivers provided transportation. The next day—the day of the Lewises' trip—the strike spread, although many private motorists were reported to be carrying passengers, for a fare, from the airport to hotels.

"We were getting hundreds of calls here," Miss Wright said from her office in New York. "Everybody in the office was taking calls, and we were trying to keep abreast of what was happening."

Many State Department advisories concern less threatening situations than labor unrest, such as temporary shortages of hotel space in popular tourist destinations. French representatives in the United States were pleased with an advisory late one August that hotel space would be critically short in Paris until the end of November because of international exhibitions.

"That's correct," said Nora Brossard of the French Government Tourist Office in New York. "People shouldn't just waltz off to Paris without confirmed reservations. It's impossible there during this season."

The Guatemalan authorities were much less happy with State

Department advice a few years ago that United States citizens traveling in Guatemala use extreme caution because of terrorist violence, although no tourists had been victims. Said a response from the Guatemala Tourist Commission: "The Government of Guatemala is taking all necessary precautions to preserve its unblemished record of providing effective security for American tourists."

At one point the State Department advised against visiting specified areas of Colombia that, it said, "are still considered dangerous due to military engagements with local terrorist guerrilla groups." Among the areas mentioned were southern Huila in the area of San Agustin, noted among archaeologists.

Asked about this, Luis Toro, head of the Colombia Government Tourist Office in New York, said it was the first time he had heard of problems there. "It is a very primitive place," he said in a telephone interview. "It has only one hotel with maybe twenty rooms. It is far away from the major cities. We do have a problem in La Guajira in the north because of the drug traffic, but in the rest of the country there is no problem whatsoever."

In the opinion of Graham A. Hornel, director of public relations for the Pacific Area Travel Association, travel advisories tend to draw much greater exposure to the negative rather than the positive aspects of tourism and can be detrimental long after they are rescinded. "I'm not saying that the State Department shouldn't consider the safety of American travelers," he said, "but the media pick up where it's unsafe, not where it's safe. People talk to each other, and it gets exaggerated."

41. Protecting Yourself Against Crime

To Roberta Sydorko, a vacation should be "a time of relaxation and excitement—not having to look over your shoulder every minute to see if you are being stalked."

"The minute you put down your guard," she said, "you get hit, or robbed, as we did. That's not a vacation to us."

Mrs. Sydorko, a medical secretary who lives in Iselin, New Jersey, was complaining in a letter to a travel editor about a vacation in Rio de Janeiro. She spoke of several misadventures of members of her tour group—victims of muggings, holdups at knifepoint, pickpockets, and the like, culminating on the last day with the theft of her own pocketbook containing money and jewelry worth about $1,500. She had placed the bag on the floor between her sixteen-year-old son and herself as she lunched at a five-star hotel just after checking out.

Such distress stories are common these days. One hears of them despite the stern warnings often given by tour operators at welcome briefings at vacation destinations: Don't ride local buses; lock up airline tickets, jewelry, and extra money in the hotel safe; don't take anything but essentials to the beach. Yet perils continue, and it is easy for vacationers to conclude, as Mrs. Sydorko did: "No more trips to faraway places."

Such decisions are a major source of concern in the travel industry. It is especially painful to the authorities in Brazil, Italy, Spain, Indonesia, and Colombia—countries that are often cited as trouble spots by American consular officials. Brazil, for example, is in severe economic difficulty and wants tourist dollars badly. The country can hardly afford a reputation that keeps travelers away.

"We have made major efforts to prevent crime and make it easier to report and hopefully to track down," said Laurence Mountcastle, North American manager for the Brazilian Tourism Authority. "But no matter how many warning signs are placed in hotels about the beach, some tourists still will take along bracelets and necklaces—things that can easily be snatched by kids."

"They hit and run, hit and run," said Amelia Medwied of the Italian Government Travel Office in New York, about the situation in some cities in her country. "By the time you go to the police and make your report, they're very hard to find."

"Pickpockets in London are a major problem, particularly in department stores and subways," said John P. Caulfield of the United States Foreign Service. "I used to issue replacement passports several times a day when I was a consular officer there."

Mr. Caulfield, who recently completed an assignment as press officer of the State Department's Bureau of Consular Affairs in Washington, said incidents were fewer in the Caribbean but sometimes more serious. "Someone tries to grab a woman's purse," he said, "and she doesn't give it up. So she gets injured as the robber rips it away. We get about one case a month like this in the Bahamas.

"But," he added, "when you think that about ten thousand Americans a month visit the Bahamas and I get only one horror story from them, I don't think that to dwell on it puts the situation in the proper perspective."

To some extent, tourists are vulnerable because they tend to be conspicuous. Walk around Times Square, for example, and you can easily spot the tourists by the way they dress, their cameras, and the way they stroll casually around, stopping often to consult guidebooks or maps. You, who would never be mistaken for a tourist in your own city, may be just as conspicuous when you go on vacation.

It is highly possible, however, to thoroughly enjoy touring Rio or Naples or Seville or London—or New York, for that matter—without being victimized if you take a little care. Based on many interviews and observations, it seems hardly necessary to tarnish a vacation by, as Roberta Sydorko said, constantly looking over your shoulder. Rather, it seems more a matter of applying simple precautions and a dose of common sense.

To help you do this—and to provide a lot of other useful information for travelers—the State Department offers an excellent thirty-page pamphlet called *Your Trip Abroad*. You can get a single copy free by sending a postcard requesting one to the Bureau of

Consular Affairs, Room 6811, Department of State, Washington, D.C. 20520.

In one succinct paragraph, the pamphlet says: "Coat pockets, handbags, and hip pockets are particularly susceptible to theft. You can prevent a potential theft from occurring by carrying your belongings in a secure manner. Women may wish to carry shoulder bags tucked under the arm and held securely by the strap. Men may wish to use their inside coat/front trouser pocket or a money belt instead of the hip pocket. In addition, if you wrap your wallet in rubberbands, it is much more difficult to remove without your feeling it. If you should find yourself in a crowded area, such as a subway or marketplace, take special precautions."

The pamphlet does not say so, but experience in many foreign cities has shown that a woman is usually safer walking at least several feet back from the curb and carrying her bag on the shoulder that is away from the street. Many women have had strap bags torn off their arms by thieves on bicycles or motor bikes whose swiftness makes them impossible to catch. Experience has also shown that the wise tourist does not carry money, passport, credit cards, air tickets, and other valuables in the same wallet, purse or pocket. Thus, if a pocket is picked, not everything is lost. In fact, the State Department particularly advises that passports be carried separately because thieves are usually not interested in them and a passport can be the best possible identification when claiming a refund or other restitution for a loss.

However, based on an assumption that most American tourists put everything in one pocket, the State Department uses statistics on passport losses as an indication of the extent of thefts generally. In fiscal year 1982, Mr. Caulfield said, 6,039 American passports were reported stolen in Europe, 1,088 in Latin America, 195 in Africa, 369 in South Asia, the Far East, and the South Pacific, and 734 in the Middle East.

Of those reported stolen in Europe, he said, 1,128 were by muggers, 1,366 by pickpockets on the street, 857 on public transportation, most of them also by pickpockets, 993 in such places as department stores and parks, 319 in restaurants, 445 in hotels and other lodging places, 681 in unattended vehicles, and 250 miscellaneous. Based on age, Mr. Caulfield reported 485 losses by Americans under eighteen, 2,132 between eighteen and twenty-nine, 1,221 between thirty and forty and 2,201 over forty.

According to insurance underwriters, baggage left in unattended vehicles is particularly vulnerable. Rental cars are easy to spot in most countries, and if parked near tourist attractions, it does not take much to guess who has rented them. Also, a lot of baggage is lost between airports and hotel rooms.

Despite increasing reports of assaults and robberies in which the victims are tourists, promoters of many leading vacation destinations seem reluctant to volunteer information about perils that travelers could face.

"In Paris," said George Hern of the French Government Tourist Office in New York, "there are usually signs in public places about pickpockets and that sort of thing." He said that he knew of no official warning literature, however, such as leaflets that a few years ago were offered by the New York City transit police about crime in the subways and how to avoid it.

Similar comments were received from half a dozen other officials of foreign government tourist offices who were asked what their countries do to advise visitors about risks.

"We have no literature," said Mrs. Medwied of the Italian office, "but when the question comes up, we don't avoid it. We don't say, 'Watch out when you go to Italy, something is liable to happen,' but we do hope people will take common precautions, just as they do at home."

Some guidance is available in occasional newspaper articles and guidebooks. For example, the 1984 edition of the *Fisher Annotated Guide to Spain and Portugal* includes a cautionary note about crime affecting visitors to Seville.

In Paris a few years ago, the American Embassy prepared a two-page warning bulletin on pickpockets. "Each year," it said, "some 1,400 Americans report their passports stolen or lost in Paris. Many of them are the victims of pickpockets operating in areas frequented by tourists, particularly museums and crowded subway and train stations."

Citing a study made by the Paris newspaper *Figaro,* the bulletin said that the subway system, the Métro, was a favorite haunt of pickpockets. It said they operate on three Métro lines in particular: Porte de Clignancourt-Porte d'Orléans, Nation-Porte Dauphine, and Château de Vincennes-Pont de Neuilly. "These three lines serve such crowded locations as the Louvre Museum, the Beaubourg cultural center, principal department stores, and several railway stations," it said. "The pickpockets' favorite days for operation are Friday, Saturday, and the day preceding a holiday."

A copy of the bulletin was mailed to *The New York Times* by Johanna P. Kovacs of Carnegie, Pennsylvania, who said she had picked it up when she went to the embassy to report a robbery. "My husband and I along with sixty other members of the American Association of Retired Persons recently spent three weeks in Paris," she said. "Out of sixty people, six were robbed. I was knocked to the sidewalk in front of the American Express Company, where we were going to report the robbery of our credit card.

"Yet we never read of the epidemic of robberies in Paris," she said. "Everyone hears what happens in New York City, but the French are very good at keeping a secret."

Jessie E. Knight of Great Neck, New York, a longtime aficionado of the Costa del Sol in Spain, complained of a recent upsurge in crime by the young there, attributable largely to unemployment. She spoke of youths who travel in pairs on motorcycles and snatch purses and bags. "I was thrown down on my face," she said, "and my bag was torn from my shoulder, cutting my face (five stitches) and breaking my shoulder in two places. A large group of retired people was at the hotel we were at, and there were similar tragedies every day."

Mrs. Knight said Spanish tourist authorities "do nothing to alert people" to dangers, "fearing loss of business." She said the American consulate in Seville advised her to write to the travel section of the *The New York Times.*

Asked for comment, Charles Ocheltree of the Spanish National Tourist Office in New York said exposure to crime was similar in most countries. "It is one of the experiences of everyday life," he said, "and one of the experiences while traveling. Common-sense practices should prevail. There is no need to take all your best jewelry and your Macy's credit card when you are traveling over-seas."

Mr. Ocheltree said his office reported to higher authorities all instances of crime in Spain that it heard about from tourists. "Responsibility for prevention lies with the cities themselves," he said. "It is not a Tourist Office function and we do not have the funds to carry out a warning program of a major scope."

In Rome, assaults such as that experienced by Mrs. Knight have been commonplace. In an article in *The Times,* Paul Hofmann said the technique was known as the *scippo*—Italian for *sudden pull.* One Easter Sunday, Mr. Hofmann wrote, the Rome police reported more than sixty purse snatchings, mostly from tourists.

Particular targets are the elderly. "It's a New York situation almost everywhere you go today," said Raymond Tanenbaum of Grand Circle Travel, a major operator of tours for the elderly. He said his organization was particularly concerned about its extended-stay programs in Italy, Spain, Hawaii, and Florida, and was warning vacationers upon arrival and "using whatever leverage we can with local authorities."

"I had my wallet picked from my front pocket on a bus in Rome," Alfred P. Gualino of Union City, New Jersey, recalled about an experience on a Grand Circle tour. "Out of fifty-six members in our group, ten that we knew of either had their pockets or handbags picked. We were told not to leave any valuables in our rooms and that we should get a safe-deposit box to keep them in. I got one and kept the key in my wallet, which was stolen from me.

"On returning to the hotel, I told the manager that I had been robbed and that the key for the safe-deposit box was in my wallet. The manager told me that for a locksmith to open the safe-deposit box I would have to pay two hundred fifty dollars, in advance. I told him it was outrageous and how could I possibly pay in advance when all my traveler's checks were in the box. He then asked me to sign a statement that I agreed to pay the two hundred fifty dollars."

The situation in Italy provoked the United States Department of State to devote nearly a full page to safety precautions in a four-page advisory notice sent with passports to travelers who had signified that they planned to go there. Of special recent concern was a rash of robberies from automobiles rented at Rome's principal airport.

In one case, Alexander Mauro, a professor of biophysics at Rockefeller University in New York, wrote to the Hertz Corporation that he and his wife, Jean, had been "helped" to change a tire, which they believed to have been deliberately forced to blow out, by "a passing motorist who managed to make off with a bag containing our passports, return plane tickets, a considerable sum of money, essential eyeglasses, etc." Dr. Mauro accused Hertz in Rome of having "refused to warn car renters of the possibility of thievery while changing flat tires, on the grounds that such advice would create a 'negative image' for Hertz."

"I would like to point out that such a possibility (of thievery) exists in any given city," Carolyn F. Esposito, supervisor of executive customer service for Hertz, replied to Dr. Mauro. "I am certain you will understand that to issue such a warning in one particular area would be against our better judgment."

John Britton, a Hertz spokesman, voiced company concern but said: "In Rome we employ local citizenry. The whole operation is run locally by Italians. The vast majority of business we do is not with Americans. But it could be, I suspect, that Americans are singled out for looting as opposed to others. If our local management took the position, 'Look out, Americans, these people are out there to fleece you,' that would not sit well with local people."

William Schechter, then vice president-public relations for Avis, said his company's chief of security for the Mediterranean region had met with Roman police officials. He said Avis had posted robbery warning signs at its airport and downtown locations and had affixed warning notices to wallets containing customer's rental contracts.

Several companies that insure travelers against loss from crime or otherwise help them, such as Sentry Insurance of Stevens Point, Wisconsin, which markets comprehensive Travel Guard coverage through travel agents, and Near Inc., provide baggage tags that bear an identifying number and instructions for reaching the company rather than the owner's name and address. A name and address can tip off burglars that a home may be unoccupied. You can get a free Near tag by writing to the company at 1900 North MacArthur Boulevard, Suite 210, Oklahoma City, Oklahoma 73127; phone (800) 654-6700.

American consular officers can help victims of crime in many ways. They can issue a new passport quickly if convinced that you are an American citizen. They cannot lend you money, but they can help you get emergency money from home. If you are injured, they can direct you to an English-speaking physician. They can tell you how to replace stolen traveler's checks, cancel credit cards, and report losses to the police.

The local authorities may be unable to help find the criminal and recover your belongings, but a copy of a police report, filed promptly and stating as specifically as possible what you lost, when, and where, may be essential to pursue an insurance claim.

42. Protecting Your Film

The confrontation at the Madrid airport was unpleasant. An American, carrying a tote bag full of film he had used on a month of travel, was asked by a security officer to put it through an X-ray machine. The traveler, fearing possible damage to the film in the form of fogging, asked that the bag be inspected by hand. The officer balked, the American insisted, and angry words were exchanged. Finally the officer seemed to submit: He personally opened each of the traveler's two-dozen cannisters, removed the 35-millimeter film cartridges and examined them—and then hastily thrust everything back into the bag and put it through the machine anyway.

Fortunately, none of the film was damaged. As the American learned later from photographic experts at home, Madrid's X-ray device was indeed safe for his relatively low-speed film, just as the security officer had contended. Nonetheless, the episode left unanswered the questions of what might have happened if his film had been high speed and whether a traveler has a right to protect it.

"The passenger has a right and in most cases it works because the Civil Guard will oblige," said Pilar Vico, a spokesman for the Spanish National Tourist Office in New York. "But in most cases one of the first things they will say is 'Don't worry too much,' and if a passenger insists on hand inspection, a lot will depend on who is in charge. It's a very personal thing; it depends on who is on duty at a particular moment."

The Madrid incident was hardly unique. In the United States, Federal Aviation Administration regulations guarantee travelers the right to have photographic equipment inspected by hand instead of by X-ray, upon request. Abroad, however, the situation is spotty; some countries do, others don't.

For example, Alta M. Cools, features editor of *Photo Weekly* and publisher of an industry newsletter, told of confrontations in

Düsseldorf and Rome and said she heard an armed guard in Brussels tell an American tourist: "You have two choices: Either put your film through the X-ray machine or stay here in Belgium."

According to photo industry experts, the risk of X-ray damage to most film has lessened substantially at most airports in recent years because of the installation of low-dosage equipment. The biggest problems are reported from the Soviet bloc.

"East Europe and the Soviet Union sometimes accede to requests for hand inspection, sometimes refuse this courtesy," reported Bob Schwalberg, a senior editor of *Popular Photography*. "A lot worse, however, is their habit of heavily X-raying checked-through baggage, the last refuge of a traveling film hound."

Based on such reports, one might expect photo buffs to have few fears these days. Considerable concern was revived, however, with the introduction in 1983 by Eastman Kodak and the 3M Company of color film with a speed rating of ISO 1000—or two and a half times the fastest film previously in common use. According to V. Glenn McIninch, who had recently retired from Kodak's film technical services division, tests indicated that the new film was three to four times as sensitive to X-rays as 400-speed film. Kodak has been including a printed warning with its new film about possible damage from X-ray exposure, and the F.A.A. has recommended that such film be removed from carry-on luggage and be inspected physically because "it is sensitive enough to be affected by the low level of X-ray energy used in the screening process."

A spot check indicated that at some foreign airports where security officers usually insisted on X-raying hand baggage, they would relent if 1000-speed film was involved. Photographic experts state, however, that one exposure to X-rays rarely damages film; it is in repeated exposures on a long trip that the real danger lies.

The main reason for security measures such as the use of X-rays is, obviously, to thwart potential hijackers. Sympathetic to this, the photographic industry treads cautiously while trying to ease the plight of camera-toting travelers. Said Thomas J. Dufficy, staff attorney and spokesman for the National Association of Photographic Manufacturers: "We have always stated that the safety of the passengers, crew, and equipment is of paramount concern. We are trying to work out a system that is compatible with not discouraging people from taking cameras with them and not having a fear that their film will be damaged by X-rays."

Mr. Dufficy pointed out that film that has been processed or developed is not subject to radiation damage. He said that in the United States, at least, undeveloped film with a speed of 400 or less could be subjected to up to five X-ray inspections during travel with reasonable certainty that it would not be visibly affected. He cautioned, however, that 1000-speed film should not be subjected to X-ray if it can be avoided.

A handy way to facilitate physical inspection, he said, is to place all film in a clear plastic bag so the inspector has no difficulty determining its nature. He added: "You might also plan your film shooting so you can present your camera, not loaded with film, to the inspector for an X-ray inspection." Others advise that you carry as much film as possible in your pockets, since it will not be damaged by the metal-detecting magnetic security devices you walk through. Metal film cartridges may make the device whine, but you can usually then put them on a tray while you walk through again.

An eternal optimist in the photo industry is Irwin H. Diamond, president of the SIMA Products Corporation of Chicago, which for ten years has been manufacturing a lead-laminated pouch called a FilmShield to safeguard most film from X-rays. With the introduction of 1000-speed film, the company came out with a double-thick pouch that it calls Super FilmShield and that it says is total protection. The suggested retail price is $11.95.

In a telephone interview, however, Mr. Diamond said it was a "very legitimate position" not to want high-speed film to be X-rayed at all. "That's one approach," he said. "We certainly don't not recommend it." Mr. Diamond and others suggested that a Film-Shield pouch be removed from hand luggage and shown to inspectors; otherwise an X-ray may show it as a formless feature in a carry-on bag and arouse suspicion, causing delay.

Mr. Schwalberg of *Popular Photography* said, "Many of us take a paranoid route—double pouch our film and put it in baggage that gets checked through." He cautioned, however, that he would not do this if passing through airports known to X-ray checked baggage, especially since some are reputed to increase the dosage if the initial radiation fails to identify the contents.

In a form letter he sends to people who inquire about the effects of X-rays on film, Mr. Dufficy says that in many instances they are not visible to the human eye "and do not affect the enjoyment or use of the photograph."

"If you believe your film has been damaged by X-rays," he says, "you may send some representative prints, slides, or negatives to us for evaluation. Many times we find that improper loading, nonrecommended storage, or defects in the equipment are the cause of the problem and not X-rays." His address is Thomas J. Dufficy, National Association of Photographic Manufacturers Inc., 600 Mamaroneck Avenue, Harrison, New York 10528.

43. Special Diets

The feeding of travelers has become so sophisticated that it is now possible, with advance notice, to meet virtually any dietary need almost anywhere in the world.

In some places it is necessary to carry special food with you because what you need is not available or not prepared as you want it. But shipping meals across the world is increasingly practical as facilities improve to keep them frozen until needed, then to heat them quickly. A growing number of tours, moreover, are finding it practical to meet special dietary needs with fresh food in places where it was not possible until recently.

For example, fresh kosher food, cooked under appropriate religious supervision, is available on tours to Egypt. It is also available on some cruises, although precooked frozen meals are more prevalent to meet dietary restrictions at sea. In a growing number of resort areas and in many major cities that have a substantial Jewish population, Jews who observe the dietary laws can always find at least one kosher restaurant or one hotel with a kosher kitchen.

Orthodox Jews are not the only travelers with special dietary needs. Members of other faiths—Moslems, Hindus, and Seventh-day Adventists, for example—observe restrictions that are being met. Vegetarians receive imaginative and tasty dishes, not just what can be blandly boiled. And people with health problems who must be extremely careful about what they eat and how it is prepared are finding they can travel with greater assurance that they will get what they need.

Most major hotels, resorts, cruise liners, and airlines are equipped to meet at least some health restrictions, such as on the use of salt, providing they have advance notice, typically at least forty-eight hours. Some trunk airlines offer up to twelve types of health diets, including low sodium, low calorie, high calorie, fat free, and low cholesterol, and three categories of meals, light, strict, and stricter, for people with ulcers. American Airlines has eight broad types of health diets.

Scandinavian Airlines says that "a tasty, satisfying selection of dishes has been worked out in cooperation with expert dieticians and specialists in metabolic diseases." It cautions, however, that those on doctor's orders that go beyond this selection "must specify their needs in detail."

Sometimes, however, meals simply do not work out as passengers requested and confirmed or as airlines promised. I have heard repeatedly of special diets on major United States carriers that were served partly thawed. Around a recent Jewish Passover holiday, several of my acquaintances told of requesting meals that were both kosher and conformed to the special dietary restrictions of the period: most specifically, no leavened bread. But instead of being served matzo, as they had expected, they were served no-no dinner rolls. When they asked airline officials for an explanation, it turned out that the food had been shipped frozen by the contract kosher caterer weeks before Passover, with no intention that it be served during the holiday, and that airline commissary personnel simply took it out of the freezer later, with no thought of whether it was appropriate at the time of serving.

If you require a special-diet meal you should make your request, with sufficient detail, at the time you make reservations, then reconfirm the request at least forty-eight hours before departure. Here is a rundown on what is being offered travelers with religious scruples about what they eat.

Jews—Until it became possible to transport frozen food over long distances, travelers who wanted to eat kosher meat were largely confined to resort areas with kosher hotels, such as Atlantic City and Lakewood, New Jersey, the Catskills, and Miami Beach, or to cities with large enough Jewish populations to support kosher restaurants.

Otherwise, such travelers had to stick to vegetables, grains, and dairy products.

With the development of frozen packaging, this situation has changed. Many cities in many countries have kosher caterers that package frozen food for airlines and cruise ships. It may be difficult, however, to get meals with meat that are both kosher and meet meticulous medical restrictions. Borenstein Caterers, in the Jamaica section of New York City's Borough of Queens, offers only two basic kosher travel diets, one with no health barriers and the other low in sodium. In each category are items that are low in fat, cholesterol, or roughage, either by their nature or by the way they are prepared.

The regular Borenstein menu offers a choice of eight appetizers, including two types of lox, chopped chicken liver, and gefilte fish. It offers five breakfast entrees, including bagels with cream cheese and lox; twenty-two dinner entrees, including boiled chicken with matzo balls, brisket of beef, and broiled fillet of sole; and nineteen desserts, including three types of sponge cake and four types of tarts.

The low-sodium menu offers three more dinner entrees than the regular one but only three breakfast choices, none with lox, which is high in salt. Kosher meals are prepared and packed in the caterers' kitchens under rabbinical supervision. Except for El Al, on which all food service is kosher, each packaged meal includes disposable utensils. Aboard airlines, kosher and nonkosher meals are usually thawed and heated together, so the entrees are double wrapped in plastic. After heating, the outer wrapping, which may have come into contact with nonkosher food, is removed.

Sidney Goldstein, food and service manager for Lou G. Siegel, the Manhattan kosher restaurant and caterer, described how his company provides cold-cut lunches and the makings of hot dinners for cruises. The biggest difficulties, he said, are with chopped liver, which must be defrosted carefully or it pulverizes, and gefilte fish, which tends to be watery after being frozen.

Several tour operators offer vacations in Europe, Mexico, Egypt, and elsewhere in which kosher food is cooked on the spot, some of it bought locally and some shipped frozen from the United States.

Moslems—Spokesmen for airlines flying to and from the Middle East said special care was taken to avoid or provide alternatives to pork and food cooked in alcohol, both forbidden to Moslems. "Instead of serving duckling à la Cointreau in first class on a flight to

Saudi Arabia," said Jeff Kriendler, who formerly headed the food service division of Pan American, "we might offer lobster thermidor or filet mignon."

Moslem travelers frequently order kosher food to avoid pork, said Muzammil Siddiqi, former chairman of the religious affairs department at the New York office of the Moslem World League. But sometimes, he added, kosher food is cooked in wine, so some Moslems avoid it and ask for vegetarian meals.

On many flights to the Middle East it is possible to order meals prepared in advance to Islamic requirements. Because of substantial immigration of Moslems into the United States in recent years, butchers who prepare meat for Moslem customers can be found in such places as White Plains, New York, and Cedar Rapids, Iowa. Commercial packagers buy meat from them and package and freeze it as they would kosher food.

Seventh-day Adventists—A spokesman for the Greater New York Conference of the Seventh-day Adventist Church described followers of the religion as strict vegetarians who do not drink beverages with alcohol, caffeine, or carbonation. They may order travel meals in advance that conform to these restrictions.

Mormons—Mr. Kriendler said Pan Am carried many Mormons on missionary trips abroad from their center in Salt Lake City. "When we get a large group," he said, "our Denver office sends a wire, 'Don't offer any liquor, wine, Coke, Pepsi, tea, or coffee,' because Mormons are not supposed to take spirits or anything that is caffeinated."

Hindus—On routes where many passengers may be Hindus, airlines are likely to offer vegetarian meals of curry and rice, so advance requests may not be necessary. It may be wise, however, to state any needs when reservations are made anyway.

44. Drinking the Water

A story is told of middle-aged American tourists who were having breakfast at the Grand Hotel in Calcutta. One of them complained that she had not slept all night because of diarrhea. "Didn't you take your Lomotil?" a companion asked, referring to a commonly prescribed antidiarrheal medicine. "Well, I was going to," the ailing woman replied, "but I needed something to swallow it with, and I was afraid to drink the water."

Travelers abroad, especially in developing countries or the tropics, are apt to be much concerned with questions of health: Is even the bottled water safe? How safe is the soda: Was the bottle that it comes in sterilized? Is it safe to eat the pork? The vegetables? How do I find a doctor if I get sick? What inoculations do I need?

The increasing importance of answering such questions was underscored by Dr. Henry Masur, former director of the International Health Care Service, a unit of the New York Hospital-Cornell Medical Center in Manhattan; Dr. Vincenzo Marcolongo of Toronto, president of the nonprofit International Association for Medical Assistance to Travelers; and others.

The specialists cited these factors in health while abroad:

- As vacationers thirst for increasingly exotic adventures, they are more and more likely to select destinations where diseases that are rare or have been eradicated in the United States—yellow fever, polio, diphtheria, cholera, and typhoid—are widespread.
- As has been widely pointed out, malaria, once believed to have been virtually eliminated, is spreading alarmingly in many areas and is often resistant to popular antimalarial medicines. It can be difficult to educate sophisticated travelers about this. For example, try to persuade an old India

hand that before, during, and after his next visit there, unlike thirty years ago, he should take a pill if he hopes to avoid malaria.

- More and more people with chronic health problems are traveling these days; in fact, some of them are terminally ill and know it yet are still able to get around, either alone or with help. They travel because they are determined to have a last fling.
- The number of elderly travelers is increasing each year. Many older people are unable or unwilling to anticipate the physical challenges that certain types of travel pose for them and to recognize their own limitations. Meanwhile, they do not know where to turn for guidance.

Many travel agents are unaware of the health risks of travel, but some major tour operators who send groups to remote places appear to recognize that a little pretravel caution is much cheaper, easier, and better for good will than having to deal with sudden illness or even death. They are increasingly taking the position that caution need not scare clients away; rather, it can capture their confidence.

More and more often, operators of adventure tours or other kinds of demanding travel are insisting that their clients present evidence of good health. Some tour operators ask for physicians' letters before they accept elderly or frail-looking travelers, but such letters are not always found to be truthful.

In seminars that his center used to run for agents, Dr. Masur distributed a photocopy of a page from a brochure of Maupintour on a strenuous vacation program in Latin America. Among other things, it warned that several places visited were 9,000 to 15,000 feet above sea level.

"We request, for your own benefit and protection," the brochure said, "that you have a physical examination and obtain your physician's advice.

"Also," it added, "ask your physician for prescriptions of medicines which can assist you to adjust to high altitudes more easily and comfortably." It suggested that a physician be consulted about precautions and remedies for intestinal disorders and that the appropriate medicines be brought from home.

Literature on international health conditions is available from the United States Public Health Service. Simply by writing to a unit of the service, the Centers for Disease Control, Quarantine Division, Atlanta, Georgia 30333, a travel agent or physician can usually get, depending on current supplies, a free copy of the annual booklet *Health Information for International Travel*. Ordinary travelers can buy a copy from the Superintendent of Documents, Government Printing Office, Washington, D.C. 20402. Write first to find out the stock number and current price, which varies depending on whether reprinting is necessary to meet demand.

The booklet, which runs about a hundred pages, lists, country by country, vaccinations required for entry. It describes the risk of malaria and gives a lot of information on specific diseases, medicines, and ways to stay healthy. For example, one recent issue had these pieces of advice:

- Vaccination against polio is recommended for people who plan to visit rural or remote sections of tropical or developing countries and are likely to be in close touch with local residents. Do not rely on a past vaccination; get a booster dose, usually oral for children, by needle for adults, before you leave.

- Tetanus remains an important health problem throughout the world, and there is no known immunity. A booster injection is recommended every ten years, regardless of age. This may not be necessary at home, where you can get medical treatment quickly if you are scratched or punctured by a rusty nail, but it could be important if you are in unfamiliar territory, even in the United States.

- Typhoid is prevalent in many countries of Africa, Asia, and Central and South America, so vaccination against it— though it is not required for international travel—is recommended if you plan to stray from the usual tourist itineraries in those areas.

- While vaccination against plague, which is spread by rodents and fleas, is not recommended for the average tourist who stays in modern hotels, there is substantial risk in rural, mountainous, or upland regions of Africa, Asia, and South America—popular areas for safaris or nature or adventure tours.

A preface to the booklet stresses the importance of considering the type and duration of travel and the nature of the areas to be visited when seeking the best ways to stay healthy. It simply is not sufficient, the booklet says, to consider only whether immunizations are required under international health regulations. Rather, it says, you should consider whether they are recommended.

The Centers for Disease Control suggests that in planning a trip to areas that may be medically risky, you list your itinerary in the sequence in which the countries will be visited. Then note the incubation period of quarantinable diseases—the minimum period for vaccination before you enter a country that requires it. For example, it takes five days before a vaccination against cholera is considered effective; six days before a shot for yellow fever is considered effective. A visitor could be placed in quarantine if his vaccination was not given early enough.

Health Information for International Travel is published as a supplement to the centers' *Morbidity and Mortality Weekly Report,* an often dramatic narrative and statistical statement on disease throughout the world, including the United States. One issue warned of the danger of eating raw fish because of parasites that can be transmitted to humans. The warning focused on salmon eaten in California, but parasitologists said there were high incidences of illnesses in Japan, Scandinavia, and the Netherlands. This does not mean that Americans visiting Japan should avoid all sushi, but care should be taken in selecting where they eat it.

Another issue of the report said that dengue fever, a virus carried by the *Aedes aegypti* mosquito, had recently been reported in Cuba and the eastern Caribbean. The Cuban strain, it said, had resulted in thirty-one deaths. Three days after publishing this, the centers issued one of their occasional advisory memos, which are intended to report and describe newly identified health problems associated with international travel.

The memo advised that dengue produces high fever, severe headache, joint and muscle pain, and rash. It said the disease is usually mild but that sometimes recovery is prolonged. Although the risk for the traveler appears to be small, the memo added, visitors to endemic regions should stay in well-screened areas when possible, wear clothing that covers the arms and legs, and apply mosquito repellent.

Because of frequent changes regarding cholera, yellow fever, and smallpox, the centers' bureau of epidemiology distributes a biweekly blue sheet to keep the annual *Health Information* booklet up to date. One blue sheet, for example, said cholera still infected areas of Burundi, Cameroon, Ghana, India, Indonesia, Kenya, Liberia, Malaysia, Mozambique, Nepal, Nigeria, the Philippines, Rwanda, South Africa, Sri Lanka, Tanzania, Thailand, Uganda, Vietnam, Zaire, and Zambia, and that Jordan had been added to the list in the previous seven days.

The sheet also noted, as did previous issues, that the world's last case of endemic smallpox was reported on October 26, 1977, and that no vaccinations of any sort were required to return to the United States.

Anyone can get a free sample copy of the blue sheet by requesting it on a postcard mailed to Office of the Chief, Sanitation and Vector Control Activity, Quarantine Division, Room 107, 1015 North America Way, Miami, Florida 33132. The sheet also contains a summary of the latest inspection results by the Public Health Service of international cruise ships.

Dr. Masur said immunizations were usually required not to protect your health but to guard the requiring country against a "politically embarrassing epidemic." If appropriate for your destination, he recommended immunization against polio, yellow fever, diphtheria, tetanus, typhoid, and hepatitis. He and other physicians noted, however, that vaccination against smallpox not only was unnecessary but it could cause irritation.

Immunization against cholera, Dr. Masur asserted, is not very effective, and you have to be "knee deep in cholera organisms" to catch the disease anyway. The only reason to be vaccinated against it, he advised, is if it is necessary to enter a country. Officials warn, however, that a country may not require you to possess a valid cholera-vaccination certificate if you arrive directly from the United States or another developed country but that it may require it if you arrive by way of, say, Central Africa or Southeast Asia, even if you are an American citizen.

"Check your itinerary," Dr. Masur advised. "If you must be immunized, better have it done at home than risk being held up at a border and being inoculated with a rusty needle."

Among the Public Health Service's health hints for the traveler are these:

- "Water may be safe in hotels in large cities commonly used by American travelers; however, only chlorinated water sources afford significant protection against viral and bacterial waterborne disease."

- "Where water is contaminated, ice also must be considered contaminated; it should also be emphasized that under these circumstances ice may contaminate containers for drinking unless the containers have been thoroughly cleaned with soap and hot water after the ice has been discarded. It is safer to drink directly from a can or bottle of beverage than from a questionable container."
- If diarrhea occurs, drugs should be avoided unless prescribed by a physician.
- Swimming in contaminated water may result in eye, ear, and certain intestinal infections, particularly if the swimmer's head is submerged. Generally only chlorinated pools can be considered totally safe places to swim.
- "Insect bites are not only a source of discomfort but are also the method by which many infectious diseases are transmitted. Insect repellents, protective clothing, and mosquito netting may be advisable in many parts of the world."

Among other common-sense hints, the Public Health Service recommends that vacationers going abroad consult their physicians at home first, take extra eyeglasses or lens prescriptions, carry a card or wear a bracelet identifying any allergies or physical condition that may require emergency care, and carry an adequate supply of any prescription medicines that must be taken to control a chronic ailment.

Moreover, it suggests, to avoid disputes with customs inspectors, prescription medicines should be carried in their original containers and be accompanied by a letter from the prescribing physician, including his or her address and phone number for possible use in emergencies. The letter should include a statement of major health problems and dosages of prescribed medications.

You may also want to join an organization that keeps this sort of information on file and is available at all times by a toll-free or collect phone call from anywhere in the world. Your doctor or your local or county medical society should be able to steer you toward them.

Probably the best-known is the Medic Alert Foundation, a nonprofit organization that offers lifetime membership for only $15.

You provide the foundation with information on your medical problems, allergies, blood type if rare, medications you take regularly, and how to reach your physician and the relative or friend to contact in an emergency. Medic Alert then sends you a wallet card with your personal and medical information and, more important, a stainless-steel necklace or bracelet on which are engraved the organization's symbol and any medical condition that should become known immediately should you be found unconscious, for example: "Diabetes takes insulin." Also engraved are your Medic Alert identification number and the foundation's phone number for collect calls.

For further information and an application form, contact Medic Alert Foundation International, Post Office Box 1009, Turlock, California 95381-1009; phone (209) 668-3333 in California or toll-free (800) 344-3226 from elsewhere in the United States. A New York City chapter is at 777 United Nations Plaza, New York, New York 10017; (212) 697-7470.

Health officials generally recommend that before you embark on a long, rigorous vacation, you consider having a complete physical examination, regardless of your age and how you feel. Also, see your dentist; getting dental help overseas can often tie you down and be of questionable quality.

Some hospitals and clinics across the United States offer preventive medical programs. For example, the International Health Care Service in New York offers a variety of immunizations at $10 to $15 each. For fees ranging from $25 to $100, the center offers pretravel preventive counseling and posttravel examinations, laboratory tests, and evaluations. If clients become ill or have unusual symptoms while traveling, they can call the center for diagnoses and suggestions for treatment.

Somewhat similar programs have been offered at the hospitals of Case Western Reserve University in Cleveland, George Washington University in the nation's capital, the New England Medical Center of Tufts University in Boston, and at Toronto General Hospital. If you live near any large metropolis, you may find a program nearby. Check the public relations or community relations department of your nearest major hospital or your municipal health department.

In general, though, medical opinions vary on how much or how little to prepare for visits to countries where contagious disease is prevalent and how much medicine to take along. And even some of the most conservative physicians concede that some travelers become so frantic about what they eat and drink abroad that they are unable to enjoy their vacations.

For example, some years ago, as a correspondent in New Delhi, I invited a visiting American couple to my home for dinner. The wife declined. "Our doctor told us," she explained, "that we shouldn't eat anywhere in India except in our hotels."

45. Guarding Against Tropical Diseases

For several years, health officials in the United States have been calling attention to malaria and other tropical diseases to try to coax travelers to take appropriate measures to avoid them. Special emphasis is put on malaria because in some areas of the world it is becoming increasingly resistant to chloroquine, a drug that has long been depended on to prevent it.

But other diseases are also getting substantial attention among medical experts as tourists tread deeper into remote areas on adventure and other specialty tours. Among those diseases are these:

- Chagas' disease is a chronic wasting disease caused by a parasite carried by insects. It is widely found in rural areas of Central and South America, especially among the poor. Dr. Vincenzo Marcolongo, the Toronto physician who heads the International Association for Medical Assistance to Travelers, insists that Chagas' disease, although mainly confined to local residents, can be and has been contracted by hikers, campers, archaeologists, geologists, and bird watchers, among others.
- Schistosomiasis, sometimes called bilharzia or snail fever, is a debilitating parasitic infection spread by contact with

infested water. The parasite must spend one stage of its life in a snail host. According to Dr. Myron G. Schultz, an epidemiologist with the government's Centers for Disease Control in Atlanta, it is endemic in about seventy countries of Asia, Africa, South America, and the Caribbean. The World Health Organization estimates that up to two hundred million people have it.

• Amebiasis is an intestinal disease spread by a parasite that is present throughout the world, particularly where there is poor sanitation. It is commonly contracted from leafy vegetables, such as lettuce, that grow on or near the ground, are contaminated by infected feces, and are not properly washed before consumption.

Malaria, which is spread by the anopheles mosquito, is receiving special attention not because the incidence is increasing among American travelers (it isn't; the C.D.C. counted 916 cases in the United States in 1982), but because of greater risk of exposure as the disease's resistance to chloroquine as a preventative spreads. In discussing this increased resistance to the drug, Dr. C. C. Kent Campbell, chief of the malaria branch of the C.D.C., repeatedly stressed that his goal was not to scare but to inform. He particularly noted the surge in adventure travel—remote treks, safaris, and the like, often in areas where malaria is prevalent.

"If you go to Nairobi and sleep only in an air-conditioned room in the Norfolk Hotel," he said, "you won't face any risk at all. But a lot of people go to Kenya with the intention of seeing only Nairobi; yet once they get there they decide to take an overnight trip somewhere, and they become exposed to malaria."

Because of such possibilities, specialists in tropical medicine generally recommend antimalaria drugs to travelers going anywhere in East Africa and anywhere in such popular tourist destinations as Haiti, India, and Thailand. An important factor in the recommendations is that for optimum protection, you typically should start taking a weekly oral dose of chloroquine a week or two before entering a malarious area and continue for six weeks after leaving. In most areas, chloroquine remains the standard preventative.

Dr. Campbell said that in East Africa, however, *Plasmodium falciparum* malaria, the disease's most virulent species, had become increasingly chloroquine-resistant. For this reason, the C.D.C.

recommends that travelers take along some chloroquine and a sulfa drug commonly marketed in the United States under the trade name Fansidar if headed for such areas as Kenya, Tanzania, Uganda, Madagascar, the Comoro Islands, or Mozambique.

You will, of course, need a medical prescription to buy either of these drugs, and in any event a physician should be consulted. Based on your medical history, your doctor may prefer something else.

When you reach an area of risk, sleep under mosquito netting unless your hotel is air-conditioned and the windows are sealed. Malarial mosquitos strike between dusk and dawn and are attracted by dark clothing, perfume, and after-shave lotion. So after sunset lean toward light-colored clothing that covers as much of the body as possible. Apply mosquito repellent to all exposed areas of your skin. And if your hotel room is not sealed and air-conditioned, ask the management to have it sprayed with an insecticide.

If, after you return home, you develop symptoms of malaria, such as high fevers and exhaustion, be sure to tell your doctor where you have been and when. This will greatly enhance the likelihood of a prompt and accurate diagnosis and the best treatment.

Parasitologists are alarmed particularly by what they call a casual attitude toward malaria, and they cite these cases:

- A California physician spent one December working in refugee camps in Thailand near the Cambodian border. Although he knew malaria was endemic in the area, he did not take any pills to prevent it. Eight days after his return, he developed a 104-degree fever. Eventually doctors diagnosed the most dangerous form of malaria. Only a large exchange of blood kept him alive.

- A seventy-three-year-old woman was brought to the emergency room of a New York hospital complaining of fever and drowsiness four days after returning from a two-week tour of Gambia, Liberia, the Ivory Coast, and Senegal with 156 other Americans. She died four days later. Public health officials determined that the tour group had been warned about malaria, but the woman had apparently not taken the prescribed pills.

- At least nine of the 360 American members of the Hare Krishna sect who went on an annual spring pilgrimage to India came down with malaria. They toured rural areas, but according to investigating physicians no antimalarial precautions were used. There were no fatalities. Attempts by public health officials to have the sect take precautions before future pilgrimages have been inconclusive.

- Six members of two travel groups from New York and Puerto Rico that visited Haiti one winter caught the disease. Investigators found that none of the seventy travelers had taken adequate pills. One illness was fatal. "If people ask us, we tell them to take pills," a spokesman for the Haiti Government Tourist Bureau in New York said. "But we do not warn about malaria in our tourist literature. Reports of recent malaria occurrences in Haiti are highly exaggerated."
- A British newspaper reporter went to Mombasa, Kenya, on vacation. Malaria was diagnosed shortly after he returned home. He was treated promptly and recovered. He asked his travel agent why he had not been warned of the malaria danger. According to the reporter, the agent replied that he had no legal obligation to make such a warning.

A major problem for the Centers for Disease Control and other health organizations is to transmit their information and expertise to travelers. How to do the job better has been a major concern of Dr. Schultz of the C.D.C. staff, and America's 23,000 travel agencies are considered to be a prime potential conduit. But in a recent count, only one-tenth of them were on the mailing list for free travel-agency subscriptions to C.D.C.'s biweekly blue sheet, mentioned earlier, which lists countries infected with diseases that the World Health Organization considers quarantinable—cholera, yellow fever, and plague.

Health information similar to that in the C.D.C.'s booklet *Health Information for International Travel* is available to both the trade and the public from the International Association for Medical Assistance to Travelers, which has headquarters at 188 Nicklin Road, Guelph, Ontario, Canada N1H 7L5, and can be reached in the United States at 736 Center Street, Lewiston, New York 14092; phone (716) 754-4883. This organization, known as Iamat for short, offers a variety of health information, including a leaflet *How to Protect Yourself Against Malaria*, a country-by-country *World Malaria Risk Chart*, a membership card in Iamat, and a directory of English-speaking physicians around the world who have agreed to a set payment schedule.

All this can be yours without charge, but Iamat's founder and president, Dr. Marcolongo, encourages donations. If you want your packet to include Iamat's twenty-four world climate charts, which tell not just what weather to expect at any time of the year but also what to do about water, milk, food, and clothing, the doctor suggests a contribution of $20.

The association has campaigned to form a travel agency group in which membership would entail a pledge to warn clients of any malaria risk before they leave on a trip. "You, as a travel agent," a brochure for the group says, "are the one professional in the strategic position to warn your clients of the risk of malaria and therefore help stop the needless deaths caused by this disease."

The extent to which travel agents have taken the pledge is unclear. Murray Vidockler, a Brooklyn agent and tour operator who is also executive director of a trade group called the African Travel Association, said: "In my personal opinion, people are being under-advised. I have no proof of this, but my own daughter-in-law got malaria after a trip to Kenya because no one told her what preventive medicine she could take. She was admitted to a hospital in Boston, and they couldn't even diagnose the disease until my son, who obviously knew where she had been, mentioned the possibility of malaria."

Mr. Vidockler said he knew of a New Jersey travel agent, the wife of a physician, who was apparently bitten by a malaria-carrying mosquito at an African airport. Despite all the warnings and the family's professional background, he said, "they never take preventive pills for anything."

In a telephone check of twenty-four major travel agencies and tour operators who send tourists to malarious areas, thirteen said they warned travelers to take preventive pills. Eleven said they would provide such information if asked. Of fifteen Asian and African government tourist offices that were checked in New York, not one could produce official literature warning against malaria, although some distributed brochures of private companies with such warnings and said they would reply frankly when asked specifically if their countries had a risk.

Extremely informative for casual pretravel reading is the 444-page paperback called *Control of Communicable Diseases in Man*, an official publication of the American Public Health Association. Using an A-to-Z format, it tells you, mostly in lay language, how to recognize and deal with specific diseases around the world. It is available for $7.50 in larger bookstores, or you can order it for that price, postpaid, by sending a check or money order to Publication Sales, American Public Health Association, 1015 15th Street N.W., Washington, D.C. 20005. C.O.D. orders are accepted by phone at (202) 789-5600.

Americans who like the tropics can also glean a lot of practical information from the *Health Guide for Travelers to Warm Climates*, published by the Canadian Public Health Association. A chart is shown for each country, detailing tropical diseases and telling whether they are a threat there or not and what is recommended for immunization. You can get a copy by sending a check for $4 (U.S.) to the association at 210-1335 Carling Avenue, Ottawa K1Z 8N8, Canada.

Dr. Marcolongo of Iamat has for several years been expressing alarm about schistosomiasis, the parasitic infection in which small worms penetrate the skin, enlarge the liver and spleen, impair blood flow, and, if untreated, prove fatal.

Some physicians at the Centers for Disease Control do not share Dr. Marcolongo's concern. "Schistosomiasis is on the rise," said Dr. Irving Kagan, the retired director of the parasitology division at the centers, "but it should not affect travelers because travelers should not be swimming in rivers in affected areas. You have to play an active role, such as by going swimming. No matter how inviting the Nile is, tourists just don't swim in the Nile."

Dr. Marcolongo, however, does not think the idea of a Nile swim to be outlandish, although he concedes that a vacationer on a luxury river cruise would probably not leap overboard for a dip. He feels the river might entice other kinds of American travelers and cites the experience of a twenty-eight-member international tour group that crossed the Sahara in southern Tunisia by camel. Upon reaching an oasis, he said, "the idea of jumping into cool water to relieve the intense heat" provoked the tourists to overlook warnings given at home. Nine members of the group, the doctor said, contracted schistosomiasis.

46. The War Over Smoking

Probably no issue causes greater emotional controversy among travelers than smoking.

Two letters illustrate the emotions involved. In one, Dr. Edward M. Clemmens, a physician from Ossining, New York, said he would boycott a major foreign airline until it changed its seating pattern to remove the health hazard of a "whole cabin filled with smoke." In the other, Frank H. Addonizio, a Washington lawyer, accused one of the largest United States airlines of "accommodating the nonsmoking public" to a point of "total abrogation of the rights and expectations of the smokers."

According to airline officials and staff members of the now-defunct Civil Aeronautics Board, smoking versus nonsmoking is one of the major sources of passenger complaints. It pits passengers against the travel establishment and against one another. It provoked the C.A.B. to comment in print: "We've concluded that it's nearly impossible to please everyone involved."

Despite widely disseminated warnings in the United States that ambient smoke may be harmful to nonsmokers, no major organization is advocating that smoking in travel be banned completely. In March 1984, however, the C.A.B. rejected proposals that smoking be banned from air trips lasting two hours or less—or roughly 85 percent of all commercial flights in the United States. Several organizations have been working hard to teach travelers who object to smoke that they have a right—a legal right—to protection from drifting smoke.

At the forefront of this campaign is a nonprofit organization called Action on Smoking and Health (ASH). Its roster of trustees and sponsors includes many people prominent in medicine and public life, among them Dr. Leona Baumgartner of the Harvard School of Public Health and Mayor Edward I. Koch of New York.

Among its primary goals, ASH literature says, is "protecting the rights of the nonsmoking majority."

In the view of John F. Banzhaf III, a professor of law at George Washington University who is also executive director of ASH, smokers do not have a right to smoke but only a privilege to do so. "Every bit of research I've done supports this view," he said in an interview. "Drifting tobacco smoke can impinge on health. A traveler has the privilege to smoke only so long as it does not interfere with someone else."

As might be expected, ardent smokers adamantly dispute this view and insist that they have rights, too. With the encouragement of the Tobacco Institute, an industry group based in Washington, some of them have organized to promote their cause. While a nonsmoker with a confirmed airline reservation has a legal right to sit in a nonsmoking section, no law or regulation guarantees a seat to a passenger who wants to smoke.

Theoretically, therefore, a passenger who insists on smoking in flight could be asked to leave a plane if there was no room in a smoking section. But airline and regulatory officials can recall no case in which this has happened. If a smoker insists on smoking in flight, he will almost certainly get his way.

"What usually happens," said Patricia Kennedy, a former staff member of the C.A.B.'s bureau of consumer protection, "is that the airlines try to keep a buffer zone of nonsmokers who don't care if their neighbors smoke or not. And when necessary, they try to see if people will trade seats. Some even offer inducements, such as free drinks, to passengers who volunteer to sit in the first row of the nonsmoking section."

Some advocates of "smokers' rights" contend that to ban all smoking from a flight would encourage passengers to sneak into a lavatory to light up—a practice that has been widely condemned as a fire hazard. In fact, in March 1984 the C.A.B. recommended to the Federal Aviation Administration, which watches over flight safety, that it require commercial airlines to place smoke detectors in lavatories.

As regulations stand at this writing, a passenger on a United States airline has a right to sit in a nonsmoking section on any flight with more than thirty seats. But an airline must honor such a request only if the passenger has a confirmed reservation and appears within a time stipulated by the carrier, usually at least ten to fifteen minutes before scheduled departure. If this is still true when you read this and you have complied with this time limit, do not be put off by an airline employee who pleads that the nonsmoking section is full.

Time limits have been strongly opposed by ASH, which contends that they could unjustly penalize a passenger who was delayed by such circumstances as a late connecting flight, a long line at the ticket counter or a traffic jam on the way to the airport.

On commercial flights in aircraft with fewer than thirty seats, all smoking is banned. Smoking of cigars or pipes is banned on all commercial domestic flights. On many foreign airlines, however, smoking of cigarettes, cigars, and pipes is freely permitted.

Most United States airlines have guideline boundaries for smoking and nonsmoking sections for the types of planes they fly, but the law requires them to expand nonsmoking sections on demand to include seats already assigned to smokers. All smoking must be prohibited on an American plane if the ventilation system is not working adequately. In addition, a passenger has a right not to be unreasonably burdened by smoke from cigarettes.

The term *unreasonably burdened* has caused some displeasure among opponents of smoking because they consider it vague. ASH interprets it as meaning any situation in which tobacco smoke causes illness, physical irritation, or serious discomfort. But many airlines have their own interpretations.

On most airlines, smoking and nonsmoking sections are divided between the back and the front, with all seats across a row being one way or the other. In each cabin, the nonsmokers are usually seated from the front backward and the smokers from the rear forward. Sandwiching nonsmokers between smokers to the front and rear is illegal. Some foreign airlines, however, have tried a configuration called longitudinal separation in which in the economy-class section of a 747 jumbo jetliner, the three-seat rows on the left side (facing forward) and the four middle seats might be for nonsmokers and the three-seat rows on the right side for smokers.

In a widely publicized case a few years ago, a Washington lawyer vociferously protested what he said were inadequate facilities for nonsmokers aboard an Eastern Airlines Air-Shuttle bound for New York. The pilot appealed for quiet but was ignored. So he landed in Baltimore and waited until a truce was reached, causing a two-hour delay in reaching New York for about 175 passengers.

"The shuttle is always a bit awkward on the smoking question because there are no seat assignments," James R. Ashlock, an Eastern spokesman, said.

Smokers and nonsmokers also run into problems on trains and buses. At this writing, smoking is prohibited in dining cars on American interstate trains. On most runs of five hundred miles or less where no reservations are required, at least half the coach space must be designated no smoking. In reserved coaches and on runs of more than five hundred miles, smoking is usually prohibited except in cafes, lounges, rest rooms, bedrooms, and certain areas in the two-level Superliners operating west of Chicago.

The Interstate Commerce Commission has limited smoking on the nation's interstate buses to no more than 28 percent of the seats, from the rear forward. Although state and local laws are supposed to take precedence, enforcement has been spotty. New Jersey law, for example, bans all smoking on all buses, but it has not been enforced on Trailways or Greyhound buses as they travel through the state. Discipline is largely at the discretion of drivers, whose toughness varies. "You can't really ask the driver in some cases to put his life on the line," said Laurie Lewis of New Jersey Transit, which regulates bus travel in her state.

Officials of many bus lines, both local and interstate, admit to a substantial problem with the smoking of marijuana. To the distress of many passengers, it often goes ignored, but not always. "I can remember somebody who was put off a bus for pot smoking in Ohio or someplace," said Dorothy Lorant, Greyhound's vice president for public affairs. "He phoned us at headquarters in Phoenix and was absolutely irate. I said: 'Good. Give me the name of the driver, and we will commend him.' "

If you are a nonsmoker and feel your rights on public transportation have been denied, you might seek guidance from ASH on how to proceed. The address is Action on Smoking and Health, 2013 H Street N.W., Washington, D.C. 20006; phone (202) 659-4310.

When "No Smoking" Pays Off

Many people seem to be responding warmly to moves to curb smoking among fliers, especially on short trips and in airport departure lounges.

Take the experience of Lamar Muse, a longtime maverick in air transportation who shook up much of his industry when, through the use of unorthodox marketing practices, he built Southwest Airlines from a small Texas carrier into a successful system embracing much of the South from New Orleans west. In June 1981 he began the first flights—between close-in Love Field in Dallas and relatively close-in Hobby Airport in Houston—of the Muse Air Corporation, of which he is retired chairman and chief executive officer. "Against the advice of all my marketing and advertising people," Mr. Muse said in a telephone interview, he banned smoking in the air completely.

"It takes fifty minutes to fly from Dallas to Houston," Mr. Muse said, "or ten minutes less than a church service. You don't think about smoking when you go to church, so why must you smoke in the air?"

Mr. Muse said he began smoking cigarettes in 1938, when he was eighteen years old, and quit early in 1981 after four sessions with a hypnotist. He said that he believed banning smoking on his flights had been "one of the best marketing decisions I ever made" and that the volume of favorable comments had been unbelievable. "If we find later that we made a mistake," he said, "we can change our policy overnight."

Mr. Muse's well-publicized claim to be running the first non-smoking air service was quickly challenged by Wes Lupien, former president of Harbor Airlines, which operates commuter services from Seattle north to Vancouver, British Columbia. In the thirteen years that his company banned smoking, Mr. Lupien said, "I don't know that we've ever had an adverse comment from a passenger."

Harbor's planes are ten-seaters, however, and lack air-conditioning. Also, their longest scheduled flight is forty-five minutes. Yet, until forced to adopt one, a no-smoking policy was not followed by most similar commuter airlines; if their planes could not carry more than twenty-nine passengers, they used to be exempt from Federal smoking rules. Speaking for the Regional Airline Association of America, its general counsel, Calvin Davison, said: "The association feels that smoking is not a subject necessary for the government to regulate."

A somewhat similar hands-off policy regarding smoking in airport lounges has been taken by the Airport Operators Council International, a trade association to which most major airports belong. Leo Duggan, the organization's vice president for technical affairs, said policies regarding smoking in airport restaurants were up to the concessionaires and in the departure lounges to the airlines who rented the space.

But John F. Banzhaf III, executive director of ASH, said his group sent letters to the presidents of twenty-three major airlines asking that they consider having voluntary no-smoking sections in their lounges and curb smoking on ticket and check-in lines. He said he was "rather pleasantly surprised by the responses." He said Northwest Airlines, for example, had advised that it already had separate areas in all of its departure lounges and American was moving toward that goal.

A spokesman for American, Alton W. Becker Jr., said the airline began providing no-smoking sections in lounges in March 1977 and now had them in at least eleven airports.

47. Sightseeing Tours

A major problem for many visitors to strange cities is how to select a sightseeing tour. They may abhor the idea of being herded about like sheep, yet few would disagree that a good tour can greatly help overcome the feeling of insecurity, even intimidation, that often accompanies arrival in a metropolis where one has no friends and where the prevalent language is not one's own.

For me, a half-day coach tour, taken as soon as possible after arrival, puts things in order. It gives me a feel of the pulse of a city and a grasp of how it is laid out. I may dislike the tour pace: too long at one sight, too little time at another, too much getting on and off the bus and too much time stalled in traffic or waiting at a stop for stragglers. But almost always I leave the tour with confidence that I have learned how to cope with the city: to find the best shops, restaurants, and entertainment and to know what museums, parks, or historic sights or interesting neighborhoods to revisit at leisure.

Organized sightseeing has become so competitive in many cities, however, and so many options are sometimes available, that it often is difficult to select the best. How does one find it? In telephone interviews, I put this question to people who ought to know: travel agents, tourism officials, and tour operators. Almost all agreed that the best recommendation is word of mouth from someone you trust, but it is not always available.

"As a starter, I always tell people to invest in a long-distance telephone call," said Robert Britton of the Schilling Travel Service in Minneapolis, who has a doctorate in geography and has spent years studying why people go where. "If they are going to a foreign city, I tell them to call the appropriate foreign government tourist office in Chicago or New York and ask them to name some sightseeing companies and send brochures. And I suggest that callers promise to send a check for a dollar or two, to be sure the material comes by first-class mail."

Mr. Britton also suggests writing to the municipal tourist office in the city to be visited and, if it is abroad, to include international reply coupons that can be bought at American post offices to prepay foreign postage. "That's a good way," he said, "to be assured of an airmail reply."

Many travelers do not realize it, but a lot of foreign sightseeing— even a two-hour tour—can be arranged through travel agents before leaving home. "I encourage my clients to book in advance," said Sylvia M. Mitwol of Schaeffer Travel in Livingston, New Jersey. "I try to find out what they want to see so that I know what their needs are. Otherwise, by the time they get around to arranging it themselves, it may be too late."

If you book through a travel agent, chances are the agent will depend primarily on two basic sales guides: those of the Gray Line Sight-Seeing Association Inc. and American Sightseeing International. Both are New York-based international associations of independently owned companies who run their own operations but have joined together to benefit from mass marketing. At this writing Gray Line has 185 members and A.S.I. 95.

"We don't admit just anybody," said Patrick R. Sheridan, Gray Line's president. "We check their equipment and the quality of their guides and how long they have been in business. We don't want newcomers, but existing, solid operators who simply need a little push. We're very concerned about any Gray Line operator who's hanging on to shabby equipment. If we find something like that, we slap his wrist and let him know it."

A major Paris sightseeing operator, Cityrama Tours, is a Gray Line member but also has its own New York office to promote business from travel agencies, to which it offers a commission of up to 20 percent. "Americans like to book in advance," said Henry Schaff, the manager of sales and marketing. "They like the security of having a program set up for them." Mr. Schaff added, however, that for a tour of a day or less, "usually if you show up without reservations half an hour before the tour begins, you will get on it."

Which, based on most interviews, is the way most Americans actually do it. Usually, the only risk of being turned away at the last minute is when meal or nightclub reservations are involved. Many travelers make reservations a few hours or a day in advance through a hotel concierge, whose advice is generally reliable despite probable kickbacks or commissions from the tour company.

In general, consider these points when selecting a tour:

Is the tour completely in English?

At peak season in foreign cities that attract throngs, you can usually depend on it for the most popular tours. But off-season, even in Paris, you may have to settle for a bilingual tour and in some places for one in four languages, all spoken by the same guide but with unequal proficiency. Sometimes you will not know the situation until you board the bus. A lot depends on the nationalities of the passengers. In fact, operators say that one reason Japanese often prefer to sightsee in groups rather than as individuals is that their language is rarely available on public tours.

Mr. Sheridan of Gray Line insists, "I've never had anybody complain about a multilingual tour." But Mr. Schaff of Cityrama said a one-language tour was distinctly preferable because "the guide will perhaps have more time to answer questions." Richard J. Valerio, vice president for sales and market development of American Sightseeing International, said he felt a multilingual tour lost warmth because of the difficulty of translating local colloquialisms and the need to be brief so that the bus was not way past a sight before the description was completed.

Is there a human guide, or does the company use tapes?

To guarantee passengers a specific language, more and more tours equip their buses with tapes that play simultaneously in up to eight languages, and each passenger, wearing a headset, dials the preferred one. Mr. Sheridan said Gray Line companies usually provide a guide to operate the tapes because "you can't always depend on the driver to synchronize them with the bus's progress."

Does it matter what day you take a tour?

Sometimes, yes. Be sure to check itineraries carefully. In many European cities, for example, panoramic tours skip major museums on Mondays because they are closed. You may not like what is substituted.

How do you get to those quaint back streets where large buses can't go?

Ask the tour operator or the municipal tourism office. Van or minibus tours are increasing for this purpose, although often you have to hire a taxi or chauffeured car or walk. Private cars are, of course, available for hire almost everywhere, and if three or four passengers share the expense, the advantage of flexibility may surmount the disadvantage of cost.

For example, Cityrama's two-and-a-half-hour tour of historical Paris, which cost $13 a person by bus in 1984, cost $70 in a three-passenger (plus driver) Peugeot. "You would get the same tour but no guide," Mr. Schaff said. "The driver would speak English and take you to all the places and stop if you want, but he wouldn't give detailed descriptions."

Then he added, "Of course, you could hire a guide in addition if you had room, but for three hours that would cost seventy-five dollars extra."

48. Tipping

When I was sixteen years old and visiting Washington with a schoolmate, breakfast at the Harrington Hotel, where we stayed, cost fifty cents for the two of us. The practice in American restaurants in those days was to tip 10 percent of the check. We did precisely that, leaving the waitress a nickel. She called after us to say "Thanks" and wish us a pleasant day.

That was in 1940, as America was emerging from the Great Depression. Even then a nickel was not worth very much. After we returned home, our parents told us that for a meal check of less than a dollar, we should have left a dime.

If we tipped as little as 10 percent today, we might well be rudely rebuffed. In much of the world, being tipped, and tipped well, has come to be considered a right rather than a reward for good service.

Restaurants and hotels in many foreign countries add mandatory service charges to their bills—typically 12 to 15 percent, with the actual rate set by either the government or the local hotel association. In American restaurants service charges are rare and nonobligatory. One reason: In many areas the total amount shown on the bill is subject to state and local sales taxes. There also is a legal question about whether service charges should be included in the restaurant's earnings and be subject to income tax.

Commercial hotels and motels in the United States do not levy service charges, but many top resorts do. At the Breakers in Palm Beach, Florida, where guests are on the modified American plan (breakfast and dinner), a spokesman said $13.50 a day was added to the bill for a single room and $16.50 for a double. Service charges, like the basic bills, are subject to the 5 percent Florida sales tax. The spokesman said plans were in progress to raise the gratuity to 17 percent of the bill plus a 2 percent resort tax.

"The proceeds of the service charge go into a special account," the spokesman said, "and are distributed to service personnel connected with the hotel, except bellmen, doormen, and valets. They are tipped separately. But the maids, the dining room staff, and elevator operators all share in the proceeds of the account, based on an approved formula."

James Searle, director of marketing at the Greenbrier in White Sulphur Springs, West Virginia, said a service charge of $9.25 per person per day was automatically added to each account to cover gratuities for housekeeping and food service personnel. The charge is subject to the state sales tax. Do guests tip maids, waiters, and waitresses beyond the service charge? "It happens if someone has given exemplary service," Mr. Searle said. "But the charge is designed to take away the burden of worrying about 'Do I tip or don't I?' "

When eating out or traveling, Americans seem to feel compelled to do right by those who serve them and thus avoid any disturbing backlash that could turn an excursion sour. In fact, when a nineteen-year-old relative of mine goes with friends to a restaurant that specializes in fancy hamburgers, one of them uses an electronic calculator to be sure that everyone pays a fair share of the tip and that the overall gratuity is fair to the waitress.

But what is fair? How do tipping practices—and expectations—vary? And how can you be sure that, as a traveler in unfamiliar territory, you are tipping—or not tipping—appropriately?

There are no easy answers to those questions. In countries without mandatory service charges, there are usually tipping norms—either stated or established by practice—for various types of service. Some resort hotels and cruise liners try to help their guests by offering what they call suggestions. In such cases, a suggestion is usually considered the rule unless an employee performs exceptional service clearly warranting something extra.

Sample resort suggestions might include $2.50 per guest per day for waiters and waitresses, $1.25 a day for busboys, $2.25 per person on check-in and check-out for bellhops, $1.25 per person per day for chambermaid and twenty-five cents per person per day for such night-maid service as supplying fresh towels and turning down beds.

As explained by Mark Grossinger Etess, former general manager of Grossinger's in the Catskills, the rationale is this: Many guests have bought prepaid group packages that include gratuities. A formula for distribution of these gratuities is included in Grossinger's union contract. The tipping rate suggested to nongroup guests conforms to the group formula.

Most cruise liners suggest formulas that your travel agent can pass on to you when you make a reservation. The aggregate usually amounts to about 5 percent of the basic cost of passage. The Holland America Line advertises a policy of "no gratuities required," but this does not mean tips are not accepted. According to Edith M. Schein, a Manhattan travel agent who books heavily on Holland America, it is customary to tip waiters and cabin stewards at least $1 a day each.

On long cruises of most lines, Mrs. Schein and other agents advise at least $3 a day each, more if you are traveling super deluxe, is common for waiters and stewards because passengers tend to be more affluent than on short trips. Also, the agents say, if the cruise lasts a month or longer, do not wait until the end of the cruise but tip every two or three weeks. They say you should tip the wine steward and the dining room captain for any special services performed, and if in doubt about the amount, ask the cruise director for advice.

More often than not when traveling, however, you are left to solve the tipping problem yourself. "Give whatever you feel like," you are commonly told, which is no guidance at all. But if you end up by undertipping, you may be vulnerable to humiliating barbs. If you can take a rude rebuff, however, there is no reason to tip for poor service.

You should, however, tell either the person who expects a tip or his boss why you choose to refrain. Management often does not know that service is bad unless patrons speak up or at least write a letter about it after returning home. My wife notes, however, that only about one in ten of the many even-tempered but critical letters that she has written to restaurants has evoked a reply.

When you feel well served and are ready to tip but do not know what is appropriate, perhaps the soundest advice is to ask someone who knows local customs. Impromptu replies, however, even from people involved with tourism, are not always reliable.

I once asked for such advice at the Barbados airport and later was sharply criticized by someone who thought I had undertipped a porter. After the criticism, I asked a spokesman for the Barbados Board of Tourism whether expectations for Americans were different from those for Barbadians.

"When an American comes in," he replied, "porters generally expect about a dollar (U.S.) a person. Barbadians might not tip the same thing, but Barbadians might not use a porter at all. They might be met by friends or relatives or carry their bags themselves to save the money altogether."

In most American cities, skycaps and bus and rail porters expect fifty cents a bag, sometimes a dollar minimum. But think a minute: While fifty cents a suitcase may be appropriate for a skycap who simply lifts the bag from your car at curbside and puts it on a conveyor belt within reach, a dollar a bag may be more appropriate if he takes your luggage several hundred yards from the customs inspection area to your car.

In the United States, according to Charles Bernstein, editor of the trade publication *Nation's Restaurant News,* there is considerable discussion among restaurants about imposing a service charge in restaurants catering to foreign tourists. Many of them are from countries where service charges are included in the bill, he said, and where it is customary to leave only 3 to 5 percent extra—even then only if service has been exceptional. So, he said, many visitors, not realizing that customs are different in the United States, leave only 3 to 5 percent here, and sometimes nothing.

Anyone who dines out much or does much traveling in the United States probably already knows that it is customary to tip waiters 15 percent of the food and beverage bill. Many diners do not realize, however, that the tip should be based on the bill before the tax is added; on some restaurant checks, the dividing line is obscure.

The situation becomes more complicated in fancier restaurants—those with a maître d'hôtel, captains, and wine stewards. A check of owners of a dozen leading restaurants around the country produced the unanimous opinion that the maître d'hôtel—the man who shows you to your table and perhaps distributes menus—is rarely tipped unless he does something special, such as seat you at a choice table on a busy night. In such a situation, you may want to shake his hand on the way out, leaving a $5 bill in his palm.

The rule of thumb with captains—the sort of superwaiters who take your order but usually let someone beneath them do the serving—is to tip them for special attentiveness. "If he does the carving," said Tony Vallone, owner of Tony's in Houston, "if he flambés or if he decants a very old wine, it's fair to leave him maybe five to ten percent of the total check."

Said John Fleming, who has operated leading restaurants in Chicago and Washington: "It all depends on how many tableside services he performs. If he just occasionally pours wine or comes over to talk—if he is just a token captain—I would not be too enthusiastic about putting across much of a tip, because he is probably there just for effect."

Ella Brennan, owner of Commander's Palace in New Orleans and Brennan's in Atlanta and Houston, said many of her guests ask in advance for special services, such as ordering items not normally on the menu or making arrangements for a party, and "they sometimes leave the captain five or ten dollars, depending on what they feel he has done for them."

"Down here we are not like New York or San Francisco," she said. "At the least, the captain gets part of the regular tip."

In New York, the general practice is that the waiter, who shares with the busboy, gets whatever money is left on the table or marked on the check or credit-card form unless a separate tip for the captain is indicated. Some restaurants, such as the 21 Club, indicate on the check or attach a card to it when a separate tip for the captain or wine steward—around 7 percent of the wine check—is considered appropriate.

About a decade ago, American Express added an extra line for captain's tip to charge forms distributed to restaurants requesting that type. Diners Club and Carte Blanche soon did the same. Do not be misled by this. Fill in the extra line only if you are convinced that the extra tip is warranted. Sometimes such forms are sent to restaurants that have no captains at all.

In American hotels, tips are usually expected by the bellhop who shows you to your room, the chambermaid if you stay more than one night, the doorman if he calls you a taxicab when you leave and helps load your luggage, and others for special services. In better hotels, bellhops expect a dollar a bag. If your bags are sent to your room separately, the bellhop expects such a tip anyway and will share it with the other staff members involved.

Many travelers rarely see chambermaids, but they would appreciate a dollar per day per room. In many hotel rooms, the regular maid leaves a card with her first name. If you write her name on the envelope that you leave behind in the room or at the front desk, chances are good that the tip will not go astray.

For meals served in your room, the standard tip is about 15

percent, the same as in a restaurant. For a bucket of ice, fifty cents is minimally sufficient.

In foreign countries, customs differ sharply. Some have mandatory service charges for hotels and restaurants, others leave the option to management, and still others leave all tipping to the discretion of the traveler. In some countries, tips of 3 to 5 percent in addition to service charges are common for exceptional services; in other countries such gratuities will be rejected. In major American cities, taxicab drivers commonly expect 18 to 20 percent of the fare up to $5 and 15 percent if more than that; in foreign countries, taxicab tipping tends to be nominal if it exists at all.

In many countries it is customary to tip attendants in public rest rooms simply for their being there. In France it is customary to give two francs (roughly twenty cents) to an usher in a movie house and five francs to one in a legitimate theater; Britain has no such practice, but in London theaters you have to buy your program from the usher.

Most guidebooks give advice on tipping in particular countries. So do most foreign government tourist offices, many of which have leaflets or detailed sections of leaflets devoted to the subject.

Sometimes the information is surprising. Etsuko Penner of the New York office of the Japan National Tourist Organization said that in her country a 10 percent service charge was added to bills in restaurants and Western-style hotels, and no further tip was expected. She said that in traditional Japanese inns, however, extraordinary service might be rewarded with a thousand yen (about $4, based on recent exchange rates) for a stay of one or two nights.

"But don't just give the money out," she cautioned. "Wrap it in a piece of paper. There is something very demeaning in Japan about handing or accepting money raw. It's just never done."

49. Driving Abroad

This section was written by John Brannon Albright, an editor of the Travel section of The New York Times.

Italian autostradas used to be notorious for the way speeding motorists would blare their horns as they passed everything in sight. But these days, according to the Italian Government Travel Office in New York, the custom is to blink the headlights and use the left-hand directional signal to let the driver ahead know you are about to pass. The law, an official said, calls only for the use of directional signals, but, to discourage horn blowing, headlight blinking has become popular at night and by day.

The custom is also practiced in West Germany and is one of many driving habits that a traveler planning to operate a car in a foreign country should know about. Some other important differences from the United States are the need in some countries for an International Driving Permit, higher minimum-age and lower maximum-age limits, driving on the left side of the road, seat-belt requirements, speed limits, mandatory driving with headlights in the daytime, and insurance requirements.

In most places, the license issued by your home state will suffice, but in at least three countries—Spain, Japan, and South Korea—an international driver's license is required, and some countries that accept home-state licenses require a translation. Among them are West Germany, Italy, and Austria. Translations can be obtained from the United States Embassy in each country, but the requirement can also be met by obtaining an International Driving Permit, which carries nine languages: English, French, Spanish, Italian, German, Arabic, Greek, Japanese, and Swedish.

The permit costs $5, is valid for a year, and may be obtained from the American Automobile Association and the American Auto Touring Alliance.

An important consideration for some travelers is the age limit for renting a car. In some countries, because of insurance company restrictions, many car rental agencies will not rent to people under twenty-five years old or over sixty. Some examples at this writing: In France the minimum age is twenty-five; in Britain it is twenty-three; and in most other European countries it is twenty-one. Residents or visitors with their own cars can drive as young as eighteen—two years older than in most of the fifty states.

In Singapore the maximum age for driving a car is sixty; in Jamaica, New Caledonia, the Philippines, and Sri Lanka, it is sixty-five; and in Australia and Tahiti it is seventy-five. In Britain and Ireland, some rental car agencies, but not all, do not rent to people over sixty-five. Among agencies in Britain that rent to them are Godfrey Davis, Avis, and Hertz; in Ireland, at least Avis and Hertz rent to people over sixty-five.

It is possible in some of the countries with age restrictions to arrange for chauffeurs. For example, in Britain, New Caledonia, the Philippines, Singapore, and Sri Lanka, Hertz offers the services of a driver for about $30 a day extra.

In at least five places, only cars with chauffeurs are available to anyone: Hong Kong, India, Indonesia, Nepal, and Pakistan.

In at least ten countries and one American and one British possession, motorists drive on the left side of the road. They are Australia, the Bahamas, Britain, Ireland, Jamaica, Japan, Kenya, New Zealand, South Africa, in both the British and United States Virgin Islands, and Zimbabwe.

As in the United States, buckling up is the practice in most of Western Europe. Seat belts are customarily required for the driver and any passengers in the front seat.

Except for the fact that speeds are posted in kilometers instead of miles, speed limits should pose no particular problem for Americans accustomed to the nationwide fifty-five-mile-an-hour law. But in West Germany there is no speed limit on the autobahns, the country's extensive, toll-free network of superhighways, except in certain areas prone to accidents. On the approach to a curve, for example, a speed limit may be posted for a short distance.

Off the autobahns, the West German speed limit outside built-up areas is a hundred kilometers an hour (sixty-two miles an hour), and motorists are expected to know the rule because the limit is not customarily posted. But in built-up areas there are signs indicating a reduced speed, usually fifty kilometers an hour (thirty-one miles an hour).

An unusual practice by American standards is the custom in Scandinavia of driving with one's headlights on in the daytime. The practice became a law in Finland in 1970 after studies showed that daytime accident rates dropped when motorists drove with their headlights on, making their vehicles more visible. Sweden followed suit in 1977. In Denmark and Norway, the use of headlights in the daytime is recommended but not compulsory, according to the Danish National Tourist Office in New York.

Sweden is considered one of the toughest countries in the world when it comes to drinking and driving. The percentage of alcohol in the blood that constitutes drunken driving is extremely low. Roadblocks are common, and jail terms are automatic for offenders. Enforcement is so strict, an official of the Swedish National Tourist Office said, that when a group goes out to a party, one member is designated the driver and that person has only fruit juice or a soft drink. When the group goes out the next time, a different member takes a turn at driving.

Tourists apprehended for driving while drunk are subject to stiff fines and, after being held overnight in jail, must leave the country or face trial.

In most foreign countries, as in most states, liability insurance is mandatory, but your policy at home generally does not cover driving abroad. Validations for driving in Canada can usually be obtained, however, and some policies cover motorists driving a few miles across the border into Mexico. But for extensive driving south of the border, a policy issued by a Mexican insurance company is required.

In almost every other foreign country a policy specifically intended for driving in that country is required, but the policy does not necessarily have to be issued by a company in that country. The American Automobile Association, for example, offers a tourist automobile policy that covers liability and property damage, collision and comprehensive. It is available to members and nonmembers.

Among other driving habits abroad, it is considered good form to beep your horn frequently when approaching a curve in the Alps, and in Britain, drivers are expected to give way to sheep and cattle on rural roads. When approaching a traffic circle, called a roundabout, drivers in Britain must yield to motorists already in the circle.

Across the English Channel in France, the rule is exactly the opposite. The car entering the traffic circle has the right of way over traffic already in the circle because of the French rule of *priorité à droite*, which means that the car on the right has the right of way. Richard J. H. Barnes, an American resident of France, says, "For those American drivers who have ever tried to exit from the Etoile traffic pattern or, worse, have ever seen Paris taxis shoot out of the narrow rue Boissy d'Anglais between the Hôtel Crillon and the American Embassy into the broad Place de la Concorde at forty miles an hour without so much as a glance at traffic already in the Place, *priorité à droite* is indeed an unsettling experience."

One tip from the German National Tourist Office: Leave autobahns to buy gasoline; it is usually cheaper in a nearby town. Eating at the restaurants on the autobahns is another matter, though. A driver's menu of less hearty fare that is not likely to cause drowsiness is usually available for $10 a person. Some stops on the autobahns have showers, facilities for handicapped motorists, and a baby room where diapers can be changed.

Here are places to obtain more information on an International Driving Permit and renting a car abroad.

American Automobile Association, 8111 Gatehouse Road, Falls Church, Virginia 22047; phone (703) 222-6334.

American Automobile Touring Alliance, 888 Worcester Street, Wellesley, Massachusetts 02181; (617) 237-5200.

Auto Europe, 1940 Commerce Street, Yorktown Heights, New York 10598; in New York State (800) 942-1309; elsewhere except Alaska and Hawaii, (800) 223-5555.

Avis Rent A Car System, 900 Old Country Road, Garden City, New York 11530; (800) 331-2112.

Budget Rent-A-Car, Worldwide Reservations Center, 3350 Boyington Street, Carrollton, Texas 75006; (800) 527-0700.

Cortell Group, 3 East 54th Street, New York, New York 10022; in New York City (212) 751-3250; elsewhere in New York State (800) 442-4481; elsewhere (800) 223-6626.

Dollar Rent a Car, 6141 West Century Boulevard, Post Office Box 45048, Los Angeles, California 90045; (800) 421-6868 and ask for international.

Europe by Car, 1 Rockefeller Plaza, New York, New York,

10020; (212) 581-3040; outside New York State (800) 223-1516; or 9000 Sunset Boulevard, Los Angeles, California 90069; in Los Angeles (213) 272-0424; elsewhere in California (800) 252-9401.

Hertz, National Reservation System, Post Office Box 26120, Oklahoma City, Oklahoma 73126; to reserve abroad (800) 654-3001; for information (800) 654-3131; for chauffeurs, ask for the Yes Desk (800) 336-4646.

Kemwel Group, 106 Calvert Street, Harrison, New York 10528; in New York State (800) 942-1932; elsewhere except Alaska and Hawaii (800) 431-1362.

National Car Rental, Worldwide Reservations, 7700 France Avenue South, Minneapolis, Minnesota 55434; (800) 328-4567.

50. Emergency Help on the Road

A growing problem for American motorists is to get emergency assistance on the road. The number of repair shops is declining steadily as gasoline stations go out of business or as their owners find it more profitable to convert service facilities into food-and-sundry convenience shops than to fix cars. The American Automobile Association counted 226,000 service stations in the United States in 1972 and only 139,000 in 1983.

Meanwhile, tow-truck operators are increasingly reluctant to sign contracts with auto clubs that bind them to send vehicles and mechanics to distant trouble spots at rates they consider too low. The A.A.A. estimates that the average towing job in the United States costs a motorist $36 if paid directly, but that the typical fee paid by a club to a contract operator in recent years has been $9.

In response to consumer pressure, programs have been developed by auto clubs and charge-card companies that promise to help the harried motorist. Some say they provide help themselves to members at no charge if you phone a number. Others tell you to find your own help, pay the bill, and submit a receipt for reimbursement, usually limited to $25 to $50.

But how good are they? Most of them do not directly address such questions as whether, on a subzero Sunday evening in February, help will be available—anywhere, at any price—or whether the amount they reimburse you will be anywhere near your cost. According to the A.A.A., the cost of one long-distance tow can easily exceed $100.

The A.A.A., through its 165-odd affiliated clubs across the nation, is both the pioneer and leader in arranging emergency road assistance. A member of any affiliated club can expect help at no charge from a service station that is under contract to whichever club is closest to the scene of distress. The motorist calls the help by phoning a local A.A.A. number or a toll-free number in use nationally. To get a local number, ask the directory-assistance operator for the emergency road service number of the nearest A.A.A. club or, if a phone book is available, look under AAA.

Usually, the club will send a contract tow truck in thirty to forty-five minutes, although the wait can be much longer in bad weather, during rush hours, or on Monday mornings when many cars that have been idle over the weekend fail to start. A club member is entitled to free towing only to the contractor's service station; if your car cannot be fixed at that station, you will have to pay to have it towed to another one.

Most A.A.A. clubs reimburse members up to $25 if club assistance is unavailable and a noncontract service is used or the full charge if the car is stuck where the law requires that a specified franchise tow service be used, such as on a turnpike or thruway.

If you break down in a rural area and are not a member of an A.A.A. club or of another organization that offers road service, ask a telephone operator for the state police. In most cases the police will put you in touch with a towing service—at your expense, although reimbursement of up to $25 is common under many auto insurance policies. In a city, check the *Yellow Pages* under "Towing" or ask the local police. The tow-truck operator will generally insist on cash or a traveler's check. Credit cards are sometimes acceptable; personal checks rarely are.

Even on Sunday or late at night, you can get towing service, but it may entail a substantial wait. Under pressure from the police and auto clubs, many tow-truck operators park their vehicles at home during off hours and are available either through answering services or by radio.

W. Allan Wilbur, director of public relations at A.A.A. national headquarters in Falls Church, Virginia, acknowledged that providing quality assistance was a continuing problem. "The biggest single continuing difficulty in this kind of operation," he said in a telephone interview, "is the relationship between the clubs and their contract operators."

The Automobile Club of New York, the A.A.A. affiliate that serves New York City and the nearby counties in New York State, "has no problem in our area securing service stations to render service to our members," said Peyton E. Hahn, its vice president for public information. He said the club operates twenty-two emergency vehicles of its own for backup.

Other programs for motorists are operated by major gasoline companies, by Montgomery Ward and Sears, Roebuck (the latter under the name Allstate Motor Club), by an independent organization called the United States Auto Club, Motoring Division, and, for their charge-card holders, by American Express and Citicorp Diners Club. The gasoline companies with programs include Amoco (Standard Oil of Indiana), ARCO (Atlantic Richfield), Chevron, Exxon, Gulf, Mobil, Shell, and Sun.

Leaflets on how to join—or at least how to get full information—on clubs sponsored by gasoline companies are usually available at stations that sell those brands. For information on the Sears or Montgomery Ward clubs, ask at the customer service office in any of their retail stores. If you hold an American Express or Diners Club card, your customer service representative can tell you about the organization's motoring plan. You can reach the United States Auto Club, Motoring Division, at 1720 Ruskin Street, South Bend, Indiana 46604.

Most clubs sponsored by gasoline companies restrict membership to holders of their credit cards. ARCO conspicuously does not, however, since it no longer issues credit cards, but you can pay your ARCO dues through a Visa or MasterCard account. ARCO and Amoco, whose auto clubs are among the biggest in the field, operate them not only under their own names but for others as well. For example, both the American Express Driver Security Plan and the Diners Club Motor Plan are administered primarily by Amoco. In fact, Amoco has a two-way arrangement with Diners that allows you to get many Diners Club benefits by membership in the Amoco Torch Club or to get Amoco benefits through the Diners Club Motor Plan. Before you choose either, however, be sure you understand the charges and exactly what you get for them.

Some clubs, such as Exxon's, primarily promote accident insurance and charge according to the amount you buy, with emergency road service as an optional extension; with other clubs it's vice versa. Most also offer frills, such as help in planning trips and central registries to record the numbers of all your credit cards and notify the issuers, if lost.

Before you select a club or charge-card plan, examine the promises carefully. Much of the accident insurance is severely limited, both in what it covers and how much it pays. Further, it may duplicate what you already have elsewhere. The frills offered are very often of nominal value or can be obtained just as easily—or even free—from other sources. Also, be sure that specific benefits are valid in your state; promised reimbursement for legal aid, for example, is usually not valid in New York.

Fees among motor clubs vary widely and are not always in direct proportion to the services offered. Such is the case with the A.A.A., for example, which you do not join directly. Instead you sign up with an affiliated club, usually the one nearest your home. Dues range from $13 to $50 a year for the primary member plus $7 to $24 for each additional member of your family who joins. Initiation fees, payable only in the first year, range from zero to $18. Membership usually covers all the cars in your household, and road service can be claimed by either a primary or associate member.

The Automobile Club of New York works somewhat differently. The dues, at this writing, of $35 a year plus $5 initiation fee for the primary member and $9 for others in the same family cover only one car, specified on the membership card. Coverage for a second car in the same household costs $20 a year extra.

Most A.A.A. clubs provide a maximum of $3,500 to $5,000 in personal accident insurance—much less than other motor programs. However, you may already have much more comprehensive accident coverage through a separate or job-related health plan. Typical A.A.A. frills are personalized trip planning, with detailed maps and regional guidebooks; personal check-cashing privileges to pay for emergency repairs; commission-free American Express traveler's checks; bail-bond protection for auto-related arrests, and the like. Many A.A.A. clubs also operate full-service travel agencies, but they usually welcome business from the general public, not just from club members.

Aware of the mounting costs and other problems in guaranteeing adequate emergency road service, the national headquarters of A.A.A. is promoting an optional program called A.A.A. Plus. For additional dues of $14 to $20 a year for primary members and $7 to $10 for others in the family, it provides free towing up to one hundred miles per incident to a destination of your choice, free emergency delivery of up to two gallons of gasoline, and reimbursement for up to $500 in emergency travel expenses if your car is disabled more than a hundred miles from home. At this writing, eight A.A.A. clubs, but none in the New York area, offer this option.

Taking Precautions

With emergency road service often not available or subject to long delay at times of great need, it behooves the motorist to take as many of these precautions as possible so that help will not be needed:

- By midautumn, be sure your car is adequately winterized to assure that it will start and keep running in the coldest weather.
- If you do not have an appropriate owner's manual, get one from a dealer or the manufacturer. Study it and keep it in the car. Carefully follow the suggested maintenance schedule.
- If you know how to use them, carry a pair of jump cables to start your car with the help of another auto if your battery goes dead. But be extremely careful. If you do it improperly, you may damage the car—even blow it up—and injure yourself severely.
- Make sure that all electrical connections are properly maintained. Particularly, keep battery terminals clean and tightened.
- Be sure that fan belts are not loose or worn. A fan belt turns the alternator, which provides the electricity that is transmitted to the battery by cable.

- Open your hood occasionally and make sure that hoses are in good condition. You do not need mechanical expertise to tell whether a hose is soft, cracked, or leaking.

If you do all that, officials of the American Automobile Association say, you will sharply cut their emergency load and enable them to provide better road service to those who deserve it most. If you still get stuck on the road, however, and need help, the A.A.A. recommends that as a first step you get your car off the road as fast as you can onto a shoulder or median strip.

The association urges that every motorist carry flares, which can be bought at nominal cost at most auto parts stores. They should be set out day or night, at sufficient distances, depending on the width and shape of the road, to alert other drivers, both for their safety and your own and to announce that help is needed.

The A.A.A. also recommends setting out warning triangles. These are red plastic devices that reflect light and stand one to two feet off the ground. Auto supply stores sell them for about $10 each.

Most toll roads and highways in the Federal Interstate Highway System are regularly patrolled by police cars and tow trucks. To attract their attention, raise the hood of your car and tie a white handkerchief to your radio antenna or a door handle or window on the side next to the highway. Then stay in your car and wait for aid. If you are lucky enough to be on one of the toll roads or interstate highways that have telephones at frequent intervals, you probably can save time by walking to a phone and requesting help.

Late at night or on a weekend, it is easier to get service on a toll road or interstate highway than on other roads. But during daylight hours on weekdays, when most service stations are open, help may come more quickly on lesser roads, especially if you have a citizens band radio or can find a telephone to summon a tow truck directly.

On lesser roads, if you cannot reach a phone easily, prepare yourself for a long delay. Getting help may involve a lot of walking or signaling to passing motorists. It is extremely important to remember the location of your car so that you can tell the tow-truck operator.

Other Towing Problems

Arranging to be towed may be only the start of your problems when your car breaks down far from home and there is no telephone nearby. If you are carrying, say, three or four passengers, what happens to you all when the tow truck finally arrives to haul the car away?

If the tow-truck operator cannot carry all of you with him, you may have to depend on him to call a taxi from the nearest town, with his radio if he has one or by telephone from his garage when he gets there. Or one of you may be able to go along with him to make the arrangements yourself or to rent a car.

In Britain and the Netherlands, according to an official of the American Automobile Association, auto clubs provide flatbed trucks to carry both disabled car and passengers, but such service is still under study in the United States.

Even a breakdown on a major highway can be emotionally draining. Not long ago a Philadelphia couple and their three children awaited a tow truck on a Sunday afternoon at a gasoline station on the New Jersey Turnpike when no mechanic at the station could repair the cracked radiator of their Toyota sedan. For $40 and $1.65 in turnpike tolls for the car, the tow-truck operator said he would take the vehicle to his station near Hightstown. He said he did not repair Toyotas but would store the car for $5 a day in his locked lot until the Philadelphians arranged to send it elsewhere.

Because of a family emergency, the family had to get to New York without delay. The husband approached drivers at gas pumps and within a few minutes arranged transportation in a station wagon at no cost. In fact the driver went eight miles out of his way to drop them off.

By telephone the next day the husband located a Toyota dealer in Trenton who sent a tow truck to Hightstown, took the car to his shop, and repaired it. Four days later the dealer phoned the family and reported that the car was ready. The wife went by train and taxi to Trenton to claim the car, paying towing and repair charges in cash. The total bill exceeded $300.

The wife paid it with almost a feeling of relief. "When that radiator cracked," she said later, "it seemed as if we would be stranded on the turnpike forever."

When You Need Repairs

The scenario is familiar: Three hundred miles from home your car suddenly begins to sputter and lose speed. You reach a service station just as the engine dies. After a quick inspection, a mechanic announces that the generator must be replaced but that he cannot get one before morning. But you cannot wait, so you leave the car, hitch a ride to a bus stop, and go home by Greyhound. Two days later, you return, pay $58 for a rebuilt replacement generator plus $60 in labor, turn around and go home, where the engine promptly dies again. You learn from your neighborhood mechanic, whom you have used for years, that the replacement was a dud.

Consumer protection officials say cases such as this arise daily. They say the only hope of getting recourse is to complain promptly and loudly with as much documentation as you can muster to everyone who might conceivably be able to help. Among the people to whom complaints should be addressed are the repair shop's owner, the local prosecutor's office, the state or local consumer affairs office, the gasoline company whose products the station sells, the local Chamber of Commerce, and the local Better Business Bureau.

If parts have been replaced, ask for and keep the old ones. It is also important to keep any written material, such as estimates and bills.

If you are still at the repair shop when a dispute arises over a bill or the work, complain then and there, advises Karl F. Lauby, former vice president-operations of the Better Business Bureau of Metropolitan New York. He says, "Call the local Better Business Bureau, if there is one, the nearest consumer protection agency, or the state attorney general right from the station to register your complaint. If they will handle the complaint over the phone, you may be able to resolve the matter while still in the locale of the station."

If, as in the case of the generator replacement, you do not discover the problem until later, write to one of the agencies he listed, providing copies of all documents that you received. Be sure the local police are kept informed, and even the district attorney's office, although Mr. Lauby commented: "Most local D.A.'s in smaller cities have far more criminal things to worry about than someone who pokes a hole in your tire when you thought you were getting air."

New York State licenses repair shops and polices them, but many states do not. Some states have put up information centers on major interstate highways just inside their borders. The centers frequently have complaint forms and will forward them to the appropriate authorities. The consumer protection offices of some states also have toll-free telephone numbers that you can call during business hours to register complaints or get advice. You can get the number for your state, if there is one, from toll-free directory assistance, (800) 555-1212.

If the station with which you have a dispute sells a major brand of gasoline, write to the oil company. You can usually get the appropriate address from the nearest sales office; check the telephone book of any major city. Be aware, however, that fewer and fewer gasoline stations are company-owned.

Most companies tread lightly in cracking down on licensees on the ground that they have limited control. They are likely to pursue complaints more vigorously if you paid with a company credit card, since under Federal law you usually do not have to pay disputed charges or accrued interest and late penalties until the matter is settled to your satisfaction or the company has rendered a judgment based on investigation. You have similar rights if you paid with another card, such as Visa or MasterCard, but the gasoline company is not likely to care so much under those circumstances.

At some point in a dispute, even when right is clearly on your side, you may have to decide between accepting a settlement, even if it is not as much as you sought, or getting nothing. The court of last resort is, of course, a court of law, but a suit can easily cost you more than you recover.

Talk to consumer protection officials in almost any state or locality and you will learn how common and widespread auto repair rip-offs are. Especially easy prey are long-distance travelers who are unlikely to be able to return to an area easily. Sooner or later, a discussion of predatory mechanics will turn to Georgia, which a few years ago was infected by a rash of roadside rip-offs that drew nationwide attention to the area: the Georgia portion of Interstate 75, which starts in northern Michigan and ends in southern Florida.

A central figure in the state crackdown was Tim Ryles, then head of the Governor's Office of Consumer Affairs, who described the techniques of the larcenous service station operators this way:

"They're not expert mechanics, they're specialists at fraud. They know how to psych out a dude, as they call their targets. They know how to damage a tire, spray oil on shock absorbers to make them look defective, pop bolts on a water pump. When the water spills over, they say, 'Sir, your water pump's shot.' Then they take it into the shop and paint it and put the same one back on and charge you eighty or a hundred dollars."

Literature is published by most state governments to tell you how rip-offs on the road can be avoided. To find out about it, ask the consumer protection bureau, if there is one, the attorney general's office, or the information section of whatever agency oversees motor transportation.

If you are far from home, however, and on the go, this often is not practical. And if your car must be left overnight, it is often impossible to heed the often-heard suggestion that you watch as the repairs are made.

Possibly the best precaution is to seek help through the state or local police. If you are a stranger to the area, they usually get in touch with a service station for you or give you the names and telephone numbers of one or more. This does not guarantee exemplary workmanship, but it is unlikely that the police will put you in touch with a cheat.

Mr. Lauby advises that before you leave home, mark auto parts in your car. "A simple, inconspicuous tick mark with a crayon or felt-tip pen on the front end of important parts," he says, "will help you tell if the part has been replaced." He suggests that you ask for parts back after they have been replaced. "Your regular mechanic may be able to determine whether or not they were defective and needed to be replaced," he says.

If you call a towing company, before you commit yourself, ask the name of the station where your car will be taken. Then, if during business hours, call the nearest Better Business Bureau, consumer affairs office, or state attorney general's office to check on the reputations of both the towing and repair companies. If there is no problem, call for the tow.

According to W. Allan Wilbur, director of public relations for the American Automobile Association, local A.A.A. clubs frequently tell a member of any affiliated club, if asked, what stations to avoid because of complaints. The association issues periodic regional emergency road service directories that are available to members on request. Each listed station or repair shop is inspected to make sure it has competent mechanics.

"If a member has a complaint against an A.A.A.-approved auto repair service," Mr. Wilbur said, "A.A.A. will step in as a mediator." He said roughly 60 percent of such complaints are resolved in favor of the customer.

Like the A.A.A., the Amoco Motor Club provides members with emergency road service by stations with which it has contracts. According to a spokesman, the club has field representatives who "see what kind of service our dealers perform." He said the club tries to resolve members' complaints but has limited ability to investigate them.

Mr. Ryles of Georgia recalled that his office cracked the Interstate 75 fraud ring by having reliable independent mechanics rig rented cars so they showed minor defects, then evaluate the work done at repair shops near the highway.

"We got access to oil company files," he said, "and found valuable information in their computers. We also encouraged widespread publicity. We licked the problem. We haven't had even a handful of complaints in the last two years. But when we do, I have a big 225-pound assistant who is our chief auto investigator. If we get word that the cheaters are back, he goes down and pays them a visit, and that's that."

51. Hotel Phone Bills

Carol Nashe knows a lot about telephones and a lot more about hotels. She is director of public relations for the 1,430-room Sheraton Boston Hotel, and it is part of her job to keep track of trends in the lodging industry. "When I'm traveling," she said in an interview, "I usually check where I plan to stay to see how much it will cost to phone from the room. Often I give my office a time when I'll be available and let them call me."

Miss Nashe's remarks referred to a relatively new practice among American hotels but one that has become common and has caused considerable distress for many guests. It is the practice of adding a surcharge to phone company charges for calls placed from guest rooms. In fact, because of technical problems that the lodging industry is striving to overcome, many guests have even been charged—at inflated rates—for calls that never went through.

A spot check of the telephone policies of five major chains and twelve hotels indicated that the Sheraton Boston was in a minority. According to Miss Nashe, it doesn't add surcharges to long-distance calls at all. At this writing, it charges a minimum of forty-five cents for a local call from a guest room, however, compared with ten cents if you use a pay phone in the lobby. At other hotels, surcharges on long-distance calls from guest rooms commonly run 30 percent of the operator-assisted rates of whatever regional company succeeded the Bell System after divestiture—even if you dial the call yourself.

If, like many people, you use hotel phones only to order ice or request a wake-up call, this need not bother you. But if you are traveling on business and have to keep in frequent touch with your office, or if you are on vacation and concerned about small children or elderly parents at home, you may need to phone often. So a hotel's telephone policy could have a substantial impact on your bill and may be worth asking about before you check in.

There has long been well-documented evidence of telephone price-gouging at many hotels overseas. In the United States, surcharges have not reached such proportions and, because of consumer resistance, probably will not. But except for small surcharges on local calls there was no problem until June 1981.

That was when the Federal Communications Commission gave hotels permission to resell the interstate telephone service they bought from the Bell System subsidiaries of the American Telephone and Telegraph Company. This meant that to meet rising costs of labor, equipment, and bookkeeping in providing phone service to guests, hotels could for the first time add surcharges to interstate calls; previously they could charge only Bell rates.

Almost immediately thereafter, A.T.&T. announced that it planned to drop the thirty-eight-year-old system under which Bell operating companies helped hotels and motels defray phone costs by paying them 15 percent commissions on interstate and international calls and, in most states, 10 percent on intrastate and local calls. An end to the payment of commissions was delayed until January 1, 1983, but hotel surcharges started almost as soon as A.T.&T.'s intention was made known.

To find out exactly who is doing what is like groping through an endless maze. Some hotel chains, such as Marriott, have company-wide policies with surcharges averaging seventy-five cents to $1.25 for direct-dialed interstate calls. Other chains, such as Sheraton, which is primarily a management company and owns relatively few of the properties that bear its name, and Holiday Inns, which is 80 percent a franchise operation, say they leave it up to individual properties.

This does not mean, however, that you cannot ask an individual hotel about its phone charges and expect an accurate answer. You probably cannot get it, however, from a chain's 800 toll-free reservations number but will have to phone or write the hotel you plan to use. If you plan a long stay and make lots of calls, one extra long-distance charge to get this information may be worthwhile.

When you first enter your room, look for a notice near your phone outlining the charges. If you don't find one, ask the front desk or the hotel operator before you make your first call. And be sure you understand what you are told, because slight differences in language can mean major differences in your bill.

For example, properties managed by the Hilton Hotels Corporation charge the phone company's operator-assisted day rates for direct-dialed calls, regardless of the hour, according to Louise Harris, public relations manager. So do the Westin Hotels, which include the Plaza in New York, according to David Ling, the rooms director. So, for example, if you called Los Angeles from New York at midnight not long ago, the hotel got the saving between the day and night rates, $1.50 for five minutes in this case, and the $1.50 charge for operator assistance, which you did not use. If you actually are assisted, Hilton adds a 10 percent surcharge to the bill.

For direct-dialed calls, the Sheraton Washington and the Sheraton Carlton in Washington charge whatever operator-assisted rate applies at that hour. Corporate-owned Holiday Inns usually charge the applicable operator-assisted rate plus 30 percent, according to Douglas Schoenfeld, director of marketing services.

Generally, hotel executives say surcharges are a way to break even, not make a profit, on the cost of providing telephone service. To pare costs, some hotels are installing microprocessors that automatically route long-distance calls to a system other than A.T.&T.—such as M.C.I., Sprint or I.T.T.—whichever is cheapest and adequately serves the area called.

Many hotels are struggling with the problem of when to start billing a room. Until recently, only A.T.&T. had the technical ability to determine when a call was actually answered. So hotel guests were sometimes charged for calls they placed but that were not completed. Conversely, some hotels timed their equipment to start billing forty-five to sixty seconds after a call was dialed, which meant that guests who talked for less than that—such as to say, "I'll be home tonight instead of tomorrow" and then hung up—were never billed.

The warning here is quite clear: Examine your bill carefully before you pay and ask when in doubt.

Here are some things to consider doing:

- Use a phone company credit card, call collect, or bill to your home or office phone, but be aware that some hotels add surcharges to these calls, too.
- Better yet, arrange for your office or spouse to phone you at a specific hour when you will be free in your room.
- Consider using an alternative long-distance service. Several, such as I.T.T., Satellite Business Systems' Skyline Service and Western Union's MetroFone, provide local access numbers in most metropolitan areas so you can call from there and be billed at your office or home. First, however, check whether the charge for a local call from your hotel room, which you will have to pay, is a flat rate or timed and/or based on distance. If timed or based on distance, costs could multiply.
- Consider buying a small device called a tone dialer. The dialer can be either screwed onto or held against the mouthpiece of a rotary-dial phone to enable it to be used like a touch-tone model and thereby give you access to alternate long-distance services. Such devices cost from $25 to $40, can be carried in a pocket, and can be used in guest rooms, lobbies, or on the street if phones have dials instead of push buttons.

You can almost always save money by using a pay phone in a hotel lobby instead of calling from your room. On occasion, of course, the comfort of kicking off your shoes while talking and stretching out on a bed may well be worth the extra cost—but it's good to know what you are paying for that comfort.

52. Rules for Avoiding Common Mistakes

As travel gets more complex, more things can go wrong, and they do. Even experienced travelers are not immune to trouble, as the following examples indicate. Some of the problems, to be sure, were unavoidable; others could have been prevented by more careful planning. The best advice: Travel cautiously. The time and money you save will almost certainly be your own.

Example—A Chicago couple took a train to Miami to join a Caribbean cruise. The train was scheduled to arrive five hours before sailing time, which seemed sufficient for them to get from the railroad station to the pier. But, if they had checked, they would have discovered that their train was frequently many hours late, as it was on the day of their trip; they missed their sailing and had the option of forfeiting their cruise fare—nearly $1,500—or catching up with the ship in Jamaica. They chose the latter, but they missed nearly two days' cruising and had to pay an unexpected $250 for air fares to Jamaica, as well as being out of pocket for a hotel room and meals.

Rule—If you have to make connections, allow extra time. Carry a book in case you allow too much.

Be especially wary of long-distance American trains. Amtrak has made a lot of progress in recent years, but on some long-distance routes, scheduling problems persist. Don't take any chances with connections unless you have a firm guarantee that your cruise or land tour will wait for you or pay for alternate arrangements if your train is late.

Example—A couple flew from Denver to Hawaii to vacation in a friend's beach house. They took some of their own supplies, including a dozen frozen filet mignons, which they packed in insulated bags in a suitcase that they checked from Denver to Honolulu. The couple had to change planes in San Francisco, where they had a three-hour layover. They made the connection easily, but the suitcase with the steaks did not. By the time the suitcase arrived in Honolulu two days later, the steaks were unfit to eat.

Rule—Lost or misdirected baggage is a matter of substantial concern to both airlines and passengers. Carry whatever you can in hand luggage, particularly perishables, unless it is feasible to ship the perishables as air freight with the airline guaranteeing to provide special treatment.

Example—A graduate student, planning his return to New York from a year in Japan, discovered that he would have a four-hour layover in Los Angeles. He arranged to rent a car at the airport and planned to drive downtown to lunch with friends. His flight from Japan arrived on time, but it took him nearly two hours to complete immigration and customs formalities and claim his baggage. The student wisely reckoned that it would probably take at least an hour to pick up his car and drive downtown and the same time to get back to the airport, which left him no time for the reunion. His friends celebrated without him.

Rule—If you are traveling internationally, do not arrange any appointments or connecting transportation without making sure that you can complete all formalities in time. At some airports at peak periods, delays of three hours or more are not uncommon. If someone is to meet you at the airport and does not have to travel far, suggest that she or he go about normal business but stay near a telephone.

Examples—My wife and I were booked on the now-defunct Air Florida from Treasure Cay in the Bahamas to Philadelphia, where we live. After the airline had taken our tickets and checked us in at the Treasure City airport, we learned that the flight had been canceled because of mechanical problems in Miami. We were transferred to a flight to Fort Lauderdale on Mackey International, but that was scrubbed when an engine malfunctioned. Air Florida paid our taxi fare between the Treasure Cay airport and a resort hotel and picked up the tab for a night's lodging, dinner, and breakfast. The next morning the airline sent us to Miami on Bahamasair and transferred us at no extra cost to a nonstop Eastern flight to Philadelphia that offered movies and dinner—frills that Air Florida flights did not provide. The airline assumed responsibility because it had failed, through its own shortcomings, to fulfill its contract to us.

Two weeks later we were scheduled to fly from Toronto to Philadelphia on USAir. Shortly before we left for the Toronto airport by taxi—two hours before takeoff time—it began to snow heavily. After our taxi crept barely half a mile in forty-five minutes, we returned to our hotel and phoned USAir to change our reservations to the following day. Our original flight had operated despite the snow, however, and we were considered no-shows.

I was traveling by full economy fare so there was no penalty, but my wife was using a discounted Freedom Fare that permitted no change in reservation; she had to forfeit the discount and pay $40 more. She was told that USAir's customer relations department would probably send her a refund by mail if she could prove that she missed the plane because of circumstances beyond her control. But, because the airline was not responsible for the delay, we were stuck for the expenses of an extra night in Toronto.

Rule—Who pays for the additional expenses incurred by a missed connection depends on several factors. Bring extra money—in the form of traveler's checks or a widely accepted credit card—for emergencies. You may get a refund later, but you may have had to lay out a lot on the spot, much of it nonreimbursable.

53. Lost Plane Tickets

Linda S. and nine of her college classmates were on the way to South America to spend their junior year abroad. At the check-in counter at Kennedy International Airport in New York, where she had been taken by friends, Linda discovered that she did not have her ticket. Although she produced lots of identification and could establish beyond any doubt that she was a bona fide member of a group in which everyone else had a ticket, airline officials said they could not carry her unless she paid $500 to replace hers.

Linda phoned home and asked her mother, who by chance is a travel agent, what to do. Her mother rushed out to the family car and found Linda's ticket between the two front seats, where it had apparently fallen the night before. The mother read the ticket number on the telephone to an airline official. After a lot of cajoling, he agreed to carry Linda without extra charge, provided the mother promised to deliver the ticket to the airline's New York office the following morning.

Linda was lucky. Misplacing or losing an airline ticket can be both annoying and costly. Different airlines have different policies and procedures, but replacing a lost ticket is usually a nuisance at best and often costly as well.

There is a sound reason. Airline tickets, like cash, can be highly negotiable. One reads frequently in travel-business newspapers about the theft of blank air tickets from airline offices or travel agencies. The thieves fill in the tickets and fraudulently cash them in for refunds or sell them to would-be passengers.

If a ticket has been bought with cash or a check, it can be turned in for its face value in cash, assuming that it is not marked nonrefundable or for restricted passage with stiff cancellation penalties. If it has been purchased with a credit card, a refund is in the form of a credit to the cardholder's account. In such a case, someone who finds a lost ticket would not benefit by turning it in for a refund but could still use it to fly.

Officials of eight major airlines, domestic and international, were asked what their airport staffs would do if a person whose name was on the passenger list could not produce a ticket at check-in time. Their regulations are similar, but some airlines give substantial discretion to their top airport supervisors.

If a lost ticket for a domestic flight was purchased for cash directly from the airlines, the passenger usually has to buy a replacement, for cash or by acceptable credit card, before being permitted to board the plane. The passenger is also asked to fill out a "lost ticket refund application." Anywhere from forty days to four months later, depending on what airline it is, the cost of the lost ticket is refunded—usually less a $10 to $25 service fee—provided the ticket has not been used. If the ticket was bought through a travel agent, however, the agent may give a refund immediately and wait for reimbursement by the airline.

If the passenger finds the lost ticket after buying a replacement, he should turn it in to the airline or travel agent as soon as possible so the refund can be expedited.

If the lost ticket has been charged to a credit card and the passenger has a cardholder's receipt and can amply identify himself, the airline supervisor at the airport may authorize issuance of a replacement ticket without charge. The reason is that the cardholder's receipt will probably show the number of the missing ticket. If the airline has the number, it can verify by computer that the passenger claiming the loss is the same person to whom the ticket was sold. Also, if the airline knows the ticket number, it can alert its sales and check-in personnel to watch for attempted fraudulent use.

Oddly, when a ticket is bought with cash directly from the airline, this procedure cannot be followed. The top coupon—the only record the airline retains that bears the ticket number—is usually forwarded within twenty-four hours to a central accounting office and fed into a computer, so no record of the number is available at the sales office or the airport check-in counter.

If the flight is international, if the lost ticket was bought with a credit card, and if the ticket number is available at check-in time, most of the airlines questioned said they would issue a replacement ticket without charge. They noted that it was harder to misuse an international ticket than a domestic one because on foreign flights passengers must usually present passports—which bear photographs—when checking in. But they said they would require the passenger to fill out and sign a "lost ticket indemnity form," which is a promise to pay the value of the lost ticket if it is misused.

It may sound odd, but if a ticket has been purchased from a travel agent rather than directly from the airline, it is usually easier to obtain a replacement without paying additional fare. One reason is that an efficient travel agency will have kept a record of the ticket number and can supply it immediately to the airline, provided, of course, that the loss is discovered during business hours. If the passenger is a regular client of the travel agent and the loss is discovered during business hours and before the passenger goes to the airport, the agent may simply write out a new ticket and give it to the client. The agent then reports the loss to the airline and assumes that the client will make good if the missing ticket is misused.

Here are a few tips that can make ticket replacement easier, should yours be misplaced or lost:

- Record your ticket number and keep the record separately from the ticket. If you buy the ticket with a credit card, the number is usually written on your credit receipt.
- If it is at all avoidable, do not pay with cash.
- Carry a driver's license and at least one other form of indisputable identification, preferably one that bears your picture.

54. Lost Luggage

Some of the biggest problems for air travelers arise from baggage. While most of it gets where it is supposed to go when it is supposed to get there, enough baggage is lost or damaged on the way to be a major source of contention between airlines and passengers. To try and get compensation from the airline can be an exercise in frustration.

At some airports, you cannot leave the baggage-claim area until a guard has matched the numbers on your ticket stub against those on the tags attached to your suitcases. At others, a chaotic honor system seems to prevail—or is it that some lines do not care?

Because of a mix-up, two passengers arrived in New York on a flight later than the one carrying their luggage. They said they found their suitcases at the back of a claim area, "with no one there to check receipts."

"There was not a soul within shouting distance," they wrote to me. "We could have walked out with more bags than our own."

In another case, more or less typical, luggage and skis disappeared between Aspen, Colorado, and Birmingham, Alabama, and recovery—of only some of the items—took many days. In the meantime, the traveler had bought replacement clothing.

These are the kinds of experiences that make passengers bristle. Sometimes the wrong flight number is written on a baggage tag. Sometimes a handler at an intermediary airport takes the wrong bags off the plane or leaves them aboard. Sometimes a suitcase disappears, never to be found or to turn up months later at an airport far from the owner's route.

As improvements in airport facilities lag behind increases in travel, more and more baggage arrives battered and sometimes rifled. If this happens to you, do not automatically assume that an airline will promptly accept responsibility and pay you what you think you should get.

As required by law, the extent of a carrier's liability is outlined on all air tickets issued in the United States and should be must reading because, for many passengers, it is grossly inadequate. It was raised in April 1984 to $1,250 from $750 on domestic flights. That is the most you can claim for damages, loss, or delay of any or all the personal property traveling with you—not the amount per suitcase and its contents.

For the liability on a flight within the United States to be higher, specific arrangements must be made with the airline before the flight, usually for an extra charge of about $1 for every $100 of declared value. Not all airlines will agree to this, however. Airlines are required to assume liability within the $1,250 total for damage to eyeglasses, contact lenses, one camera for each passenger, and "reasonable quantities of toiletries," but not for many other fragile items or perishables that spoil.

On most international flights or on domestic legs of international flights, liability is governed by the Warsaw Convention of 1929. This limits liability to $9.07 a pound ($20 a kilogram) for checked baggage and $400 a passenger for unchecked belongings unless a higher value has been declared in advance, at a surcharge. The normal maximum liability for sixty pounds of checked belongings is therefore $544.20.

Liability should not be confused with insurance, which usually covers luggage wherever it is lost or damaged. To establish liability, however, you must prove that the carrier was at fault. Because of the limitations, your best protection is probably insurance of your own.

If you own a home, study your homeowner's insurance policy; many of them cover losses of personal effects outside the home as well as inside. If you own valuable cameras or jewelry, they should be covered by what the insurance industry calls a "personal articles floater"—a policy that protects you wherever a mishap occurs.

If you do not own a home and a personal articles floater is not suitable, consider buying baggage insurance for a specific trip. Several nationwide companies offer it, usually through travel agents, with premiums based on the length of the trip and the maximum coverage you want. A typical policy provides up to $1,000 of coverage for thirty days for a premium of $45 to $50.

Even if liability is established, airlines, bus lines, and railroads do not pay full replacement cost for lost or irreparably damaged belongings but deduct depreciation for wear and tear. They do not reimburse for money, jewelry, or other valuables in checked bags. Clearly, it is better to take only what you need and leave most valuables safely at home.

An airline may refuse to check certain items—such as musical instruments or antiques—that are too big or too fragile to be inside baggage unless you sign a waiver releasing the company from liability for damage. Or it may require that you pay a surcharge above your fare and place such an item in a seat beside yours. Only certain designated seats in a plane can be used for luggage, so arrangements must often be made far in advance.

On domestic flights, the typical surcharge is 75 percent of your fare, although sometimes it is higher; on international flights it is 100 percent. On buses, if the seat next to you is available, you may use it for large and important luggage for a 65 percent surcharge; no such arrangement is available on trains, where you simply take your chance on finding an empty seat.

Any claim, whether against a transportation company or for reimbursement through insurance, should be lodged promptly and be as well documented as possible. For example, if you are still in the baggage claim area when you discover damage or pilferage, show the evidence at once to an airline representative and fill out a form that should be readily available for the purpose. That way, it will be easier to substantiate your claim later.

Also immediately report missing luggage. If it contains items that you need immediately, such as toilet articles or a change of clothing, ask the airline if it can provide an overnight kit or cash to buy replacements. Only if you ask are you likely to get such reimbursement. If the airline does not make such on-the-spot aid available and you are forced to go out and buy a shirt or cosmetics, keep all your receipts to establish your claim for later reimbursement. Above all, keep all ticket receipts and baggage checks as evidence in case missing possessions never reappear.

If your baggage is not lost but you discover, after reaching home or a hotel, that it has been rifled, report it to the carrier as soon as possible. The quicker you do so, the easier it is to investigate. And remember that in handling any baggage claim, a carrier looks carefully for any evidence of inconsistency, exaggeration, or fraud.

The question of when "missing" becomes "lost"—when the traveler can expect compensatory payment from an airline—depends upon when the airline gives up the search. Generally, experts say, if missing luggage is going to be found, it is found within three days, although some airlines may continue a search as long as two weeks.

Then, after the line concedes that the luggage is unfindable, there are further problems in getting compensation. Just because you lose belongings that you think are worth the maximum does not mean that the airline will concur. You will be questioned about length of ownership and usage, and airlines commonly try to deduct as much as they can for depreciation. Sometimes it is necessary to go to small claims court or get a lawyer to settle a claim justly.

With American carriers, you have at least forty-five days after the discovery of loss or damage to file a claim. Foreign rules vary, but the best protection against loss or damage is to keep it from happening. Here are some ways to do that:

- If you do not need a lot of clothes, try to pack everything into a carry-on bag that you keep with you.
- Have your name on the inside of checked suitcases. Should an identification tag on the outside be torn off, a note inside will identify you as the owner. The identification tag on the outside should *not* include your address, however, or any other information that could indicate to loiterers that your house may be vacant.
- If an airport is especially busy, like Atlanta, Los Angeles, Chicago's O'Hare, or New York's Kennedy, and if you are changing not only planes but also airlines, the more time

you can allow for the connection the better. In many cases it may be safer not to check your bags all the way from your point of origin to destination but to reclaim them at the transfer point and recheck them for your next flight.

- If your trip involves extensive air travel, use baggage with the sturdiest frames available to avoid damage.
- If your suitcases look like many others, distinguish yours by some markings, such as strips of bright tape. This greatly lessens the risk that your bag will accidentally be taken by another passenger.
- Unless you have an unusually keen memory, keep a list of the contents of your baggage. That helps when you file a claim.

Carry-On Luggage

Every airline has its own rules and practices governing what baggage you may carry and where on the plane it must go. Often the rules are blatantly ignored, however, by check-in clerks and in-flight personnel.

How much you can carry free is usually set by governmental or industry regulations, but these can vary substantially between domestic and international flights and can depend on the rules of the country in which your flight begins.

Having read this far, you have some idea of what is meant by baggage confusion. Let's look now at an example that occurred a few years ago.

Richard Swift Glassman of Media, Pennsylvania, flew from New York to Salvador, Brazil. His baggage allowance was based on the so-called piece concept, which meant that he was allowed to check two bags without charge. The length plus height plus width of the larger bag was not to exceed 62 inches and the total dimensions of the two were not to exceed 106 inches. He was also permitted to carry on one bag measuring up to 45 inches, provided it could be stowed under his seat. No bag could weigh more than seventy pounds.

For Mr. Glassman, as for most travelers, this allowance was more than adequate. But when he returned to New York, the situation was drastically different. The airline that carried him, Varig of Brazil, charged him $195 for exceeding his allowance.

Mr. Glassman bridled and wondered how that could be. After

long correspondence with Varig, the Civil Aeronautics Board, his Congressman, and others, he learned to his frustration not only that it could be but that it also was common practice, although views differed on whether it was legal.

Explanation: His outward and return trips, although both involving Varig, were based on different baggage rules. Under a C.A.B. ruling of March 1976, the free baggage allowance on all flights within or from the United States was under the piece concept. It did not matter whether the airline was American or foreign.

But at issue at the time was whether the board could govern what foreign airlines charged on flights originating abroad. Most European airlines had adopted the piece concept, but many others, including most in Latin America, still clung to the weight concept, adopted when the load that airplanes could carry was not nearly what it is today. The weight concept generally limited the free allowance to a total of forty-four pounds for economy-class passengers and sixty-six pounds for those flying first class. Each kilogram (2.2 pounds) in excess of those weights was assessed at the rate of 1 percent of the first-class fare to the destination. In Mr. Glassman's case the excess-weight fee amounted to $195.

Since then, rules have become a little more standardized but not much. In 1984, the C.A.B. blocked a move by the International Air Transport Association to revise the piece-related system on flights to and from the United States. The move would have lowered the maximum weight allowance for the total number of pieces carried by each passenger and would have had the effect of raising excess-baggage charges substantially.

The lesson in this for you, the traveler, is to check the current baggage rules when you make your reservation, if there is even the slightest possibility in your mind that your baggage may exceed the free allowance for size per piece and for overall weight. Also, be sure you understand what variations in rules apply to every leg of a trip abroad. If you plan to carry anything that requires special handling, be sure you know of any special rules—or charges—that apply. And if you plan to carry any baggage at your seat rather than check it, ask your travel agent or the airline how small it must be to fit under the seat in front of you or whether the plane will have an enclosed overhead bin in which you can stow it.

While all domestic airlines in the United States follow the piece concept, regulations regarding dimensions vary. Charges as well as rules vary widely for extra pieces, sometimes with a single airline applying different rules to different routes. Rules can differ according to the type of aircraft, the time of the flight, and the way items must be packaged. Special rules govern fragile items, such as electronic or photographic equipment, musical instruments, or pottery, and again each airline has its own rules.

Sporting equipment is covered by separate rules. Take bicycles. Most airlines accept only nonmotorized touring bicycles with single seats, but a few also accept those with tandem seats. Some airlines require that the handlebars be fixed sideways and the pedals removed and placed in a container—the type of which varies according to the carrier. A few airlines require that the entire bicycle be placed in a cardboard container. Some airlines carry a bicycle free in lieu of one bag; others charge $20 or so extra. Other varying rules apply to equipment for golf, scuba diving, skiing, fishing, or whatever. Still other rules apply to pets, which sometimes are allowed in the passenger compartment but usually must be carried as cargo.

The person who travels reasonably light and carries only the usual personal effects need rarely be concerned about conflicting rules. But the bicyclist, the musician, the fisherman, the scuba diver, and dozens of others who want to pursue their interests away from home face substantial difficulties if they take their own equipment with them. They may find, for example, that on a winter vacation trip from, say, Kansas City to Austria, they may be unable to check their skis through to their destination because different airlines are involved, each with different rates and rules. So such passengers may have to reclaim the skis in New York and recheck them, a time-consuming nuisance.

The person who intends to travel with anything other than ordinary baggage may ease potential problems by following these rules:

- If a trip involves several different flights, arrange the routing to involve the fewest number of airlines.
- If you are going abroad, find out whether any excess charges for the return portion are based on the United States dollar or on local currency. Usually American carriers levy dollar rates anywhere in the world, but foreign airlines do not. When the dollar is weak, payment at a foreign rate can

substantially increase the cost; vice versa when the dollar is strong.

- If two or more people are traveling together in or from a country where the weight system applies, remember that baggage weight can be pooled. Thus, if one person has fifty-five pounds and the other twenty-five pounds, the total of eighty pounds is less than the eighty-eight-pound limit for an economy-class couple, so no excess charge should be involved. The same logic prevails under the piece system if you exceed the maximum overall weight allowance.

On Buses and Trains?

As if the baggage liability limits of airlines are not meager enough, those for ground travel in the United States are lower yet. On interstate buses, the ceiling of $250, approved by the Interstate Commerce Commission for each adult passenger and limited to two checked bags, regardless of the value of their contents, is far below that on any other form of long-distance American mass transportation. The ceiling is only $125 for a half-fare ticket.

Amtrak automatically assumes a maximum liability of $500 a passenger for checked baggage for every ticket-holder with a maximum total of $2,500 for those traveling under a family plan. A traveler has the option, however, of increasing the limit by buying insurance at the rate of fifty cents per hundred dollars of additional evaluation up to a maximum of $2,500. Amtrak sets its own limits, free of outside regulation; the additional insurance can be bought from ticket agents at the station of departure.

55. When Companies Default

The failure of the travel industry in 1983 to help thousands of holders of useless tickets on Continental Air Lines and in 1984 on Air Florida illustrated how vulnerable consumers could be to financial loss and how weak were the measures to protect them. By the time you read this, the industry may have produced a sound program to assure that if a carrier defaults after you have paid for a ticket but before you go, you either get your money back quickly or have your ticket endorsed over to another airline so that you can reach your destination with minimal delay and no extra charge.

For years, everyone in the industry seemed to agree that some such program was badly needed. Everyone seemed to disagree, however, about how to pay for it. The Continental case brought this discord into sharp focus because it involved the bankruptcy of a major carrier and the failure of the airline industry, leaning on a technicality, to invoke a default plan it had developed to protect consumers under presumably just such circumstances.

These were only two of several major defaults in recent years, however, in which tens of thousands of travelers were hurt sorely. At best, they ultimately reached their destinations after substantial disruption or because travel agents voluntarily assumed financial responsibility as gestures of good will. At worst, many travelers continue to be out hundreds, sometimes thousands, of dollars each as they wait for slow-moving bankruptcy courts to dole out a pittance.

Some large defaults have been chalked up by tour operators whose abrupt suspensions of operations have cost would-be passengers their vacations and the cash they prepaid for all-inclusive arrangements. Even where bonding and escrow laws have been scrupulously observed, there often has been far too little in the kitty to allow more than token refunds.

In airline bankruptcies before Continental's, the most fortunate consumer-victims were those who bought their unused tickets through travel agencies. Under an airline default protection plan that became effective in March 1982, more than a hundred United States carriers guaranteed to honor, within one year of purchase but usually on standby, tickets issued by agencies for travel on a carrier that later went under. Many airlines even honored tickets that had been bought directly from the defaulting carrier.

According to William E. Jackman, a spokesman for the Air Traffic Conference, an industry regulatory group that has been replaced by the Airline Reporting Corporation, thirty-one airlines honored nearly 65,000 tickets valued at $8.5 million for travel on Braniff International, which went out of business in May 1982. It was revived as a much smaller company and under different owners nearly two years later. He said that at least seven airlines honored more than 2,000 tickets valued at $385,697 on Altair Airlines, a regional carrier in the Northeast that defaulted in January 1983, and that eight lines had honored an undetermined number of tickets on Golden West Airlines, a southern California company that defaulted in April 1983.

But consumers who could not get alternate transportation or who canceled their trips and sought refunds were left waiting at courthouse doors. There they joined the 17,000 or so would-be passengers plus other creditors who have been trying to collect $380 million to $500 million (reports differ) from the shambles of Laker Airways, which defaulted in February 1982. Lawyers said this case could go on for years.

In the Continental case, the default protection plan did not work. The Air Traffic Conference contended that even though Continental had filed in late September 1983 for reorganization under Chapter 11 of the Federal Bankruptcy Code, it had not technically defaulted because it continued operations, although they were sharply reduced. As a result, few carriers accepted Continental tickets. Under its reorganization, Continental gradually increased service and offered credits for future travel in place of refunds. Such credits were useless for many ticket holders, however, either because they had completed their trips by other means at additional expense or because Continental no longer flew where they wanted to go.

With the breakdown of the system in the Continental case, most people holding Air Florida tickets when it failed were not protected at all unless they had insurance or their travel agents helped.

At this writing, the hope for consumers in future defaults seems to lie in proposals for some form of insurance financed by a small surcharge on air tickets or paid by the industry to cover the cost of providing alternate transportation or refunds if a carrier goes bankrupt. In May 1983, the American Automobile Association introduced such a plan for air tickets purchased through the travel agencies of participating member clubs.

Meanwhile, consumer insurance to cover most kinds of travel default is sold by many travel agencies. Also, if you are going on a tour it is wise to ask an agent about the tour operator's track record and whether travel by chartered plane is involved.

Under Federal regulations, a charter operator is required to post a $200,000 surety bond and to keep payments from travelers in an escrow account until a trip is completed. But noncharter operators are governed essentially by rules and ethics of their own. The United States Tour Operators Association, whose thirty-odd members are among the biggest in the field, has a default protection plan that requires a $100,000 bond and covers all consumers. The American Society of Travel Agents has a similar plan but invokes it only for consumers who have bought packages through ASTA members and only for money lost, not for complaints about the quality of a tour. Under either plan the settlement process can be long and complicated. Ask your travel agent which operators are in each plan; participation indicates reliability.

How much you are likely to get depends largely on how much the defaulting tour operator has paid the hotels, sightseeing companies, airlines, and other suppliers involved in the package purchased. In the United States and many foreign countries, commitments by tour operators are made largely on credit and much prepaid money may long remain intact. The Chinese Government, however, usually insists on cash up front.

If a tour operator defaults while you are traveling on one of his programs, you probably will not be stranded but your trip may be abruptly halted. Situations vary, but usually an airline flies you home at no extra cost, although probably on standby. Expect hotels and suppliers to refuse to honor vouchers unless the tour operator has already paid them.

If a travel agency goes bankrupt after you have prepaid your vacation but before you have taken it, your degree of protection varies. According to an ASTA spokesman, airlines usually honor tickets sold by such agencies, regardless of whether the carrier has been paid. He said some cruise lines also honor tickets, "although that situation is a little more fuzzy." Whether tour operators, hotels, and other suppliers would honor the agency's vouchers, he said, would probably depend largely on whether they had been paid.

Robert E. Whitley, executive vice president of the tour operators association, said he thought its $100,000 bond was sufficient because little money had to be paid up front. He acknowledged, however, that more than nine hundred customers who had paid about $1.2 million were hurt when Travel Headquarters of San Ramon, California, defaulted in 1982 because it had had to pay China in advance for tours there but fell far, far short of its sales goal.

Thomas Mahoney, who was a senior attorney for the Civil Aeronautics Board, said claims totaling $640,000 were at stake in a class-action suit in behalf of 2,100 people against the First Charter Corporation of Philadelphia, a tour operator that defaulted in April 1983. "But there is only $250,000 in the kitty," Mr. Mahoney said, "and 640 doesn't go into 250 very easily."

Sometimes even major victories prove elusive, at least for a while. Thomas A. Dickerson, the attorney who steered successful class-action litigation against the Nationwide Leisure Corporation of Melville, New York, which defaulted in August 1978, said $470,000 was put in court custody in 1979 but had not been disbursed to consumers pending the consolidation of various claims. "The money has been rolling over in ninety-day Treasury bills ever since then," Mr. Dickerson said five years later, "and it amounts to at least $650,000 right now. So the longer the case goes on, the more money there's going to be."

56. Getting Bumped

To be bumped from an aircraft is to be denied a seat when a flight is overbooked, even though you hold a confirmed reservation. Strange as it may seem, this is more likely to happen on a route on which an airline operates many flights than on others.

Between New York and Chicago, for example, or Chicago and Los Angeles or New York and Miami, where there are wide choices of flights, many travelers, uncertain exactly when they can leave, make several alternate reservations. Obviously, they can use only one, so on the other flights they either cancel or simply do not appear at departure time.

It is to compensate for cancellations and no-shows, which they are mechanically unable to detect in advance on busy routes, that airlines deliberately and admittedly overbook in the first place. The large airlines profess to base their overbooking on careful computerized studies of traffic patterns. They contend that they can usually predict accurately the number of no-shows and overbook accordingly. But at best there is a risk, and sometimes a prediction proves very wrong.

A lot of the furor against overbooking stems from the bumping of the consumer advocate Ralph Nader from a Washington-to-Hartford flight of Allegheny Airlines, now called USAir, in April 1972. The bumping forced him to miss a fund-raising rally in downtown Hartford. As a result he sued Allegheny, charging that it had fraudulently represented his reservation as having been confirmed. He won $10 in actual damages and $25,000 in punitive damages for the group that sponsored his visit.

Until a few years ago, the last passengers to arrive were customarily the ones bumped if the plane was full. Then the Civil Aeronautics Board introduced rules requiring United States airlines to seek volunteers who were willing to be bumped in return for a seat on a later flight and some sort of compensation—a cash payment or a free trip on another day. Involuntary bumping was permitted only if there were not enough volunteers. Passengers whose travel was least urgent were to be bumped first, based on a priority schedule established by the airline and open to public view.

With a few technical exceptions, airlines are required at this writing to provide alternate transportation and compensate anyone bumped involuntarily and delayed more than an hour beyond the scheduled arrival time in reaching his or her destination. Compensation must equal the cost of a one-way ticket, with a minimum of $37.50 and a maximum of $200, if the passenger reaches the destination within two hours of the scheduled time on domestic flights and four hours on international trips. If alternate travel takes longer, the compensation is doubled.

You usually cannot claim compensation, however, if you are bumped because the government requisitions space or because a smaller plane is substituted for the scheduled one. The C.A.B. permitted this loophole on the theory that if a company must compensate many passengers because it substitutes a plane, it will probably cancel the flight. Compensation has not been required in case of cancellation.

That's where a rub has come, and a few years ago it was a big one. During the grounding of DC-10's in the summer of 1979 after several major crashes, thousands of frustrated passengers were left virtually to fend for themselves—often at substantial discomfort and extra cost—because of substitution of smaller aircraft and long delays. Thousands of others were similarly inconvenienced when their flights were canceled because of fuel shortages or because of mechanical problems caused by heavy use of planes.

Among the victims of the DC-10 grounding was Marna Walsh of Brooklyn. She said that when she checked in with Icelandair that July for a flight from Luxembourg to New York, she was told that a DC-8, a much smaller plane, had been substituted for the scheduled DC-10. Because of this, the airline said in a written notice addressed "Dear Passenger," she could not fly until the following day. "We regret to inform you," the notice said, "that our company is not able to pay for any hotel accommodations, since the grounding of the DC-10 is a situation beyond our control and does not involve our responsibility."

"There were young people stranded with practically no money,"

Mrs. Walsh recalled later. "Some of them missed connections in New York and were forced to spend the night at Kennedy or La Guardia because they had no money for a hotel room."

According to Teodor Lopatkiewicz, then a spokesman for the C.A.B. in Washington, the circumstances cited by Mrs. Walsh did not apparently call for compensation because, for one thing, Icelandair was not a United States airline and did not have to observe the bumping rules. He said, however, that the agency had received many such complaints about American carriers and that it was investigating the possibility that some airlines were doing what they all denied: accepting and reconfirming reservations on DC-10's for dates when it was extremely doubtful such planes would be permitted to fly.

The investigation proved inconclusive.

57. Why "Full" Planes Aren't

Look what happened to Anita G. Henry.

One March, Mrs. Henry, a drapery designer from Manhattan, decided it was time to make plane reservations to go to the Caribbean for Christmas, nine months later. She asked her travel agent, Ann Greenfield of Continental American Travel, to reserve her a seat shortly before the holiday to any of several islands from which she could transfer to a plane small enough to land in Saint Kitts, her destination. Mrs. Henry said her agent was told that nothing was available and that even waiting lists were closed.

"Miss Greenfield is excellent," Mrs. Henry said. "She kept after the airlines and kept me informed. On December 18 I went to her office in desperation. She called American Airlines; one seat had just been released for the next day on a flight to Saint Martin.

"Imagine my astonishment and annoyance when I got on the plane and realized it was one-third empty!"

When Alton W. Becker Jr., an American Airlines spokesman, was asked about this, he said Mrs. Henry's account was "probably accurate." He explained the episode this way:

The demand for pre-Christmas flights to the Caribbean is tremendous, and reservations are accepted a year in advance. The peak days are December 20 to 24.

A couple of months before Mrs. Henry's trip, airline specialists began examining the situation closely, including the economic implications of the fact that planes that flew fully loaded to the Caribbean just before Christmas might return nearly empty. The reverse situation is likely around New Year's. The airlines did not want to add flights unless they were likely to be full in at least one direction. In late October, American began to add extra sections to some Caribbean flights scheduled between December 20 and 24. Ultimately, these additions meant that some passengers who were booked for December 19 to Saint Martin were able to switch to preferable later flights, freeing seats for Mrs. Henry and others.

If pre-Christmas flights were fully booked by March, however, why wait until fall to add sections? "There are other factors to be considered besides apparent passenger demand," Mr. Becker said. "It is difficult to project far in advance how many passengers will show up for flights and what the availability will be in terms of planes, pilots, flight attendants, and fuel."

American, of course, had intended the December 19 flight, the one carrying Mrs. Henry, to be full. So why the empty seats? Mr. Becker explained it succinctly: "No-shows."

In the scheduled airline industry, no-show is synonymous with bad guy. People who make reservations and pay for them, then fail to show up at flight time without bothering to cancel can in most cases, even with many bargain fares, claim full refunds later. They cannot claim refunds for charter flights or when transportation is part of an air-ground package.

According to official airline estimates, the overall annual no-show rate has run as high as 20 percent of total capacity of scheduled flights. Said William J. Dunn, then public relations director in New York for BWIA International, formerly British West Indian Airways, a major Caribbean carrier: "It is our biggest headache. We just don't know how to lick it."

Some airlines maintain it can be licked by forcing no-shows to pay a penalty when they seek refunds. Some bargain fares have been subject to cancellation penalties, but generally such moves by one or two carriers have soon been rescinded because the rest of the industry refused to go along.

Miss Greenfield of Continental American Travel warned of one danger regarding no-shows. "If seats are hard to reserve, some agents don't tell the airline when a client cancels a flight," she said. "Instead they give the seat to another client, using the canceled client's name. But to me, that practice is terribly dangerous, and I firmly discourage any client of mine who suggests it.

" 'What happens,' I ask them, " 'if there is an accident? There will be no record that you were on the flight, so what are the insurance people going to say when you or your family files a claim? If you have a family, flying under a fictitious name is a dumb thing to do.' "

To the distress of many travel agents, some airlines allow favored agents and tour packagers to book large blocks of seats far in advance, removing them from general sale. This means that six months before the Presidents' Day weekend, say, your own agent may be unable to book you to Barbados, but you may suddenly learn through a friend that space is available through Packager X, provided you buy hotel accommodations at the same time.

"When that sort of thing happens to a client of mine," a Cleveland agent said, "it sure makes me look stupid."

Mr. Dunn of BWIA said some agents and packagers cannot be turned down. "They may book twelve, nineteen, twenty-two seats on a single flight," he said. "They are damn good agents—the backbone of our business."

Based on a spot check, airlines that permit block booking also usually require that the seats either be paid for by a certain date or be turned back to the airline. This, along with the addition of extra flights during peak periods, is why seats that were unavailable eight months in advance suddenly materialize as departure nears.

An alert travel agent keeps in touch with an airline if a reservation cannot be obtained at once and if you, the client, are willing to wait and take your chances. But this alone does not beat the no-show problem, since the number of dropouts often cannot be determined until a few minutes before flight time.

Airlines commonly try to compensate for anticipated no-shows by overbooking, but they face formidable penalties if confirmed reservations are not honored, so beyond a certain point they usually dare not gamble. The result: Supposedly jammed flights go partly empty.

One official of an airline with heavy New York-Florida traffic suggested that if you were unable to get a confirmed reservation, the best solution was to go standby. "I tell people, 'Never mind about reservations, just go to the airport,'" he said. "The chances are usually very good that they will get on."

Generally, however, it is best to consult an expert before making the trek to an airport based on hope. While no-shows are flagrant on some routes, the airline industry is struggling to economize by eliminating marginal flights. So the general trend now is toward jammed planes.

58. Canceled Tours

Little in the travel business is as murky as the question of what you are entitled to when a vacation package or tour is canceled or substantially changed because of an act of God.

Strikes against airlines or governmental aviation authorities have severely delayed or forced the cancellation of tours. So have all sorts of natural and man-made calamities such as earthquakes, blizzards, floods, and wars. Because your own vacation can be disrupted by circumstances that seem beyond your control, it is useful to examine the possible consequences.

Travel packages are usually paid for in full before you leave home. These arrangements can vary from simply a few nights at a hotel and use of a rental car for a specified number of days to a very elaborate escorted tour, including most meals, sightseeing, and the services of a professional escort. Unlike the fully independent traveler, who arranges each element of a trip separately, the purchaser of a tour or package can pay thousands of dollars in advance, much of which can be unrecoverable if a trip is severely disrupted by an act of God.

If a strike or natural disaster delays an independent traveler's arrival in Paris, say, the most he or she may lose at a hotel is the cost of the first night's stay because that is probably all that was prepaid. The airline will refund the air fare but will not assume responsibility for the hotel payment unless the carrier can be proved to be responsible for the delay. If an act of God makes it impossible for you to comply with the restrictions of reduced-price fares sold under such names as "super saver" or APEX, your ticket will probably be honored later.

A common term to describe acts of God is *force majeure*. It came from the French and means *overpowering force* or *coercive power*. As applied in the travel industry, it means events considered wholly outside the control of an airline, tour operator, hotel, or sightseeing company. Virtually every tour brochure contains a disclaimer of responsibility by the operator for almost everything a supplier of travel facilities might do wrong, whether consciously or as a result of force majeure.

Some tour operators include strikes under the force majeure umbrella. Others, however, unsure whether this is legally sound because a strike can be avoided, publish special disclaimers of responsibility to cover strikes.

In considering all this, the important thing for the traveler to ponder is what a canceled tour could mean not just to the time you have allocated for your vacation but also to the money—often thousands of dollars—that you have paid in advance. The more established tour operators can be expected to do as much as they can to provide a substitute vacation, a refund, or a credit on a tour next year, but largesse has a limit. They cannot be expected to try to keep you happy if it forces them into bankruptcy.

You may decide that you have no recourse but to go to court and sue. You may find, however, that litigation takes years and produces scant return. Thomas A. Dickerson, a Manhattan lawyer who has steered class-action suits in the travel field, goes after everyone with any involvement in a tour. He strongly advises that you keep all pertinent records and that you complain promptly, in writing, to the tour operator, your travel agent, the American Society of Travel Agents, and the Department of Transportation. If your tour involves a charter flight, he urges that you complain also to the insurance company named in the brochure as having issued the operator a surety bond, which is legally required of charters.

Probably your closest ally when a tour is disrupted or canceled because of force majeure is the travel agent who made your arrangements. The agent is on the front line in confronting your ire; most agents' lifeblood is repeat business, and they do not want to lose it.

Next up the line is the tour operator, the company that assembled all the elements that went into the tour. The tour operator chartered the jetliner or reserved blocks of seats on scheduled flights, committed himself to blocks of hotel rooms, often for an entire season, hired sightseeing buses and guides, and bought tickets for you to attend special events such as the Salzburg Festival in Austria, the Olympic Games, wherever they may be, or the Passion Play at Oberammergau, Germany.

The tour operator, however, usually has few assets beyond your money and his business acumen. When a supplier fails to deliver because of force majeure, an operator who has already paid him can often only hope to get something back but cannot insist on it. Where possible, operators do not pay until facilities are used or services are delivered, but sometimes they have to pay in advance, leaving little if anything to refund to you.

If your tour involves a charter flight, however, regulations require that your payments be made to an escrow bank account. The operator pays his suppliers from this account, but he cannot take his profit until two days after the trip is successfully completed. If the trip is not successfully completed, he may never get his money, so he has nothing to return to you, although you may ultimately get something back by hiring a lawyer to go after what remains in escrow.

Arthur Frommer, who has long been prominent in tour operation but whose company is now owned by somebody else, put it this way in a telephone interview: "There is no way to refund seventy-five thousand dollars to a group if we have to pay out seventy-five thousand dollars to a hotel or airline."

"We refund that part of the traveler's payment that is recoverable from our suppliers," said Brian King, head of the New York office of Maupintour, one of the most highly respected operators of escorted tours. He said his company's record was probably better than most because "ordinarily we give suppliers such extended business that they're very considerate."

Extensive questioning of travel industry executives and Federal officials produced the following picture of what you can expect if, at some time, force majeure impedes your vacation tour.

Air Travel—If the start of your tour is delayed—by a strike, blizzard, or whatever—you will probably not be compensated for lost time. If you are a day late in reaching Paris, for example, the tour operator may throw in an extra dinner some evening. Or he may simply plead that, to help you overcome jet lag, he had not scheduled much for the first day in France anyway, so you did not miss much.

The airline usually has no responsibility unless it must cancel your flight completely. If the reason is mechanical, it will probably assume responsibility and make alternate arrangements; if the reason is a controllers' strike that has disrupted all air traffic, the carrier will not assume responsibility but will probably refund the tour operator's money anyway to be passed on to you. The air controllers' strike in 1981 did not put this to the test—most passengers were able to get to their destinations—but half a dozen airlines that were queried said that they would not keep tour money if they could not operate a flight. "We are not going to do business that way," said Dan Mahoney, a spokesman for United Airlines.

If your flight is a charter, the airline is not obligated to make alternate travel arrangements unless departure is delayed at least forty-eight hours, so you could lose up to two days of your tour without compensation. But if you take action against the charter operator—the company that hired the airline—you may find that his disclaimer of responsibility for delays will not stand up in court.

If a delayed or canceled flight strands your tour far from home, expect the airline or tour operator to make the best alternate arrangements possible. If no flights are operating, however, it is not at all clear who will pay your extended hotel and meal expenses; it could well be you.

If a tour begins, say, from Denver but force majeure prevents you from reaching there in time from another part of the country, the operator will probably arrange for you to catch up with the group. Do not expect a refund for time lost, however, and do not expect either the airline or the tour operator to pay for any overnight hotel stays at connecting points.

In the opinion of Clifton N. Cooke, a former airline executive who now publishes *Jax Fax Travel Marketing Magazine*, a monthly directory of air tours, a carrier that must curtail but not cancel all operations will probably give priority to charters. "They are looking for marginal flights to cancel," he said, "not charters, which usually are full or close to it. I think they would much prefer to cut back on the flight they know is a bummer—just take the crew off and save the gasoline bill."

Hotels—Here the outlook seems bleakest. Said Mr. Cooke: "I doubt that some hotel in southern France, for example, is going to refund money that was paid far in advance but then a tour operator didn't actually bring the people in." Mr. Frommer and others expressed similar views.

Discussing lodging in the United States, Albert E. Kudrle Jr., former director of public relations for the American Hotel and Motel Association, said every chain or individually operated hotel had its own policy on refunds and that a lot depended on the type of establishment, the nature of the tour, the terms of the contract, and the hotel's experience with the particular tour operator. The thorniest problems arise, he said, with a major convention or a resort hotel. "It all goes back to the old story of whether the hotel can re-rent the rooms," he said.

In short, do not expect your tour operator to get you refunds from resort hotels in the United States or overseas where a stay has been fully prepaid. If you get one, consider yourself lucky. But remember, the bigger and more prestigious the tour operator, the better your chances.

Tour Buses—As with hotels, refunds are often difficult to obtain from the bus companies, especially foreign ones, that provide the coaches that take you to Amsterdam on Monday, Brussels on Tuesday, and Paris on Wednesday. If the tour operator does not get a refund, neither, probably, will you. On an escorted tour of Europe, the amount can be substantial.

Local Sightseeing and Special Events—A similar situation prevails here, but the amounts involved tend to be relatively insignificant. Mr. King of Maupintour pointed out, however, that one ticket to one performance of the Salzburg Festival could run $125 to $150. "If a passenger or a tour doesn't make it," he said, "and the ticket cannot be resold, that's it."

59. When You and Your Hotel Disagree

The hospitality industry—hotels, motels, country inns, guest-houses, and the like—is one of the least regulated segments of the business of travel. The name "hospitality" conjures up visions of friendliness, and often hotels have excellent records to prove that they are living up to what the word means. But sometimes hospitality is overshadowed by abuse.

Laws, ordinances, and legal codes in many American states and municipalities and some foreign countries cover fire safety and sanitation standards and antidiscrimination in employment and treatment of guests. The degree to which such regulations are enforced, however, varies widely.

Some laws require that current room rates be posted prominently. In most places, however, hotels have virtual freedom to set and change their rates at will and establish their own policies on reservations and overbooking, deposits, mode of payment, and minimum lengths of stay. Furthermore, there are no uniform standards in the United States by which hotels are rated, although some other countries have government-regulated rating systems.

The traveler, therefore, must find out, when arranging a hotel stay, what may lie ahead. Many simply neglect to ask enough questions about where they are going and what their rights and means of recourse will be if, for example, a hotel clerk, when confronted at midnight with a reservation slip guaranteeing that the holder will pay for a room even if it remains vacant all night, shrugs his shoulders and simply insists that nothing is available. Many vacationers let themselves be enticed by advertising that may promise more than can be delivered for the big-print price.

"Ultimately, you get only what you pay for," said John H. Keller, president of Caribbean Holidays of New York, one of the biggest wholesalers (he sells only through travel agents) of hotel space in the Caribbean, Bahamas, and Mexico. "You don't get champagne for beer money."

Melody Lukaszak is a ski buff. She and her husband, Phillip, live in Orland Park, Illinois, a suburb of Chicago, so for their winter vacations they have a choice of two major ski regions that are almost equidistant from their home: the Rockies or New England. A few winters ago they and two friends, Jackie and Paul Dziubek, chose Killington, Vermont, and sent a deposit of $100 a couple to reserve two rooms for the week of February 22 to March 1 at the Grey Bonnet Inn there.

Then, when the two couples canceled their reservations because of poor skiing weather, they ran into a problem that besets many travelers who feel they have been wronged by a hotel and try to get recourse. When they tried to recover their deposit, the hotel refused.

Defaulted deposits are among the many problems that travelers have with hotels. The vast majority of hotel experiences, both in the United States and abroad, probably range from satisfactory to gratifying. I say "probably" because newspapers rarely hear about the happy experiences. But editors' files hold many complaints from people who feel aggrieved because of overbooking that denied them a room, because the facilities were inferior to what they expected, because they got inadequate or incompetent service, because the food was substandard, or because they had disputes over bills.

There are ways to get recourse, but many disputes end in consumer frustration because, in effect, both sides are right: The traveler has indeed been aggrieved, but the hotel has fulfilled its legal obligations.

The problem with the Lukaszaks' ski vacation in Vermont was that it rained instead of snowed and temperatures that February ran up to close to sixty degrees. Mrs. Lukaszak said that on February 20, two days before their arrival time, she and her friends decided to cancel—on the basis of information received from the National Weather Service in Burlington, Vermont.

"Since then," the Lukaszaks and Dziubeks said in a joint letter to *The New York Times,* "we have talked a number of times (long distance) with various managers, and on March 19 with the owner of the Grey Bonnet Inn in an attempt to get our deposit back. We even suggested a compromise of half the deposit. They absolutely refused. They say they can't control the weather; well, neither can we."

In a telephone interview, Russ Latherow, then reservations manager of the Grey Bonnet, did not dispute the two couples' account. He said the inn could not afford to have a no-snow refund policy. "We need three weeks' advance notice to cancel a reservation without loss to the client," he said, "or at least we must be able to resell the room. In any event, we have their deposit on file, and they can use it at a later date if they choose."

Mr. Latherow added: "We guarantee rooms and time but not the weather. Incidentally, Killington was never closed. There was skiing all the time, but granted, it was skiing in the rain."

The couples' letter said ski resorts in the Rockies often had no-snow policies under which at least part of a deposit could be reclaimed. Asked about this, Peggy Grandin, director of public relations for Colorado Ski Country, a trade association, said such policies were not typical. "As a general rule," she said, "most cancellation policies involve at least thirty days' notice."

If the couples had asked before making their reservation, they could have determined the policy of the inn on cancellations. Some hotels volunteer such information, but, because business is business, you cannot expect it. Some states, such as New York, have truth in advertising laws and require that travel contracts, reservations forms, or both spell out conditions and penalties, but experience has shown that many consumers do not read them with care.

Some advertising stretches the truth to the legal limit. Much of it is placed by wholesalers or tour operators with vacation packages to promote, rather than by hotels themselves. Mr. Keller of Caribbean Holidays called it "price-oriented, low-ball advertising that leads people to believe that they will get something that is not warranted." He exhorted first-time visitors to Caribbean or Mexican resorts to determine exactly what they are buying. Is the room oceanfront or part-ocean-view or no view at all? Is there tennis on the premises? How far is it to town? Is there a gambling casino or a discotheque? If the ad or brochure does not provide specific answers, Mr. Keller and other travel professionals advise, ask your travel agent. If your agent does not know, insist that he find out.

Here are a few hotel situations in which problems are common and some suggestions on how to deal with them.

Payment of Deposits—At nonresort hotels, it is usually sufficient to pay for only the first night in advance and sometimes not even for that if you plan to arrive before six P.M. One night's deposit is often advised, however, to guarantee your room regardless of what time you arrive and to ease your own anxiety about getting there by a specific hour. In lieu of a deposit, major hotels and resorts usually accept a charge card number that you provide by phone.

If your reservation at a nonresort hotel is for a week and you decide to stay only a day or two, simply pay what you owe for the time you stayed and leave. You owe nothing more. If you book through a travel agent at such a hotel, you should not have to pay the agent more than one night's deposit.

If you are going on an escorted tour, however, or buying a resort package that stipulates the number of nights you agree to stay, you will probably have to pay the entire bill in advance. If you are required to do this, it is imperative that you understand cancellation policies and penalties and that you expect hotels—as businesses, not dreamboats—to observe them to the letter.

An act of God, such as the absence of snow at a ski resort, may not relieve you of your obligation, and in some cases a hotel can upset your plans drastically but need do little to make good. For example, two months in advance of his family's proposed arrival, Rudolf Maschke, a Long Island publisher, sent a $50 deposit to the Pines, a leading resort in the Catskills. He received a written confirmation. Three days before he was to go, however, the hotel told him by telephone that it had had to cancel his reservation on realizing that it needed the rooms for a detectives' convention. The hotel returned his deposit and said, as it had a right to, that it could do nothing more.

Irving Gevirtz, then reservations manager of the Pines, confirmed in a telephone interview that an error had been made and that the convention had taken over the entire hotel.

Overbooking—In some years, confirming more reservations than there are rooms has been a common practice at many resorts, such as in Hawaii, Mexico, and some Caribbean islands. A lot depends on the economy—whether, for example, a lot of Americans can afford to travel far that year, or whether local economies have been ailing to the point that currency devaluation, such as in Mexico not long ago, has created tremendous bargains for travelers with United States dollars.

When You and Your Hotel Disagree • 331

Although you can book directly at most resort hotels, you are likely to get a lower rate at a major property in the Caribbean or Mexico if you buy a charter package that includes room, airport-hotel transfers, and round-trip air transportation from home, or a wholesaler's package that basically covers room and transfers, sometimes meals, and maybe such extras as a "manager's rum swizzle party."

Your susceptibility to overbooking and other problems is often directly related to the clout the wholesaler has with the hotel and in the travel industry generally. A major hotel is unlikely to willingly irk the major producers of its business.

Therefore, if you are buying a package, question your travel agent about the size, reputation, and stability of the wholesaler and how long the company has been in business. If the package price seems astoundingly low, be especially suspicious. Chances are there is an asterisk by the price and small print below stating that the accommodations are at a minimum-grade hotel, with upgrading available at higher prices. And if the hotel is full of guests who are paying more than the rate negotiated with the cut-rate wholesaler, guess who will be "walked" first if there is overbooking.

According to Mimi Alexander, a major wholesaler of hotel space in Mexico, she sometimes has not become aware of overbooking problems until the night before a group was to leave New York. Sometimes problems arise, she said, because plane schedules are disrupted and a group that is supposed to leave a Mexican resort is still there when another group arrives to take over the rooms.

"One hotel caused us special pain because of deliberate overbooking," Mrs. Alexander said. "It wasn't our fault. I told the hotel I can't stand it anymore. We dropped them completely—canceled the contract—but we're going back to them for the summer." One of Mrs. Alexander's clients, Robert L. Spiewak, a Manhattan clothing manufacturer, wrote to Rodolfo Casparius, director general of El Presidente hotel chain in Mexico, about overbooking at the company's establishment in Cozumel one February. The letter, signed by sixteen travelers, said they had been sent to "substandard accommodations, ranging from second to tenth class."

"I got back a letter of apology," Mr. Spiewak said. "The director accepted blame and offered my wife and myself a free week at any of his hotels."

Disappointment—Suppose, when you reach your hotel, having paid in advance for a week or more, you simply do not like it. The room, facilities, service, food, or whatever is not what you hoped for. What can you do to get out of it? In most cases, you will lose at least what you have paid for the first night plus, if applicable, the first day's meals. You can claim a refund for the balance, but do not expect it in cash from resorts, at least not until you have undergone a long period of well-documented complaining to top management and possibly to trade and governmental authorities as well.

Sometimes, however, the system works faster. One May, Barbara Capobianco of Worcester, Massachusetts, wrote to E. David Brewer, vice president and general manager of the Caneel Bay resort on Saint John, Virgin Islands, that the night after she and her husband arrived at the resort two weeks earlier, they were awakened by a bat in their room. She said her husband captured the bat in a sheet. They were moved to another room, she said, and there they encountered a rat. She added that after a sleepless night, they made arrangements to move to another resort and were claiming a refund of $117 for unused time at the resort.

"Throughout this most unfortunate experience," Mrs. Capobianco wrote, "the quality of service we received from your staff was unacceptable." She detailed treatment that she considered casual, negligent, and otherwise inappropriate.

In a letter of reply, Mr. Brewer sent "profound apologies," and a refund of $558, covering the couple's total bill. "I am sure that you understand," he wrote, "that we do live in a tropical climate and that such vermin as rats and bats are not terribly uncommon to this area. We do admit that from time to time they enter rooms, and we make every effort to correct the situation as quickly as possible.

"It does seem, and I agree with you completely, that we handled your situation most inappropriately. There was absolutely no excuse for the way the staff treated this situation, and you may be assured that this will have my personal attention."

Mrs. Capobianco, reached by telephone, confirmed receipt of Mr. Brewer's letter and the refund.

In a letter to me accompanying a copy of Mr. Brewer's reply, George Bradley Jr., vice president for marketing and sales of Rockresorts Inc., which owns and operates Caneel Bay, said that the problem of vermin is "one that we do experience on occasion due to our environment, unique accommodations, and mode of operation, which is most desirable to our extremely high percent of repeat clientele."

If you are not a repeat customer but visiting a foreign resort for the first time, to get the greatest value for your dollar you probably will have to buy a wholesaler's package and receive his prepaid voucher from your travel agent to present to the resort on arrival. According to a spokesman for Gogo Tours of Paramus, New Jersey, a major wholesaler of accommodations in Mexico and elsewhere, one of three things may happen if you check out after the first night.

The hotel will return your voucher and request that you pay in cash for the night; the hotel will keep the voucher and pay your bill for comparable lodgings in another hotel, which is a frequent way of dealing with overbooking; or the hotel will give you a refund voucher to be presented to your travel agent at home for reimbursement through the wholesaler, which is sometimes a cumbersome process, indeed.

If, to begin with, you have a voucher from a major wholesaler, probably several hotels in the area will accept it, provided they have room. If, in switching, you get a higher-priced room, you will be expected to pay the difference. Major wholesalers usually have representatives at resorts who can make alternate arrangements for you.

In the Caribbean, according to Mr. Keller, your original hotel will usually endorse a voucher over to another establishment, but in Mexico some hoteliers balk. On a charter tour, your options to switch may be limited or nonexistent because the operator may be locked into a hotel contract and may not have other arrangements.

How to Complain—Several trade sources who were questioned agreed that if you have a dispute with a hotel, it is wise to try to settle it on the spot, where you may have the option of simply refusing to pay charges that you feel are unfair. "Try to see the manager eye to eye—that's the best way," said Mr. Kudrle of the hotel association. The trade sources also agreed, however, that sometimes an on-the-spot settlement may not be possible because a responsible official is not available, you have to rush off to catch a plane, or, in some distant places, you are threatened with intervention by the local police, who are unlikely to be on your side.

In such cases, the best advice is to complain, soberly but firmly, with the fullest possible documentation, including names, dates, places, photocopies of vouchers, confirmation slips, and other material, to a variety of places as soon as possible. Complain to your travel agent and the head of the wholesale company, if you have dealt through them. Complain to the managing director of the hotel and, if it is part of a chain, to the president or chairman of the overall company. Complain to appropriate trade associations and, if a foreign country is involved, to the head of its official tourist office in New York.

All this may take time, but some sad vacation tales have had relatively happy endings. When Prof. Ingo Walter of the New York University School of Business Administration felt he was over-charged at the Frankfurt Inter-Continental Hotel in Germany and could not get satisfaction at the hotel, he wrote to Hans Sternik, president of the worldwide Inter-Continental Hotels Corporation. He received a letter of apology and a check for $110.50, the amount he claimed.

60. Complaints and Your Legal Recourse

Late one summer, Sidney Tishler of Baltimore was driving his family home from a New England vacation and decided to spend a night in Cape May, New Jersey. He had read about the Victorian seaside resort and said he thought it sounded "so beautiful."

But the Tishlers' visit did not prove to be beautiful at all; it was nightmarish. In a letter to Robert C. Patterson Jr., then executive vice president of the Cape May County Chamber of Commerce, Mr. Tishler said that with the help of a chamber aide, he had selected a motel that would take him without a reservation. Upon arrival there, he said, the owner demanded $42 cash in advance and was rude to him and his daughters, eight and four years old.

Shortly before midnight, Mr. Tishler said, the owner angrily awakened him, insulted him, and physically threatened him in a dispute over use of an air-conditioner. The owner later apologized, he said, but, "neither my wife nor I could sleep" and "the next morning we were in no condition to go to the beach or to explore the beauties of Cape May."

Mr. Tishler told Mr. Patterson that he did not plan to sue, but that he wanted the Chamber of Commerce to "be made aware of the quality and caliber of service being provided by one of its members to a guest." He said he also hoped that Mr. Patterson "or others who receive copies of this letter can advise me as to what protection or 'rights' a hotel guest has" when the owner-manager behaves in an "irrational" manner.

The six-page letter named the motel and its owner, but for legal reasons the names are not being published here. Copies of the letter were sent to the Mayor and to the police chief of Cape May, the Governor of New Jersey, the Better Business Bureau of South Jersey, the American Hotel and Motel Association, and others. Mr. Patterson was the only one to reply.

In a letter written after I had asked his office about the matter, he told Mr. Tishler that the motel owner "has been warned that we will not make visitor referrals to his motel if his policy and treatment do not improve." When asked in a telephone interview to amplify this, Mr. Patterson said that referrals would continue "unless we get further complaints." He added: "We have no authority to take other action. We have no law enforcement behind us. On the few occasions when we've tried to take action, we've been threatened with lawsuits."

Mr. Tishler's misadventure is only one of hundreds that have been described to me. Many people ask essentially the same questions he did: What are a traveler's rights and what can be done to protect them or to gain restitution when they are violated?

The truth is that laws and regulations in the travel field, such as they are, are stacked much more in favor of the suppliers of travel facilities than the traveler. Much of the field is simply unregulated, notably in the United States. Nonetheless, a large number of travel agencies, tour operators, hotels, and airlines have made a point of responding positively to substantiated complaints and paying refunds promptly. Sometimes, in questionable cases, they even give the consumer the benefit of the doubt. But more often than not, complaints are ignored or the restitution offered is insultingly nominal.

For example, the old Nationwide Leisure Corporation, a charter tour operator that had a meteoric rise and rapid downfall a few years ago, commonly switched hotels on its London tours and provided accommodations that were inferior to those it advertised. To travelers who complained, it offered refunds of $25 in cash or a $50 credit on a future tour. Only under strong legal pressure did it ever do more.

Until recently, aggrieved air travelers had a solid friend in the Civil Aeronautics Board, which maintained field offices around the country that could frequently deal with consumer problems by telephone while they were occurring. The C.A.B. long had substantial clout with the carriers, but under the Airline Deregulation Act of 1978, its power gradually waned. At this writing there was uncertainty about how the Department of Transportation would handle the board's consumer protection role, which it inherited when the C.A.B. went out of business at the end of 1984.

But even with C.A.B. protection, the justifiably aggrieved consumer did not always find justice on his or her side. A traveler once complained that he was booked on a Pan American flight from Los Angeles to New York but that departure was delayed fifteen hours because of mechanical difficulties. He wanted Pan Am to switch him to another airline, but the company refused.

"That's right," a Pan Am spokesman said later. "The traveler had bought his ticket at a promotional fare of $99 a round trip—half the lowest fare of any other air service, scheduled or charter. If we had switched all 101 of the $99 passengers on that flight to another airline, we would have had to pay the difference in fares, at a cost of at least $10,000. As it was, we laid out about $3,000 for hotel rooms, meals, and ground transportation to make the waiting time easier."

The C.A.B. decided that Pan Am had acted properly.

Many consumer protection agencies lack the staff and budget to make more than a superficial investigation of complaints and lack the legal power to take much action. In many states, the greatest strength lies with attorneys general or their equivalent. But they need adequate laws to back them, and they often will not press a charge unless it involves many complainants, such as all the members of an escorted tour.

The American Society of Travel Agents has an intricate procedure for dealing with complaints against any of its 23,000 members, which include agents and 11,000 travel agencies in the United States. But according to H. William Cordes, who recently retired as the society's director of consumer affairs, an aggrieved traveler should get in touch with ASTA's consumer affairs office quickly because as an unresolved complaint ages, the management of a hotel or the ownership of a travel agency may change, and "we end up with egg on our faces."

The society has a board of arbitration for tough cases and can "pink sheet"— publicize to its members—that one of them has erred unapologetically. But Mr. Cordes described this as a "very judicious and careful undertaking," one that seldom happened because "our lawyers were always looking over my shoulder to make sure that we gave due process."

So if a settlement of your complaint cannot be reached easily, the next step may be to sue. In most individual cases the compensation sought is less than $1,000, which usually means going to small claims court. And in many states that can be a frustrating route indeed.

Take New York. At this writing, it costs only $4.55 to take a case to small claims court, and a consumer who can substantiate a complaint can easily get a judgment in his favor. But collecting on that judgment, which is the job of the local sheriff's office, is another matter.

If the consumer can point the sheriff to a defendant's bank account, the sheriff can garnish funds, but such money is often difficult to pinpoint. As an alternative, the sheriff can theoretically auction enough of the offender's business property to cover the judgment plus costs.

To get such action in New York, however, usually costs an advance payment of $300 to the sheriff's office to start an action plus the cost of advertising the sale. And often the defendant can obtain a last-minute stay of execution, which can cost the consumer additional time, frustration, and fees for legal advice on how best to proceed. So the result of all this is that small claims court often brings nothing but a waste of time.

Thomas A. Dickerson, the New York lawyer who specializes in travel law, advises that anyone claiming more than $1,000 hire a lawyer from the start, but this can be costly. Some hope of easing the burden arose, however, with a ruling in 1976 by the New York State Supreme Court. For the first time, an American court permitted what is called an "open class-action" suit in the travel field. The New York court allowed 219 people who had been on the same or similar charter tours to the same resort to be represented collectively in a single suit charging misrepresentation.

The suit, which resulted in the plaintiffs' getting most of their money back, was pulled together by Mr. Dickerson, who was a passenger on one of the tours. Class actions, he feels, can bring legal recourse within the means of the average aggrieved traveler because the costs involved are shared with many others and because the total size of the claims makes expensive litigation feasible.

Many travel complaints involve hotels, and most are from vacationers who bought bargain packages that included round-trip travel by charter jetliner plus seven or eight nights' accommodation. A common complaint is that the hotel was not so good as was depicted in the brochure or that, because of overbooking, the traveler was switched from a convenient, comfortable hotel to a distant, inferior one.

While many package vacations have been acclaimed by travelers, a few large tour operators—the people who assemble all the elements of vacations and market them through travel agents—have been frequent targets of complaint. Many such complaints are ignored; rather, the tour operators devote a vast proportion of their human resources into one field: selling. That's where the money is.

Some pay astronomical telephone bills so that reservations can be received efficiently, at no cost to the caller. Processing those reservations, however, is sometimes slipshod and fraught with error. Tour operators commonly strive to minimize clerical costs. Some seem unwilling to spend much, if anything, on investigating consumer complaints and making restitution, even if the company knows it is at fault. When such operators do make restitution, it rarely comes close to compensating for the anguish of a spoiled vacation.

Tour Complaints

Wilfred Minkin felt aggrieved. One August he took his wife and three children on a fifteen-day escorted bus tour of Europe. As a result of food eaten at a hotel in Geneva, he contended, at least twenty-four of the twenty-nine passengers on the tour became violently ill and "our two days in Paris were ruined." For nearly eight months, he sought a refund for this lost portion of the vacation, but he was unable to get anyone to assume responsibility.

His case is illustrative of hundreds of complaints that are lodged each year against the companies that package and operate tours. Actually, the number of travelers who complain is small in comparison with the large number who take tours and are apparently satisfied. The record of most major tour operators is good, considering the complexities of putting together packages, which require dealing with dozens of suppliers.

Airlines, hotels, long-distance coach operators, bus and jitney services that move groups to and from airports, sightseeing companies, restaurants, producers of entertainment—they are only some of the independent parties whose services may be components of a package tour. The tour operator is the middleman who brings these services together in packages that he hopes will make him a profit.

In dealing with so many components in so many places, however, something often goes wrong. Tour operators contend that an educated traveler will be realistic about this and focus on everything that goes right.

Many consumer complaints, when examined closely, are obviously unreasonable—the work of "sharpshooters," as the tour operator Arthur Frommer calls them. But there are sharpshooters among the tour operators as well, and too many operators shield themselves behind legal technicalities or offer token compensation that only aggravates the traveler's feeling of grievance. Indeed, the operators are so shielded that it can be difficult if not impossible to get substantial compensation from them, even if one takes them to court.

The complaint of Dr. Minkin, a dermatologist in White Plains, New York, was supported by letters from several of his fellow passengers who insisted that they, too, became ill under the same circumstances. One passenger, an Illinois businessman, wrote that his family had to get medical treatment in Paris that cost $200. The businessman's son, a fourth-year medical student, who also became ill after the Geneva meal, was told by the doctor that the food poisoning was from bad meat.

The complaints of Dr. Minkin and the others were directed primarily at a Swiss company that operated their tour. Copies of much of the correspondence were sent to *The New York Times*. I named the company when I first wrote about the case, but because of organizational changes since then, its response might have been different today. Therefore, the name is being withheld.

The company wrote to the hotel in Geneva, which rejected any possibility that it might have served tainted food. Just after Christmas, Dr. Minkin received a letter from an American insurance company of which the tour operator was a client. "Since the hotel involved is owned and operated by an independent contractor," the insurance company wrote, "it is our opinion there is no legal liability on the part of our insured. We must decline all claims directly or indirectly related to this incident."

In the opinion of the tour operator, that just about ended the matter. The head of its office in the United States acknowledged in a telephone interview that there was "some evidence" that "somebody was ill and had been treated locally from outside." "We are in the tour business," he said, "and we can't have unhappy people. But from the standpoint of the company, I feel I need further substantiation. Not everybody got sick. Of those who did, did they get it from the meal? Did they eat someplace else? Where did they get sick? Show me somehow that maybe this came from the meal."

Even if it could be proved that the travelers became ill from food at the Geneva hotel, the tour operator would have no legal responsibility, although its United States representative indicated that he might do something for good will.

"The travelers could sue the hotel," another spokesman for the tour operator said, "but presumably that would have to be in a Swiss court, which would not be very practical."

It is difficult to say whether the Swiss company's position typifies that of major tour operators. When asked what they might do in such a situation, the heads of several other companies indicated that they might offer good-will refunds, but there seemed to be a reluctance to assume responsibility or to pay substantial amounts as compensation.

"The degree of a good-will refund varies," said Alexander W. Harris, then president of General Tours of New York, which specializes in travel to Eastern Europe, the Soviet Union, Egypt, Israel, East Africa, and China. "It depends on how much the person paid for the entire tour. Many people don't realize that the major portion of the total cost is for transportation, not land arrangements, and they get the transportation whether they are sick or not."

Mr. Harris and the others who were questioned are members of the United States Tour Operators Association, which lays down codes of conduct and ethics for the trade and requires proof of financial responsibility. In its "principles of professional conduct and ethics," the association pledges, among other things, that representations by its members to the public "shall be truthful, explicit, intelligible, and avoid deception."

In a paper presented to the Civil Aeronautics Board a few years ago, the association said that "it is accepted that the consumer should be entitled to an appropriate refund in cases in which the tour operator has breached the terms of agreement." "The tour operator responsibility," the paper said, "should be in accordance with applicable contractual law."

A typical clause in tour contracts states, however, something like this: "The participant (consumer) waives any claim against the tour operator for any damage to or loss of property, or injury, or death of, persons, due to any act of negligence of any airline, hotel, or any other person rendering any of the services of accommodations included in the ground portion of the itinerary."

Moreover, the courts have never firmly decided whose agent the operators are, according to leading tour operators. "Do we represent the customer or the airline or steamship company or hotel that appoints us to sell space?" one asked. "We are caught between the customer and the supplier, and with the best of intentions, there are certain circumstances that arise that are beyond our control."

In discussing the handling of consumer complaints, tour operators speak of the value of repeat business and especially of their need to satisfy the travel agents who retail their packages. "If we do not respond to a justifiable complaint," Mr. Frommer said, "it's not simply that we lose the business of the passenger, we lose the business of the travel agent, and that can mean hundreds of passengers a year."

However, when they try to satisfy complaints, the tour operators sometimes find that they do not have much influence with suppliers of travel services. For example, hotels, even those linked to some of the world's biggest chains, frequently overbook to compensate for the anticipated last-minute cancellations or no-shows. If such a hotel is in a popular resort where space is tight in high season, a tour operator who wants to be sure his reservations will be honored may hesitate to complain loudly to the management on behalf of an aggrieved traveler.

All the tour operators who were questioned expressed the belief that many travelers are unrealistic in their expectations. "Passenger expectations are high," one leading operator said. "That's why people take vacations. They need an uplift in spirit and body. There is an implication of something heavenly, but travel is not like that. Travel is normal living. Many people wrongly assume that a vacation will remove all the frustrations of daily living."

342 • On the Road

One way to make sure your expectations are realistic is to read the tour brochures carefully, especially the small print in the back. Some tour operators readily acknowledge that the main object of brochures is to lure, not repel, but they stress that in literature of association members, the small print in the back states explicitly what the tour includes and what responsibility, if any, the operators will assume if something goes wrong.

If you conclude from all this that tour operators are hard-nosed businessmen, you are correct. Even big operators could be wiped out if they had to pay big refunds to all the members of a large tour group. Therefore, their interpretation of what constitutes a legitimate grievance may be far different from yours.

There is no way you can assure yourself of a trouble-free tour, but here are some suggestions that may help you avoid problems:

- Before you go, check out the tour operator as thoroughly as you can. Is he a member of the U.S.T.O.A.? What does your travel agent say about him? Does the Better Business Bureau, the American Society of Travel Agents, or your local consumer affairs office know of complaints against him?
- Study the brochure carefully and do as much homework as you can about your destination. What meals are promised? What type of accommodations? Do not expect hotels in the interior of developing countries to be as well run as deluxe establishments in Paris or New York.
- Find out what protection, if any, is offered against changes of hotel or itinerary. What penalties must you pay for last-minute cancellation or if illness forces you to leave the tour and return home? What insurance is available to cover penalties and additional costs?
- Know your own limitations. If the tour obviously involves a lot of walking but you tire easily, think twice before you sign that contract.

Do not hesitate to complain if you believe you have been treated unfairly. Be prepared, however, to document your complaint as fully and authoritatively as possible. Let established facts, not impassioned language, plead your case for you.

If, in your opinion, you are denied satisfaction, complain to the United States Tour Operators Association, which has offices at Suite 4-B, 211 East 51st Street, New York, New York 10022; phone

(212) 944-5727. If the tour operator is not a member of the association, get in touch with the American Society of Travel Agents, 4400 MacArthur Boulevard N.W., Washington, D.C. 20007; (202) 965-7520. You also might try your local consumer protection office or your state attorney general.

Such steps may result in satisfaction if the intervening agency is persuaded that your claim is justified. But you might decide ultimately that your only recourse is to go to court. Your lawyer is the best person to consult on the advisability of a suit. Be aware, however, that if a large amount of money is involved and many travelers besides yourself are lodging similar claims, the tour operator will almost surely fight the suit. That could make suing costly for all of you, although class-action litigation may be possible.

61. Traveler's Aid

Though not so visible as they once were, Traveler's Aid Societies throughout the United States continue to provide services for thousands of travelers each year. They help cope with all sorts of crises, some of them almost endemic because of the nature of travel today.

"One of our biggest problems is with people who expect to arrive at one airport but actually land at another," said Ann Ingram, director of volunteer services for Traveler's Aid in Washington. "We have three airports in the Washington area. Often when a traveler buys his ticket, he neglects to ask which airport he will land at, and the agent doesn't volunteer the information. So he arrives and suddenly becomes aware that the person who was supposed to meet him has gone somewhere else. Then he comes to us for help."

"We telephone around," Mrs. Ingram said, "and try to get the meeter and meetee together. But we don't step out of the case until we are sure they both understand clearly where they will finally get together. We have had the experience of each one hurrying to the other airport and unknowingly passing each other on the road."

Pauline Dunn, head of Traveler's Aid in Washington, says the confusion can even be worse. "We've had people show up at Dulles who want to be in Dallas, Texas," she said. "Sometimes their tickets were written wrong or somehow they got on the wrong plane or got off at the wrong place."

As explained by Traveler's Aid executives in a check of half a dozen societies, the main accent is on helping people to help themselves. "We provide whatever is necessary and appropriate while we are helping the person solve whatever problem he faces," said Vincent DeSanti, former director of professional services for the society in New York.

Essentially, each of the country's seventy-odd Traveler's Aid Societies is independent and responsible for its own finances, although often with United Way help. Much of the work is done by volunteers. National standards are set and activities are coordinated from the Des Plaines, Illinois, headquarters of the Traveler's Aid Association of America.

The network was spawned in Saint Louis in 1851, according to Richard Gelula, national program director. The money came from the estate of Mayor Bryan Mullenphy, who, while sitting in a bar, wrote his will on a napkin, bequeathing about $1 million to help the needy.

Today some societies have fatter budgets and more workers than others. Therefore, the degree of help they can give varies substantially.

In Manhattan, for example, the society no longer has counselors at railroad stations or the Port Authority bus terminal, but it does have a staff in the International Arrivals Building at Kennedy International Airport and at society headquarters, 204 East 39th Street. It serves about thirty thousand people a year.

Actually, Traveler's Aid is involved in much more these days than helping vacation or business travelers. Many of its clients are runaway minors, the mentally deranged, or jobless drifters—"the center-city fallout from the mass mobility of our society," as Mr. Gelula puts it. Also, the network has been heavily involved in the resettlement of Indochinese refugees.

But in many places it is still able to help travelers handle an unexpected and temporary crisis, although often only if the crisis erupts during normal business hours—between nine A.M. and five P.M. Monday through Friday and never on holidays. Some societies have twenty-four-hour telephone answering services with social workers on call, but in many cities about the only place a person can turn for guidance and help at off hours is the police.

A basic assumption is that most travelers in trouble have human or financial resources at home or at their destination to help solve a crisis, but it may take hours or even days to tap these resources. "The problem is," Mr. Gelula said, "that when the emergency happens—a lost ticket or a stolen wallet—some people lose the ability to decide what to do next in a rational way."

"Sometimes the ego that keeps us going just falls apart," said Harriet Ament, who heads the Traveler's Aid office at O'Hare International Airport just outside Chicago. "Our first job is to provide tender loving care—to show travelers in trouble that there are people who care, and to get them to think straight again."

Mrs. Ament tells of once having helped "an exceedingly well-dressed, young attractive bride who was also hysterical." She was supposed to fly to New York to meet her husband and be introduced to her in-laws for the first time, and she was somewhat distraught to begin with.

"She parked her car at the airport," Mrs. Ament said, "took her suitcase from the trunk and then locked the trunk with her purse inside. It had her keys, her ticket, everything. She missed her plane and came to us in panic. We talked awhile, and finally she agreed that it was not the end of the world.

"Then we tried to reach her in-laws, but we failed because they had already left home to meet her. Finally we got an airline to contact her husband at the airport in New York, and he paid for a replacement ticket for her. We got her on the first possible flight and made sure that her relatives knew exactly when it would arrive."

In the opinion of Wynn Kenton, a former New Yorker who was once a volunteer counselor for Traveler's Aid at West Palm Beach Airport, many people who land at unfamiliar airports are disoriented to some extent. "They can't find the baggage-claim area," he said, "even though there are signs. They don't know how to shop around by phone for car rentals or to arrange for an off-airport rental agency to pick them up. They come to us with everyday, mundane questions. You'd be surprised at the number of people who get panicky."

The strength of Traveler's Aid lies largely in counseling—in calmly discussing the emergency and exploring possible solutions. A thick directory published by the national association gives details on social service organizations—not just Traveler's Aid Societies—in the United States, Puerto Rico, Canada, and Australia that can help. In many countries, Traveler's Aid can call on branches of International Social Service, a Geneva-based organization, which works with local governments, voluntary agencies, and American consulates.

The material aid that Traveler's Aid can give depends largely on local policy and resources. Often it goes little beyond making a long-distance phone call, at the society's expense, to a social service agency that can ask a friend or relative to send money or other help. Some societies, however, will advance money for a night's modest lodging or a couple of meals.

"We expect you to repay us if you can," said Mr. DeSanti, "but we don't have a collection agency to send after you to pick it up."

"We can't lend someone a hundred dollars," said Mrs. Ament, "but if your wallet is lost or stolen and you need five dollars to get to town, we might be able to help."

"Sometimes we would be willing to take a chance where a bank would not," Mr. Gelula said, "and cash a personal check. Obviously, though, you would have to have good credentials. We might cash a check for twenty-five dollars just to get you through the day."

"But I don't know if I'd want to advertise that to the public," he added, "because we could be besieged. But banks are not very responsive to that sort of situation."

Traveler's Aid will also arrange to meet children who are traveling alone. Many offices have teletypewriters that the deaf can use to get in touch with their homes or deaf friends, as many people with impaired hearing have teletypewriters instead of telephones in their homes. Once the Traveler's Aid office at Logan International Airport in Boston, without advance notice, arranged a five-hour tour of the city for a group of sixteen travelers who were blind.

What you should know if you ever face a crisis while traveling in the United States is that, at the least, Traveler's Aid can probably steer you in the right direction, but you may have difficulty finding a society office or booth. According to Mr. Gelula, only thirty-five or so airports, thirty-five or so bus stations and two railroad stations—Chicago's Union Station and Washington's Union Station—have them, and they are often tucked away from the mainstream of traffic.

The societies do not pay rent, and airports and stations are reluctant to give away prime commercial space. Many airlines, however, are putting in a pitch for Traveler's Aid because the societies deal with many problems that otherwise might be thrust upon clerks at check-in counters. Many carriers, hard hit by lean years and rising costs, have laid off many service employees.

At some major bus stations where there is no Traveler's Aid booth there are signs directing travelers to the nearest office. If there is no sign, travelers should check the local telephone directory under "Traveler's Aid" and pray that someone will be available. If not, they should try the police.

If you are in trouble at a major railroad station, go to the stationmaster's office or ask if there is a passenger service manager around. According to an Amtrak spokesman, passenger service managers, who are said to be trained to deal with personal crises, are stationed in Albany, Boston, Chicago, Detroit, Los Angeles, Miami, New Orleans, New York, Oakland, Philadelphia, Saint Louis, Seattle, and Washington.

Why has there been no Traveler's Aid office at Penn Station in New York, where society officials have felt one could be exceptionally useful? Said the Amtrak spokesman: "Our real-estate department is under pressure to utilize space for maximum revenue. We get Federal aid, and we have to justify every penny we spend. To rent space to a restaurant or to off-track betting would be preferable."

62. American Consulates

This section was written by Margot Slade, assistant editor of The Living Section of The New York Times.

Contrary to what seems to be popular opinion, American embassies and consulates are not travel agencies, law offices, Red Cross stations, banks, or hostels for the weary of foot and empty of pocket. Their staffs will not change hotel reservations, post bail, tend the sick, lend money, or provide sleeping bags to ease the discomfort of sleeping on their foyer floors. "American travelers' expectations of what consuls can do can be extraordinarily high," said John P. Caulfield, a consular officer who recently completed an assignment as press officer for the State Department's Bureau of Consular Affairs.

"People must recognize we have limited resources and must concentrate on travelers who need the most assistance," said Dena K. Cowdy, supervisor of the special consular services unit at the United States Embassy in London. "Americans abroad," Mrs. Cowdy said, "must understand that certain things just aren't our province. Uncle Sam, for example, won't finesse a change of charter flight tickets for people who want to extend their London stay."

This is not to say American consulates are worthless to travelers in trouble. Whether you've been mugged in Madrid or lost your passport in Paris, consular officials can reduce a devastating experience to manageable proportions. They can offer comfort—an undervalued currency—and guidance on putting your vacation back together.

A day at any consulate includes a grab bag of problems to be solved. In London, Mrs. Cowdy said, one request came from a young man who had run out of money and wanted the embassy to help him sell a kidney; the embassy, he was told, could not facilitate an organ transplant but could help with a money transfer from the United States.

More common, Mrs. Cowdy said, are the older people who get lost. As Mrs. Cowdy explained: "They arrive in London from a long flight, take a nap and then a walk. The next thing they know, they can't remember where the hotel is or its name." If they're lucky, consular officials can help them recall the location of their hotel. Where luck runs out, Mrs. Cowdy said, a traveling companion or tour leader "usually has enough sense to call us and report the person missing or to call the police, who contact us."

For most consular officers, troubled Americans come with one of several problems: lost passports, stolen wallets, no money, illness or injury, natural disasters, and running afoul of the law.

Americans expect more help than they get with legal problems abroad. When you travel outside the United States, you are subject to the legal system of the host country; if you break a law in a foreign country, there is little your government's representatives can do. They cannot serve as attorneys or give legal advice; they cannot get you out of jail. They can get you legal counsel. According to Mr. Caulfield, embassies in most capital cities and consulates in many major cities maintain lists of local attorneys and can put you in touch with one of them.

Most foreign governments notify American officials if you are arrested. Someone from the embassy or consulate will visit you in jail, advise you of your rights under local law, and contact friends or family if you wish. They can try to transfer money, food, and clothing from family members to you to ease incarceration. They can try to get relief if you are held under inhumane conditions or are singled out for punishment. But that's about it. As one consular officer put it: "Don't expect white knights who will rescue prisoners from the castle keep."

Amid natural disasters or civil disturbances, consulates function primarily as information centers. "They say what the situation is and advise the best course of action," Mr. Caulfield said. "The rest is up to you." In a flooded Florence, for example, they can tell stranded Americans where the nearest disaster relief area is or what arrangements are available for leaving the city. "Americans who called the embassy in Sri Lanka during the unrest were told the airport was closed and to stay put," Mr. Caulfield said of trouble there in 1983. "Meanwhile, the embassy talked to the airlines and tried to book Americans on the first flights out once the airport was operating."

Being sick is no fun. Being sick in a foreign country can be frightening. Consular officers can help. They maintain lists of doctors, including their specialties and English-language competency, most of whom have been interviewed, all of whom are considered reputable. The consul will also inform family or friends of your condition. For the seriously ill and elderly, transportation back to the United States, with an escort, might be arranged. The costs, however, would be borne by the traveler or the family.

Wealthy Americans are what some foreign countries expect; destitute Americans are what consulates frequently see. In theory, the best they can do is facilitate money transfers; in an emergency, this is generally done through State Department transfers in which someone at home deposits money with the State Department, which notifies the consulate, which is then free to give money to you. You are allowed a collect telephone call to whoever can send the necessary money.

In practice, many consular officials go beyond the call of duty. Mr. Caulfield, for example, recalled persuading a local hotelier to carry an impoverished American for the night. Then there was the young man who insisted he had no place to stay and no money. Mr Caulfield did not believe the tale, "but I couldn't leave him there." The solution? Directions to a Salvation Army center.

"Oh, no! My wallet's gone." And with it maybe passport, credit cards, traveler's checks, and currency. Some 8,400 American passports were reported missing in 1982. Every day brings reports of Americans whose vacation balloons went bust when their pockets were picked or their hotel rooms rifled.

In such cases, American consular officials are the facilitators of first resort. They can tell you where to get traveler's check refunds and replacement credit cards and may often call ahead to let those offices know you are coming. If the victims are elderly or genuinely helpless, consular officers may negotiate for them. Again, they will let you place collect calls to someone in the United States who can report cards lost or stolen for you.

People who can prove they are American citizens and who have lost their passports should have no trouble getting new ones within a few hours, and an emergency usually speeds the process. More often, Mr. Caulfield said, "consuls may need more time to satisfy themselves that you are who you say you are."

Consulates are closed at night and on national holidays—American national holidays, too. However, troubled travelers can always leave messages for the duty officer, who, the State Department says, will get back to you. As with any government agency, however, the quality of help you receive depends on the ability of the person giving it; as Mr. Caulfield noted, for every letter of complaint sent to the Bureau of Consular Affairs, there is a letter of praise.

His advice: Take preventive action. For example, keep records of all credit card and passport numbers and the numbers to call if they are lost or stolen. Do not let one member of the party carry everything, and do not have all the traveler's checks in one person's name.

There is more you can do for yourself, so your government need do less. For advice write for the free booklet *Your Trip Abroad* by sending a postcard with your name and address to the Bureau of Consular Affairs, Room 6811, Department of State, Washington, D.C. 20520.

What They Will Do

Much of what an American consul can and cannot do for American citizens abroad is governed by United States and foreign laws. For example, consuls can and will do these things:

- Issue a replacement passport for one lost or stolen. Under recently simplified regulations, the replacement is normally valid for ten years—the same as the missing one. If you cannot pay the $42 fee—$35 for the passport and $7 for preparing it—it is issued free but is limited in duration to completion of your trip. If you cannot adequately establish your identity and United States citizenship, the consular office will, at its expense, cable or telex the State Department for instructions.
- Assist in finding appropriate medical services, including English-speaking physicians, in case of injury or illness, and help inform relatives or friends about your plight and ask them for guidance or money.
- Help a destitute American get in touch with relatives,

friends, bankers, or employers and advise on the best way to transmit emergency money. The consular office can also advise on how to inform the local police about stolen money or inform the issuing authority about missing traveler's checks.

- Provide notary services.
- Assist in casting absentee ballots in elections at home.
- Help locate missing Americans.
- Help traveling Americans during local civil unrest or in natural disasters.
- Provide restricted aid in a dispute that could lead to legal or police action. A consular officer can provide a list of reputable local lawyers, assist in obtaining adequate legal representation, and try to prevent discrimination under local law.
- If an American is arrested, visit him in detention, notify relatives or friends, provide a list of lawyers, and try to obtain relief if conditions are inhumane or unhealthy. Also, under new legislation, consular officers can pay for, usually with reimbursement later, emergency medical care for American prisoners and provide them food and supplementary diet items.

Through passport offices in the United States, the State Department also warns prospective travelers about contagious diseases, visa problems, currency requirements, and hotel shortages in countries they may plan to visit.

What They Won't Do

Consuls cannot do these things:
- Give or lend money or guarantee or cash personal checks.
- Provide direct legal representation or advice.
- Do the work of travel agencies, information bureaus, or banks, search for missing luggage, settle disputes with hotel managers, or help get work permits or find jobs.
- Act as couriers or, in general, as interpreters.
- Provide bail or get you out of jail.
- Arrange for free medical or legal service.

"Especially during the tourist season," a State Department leaflet warns, "consuls are likely to be working under heavy pressure and must give priority to cases of grave emergency or distress."

For this reason, department officials suggest that a traveler take a few simple precautions, such as carrying a little extra money, preferably in traveler's checks, to cover unexpected emergencies, leaving a copy of the itinerary with a relative or friend, carrying an identification card for any health insurance coverage that embraces foreign travel, and becoming familiar with local customs and laws, especially those governing currency and drugs.

Travelers are strongly advised to avoid areas of unrest or disturbance. If they plan a long stay in a foreign country, they are urged to register with the nearest consular office so they can be reached quickly in an emergency. If arrested, they are urged promptly to ask permission to notify the nearest American consular officer and to persist if turned down.

The Bureau of Consular Affairs at the State Department in Washington maintains a Citizens Emergency Center, phone (202) 632-5225. It can be useful for relatives or close friends of travelers for these reasons:

- To ask questions about arrested Americans and how to get money to them.
- To transmit money to destitute Americans abroad when commercial banking facilities are unavailable and to arrange medical evacuation.
- To find missing Americans about whom there is special concern or to transmit emergency messages.
- For help when an American dies abroad.
- For civil judicial inquiries and assistance.

At night and over weekends in bona fide emergencies, phone (202) 632-1512 if you cannot get adequate help from the emergency center.

63. Speeding Through Customs

This section was written by Margot Slade, assistant editor of The Living Section of The New York Times.

Europe was great. The plane trip was fine; even the in-flight movie was one you hadn't seen and rather enjoyed. Now comes customs.

Customs—the word conjures up images of world-weary travelers returning in the dead of night only to stand in line for hours having their baggage inspected—some would say ransacked—down to the toothbrush they bought in Paris when their own American-made bristles went astray. It is an experience travelers do not relish and pray fervently, though hopelessly, to avoid.

Not so hopelessly, it seems.

"Much as we like people coming through Kennedy, we want to move them out as quickly as possible," said Anthony M. Liberta, the area director of customs at Kennedy International Airport in New York.

"We want to get the honest travelers on their way," said Larry K. Shirk, former program manager for passenger enforcement and facilitation at the United States Customs Service in Washington.

Music to an honest traveler's ears. In airports throughout the United States, customs agents are changing the way they work to ease the passenger's entry into the country while stopping contraband at the door. The final returns are not yet in, but airline operators, passengers, and customs agents suggest the processing has been speeded at least 55 percent in recent years.

In a nutshell, the procedural changes under the new system are limited to combinations of and variations on these features: "citizens bypass," which separates those with American passports from those without; "red-green lanes," which separate people with something to declare who declare it from those with nothing to declare or who do not declare it; and a giant one-stop screening process after claiming baggage.

According to Mr. Liberta, the system not only moves passengers through customs faster but is also far more successful in terms of enforcement. He reports tremendous increases in seizures of narcotics, other contraband merchandise, and currency since 1982. Red-green lanes have now been instituted at most major international airports in the United States.

According to Mr. Liberta, approximately 50 percent of passengers coming through Kennedy Airport on international flights hold American passports. Citizens bypass, he said, "means that fifty percent won't be interviewed twice—once by immigration, once by customs."

Kennedy Airport, with more than seven million overseas arrivals a year—more than any other airport in the nation—pairs the bypass system with red-green lanes. Mr. Shirk describes this as a kind of self-selection process similar to "choosing the express line—eight items or less—at the check-out counter in a supermarket."

Red-green lanes were introduced experimentally at Kennedy in March 1983. Three months later, the system went into effect permanently at the airport's International Arrivals Building and at its overseas terminals for British Airways, American Airlines, Pan American World Airways, and Trans World Airlines.

At Kennedy, the system works like this: Most airline passengers must choose between two types of designated lanes: red for those with items to be declared and green for those with nothing to declare. While there are signs describing what is and is not declarable, in the hubbub of arrivals it helps to know beforehand. The booklet *Know Before You Go* provides this and other information. It is available free by telephoning (212) 466-5550 or writing the United States Customs Service, Public Information, Room 201, 6 World Trade Center, New York, New York 10048.

Arriving at the customs area, you head for a red lane if you were on a farm while abroad and have agricultural products; if you have more than $5,000 in currency or monetary instruments; if your purchases abroad totaled $400 or more; if you are a visitor to the United States and are bringing gifts valued at $100 or more; or if you are carrying more than a liter of alcoholic beverages (a little over a quart). In the red lane, you will be interviewed by customs inspectors, who will decide whether and to what extent they will examine you further.

If you don't fall into one of the above categories, march over to a green lane. Expect customs inspectors to interview you, but you will be dealt with as a traveler who is probably innocent of wrongdoing and deserves to leave the building with all due haste.

Other factors, usually in the form of "roving inspectors," can intervene. At Kennedy Airport, Mr. Liberta said, "the rovers are the key to the system and its success." The job of high-risk rovers is to spot people who might be carrying contraband and to intercept them. Low-risk rovers focus on the majority of travelers. They may interview you at the baggage carousel or pull you out of line at a green lane, ask you a few questions, and sign you out there and then. Members of the Customs Service's so-called contraband enforcement team are rovers out of uniform who mingle with airline passengers and size them up, considering whether or not they may be smugglers.

At peak summer periods, as many as three thousand passengers pass through Kennedy's International Arrivals Building in an hour. "That's about the maximum we can handle," Mr. Liberta said. In the past, customs authorities report, bottlenecks often formed when high-risk flights, which had taken off from countries suspected of being the source of contraband or agricultural products, were followed by low-risk flights. In such cases, a host of probably innocent passengers found themselves trapped behind the more suspect earlier arrivals.

Under the new procedures, officials maintain, this can no longer happen; passengers simply head for their prescribed area. A one-stop screening process before claiming baggage quickly became the pride of Los Angeles airport, and elsewhere it has been coupled with red-green lanes. The one-stop procedure provides for all passengers to enter a primary inspection line staffed by inspectors who are trained to screen for the Immigration Service, the Customs Service, and the Agriculture Department. Inspectors review each passenger's declaration statement and ask a few questions; they may examine carry-on baggage.

Passengers not requiring secondary screenings can pick up their checked baggage and leave. Their less fortunate compatriots—often people who fit a certain passenger profile, whose origin of flight raises eyebrows, or who were singled out in a random sampling—must pick up their baggage and go to a secondary inspection area for what Mr. Shirk termed a "more extensive workup."

"We never got a lot of complaints to start with, at least not as many as most people think," Mr. Liberta said. "But I've been in customs since 1971, and, certainly at Kennedy Airport, I've never seen everyone—passengers, inspectors, supervisory personnel—so pleased."

What Is Permitted and Banned

This section was written by Stanley Carr, an assistant editor of the Travel section of The New York Times.

On the last day of her vacation in Paris, Anita Evers splurged on a can of pâté de foie gras, which she planned to serve to friends in her Maryland home. But as she was going through customs at Washington's Dulles International Airport, the pâté was discovered in her suitcase by a customs agent and confiscated. Mrs. Evers did not see herself as a smuggler. In fact, she saw no reason why canned goose liver should not be allowed into the United States because she had been snacking on similar pâté in France and had come to no harm.

What she did not know was that most pâtés are made with a tiny amount of pork, even though this may not be mentioned on the label, and that because swine fever is reported from time to time in France, travelers are not allowed to bring pâté into this country. It could spread the disease to animals in the United States.

The problem has become so severe that travelers now face fines of up to $1000 instead of simple confiscation.

Bert Hawkins, head of the Animal and Plant Health Inspection Service of the Department of Agriculture, told Irvin Molotsky of *The New York Times*: "Heretofore, we just had the authority to slap wrists and confiscate the material being brought in. It did not seem to be a deterrent. They try to slip it past us, and we know that some gets by. We are serious about this and we will impose penalties."

The maximum penalty can be imposed by a Department of Agriculture administrative law judge under a new procedure. At this writing, the full impact of the procedure is still to be felt, but in the first six months the new system was in effect, 8,545 fines were collected. The program was in effect at all international ports of entry in the United States.

Travelers with a taste for foreign delicacies can save themselves disappointment—and money—by arming themselves before they go overseas with free booklets available from the United States Department of Agriculture and the Customs Service. The booklets provide a wealth of information not only on what you may or may not bring into the country but also on such topics as the danger of buying counterfeit goods overseas and mailing gifts home. First, though, just how much can you bring back?

Allowances—A returning resident may bring in, free of duty, $400 worth of goods bought abroad. Residents returning from a United States insular possession, such as the United States Virgin Islands or Guam, may bring in $800 worth. Residents of the United States who exceed the exemptions are charged 10 percent on the next $1,000 and 5 percent on purchases made in an insular possession. Anything above the $1,000 ceiling is charged at the regular duty rate, which varies from 2 percent to as much as 50 percent if the goods were acquired in a Communist country.

Food and Plants—The task of the agricultural representatives at each customs station is to keep out foreign pests and diseases that might affect American soil, plants, or animals. In this quest for a healthy America they daily seize salamis from Italy, knockwurst from Germany, pork pies from Britain, luscious-looking fruits from South America, whole coconuts from anywhere, and sometimes leis from Hawaii, usually leaving annoyed and bewildered passengers in their wake.

The possibility of a can of pâté being responsible for infecting a farm with swine fever might seem remote, but Jack Mahancy, a staff officer at the Department of Agriculture in Washington, explained: "Suppose the pâté ended up on the supper table at a farmer's home. Some scraps might be emptied into the pigs' food or accidentally dropped near their pen. If the pâté was infected, the disease could spread instantly among the farm animals. These are the sort of risks we have to guard against."

Secretary of State George P. Shultz was criticized for bringing home some sausage from Ireland, but Ireland is the one country from which you can bring meat because it is regarded as free from the livestock diseases the United States wants to keep out.

While meat products are the agricultural items most often confiscated, plants, fruits, and vegetables run a close second. Some travelers, often for sentimental reasons, try to carry home growing plants from other countries, and a few even try to bring in bags of soil in their suitcases. Fresh-cut flowers and most dried foliage are allowed, but many berries, bulbs, and seeds are not. You can bring in shells unless they contain escargots; dried spices are permissible; soup mixes with meat may not be.

Bonnie Aikman, an Agriculture Department representative, said, "Even well-traveled people think you can bring in any canned product, but they are wrong. It has to be hermetically sealed, shelf-stable without refrigeration, and it has to say so on the label."

You can bring home breads, cakes, cookies, and cured cheese, such as cheddar, Stilton, Brie, and Roquefort, but cottage cheese and similar cheeses are not to be admitted. Miss Aikman said: "Feta probably is not going to be allowed in. If it looks suspect, we have to take it."

To clear up any confusion and to avoid possible embarrassment, officials suggested that tourists write for the pamphlet *Travelers' Tips*, which is published in English, Spanish, Japanese, and Italian. It is free and may be obtained by writing to the Department of Agriculture, Animal and Plant Health Inspection Service, 732 Federal Building, 6505 Belcrest Road, Hyattsville, Maryland 20782.

Carrying Currency—It is legal to bring in any amount of United States or foreign currency, but a declaration of the amount must be made if it is the equivalent of more than $5,000. Travelers leaving this country with $5,000 or more in currency should also declare it—to the airline or shipping firm.

Counterfeit Products—To protect the trademarks of foreign companies registered in this country, customs agents have the right to confiscate property they believe to be unauthorized copies. With the worldwide growth in counterfeit merchandise, from jeans to handbags to fragrances, travelers should be on their guard when shopping overseas. If the "Vuitton" suitcase you buy turns out to be a fake, a customs official can impound it—and you could end up carrying home your belongings in a plastic sack. If you are wearing fake Gucci loafers, you could find yourself walking barefoot.

When a company registers a trademark in the United States, it also specifies how many or what value of its products a person can import at one time. The Customs Service's *Trademark Information for Travelers* brochure points out that importing such fragrances as Shalimar, Mitsouko, and Chanel No. 5 is limited to one bottle of perfume and one of each toilet preparation per person. Is this enforced? Strictly speaking, yes, but following the letter of the law sometimes depends on the port of entry and the products customs agents concentrate on at a particular moment. There is no restriction on Yves Saint Laurent and many other fragrances. Items such as cameras and silverware also have trademark import restrictions.

Liquor Limitations—Although the Federal Government allows residents to bring home one liter (just over a quart) of spirits duty-free and any amount as long as they pay duty on the rest, individual states can impose their own laws, so your point of entry can affect your liquor allowance. For example, on entering at Kennedy International Airport in New York State, the traveler can bring in one quart without paying duty, but twenty-five miles away at Newark International Airport in New Jersey, the traveler may bring in no more than two quarts every twenty-four hours. Passengers entering the country in Miami are allowed only one gallon at a time; in Chicago the limit is one gallon a year. *State Laws on Importing Alcoholic Beverages*, available from the Customs Service, lists all the allowances.

Mailing Gifts—A gift valued at up to $50 and sent to a friend from overseas is not included in a traveler's duty-free allowance. The limit is $100 from insular possessions. Customs duty is charged, however, if you have a store mail a purchase to you, whatever its value. You pay the duty when you collect the package at your local post office. For information about traveling abroad and importing goods, write for *International Mail Imports* from the Customs Service. It explains how travelers can file a claim if they think the duty is too high or the goods were damaged in transit.

For all these booklets, including *Know Before You Go*, a general summary of the traveler's rights and obligations, write to the Customs Service and ask for the "Travel Pack."

PART III
SPECIAL TRIPS

E very once in a while, a very special trip is in your plans. Perhaps it involves a special interest, such as pursuit of a sport. Perhaps it is a visit of a lifetime to distant, strange lands.

How do you go about arranging it? Where, in fact, do you begin? What sort of help is available—but more important, what should you determine about your own needs, hopes, inhibitions, and physical limitations before you seek it out?

This is especially important when you visit the so-called third world. Cultures, customs, and traditions are different there from what most Americans or Europeans know. Many third world countries have long been poor and are struggling against heavy odds to catch up with the industrialized giants. Some are doing so democratically; others under political systems that much of the world abhors. Some are eager for tourists and warmly welcome them as friends; others lack the facilities and trained personnel to promote tourism, even if they want to.

By no means, however, need you stay away. All this simply emphasizes the need for preparation, the need to get as accurate a picture as possible of what to expect and how to deal with it. As a starter, it means, for example, do not arrange to go to back-country Africa when the rainy season washes out many key roads, and do not pursue a favorite sport or pastime when it is out of season or where there are not enough facilities to go around. In short, apply a modicum of common sense, and a lot of enjoyment can lie ahead.

64. Traveling in South America

Some of travel's biggest thrills and challenges lie in South America. It is a continent of extremes: modern cities and amazingly preserved ancient ruins; gleaming ocean beaches and some of the highest cities in the world; urban sophistication and remote jungles and mountains where the people speak languages familiar only to themselves; ostentatious luxury in the shadow of desperately poor and politically explosive slums.

There is no real common denominator in South America: It offers virtually every kind of scenery, every type of climate, every way of life. Yet if it seems ideal for tourism, most of it has not exploited its charm. According to a May 1983 report by the Organization of American States, "South America is capturing a mere 2 percent of world tourism, a very small share indeed once the potential of the area is accepted."

The O.A.S. report placed part of the responsibility on what it called the "wide discrepancies among countries in the quality of tourism services and in the level of technical and managerial expertise of public and private groups in tourism." Based on interviews with travelers, writers, and tour operators who know the continent well, that indeed seems to be part of the answer. A substantial obstacle, however, has been the great distances and logistical problems involved in getting from the United States to some of South America's major tourist attractions and the relatively high cost. For example, New York to London is 3,456 miles and at this writing you can go on a scheduled flight for as little as $318 for a round-trip; New York to Buenos Aires is 5,302 miles and the lowest round-trip fare is $804.

Anywhere in the world, however, how you travel and how much you pay are almost always subject to sudden and sometimes drastic change. South America is particularly in a state of tourist flux, and recently air fares have been dropping as local governments seek to tap the seemingly vast potential tourist market. Meanwhile, critically ailing economies in such countries as Argentina, Brazil, and Peru have made prices of hotels and other travel facilities extremely attractive to spenders of United States dollars. This could change if the value of the dollar falls.

In 1984, the government of Peru balked at heavy United States pressure, brought primarily in behalf of Eastern Airlines, to increase substantially the South American services that Eastern could fly via Peru on routes it acquired from the old Braniff International Airways, now Braniff Inc. By the time you read this, the matter should have been settled to allow the introduction of multicountry South American tours at air fares and ground rates that, a few years ago, would have seemed impossible. For example, one eighteen-day program in Eastern's program, subject to change, would allow two people traveling together to tour Peru, Chile, and Argentina for $1,145 a person for all accommodations, deluxe where available, many meals, airport transfers, and sightseeing, including a side trip to Cuzco, the 11,207-foot-high capital of the ancient Inca empire, and Machu Picchu, the preserved Incan citadel city perched on a Peruvian mountain. The greater the number of people traveling together, up to a maximum of ten, the lower the per-person land rate. Air fare for this trip was initially pegged at $1,129 a person round-trip from Miami, plus $55 from anywhere else in Florida, $125 from the Northeast, or $150 from elsewhere in the United States.

If you are going to South America for the first time—especially beyond the major cities—you will probably fare better by taking an escorted tour or by buying a transportation-accommodation package from a travel agent than by trying to put a trip together yourself. Air, rail, and bus schedules in the continent are subject to frequent change and, in some countries, overbooking is prevalent and there is little an individual can do to overcome it. As in much of Africa, tour operators who provide a lot of business in South American countries have clout with transportation companies and hotels that individual travelers usually lack.

This is especially true at smaller hotels near popular tourist attractions at peak season. "In peak season everything operates on the force of personal relations," said John Tichenor, director of South American programs for Sobek Expeditions Inc. of Angels Camp,

California, which operates adventure-type tours. "Friends help friends," he said. "A tour operator has the leverage of a long-term business relationship and the ability to provide large groups."

"Certain countries are harder than others for the individual to travel in," said William Abbott, who grew up in South America and is now an owner of Wilderness Travel of Berkeley, California, which operates tours to the Andes, the Amazon, and elsewhere. "Peru, Ecuador, and Bolivia are among the more difficult," he said. "Brazil, Argentina, and Chile are much easier."

Planning a South American journey should begin with considering what sort of experiences you hope to have and what you hope to see. Do you want to sample the whole continent, for example, or have you a special interest, such as the beaches, the jungles, history, or modern cities? Once such questions have been answered, you can turn to these other matters.

Entry Requirements—United States laws do not require that you carry a valid passport to visit South America, but countries there usually insist that you have one and often a visa as well. Regulations can change, however, so before you go, check the nearest embassy or consulate of each country you plan to visit or ask your travel agent to do it. Also ask about any immunizations that may be required and whether to ask your physician for antimalaria pills.

Crossing land frontiers in South America can sometimes be tricky. Said George N. Bradt of Cambridge, Massachusetts, a guidebook publisher and distributor who knows South America intimately: "Long before the Falklands war, my wife, Hilary, and I presented ourselves to Argentine customs. Hilary, traveling on a U.K. passport, was scarcely glanced at. I was summarily refused entry because I didn't have a visa in my American passport. Thinking this was a minor problem, I asked where I could get one. New York, was his reply. This was on a remote crossing between Bolivia and Argentina, and after siesta the staff changed, so of course I tried again and was waved through."

Safety—Of the people interviewed who know South America well, all agreed that petty crime, such as purse-snatching and pocket-picking, is endemic in some major cities, notably Lima, Peru, and Rio de Janeiro and São Paulo, Brazil. Few muggings or other violent crimes were reported, however, so the general advice was to keep valuables locked in hotel safes or, better still, leave most things but your money at home.

When to Go—Generally speaking, when it is winter in North

America it is summer to the south, but this can mean little in some parts of South America. Some are rarely warm because of the altitude. At 11,909 feet, La Paz, Bolivia, is the highest large city in the world and the nights are cold. Some places are arid, and some have long rainy seasons when roads to popular attractions are impassable and flights must sometimes be suspended. In Cuzco, for example, the gateway to Machu Picchu, the rains run from November through April, but July and August are especially clear.

Paying Bills—Before leaving home, ask the foreign exchange department of your bank or a currency dealer about currency regulations where you plan to visit. If there is an officially condoned although technically illegal black market, such as has been the case in Brazil, you may fare much better by changing United States currency or traveler's checks in a hotel or store there than by using a credit card, with which purchases will probably be billed at the official exchange rate.

Tours—Ask a travel agent about Eastern's new tours, which are in conjunction with such tour operators as Ladatco Tours and Crillon Tours of Miami, Galápagos Tours of South Miami, Ipanema Tours of Los Angeles and Unique Adventures of San Francisco. Also ask about American Express tours, which are priced for 1985 below those of a year earlier and some of which are in conjunction with Sobek Expeditions of Angels Camp, California. Other prominent tour operators include Olson-Travelworld, Travcoa, Hemphill-Harris, and Four Winds; all sell through travel agents.

Suggested Reading—The basic bible is the annually updated, British-published *South American Handbook,* a country-by-country rundown, including Central America and the Caribbean, of background and practical information. The 1984 edition has 1,458 pages and retails for $24.95. It's bulky to take along; some aficionados suggest that you tear out and carry only the pages you need; the hard binding can withstand this. Also worth examining are *South America on a Shoestring* by Geoff Crowther (Lonely Planet, $12.95); *Heading South* by Verne Reaves (Second Thoughts Press, $6.95); *A Traveler's Guide to El Dorado and the Inca Empire* by Lynn Meisch (Penguin, $14.95), and, for the big-city visitor who wants to know a lot in a hurry, *Rio Alive* and *Caracas Alive* by Arnold and Harriet Greenberg (Alive Publications, $4.95 each). All except the *South American Handbook* are paperbacks and can be obtained or ordered through stores that specialize in travel books.

65. Traveling in Africa

Africa is at once magnificent and daunting. The prospective traveler is attracted by the countryside, the wide variety of wildlife roaming free, and the vitality of tribal ways in many localities. But the thought of the remoteness of many parts of the continent, the widespread primitiveness and poverty, the health hazards, and often rudimentary and uncertain communications give the unseasoned traveler pause.

The focus of this report is the vast heart of the continent rather than the more frequently visited countries on the Mediterranean, such as Egypt and Morocco and, at the southern tip, South Africa. Most experts on tourism in this area agree on one point, at least: Africa is probably not for your first trip abroad. It is better to get your travel legs by going to Europe, the Far East, or Australia and New Zealand.

"There's a kind of confidence that you have to have," said Murray Vidockler, founder and executive director of the New York-based African Travel Association, a trade group set up in the early 1970s to promote tourism. "Most African countries are very far behind by our standards. They are developing a tourism infrastructure but on an uneven base. It takes time to build hotels and at the same time to train the people who are needed to provide travel services."

The experts also agree that in most cases Africa is not for tourists who insist on traveling on their own. You may normally abhor group tours, but if you are thinking of going to Africa, think again unless you are especially vigorous, adventurous, and resilient—in short, unless you delight in the unfamiliar and don't really care where you stay and how you move about. In many countries, even in their capitals, hotel space and internal transportation are sorely limited. It often takes the clout of a major tour operator to get assurances that you will be able to travel from Point A to Point B when you wish and that you will be guaranteed a place to stay when you get there. The tour operator can help you surmount language barriers and deal with unfamiliar currencies and can get you all the required visas—an often-tedious and long process if you do it yourself.

Here are some tips on ways to help make an African journey workable.

Visas—Most African countries require an entry or transit visa before arriving. Often it is necessary to apply for one far in advance—at least sixty days for Ethiopia, for example. The best handy source of information is the frequently updated yellow leaflet *Visa Requirements of Foreign Governments,* available free at most United States Passport Agencies or by mail from the Bureau of Consular Affairs, Room 6811, Department of State, Washington, D.C. 20520.

Even in this leaflet, some information is sketchy and most is subject to sudden change. Sometimes African consular officers in the United States lack accurate information about entry requirements of their own countries. While it is usually best to arrange for your visas before leaving home, sometimes the requirements to enter a country differ depending on where you apply. At times it may be easier for an American to get a visa for Zaire, for example, in Brussels than in Washington—or vice versa. If your visa application must be referred to the home government, delays can be long. Experienced tour operators, however, can break through most bureaucratic tangles or obtain the help of reliable local representatives in the countries involved.

Health Preparations—You may need several immunizations—particularly against yellow fever and cholera—to enter certain countries in Africa, though none are required for re-entering the United States. Also, prophylaxis against malaria is generally advisable; consult your physician about which medicine to take. The best compact country-by-country source of information on immunizations is the booklet *Health Information for International Travel,* available for $4.25 from the Superintendent of Documents, Government Printing Office, Washington, D.C. 20402. Ask for Stock No. 017002300147-7.

Getting Around—Most countries have internal air services connecting major cities and towns, and many have trains and buses of varying quality as well. The major problems arise when you try to get from one country to another—even a neighboring one, but particularly if you want to go from East to West Africa or vice versa—because air and ground services for this purpose are at best infrequent and sometimes nonexistent.

Weather—In many African countries the rainy season can ruin a vacation by making roads to popular sites impassable. A good tour operator schedules his tours to avoid this, but it is wise to check a guidebook or other tourist literature to make sure.

Tours—A travel agent can steer you toward them, since most are booked through agents, not directly with the tour operator. Be wary of tours that are being offered for the first time, even by established operators. You are more likely to run into snags that only experience operating that particular program can eliminate. Among the respected operators of African tours are Travcoa, Hemphill-Harris, Olson-Travelworld, Percival, Lindblad, Maupintour, Special Expeditions, and Abercrombie & Kent.

Suggested Reading—Good guidebooks to sub-Saharan Africa are few and can usually be found only in large bookstores or those that specialize in travel. The British *Travelaid Guide to East Africa,* distributed in the United States by Hippocrene Books of New York and sold for $9.95, is outstanding. For the traveler determined to go it alone, so is *Africa on a Shoestring* by Geoffrey Crowther (Lonely Planet Publications, $12.95). Less detailed are Thornton Cox's *Travellers' Guides* to East Africa and Southern Africa ($6.95 each), published by Geographia Ltd. in Britain and distributed in the United States by Hastings House of New York. Also worth checking are three *Traveller's Guides* published by IC Magazines of London and distributed by Franklin Watts of New York: to East Africa and the Indian Ocean, to Central and Southern Africa, and to West Africa ($12.95 each).

Pictorially lavish are *Ivory Coast Today* and *Zaire Today* ($14.95 each), published in English by Editions Jeune Afrique of Paris and distributed by Hippocrene, and the *Cultural Atlas of Africa* ($35), produced in Britain and published in North America by Facts on File Inc. of New York.

An excellent source of practical information on twenty-six countries in western, central, and southern Africa is the *Africa Travel Guide,* published in French and English by U.T.A. French Airlines and available by mail if you send a check for $7, made out to the company, to its office at 509 Madison Avenue, New York, New York 10022.

66. Traveling in China

While China remains for many Americans one of the most exotic destinations, the increasing number of travelers bound for Peking has severely taxed the resources of a country where tourism was all but unknown a few years ago.

Many travelers have enjoyed themselves immensely. But others—especially if they have toured China in the peak tourist months of May and October—have brought home tales of inadequate internal transportation, overbooking of hotels, insufficient interpreters, bureaucratic confusion, and a conspicuous dose of commercialism. It is also apparent that some tour packagers have been treated more equally than others—so it behooves the traveler contemplating a trip to the Middle Kingdom to know exactly whom he is dealing with.

In 1982, shortly after the problems first surfaced widely, China's leading tourism representative in the United States readily admitted that substantial problems existed. "We don't have enough expertise and experience for the expanding number of tourists," Liu Zihan, a deputy director of the China International Travel Service, said in an interview in his office at 60 East 42nd Street in New York. "But recently," he added, "the emphasis has been on better planning and better service to insure greater comfort."

Mr. Liu and others stressed, however, the importance of shopping carefully before selecting a tour of China. Compare the prices and experience of various tour operators, understand what is promised and what you can reasonably expect, and be aware that itineraries are often subject to sudden change. Also, keep in mind Mr. Liu's warning—still essentially valid—that although some tour operators offer individually tailored itineraries for Americans who dislike being herded in groups, China's shortages, especially of English-speaking guides, have until recently ruled out that sort of travel except for business people, state guests, and a few others willing to go in midwinter.

When China began to edge into tourism in the 1970s, Mr. Liu's Peking-based organization, known in Chinese as Luxingshe, was given responsibility for arranging the internal travel, accommodations, meals, and sightseeing of most foreign visitors to China. In 1980, however, many other national and local organizations were also authorized to arrange tourism. By many accounts, what followed was a chaotic scramble for very limited facilities, which were promised to many more tour groups than the country could possibly handle.

It became commonplace for accommodations to be switched and downgraded and itineraries to be drastically altered without advance notice to visitors who had paid thousands of dollars each. One of the staunchest supporters of tourism in China—and an outspoken critic of what has happened to it—is Norval Welch, president of the New York-based Special Tours for Special People. In 1972, he began the first American tour programs to the country.

In a letter a decade later to Han Ke-hua, a government official in overall charge of travel and tourism in China, Mr. Welch spoke of "souvenir sellers and peddlers everywhere." He added, "There is a difference, between serving tourists and harassing them!"

On the positive side, however, is the feeling that, as a result of several major conferences in Peking in the last few years, problems may have eased. At best, though, visitors will still rarely find tourism in China to be anywhere near American standards. But in the view of Sidney Rittenberg, a native of South Carolina who lived in China thirty-four years and has conducted tours there: "Often the Chinese will do their best for you if you talk nice, not hard and tough. Rapport is very important, especially in your relationship with Chinese guides."

The experience described below is not new, and when I first wrote about it, readers were divided in their reactions. Some recalled similar misadventures; others felt it was an isolated incident and therefore unfair to China. But for more than a year afterward—in fact, until the writing of this book—I continued to hear from travelers to China who had problems that were at least this formidable and sometimes worse. Several Americans who had been to China several times and arranged or led tours there in 1983 and 1984 complained that despite all the recent hotel construction and training of guides, conditions in peak travel months were deteriorating, not improving, and were damaging the reputations of both China and several major tour operators in the United States.

On the mid-April tour about which I wrote, when thirteen Americans arrived in Guilin, southern China, their first stop on a trip out of Hong Kong, the guide who was supposed to meet them was not there. "After a three-and-a-half-hour wait at the airport," Stanley H. Forster, a financial consultant who lives in Fort Lee, New Jersey, said in a letter, "a young Chinese man, Chow, appeared. He announced that he was our National Guide, and the very young girl with him, who spoke very little English, was our Guilin City Guide (with no experience as a guide). We learned from Chow that he was a university student on a two-week field trip to learn more English by acting as our guide."

Mr. Forster's letter was addressed to Morris Schuster of the Cortell Group of New York, a major tour operator from whom he had bought his package tour. In other letters of protest to the United States Embassy in Peking and Friendly International Tours of Hong Kong, which had packaged the tour that Cortell sold, Mr. Forster and his wife, Dory, a free-lance writer, were joined as signers by seven other tourists. They complained of persistent problems with guides, of inferior meals, of hotel switches and of accommodations in dismal, hostel-like cubicles intended for backpacking youths.

It transpired that their travel in China had been arranged not by Luxingshe, as they had expected, but by the China Youth Travel Service, whose programs were intended primarily for students and others under thirty years of age and whose standards were relatively austere. Referring to the Youth Travel Service, Mr. Liu of the Luxingshe office in New York commented, "Their emphasis in food is more on quantity than quality."

He said the Youth Travel Service charged foreign tour operators "a little less" than Luxingshe, yet the Forster party paid from $20 to $50 more for each day in China than they would have for comparable Luxingshe tours marketed through such operators in the United States as General Tours, Pacific Delight, and Special Tours for Special People. Also, the Forsters paid for at least two days in Hong Kong and $200 to fly from Peking to Hong Kong when they left China—expenses that are often included in other offerings at the same per diem rate charged within China.

Reached by telephone in Hong Kong, K. S. Lau, president of Friendly International, said the $1,229 each that the Forster party paid for an eleven-night tour of China was justified. He spoke of markups and commissions that he said were normal in the travel trade. He said he had to pay the Chinese authorities $50 to $60 a day for lodging, food, and sightseeing (a figure the Forsters strongly questioned, based on what they say they were told in Peking by Hu Huan-zhang, vice president of the China Youth Travel Service), and that he paid extra for internal intercity transportation.

Asked why the visitors had not been told they were to be under the wing of a youth organization, he said that "we seldom disclose" such information because Friendly International uses several internal operators, all of whom are "official" and, in his view, provide similar offerings.

The Forsters say they had never heard of Friendly International until reaching Hong Kong on the way to China. The Cortell brochure that advertised the tour did not identify Friendly. In view of what he called "the long-existed fine cooperation between us," Mr. Lau agreed, in a letter to Mr. Schuster of Cortell, to refund $18 to each of the five Cortell clients on the tour—a refund that Mr. Schuster told this reporter he had rejected pending further investigation. The Forsters, meanwhile, want "complete reimbursement for the price of the trip" plus damages.

All this points up the importance, when shopping for a tour of China, of knowing who will make the internal arrangements and of knowing whether particular American operators deal directly with the authorities in China or through middlemen in Hong Kong or elsewhere. Most American tour operators specify the China International Travel Service in their brochures. If no organization in China is specified, warily ask why. Also, be aware that among American operators, the authorities in China prefer to deal with "old friends" who have sent many tourists their way.

Despite the persistent shortages of tourist facilities, Mr. Liu of Luxingshe in New York confirmed that some "old friends" have much greater ability than other operators to obtain the best hotel rooms, the most lavish meals, the choicest space on Yangtze River cruises, and the most reliable air schedules that China can offer.

67. Traveling in the Soviet Bloc

For travelers, there is no such thing as a Communist monolith. Americans who visit Eastern Europe or China find that conditions affecting travelers vary substantially from one country to another. The one common denominator is that in every Communist country except, perhaps, Yugoslavia, touring is markedly different from what it is like in the developed countries of the West.

Accordingly, anyone planning a vacation in a Communist country has many things to consider, among them visas and currencies, the attitudes and policies of government officials, the pros and cons of traveling in a group or alone, and the quality of services and accommodations. Travel in the Soviet Union, for example, is far more restrictive than in virtually any other country in the world that encourages tourism. By contrast, China, as it gradually expands transportation, hotel, and sightseeing facilities, is allowing foreign visitors to do more and more on their own.

"The Chinese are very open," said Graeme Clarke, who has had top-flight group tour experience with American Express. "You never have the feeling of anybody watching you. Rather, the Chinese people are encouraged to meet you. In Russia, however, you are almost totally isolated from the people. You are sort of in a cocoon."

In most Communist countries, service is substantially below the levels expected in the West, and you often have to be firm though not visibly angry with cumbersome bureaucracies to get what you feel is your money's worth. Even if a major American travel agency makes your arrangements, you are likely to find at your destination that the conditions of your stay are controlled by an official government tourist department from whose rulings there is no practical appeal.

If customs or immigration officers or local policemen seem

especially abrasive or obstructive, it is important to remain cool. In a dispute, make your viewpoint known but remember that heated resistance is more likely to lead to further trouble than to a resolution of the problem. Remember, too, that you can always seek help from the nearest United States Consulate, although there are limits to the help you can be given.

Chances are, however, you will encounter little trouble provided you follow the rules. Most Americans pass through customs easily, for instance, even in the Soviet Union. But in any Communist country you are likely to be subject to an extremely thorough check if it is a time of exceptional diplomatic strain with the United States, if you are a journalist, or if you are suspected of planning to establish contact with political dissidents. Even if none of these descriptions fit you, literature you carry will often be perused and sometimes confiscated for no apparent reason. Nonetheless, your travels will be enhanced if you carry an English-language guidebook from home, since you probably will not be able to buy a good one in a Communist country.

On a four-month tour of Eastern Europe and the Soviet Union a few years ago, I always assumed that my hotel rooms were bugged because I am a journalist, although I never knew for sure. Only in Alma Ata, in Soviet Kazakhstan, not far from the then tense Chinese frontier, was I conscious of being followed. I kept seeing the same young man throughout my day there—even at the ballet, where he sat directly behind me and followed me to the lobby, the rest room, and a nearby coffee shop.

One of the pluses of travel in the Communist world is that it is relatively cheap. Except when the dollar has been particularly strong, tourists find that it costs 30 to 40 percent less to travel in most of Eastern Europe than it does for a comparable vacation in the West, although in some countries, notably Hungary, the price gap is narrowing. And the Communist governments have tried to preserve natural beauty and historic relics and monuments.

In areas that are attractive to tourists but where facilities are short, visitors will probably find it easier and cheaper to join an escorted group tour arranged by a major packager than to travel independently. However, one major operator of escorted tours to Rumania, Hungary, and Czechoslovakia, who for business reasons asked that he not be identified, cautioned that "these tours appeal to a certain type of traveler and are not suited to everyone."

"These are still Communist countries," he said, "and comfort as we know it in the United States—including service—is not available, nor should the prospective client expect it."

According to frequent travelers to Eastern Europe, however, in Hungary, Rumania, and Yugoslavia it has become easier, and is often more fruitful, to travel wherever and whenever your personal interests dictate—provided you make sure that accommodations are available for overnight stops. Advance reservations are usually advisable.

In the seemingly unchangeable Soviet Union, the group, as always, is king. According to frequent visitors there and my own experience, it is not so much that facilities are short or that Big Brother wants to keep an eye on you but that traveling by "delegation" is the way the Russians themselves have been getting around ever since the Bolshevik Revolution, and it is their way of life.

The Soviet Union, says E. Wallace Lawrence III, who heads the Russian Travel Bureau, an American-owned tour company in New York, is not so much a vacation destination as a place for historic and cultural exploration. Mr. Clarke of American Express put it this way: "Western Europe is interested in maximizing its dollar income from tourists; other countries, such as the Soviet Union, are more interested in making converts. I've never seen a French tour that took you to a kindergarten or a shoe factory."

It is, of course, possible to travel independently in much of the Soviet Union, and Americans have been doing it for years. A recent check showed that you and your spouse can visit Moscow or Leningrad in what the Russians call deluxe style for about $125 a person a day, including lodging, breakfast, and transportation between the airport or railroad station and your hotel. In other cities, it may cost up to a third less. Sightseeing, at extra charge, is probably by chauffeur-driven car with private guide.

For about half the deluxe individual price, however, the group traveler can get nearly twice as much value for his ruble. The accommodations might be more modest and the sightseeing by bus instead of car, but you are guaranteed a lot of convenience and experiences that an individual might not be able to get from Intourist, the Soviet Government tourist agency.

In hotel dining rooms, a group finds tables waiting perhaps adorned with small American flags, and its members are likely to be assigned a waitress who speaks enough English to help explore the Cyrillic menu.

The independent traveler, however, may have to stand in line at the door, as individual Russians do, and ultimately be shown to a table to share with strangers. An opportunity to meet local people? Hardly. As an independent traveler in the Soviet Union, I found that few of my tablemates spoke English and many appeared to be visitors from distant provinces who were taking their travel with generous assistance from vodka. I had to make choices from incomprehensible menus and hope for the best.

In Moscow, I could not get a ticket to see the May Day parade because I was not with a group. Intourist suggested that I watch it on television in my room at my hotel, two blocks away. I could not see the Bolshoi Ballet because all performances during my stay were sold out to groups. Fortunately, I did get to see some spectacular ballet, but in Novosibirsk, Siberia, where by luck a top company was on tour while I was there. I was denied a visit to a collective farm and to a youth camp because I was not with a group. "You could hardly expect them to arrange the necessary hospitality for only one person," I was told.

According to recent travelers and several tour operators who arrange group visits to the Soviet Union, the situation is basically unchanged since I was there. There are a few more modern hotels, and foreigners can dine relatively well in restaurants that accept only foreign currency. And according to Mr. Lawrence, Soviet tourism officials learned a lot from dealing with foreign spectators at the 1980 Olympic Games, which for his company were disastrous because of the many cancellations of reservations by American tourists after the Soviet invasion of Afghanistan.

Still unchanged, however, is the Soviet policy of closing many areas to Americans. Much of the Urals and big stretches of Kazakhstan, for example, are off limits. The United States has taken reciprocal action and closed many cities, including Dallas and Cleveland, to Russians. Sometimes, even when a Soviet city is open to tourists, its airport remains closed, and this effectively bars visits.

When applying for a visa to the Soviet Union, it is necessary to specify the day and place you plan to arrive, when and where you plan to leave, and what cities you want to visit. If you are joining a group tour, these arrangements are made by the operator; if you are traveling independently, Intourist must approve your itinerary before you get a visa.

In most of Eastern Europe, depending upon the availability of accommodations, you can travel virtually at will these days. The exception is Albania, which has been so tightly closed to American tourism since World War II that there is no point in even applying for a visa.

But because there is still a wide gap between conditions in most of Eastern Europe and the West, be sure to consider the following points.

Visas—All Eastern European countries except Yugoslavia require United States citizens to have visas. Some countries, among them Czechoslovakia, Poland, and the Soviet Union, insist that you obtain visas in advance, and this can take a week or two; others, such as Bulgaria, Hungary, and Rumania, allow you to pick visas up when you arrive. The rules are subject to change, however, so it is best to check a month or so before you leave home and to get visas in advance whenever you can.

Margaret N. Peterson of Summit, New Jersey, executive director of a nonprofit organization called Music Education for the Handicapped Inc., told of a harrowing experience one summer when a young border guard ejected her and her luggage from a Warsaw-Prague train at two A.M. because her Czechoslovak visa lacked a required stamp. She said she had to return to Katowice, Poland, the nearest city with a Czechoslovak consulate, and get the stamp before being allowed to proceed, much later that day.

Several months after she returned home, Mrs. Peterson said that the official Czechoslovak tourist agency had given her a refund for unused hotel accommodations in Prague and that her American travel agent had sent her $150 as compensation because it assumed responsibility, although it may not have been at fault, for not having made sure her visa was in order.

Mrs. Peterson's difficulty illustrates the importance of scrutinizing your Eastern European travel documents as soon as you receive them and of contacting your travel agent or government authorities if anything seems amiss.

Passports—Travelers in Eastern European countries are asked to present their passports for inspection more frequently than they are in much of the rest of the world. Many American travelers are prepared for this but are somewhat disconcerted by the length of time the passports are kept by the local authorities. Passports collected on trains or at hotels are routinely held several hours. It is extremely rare, however, for a passport not to be returned.

Money—In some countries you have to commit yourself in advance to spend a certain amount of the local currency. Poland, for example, requires that if you are traveling independently, without relatives in Poland, and with no prepaid reservations, before you receive a visa you must buy travel vouchers or exchange orders from Orbis, the official government travel agency, amounting to $15 for every day you plan to spend in the country. Your travel agent can arrange this. You can spend the vouchers on many things in Poland, but they are not refundable, even if you stay and eat with relatives or friends.

There is usually no limit to the amount of foreign currency you may take into a Communist country, but most permit neither the import nor export of their own money. Some New York banks, such as Republic National, and foreign exchange dealers, such as Deak-Perera and Manfra Tordella & Brookes, sell Eastern European currencies, usually at a substantially better rate than you can get inside those countries. But while it is legal to buy such money in New York, it is not legal to take it to Bucharest or Prague or Warsaw. You may get away with carrying money into a country illegally, but if you get caught the money probably will be confiscated and returned to you only when you leave. And if you try to resell the money to a dealer when you return home, you will lose substantially in the transaction because of the gap between rates for selling and buying.

Do not change money on the black market; it could be a trap. Retain your receipts for all exchange transactions. If you produce these receipts at the airport or border when you leave the country, you should be able to change your surplus local currency back into dollars. But not always. The best idea is to estimate as closely as possible how much local currency you will need and to exchange only enough dollars so that you have few forints (Hungary), zlotys (Poland), or korunas (Czechoslovakia) left over.

When they visited Hungary, Arlene and Bruce Jacobi of Manhattan did not realize that Hungary limits to $50 the amount of forints that can be re-exchanged. The customs officers at Budapest Airport refused to exchange anything, but simply confiscated the Jacobis' excess 1,100 forints (then worth about $36) and told them they could collect their dollars from the New York office of the National Bank of Hungary. In New York, the bank's agent pointed out that the receipt said they should write to the National Savings Bank in Hungary. "We did so," Mrs. Jacobi said, "and never heard a thing."

Accommodations—Although there has been a lot of deluxe hotel construction in recent years, the more appealing capitals, such as Budapest and Prague, are still often short of accommodations that most Americans would consider suitable. In contrast, some Black Sea resorts in Rumania and Bulgaria have been overbuilt, and for several years there have been more-than-ample accommodations in Polish cities because political disturbances have frightened tourists away.

Be careful about so-called budget accommodations. Unless you are really prepared to rough it, what Eastern Europeans call tourist-class lodgings may be rudimentary indeed. As a sometimes gratifying alternative to better hotels, however, consider being a paying guest in a private home, which government tourist offices and some travel agencies can arrange.

Travel Agents—It is usually much easier to have a travel agent make all your Eastern European arrangements, including obtaining visas, than to do it yourself. If you prefer a group tour, the government tourist office in New York of the appropriate country should be able to direct you to the principal operators of tours from the United States, although they rarely make recommendations.

For independent travel, there may be an advantage in using a so-called ethnic travel agent—one who specializes in the country you plan to visit. For accommodations, however, the ethnic agent is likely to go to the same large American wholesaler that any other travel agent would use. It is the big wholesalers, or the national travel organization of the country to be visited, who have the clout to provide hotel reservations when space is tight.

Auto Rentals—In Eastern European countries except the Soviet Union, you can usually rent cars from agents—mostly government controlled—of one of the international companies, such as Avis or Hertz, or the government tourist agency. Before you rent, however, ask about availability of gasoline and emergency road service, including hours of operation, overnight lodging on the routes you plan to take, liability insurance, and prospects for emergency repairs. Also, be sure you have an appropriate driver's license or endorsement.

According to a spokesman for the Hertz Corporation, you will probably be rented a Western European car with a license plate that indicates you are a foreign tourist. The plate can be helpful, he said, in attracting attention, particularly from the police, if you have mechanical trouble. You can rent a car in Western Europe, he said, and drive it to the East and back, but if you rent in an Eastern country, you will probably not be permitted to take the car across the border.

The spokesman said American credit cards were usually accepted to pay for car rentals, but that gasoline generally had to be bought with cash. "Make sure your tank is full whenever you leave a major town," he advised.

In most countries visitors can drive where they want, but in the Soviet Union they are subject to the same sort of itinerary restrictions as tourists using public transportation. The Hertz spokesman said that renting a car in the Soviet Union required "very high official clearance" and "is not for the guy in the street."

Photography—You can usually photograph at will, even in the Soviet Union, except at airports and military installations. According to recent reports, Soviet sensitivities about filming the old wooden buildings that are common just behind main city streets have largely disappeared. But wherever you are, do not photograph soldiers, policemen, or anything that might be considered military equipment. It may be permissible, but unless you are sure, it is not worth the chance.

It is generally preferable to carry color film from home and to take it home for developing, but before you go, find out if the amount you can carry is limited. Do not pack film in suitcases to be checked, and try not to permit any film to be screened by X-ray machines. Airport officials may tell you that their X-rays are not strong enough to damage film, but if you are doing a lot of traveling, the cumulative effect may well be damaging. So ask to have your camera and film examined by hand. Usually, though sadly not always, your request is honored.

68. A Trip Around the World

A round-the-world trip can be a lot quicker now than in Jules Verne's day, but planning it is not necessarily easier. So many options are available by air that it can take hours of study to find the most appropriate combination of routing and price.

It is possible to skirt the globe in less than two days—one-fortieth the time that Verne allowed Phileas Fogg, the hero of his book *Around the World in 80 Days.* The great advantage of most of today's offerings is not speed, however, but the fact that if you have the time, the money, and a spirit of adventure, they usually allow you to ramble up to half a year, stopping in many countries along the way.

Such travel is an excellent way to visit the Far East and southwestern Pacific. For example, a global air ticket can be much cheaper and more convenient than a round-trip halfway around the world—from New York to Singapore, say—in which you go and return by the same route.

At least forty global tickets are being offered by airlines that have paired up so that one picks you up where the other's route ends. Prices are subject to sudden change depending on season and degree of competition and in what country you buy the ticket because of fluctuations in the value of local currencies in relation to the United States dollar. So the dollar prices given here are simply to give some idea of what you can find.

At this writing, for example, prices in the United States for joint global tickets begin at $1,999 in economy class and $3,222 in first. But because such tickets bear restrictions and possible penalties if they are amended, wealthier travelers often prefer what the trade calls normal round-the-world tickets. These are based on International Air Transport Association fares of at least $2,600 in economy and $4,500 in first class, depending on route. They carry few if any restrictions and usually allow up to a year's travel within a generous mileage allowance on your own varied choice of airlines.

Edward H. Darrach, president of Manhattan's Bristed Manning Travel Service, said that while a joint ticket "is probably a very good buy if someone knows exactly what he's doing," only a few people find them suitable.

With a joint ticket, you must travel on only the two airlines that sponsor it and in the same general eastward or westward direction, without backtracking. Usually stopovers are unlimited, but travel must be completed within 180 days. You must buy your ticket and reserve your initial flight at least twenty-one days before departure, but the rest of the itinerary may be left open, to be booked as you go along. This is a strong advantage. Under most joint plans, you are permitted to change an itinerary only once at no charge; additional changes are subject to a $25 fee for each flight coupon affected of the five or six that are usually issued.

The pioneer in special round-the-world tickets was Pan American World Airways, which established one when it had a global route all its own. It has since dropped the leg between India and Hong Kong. At this writing, as outlined by Ignacio Maza of its pricing department, it has joint arrangements with Cathay Pacific, Saudi Arabian Airlines (Saudia), Swissair, and Thai Airways International, but you, the passenger, can choose only one of them. Following are some of the options.

Cathay Pacific—Pan Am officials said this option costs $1,999 in economy and $3,499 in first class and has been a best-seller because it offers the widest choice of destinations in Southeast Asia. For example, you might fly Pan Am westbound from New York to San Francisco, Honolulu, and Tokyo. There you would switch to Cathay Pacific and could go to Taipei, Hong Kong, Jakarta, Singapore, and back to Hong Kong to change planes, then to Bangkok and Bombay. Then back onto Pan Am to Dubai, Frankfurt, London, and New York. Or you could take the same trip in reverse or begin and end in any of the cities mentioned.

Swissair—Flying eastbound, you would go from New York to Paris on Pan Am, then switch to Swissair for the flight to Geneva or Zurich or both, depending on scheduling, then fly to Athens, Bombay, Colombo, and Singapore. Then back on Pan Am to Hong Kong, Los Angeles, and New York, possibly via Miami if you preferred. The Swissair option, however, is available only in economy class.

Thai International—On an eastbound journey you would fly to New Delhi on Pan Am with stopovers en route, then switch to Thai International for the flight to Bangkok and Hong Kong, then return to Pan Am to fly across the Pacific to the United States.

Saudia—You could fly from New York to Zurich on Pan Am, then Saudia to Jidda and Singapore or Manila, then Pan Am the rest of the way eastward.

For $300 to $500 extra in economy class, Pan Am offers optional extensions on routes of its own to Australia and New Zealand, Mexico, and Central and South America, the Caribbean, the Bahamas, and East and West Africa. Such options should be examined with extreme care, however, before committing yourself. Sometimes, because of a promotional fare between two points, it is cheaper to buy separate passage to an optional area rather than extend a global ticket.

Sometimes flight schedules restrict the number of places you can visit on an extension, even though stopovers are theoretically unlimited.

At this writing, other airlines have these joint global tickets;

• Northwest Orient, jointly with Air France, Air-India, British Caledonian, C.A.A.C. (Civil Aviation Administration of China), Cathay Pacific, Garuda Indonesian, Gulf Air, KLM, Kuwait Airways, Malaysian, Pakistan International, Sabena, South African, or Thai International. Economy fare in most cases is $1,999 if paid in dollars; first class is typically $3,222. A ticket restricts you to Northwest and only one of the other airlines.

• Trans World, jointly with Japan Air Lines, Singapore Airlines, or Qantas.

• CP Air of Canada, jointly with Alitalia, Cathay Pacific, Swissair, South African, Gulf Air, or Philippine Airlines.

In addition, there are Air-India's arrangement with C.A.A.C., the airline of the People's Republic of China; British Airways's with Air New Zealand; Air Canada's with Singapore, and others.

A global ticket can begin and end anywhere on one of the two lines that sponsor it. If one of them does not stop at your home city, however, you will probably have to pay extra to go to and from the nearest place it serves.

If you spend the $600 or so extra for a normal round-the-world ticket in economy class, travel can start and end, at no extra charge, in virtually any city served by a scheduled airline. Your fare is based on going to the most distant point via the Atlantic and returning via the Pacific or vice versa. You are given a mileage allowance, which in the case of New York to New York via Singapore is roughly 24,700. You can choose your own route within the mileage and change it and airlines at will without penalty; you can probably have as many stopovers as you wish, although there have been restrictions via the Pacific.

Based on Pan Am fares at this writing, a round-trip ticket from New York to Singapore, going and returning via the Pacific, costs $2,574, or nearly $600 more than a joint global ticket with Cathay Pacific. Under temporary promotional fares, however, you can buy a round-trip ticket between New York and Los Angeles for $379 and combine it with a $1,000 round-trip between Los Angeles and Singapore for a total of only $1,379. The problem is that travel on the New York–Los Angeles sector must be midweek, must be completed within fourteen days, and must have no stopovers. On the Pacific sector, you can make only one free stopover in each direction; each additional stop costs $50, and none is permitted in Japan.

Index

what they will do, 352-53
what they won't do, 353
American Express, 20-21, 25, 166, 175
  receiving mail through, 185-86
  tours, 57-58, 369, 377, 379
American Express charge cards, 149-50,
  155
  cashing personal checks using, 171-72,
  176
  Driver Security Plan, 289
  foreign currency conversion and, 157-59
  payment of travel expenses with, 161,
  162
  tipping and, 281
American Express Pocket Guides, 5-6
American Express traveler's checks, 146,
  149-50, 175, 290-91
  theft and fraud, 151-54
American Hotel and Motel Association,
  119, 161, 327, 336
American Land Cruisers, 84-85
American Public Health Association,
  266-67
American rail travel, see Amtrak
American Sightseeing International, 9,
  274, 275
American Society for the Prevention of
  Cruelty to Animals (A.S.P.C.A.),
  221, 222, 225
American Society of Civil Engineers, 119
American Society of Travel Agents (ASTA),
  18, 19, 20, 25, 33, 135, 163, 237,
  238, 316, 324
  consumer complaints and, 337-38,
  344
American Telephone and Telegraph
  Company (A.T.&T.), 298
  alternatives to, 299, 300
American Tourister luggage, 203
American/Wolfe International, 122
Amoco Motor Club, 117, 289-90, 296-97
Amtrak, 40, 60, 66-69, 223
  All Aboard America fare, 68
  arrangements offered by, 68
  Auto Train, 68
  children on, 212
  delays on, 66
  discounts for older travelers, 68, 125
  family plans on, 67-68
  fares on, 67-68
  fine print on tickets, 131
  focus of, 66
  infants on, 219
  information on, 69
  making connections via, 301
  meals on, 66

overnight travel between New York and
  Washington, 68-69
  payment to, 162
  refunds and, 129
  stations, 66-67
  time factor and, 66
  Traveler's Aid and, 348
  unaccompanied children on, 216
  Week of Wheels and, 68
Andiamo luggage, 203
Answers to the Most Asked Questions About
  Cruising, 90-91
Apollo computer system, 30
Arab countries, 181, 182, 253-54
ARCO auto club, 289
Argentina, 168, 180, 183, 187, 224, 367,
  368
Armchair Traveler, 6
ARM Coverage Inc., 135, 137
  ski insurance of, 140-42
Around and About Travel, 6
Around the World in 80 Days (Verne), 385
Arrow Airways, 38, 125
Ashlock, James R., 39, 271
Assist-Card Corporation of America, 137
Association of Informed Travelers, 117, 119
Association of Retail Travel Agents, 33
ASTA Notes, 237
Atlantic City, 78-79
Atpac Tours, 85
Aurichio, Rosemary, 232
Australia, 196, 222, 284
Austria, 283
Auto Europe, 85, 106, 286
Automobile Club of New York, 40
  emergency help from, 289, 290
Automobile transporters, 41
Auto rentals, see Car rentals
Auto Train, 68
Avis, 98, 102, 286
  compared to renting a "wreck," 109-10,
  111
  crime in Rome and, 247
  discounts for older travelers, 127
  in Europe, 103-106, 284
  fine print on contracts, 132
  payment to, 163

Baedeker, Karl, 191
Baedeker guidebooks:
  new, 192
  original, 190-91
Baggage, 35
  allowance for, 310-11
  carry-on, 310-13

plane substitution and, 319-20
volunteers for, 234, 318-19
Bundy-American Corporation, 111
Burdine's department stores, 147
Burma, 182
Burt Franklin & Company, 69, 73
Buses, 40, 73-77
baggage on, 308, 313
charter, see Charter buses
children's fares on, 212, 215
competition between lines, 73-74
cut-rate fares, 74
discounts for older travelers, 125
escorted tours via, 56, 75-77
fine print on tickets, 131
friendliness aboard, 75, 77
infants on, 219
long-distance travel by, 74-75
payment for, 162-63
questions to ask about, 76-77
reservations for, 75
smoking on, 271
Traveler's Aid and, 348
unaccompanied children on, 213, 215-16
see also Sightseeing tours
BWIA International, 321, 322

California, 84, 85, 92
California Parlor Car Tours, 76
Camalier & Buckley, 207, 209
Campbell, Dr. C. C. Kent, 263
Campers and other RVs, 83-86
campgrounds for, 86
capacity of, 85-86
costs of, 83-86
range of choices in, 84
renting, 83-85
Canada, 69, 76, 177, 183, 184, 285
guidebooks to, 197
maps of, 199
Canadian Public Health Association, 267
Canceled tours, 323-27
act of God and, 323-27
air travel and, 325-27
charter flights, 50-51, 54, 55, 325,
326-27
hotels and, 327
lawsuits due to, 324
local sightseeing and special events and,
327
refunds from, 324, 325
strikes and, 323, 324, 326
tour buses and, 327
tour operators and, 324, 325, 327
travel agents and, 324-25

Caneel Bay resort, 333
Cape May, New Jersey, 335-36
Capitol Airlines, 45
Capobianco, Barbara, 333
Cappadona, Carmen, 230
Caracas Alive (Greenberg and Greenberg),
369
Caravan tours, 57
Cardoza, Paul, 43-44
Carefree David Travel Company, 48
Carefree travel insurance, 135, 137
Carey, William, 16
Caribbean, 50, 51, 177, 242
disagreements with hotels in the, 331,
332, 334
pre-Christmas flights to the, 320-22
Caribbean Holidays, 14-17, 46, 329, 330
Caribbean Tourism Association, 237-38
Carla C, 93
Carnival Cruise Lines, 87, 92
Carnivale, 87
Carr, Stanley, 358-61
Car rentals (in Europe), 103-107
age restrictions on, 284
confirmation of, 106
costs of, 103-107
crime and, 244, 246-47
driving laws and, 107
drop-off charges, 107
in Eastern Europe, 383-84
exchange rates and, 104, 105-106
gasoline, 105
hotel reservations and, 121, 123
information on, 286-87
insurance, 105
leases versus, 107
special needs and, 104-105, 106
taxes, 105, 107
travel agents and, 103-104, 107
see also Driving abroad
Car rentals (in the U.S.), 94-103
air fares and, 40, 95
Amtrak and, 68
case history of mixup in, 99-101
collision insurance, 98
contract for, 95-96
discount, 96, 126-27
drop-off charges, 98-99
fine print on contracts, 132
"free," 95
gasoline, 97
liability insurance, 97-98
mode of payment for, 96
payment for, 163
personal accident insurance, 98
rates for, 9

Car rentals (in the U.S.) *(cont'd)*
  through travel agents, 95, 96
  unexpected charges for, 94-95
  weekend, 101-103
  "wrecks," *see* Renting "wrecks"
Cartan tours, 58, 76
Carte Blanche, 281
Case Western Reserve University, 261
Casparius, Rodolfo, 332
Casser bus tours, 76
Cathay Pacific, 386
Catholic Travel Office, 64
Caulfield, John P., 242, 243, 349, 350-51, 352
Centers for Disease Control, 257, 258, 263, 267
  chloroquine-resistant malaria and, 263-64
  transmitting information to travelers, 265
Central Holidays tours, 58
Certified travel counselor (C.T.C.), 19, 23
Chad, 136, 237
Chagas' disease, 262
Chamber of Commerce, 76, 79, 124, 127, 294
Chapman, Alexandra, 194
Charge cards, *see* Credit cards
Charter buses, 74, 78-82
  arrangements for, 79-81
  cancellation of, 327
  examples of tours, 81-82
  gambling and, 78-79
  I.C.C. license and, 80-81
  one-day, 79, 80
  rates for, 81
  recreation and, 78
  shopping and, 78, 80
  sightseeing and, 78, 79
  tour brokers and, 79-80
Charter flights, 47-55
  adjustments to charter contracts, 51
  buying later rather than earlier, 49-50
  cancellations of, 50-51, 54, 55, 325, 326-27
  children and, 54, 212
  delays by an act of God, 53-54
  differences among programs, 51-52
  discounts on, 49-50
  examples of savings from, 47-48
  to foreign countries, 49, 50-52, 53
  in-flight services, 55
  land package for, 51-52
  opinions on, 50
  penalties for cancellation, 54
  popular destinations of, 50

  pricing formula of, 49
  protection against surcharges, 54
  questions to ask about, 52-55
  responsibilities for feeding and lodging due to delays, 55
  restrictions on, 49, 52
  return flight cancellation, 54
  scheduling of, 49
  tour operators and, 48-50
  travel agents and, 51, 52
  which airline will operate the flight?, 53
Chase Manhattan Bank, 174
Chicago, 115, 361
Children, traveling with, 209-19
  charter flights and, 54, 212
  children's fares on airlines, 211
  cruises and, 212
  flying to Florida, 210-11
  help at airports and in flight, 217-19
  hotels and, 212
  infants, 217-19
  on international flights, 211-12, 218
  package plans and, 212
  restrictions on discounts, 210-11
  seating together, 211
  type of aircraft and, 219
  unaccompanied children, *see* Children traveling alone
Children traveling alone, 212-16, 347
  by air, 213-15
  on Amtrak, 216
  by bus, 213, 215-16
  common rules for, 214
  divorce and, 213
  Eastern Airlines procedures for, 214-15
  fares for, 214
  infants, 213-14
Chile, 168, 367, 368
China, 133, 172, 192, 316, 317, 373-76
  misadventures in, 374-76
  openness of, 377
  problems with tourism, 373-75
  tour operators and, 373-76
China International Travel Service, 373, 374, 376
China Youth Travel Service, 375, 376
Cholera, 255, 258, 259, 265, 371
Christmas tours, 62-64
  Colonial Williamsburg, 63
  cruises, 64
  the Greenbriar, 63
  the Homestead, 63
  international, 64
  Mohonk Mountain House, 63-64
  Pennsylvania Dutch country, 63
Christopher's Travel Discoveries, 208

Guidebooks (cont'd)
  bed-and-breakfast, 196
  bookstores for, 6, 195
  discount, 6-7
  nature, 196-97
  offbeat, 194-97
  types of, 5-6
  used by travel agents, 8-9
  walking tour, 193-94
  Guide to Eastern Canada (Pratson), 197

Hahn, Peyton E., 40, 289
Haiti Government Tourist Bureau, 265
Halliday, Stephen D., 166
Hallwag maps, 200
Hammond Map Store, 198, 200, 201
Harbor Airlines, 272
Hardach Travel Service, 25-26
Hare, James F., Jr., 29
Harouche, Gilbert, 22
Harper, Andrew, 189
Harrington, Ed, 144
Harris, Alexander W., 341
Harris, John, 197
Harris, Louise, 299
Hartman luggage, 203
Harvard Student Congress, 5, 123
Hastings House, 197
Hawaii, 50, 222-23, 246, 331
Hawkins, Bert, 358
Heading South (Reaves), 369
Health, 255-62
  air ambulances, 133-34
  in Africa, 371
  American consulates and, 351
  customs and, 358, 359
  factors in, 255-56
  hints, 259-60
  immunizations, 257, 258, 259, 261,
    371
  insurance, 136-38
  literature on, 256-59
  Medic Alert Foundation and, 260-61
  old travelers and, 256
  physician's OK before travel, 256, 261
  preventive medical programs, 261-62
  questions about, 255
  specific illnesses, 257, 258-59
  tour operators and, 256
  travel itinerary and, 258, 259
  water and, 255, 259-60
  see also Tropical diseases, guarding against
Health Care Abroad, 137
Health Guide for Travelers to Warm Climates,
  267

Health Information for International Travel,
  257, 258, 371
  blue sheet up-dates to, 258-59, 265
Hemphill-Harris tours, 57, 369, 372
Henry, Anita G., 320-21
Hepatitis, 259
Hern, George, 244
Hertz, 98, 102, 287
  compared with renting a "wreck,"
    109-10, 111
  crime in Rome and, 246-47
  discounts for older travelers, 126-27
  in Eastern Europe, 383-84
  in Europe, 103-106, 284
  payment to, 163
Herz, Ralph, 100
Hess, Ethna, 231
Hetz, Tim, 100
Heydt, Steven, 16
Hickman's World Air Travel Guide, 217
Hidden-city ticketing, see Flyover,
  point-beyond, or hidden-city ticketing
Hideaway Report, The, 189
Hillman, David K., 43
Hillsborough Boarding and Grooming
  Kennels, 225-26
Hilton Hotels Corporation, 166, 299
Hilton International Schiphol Airport, 116
Hindus, special diets for, 254
Hippocrene Books Inc., 197
Hlavacek, Pegge, 57
Hoag, Charles, 139
Hofmann, Paul, 245
Hogg, Russell E., 157
Holiday Inns, 117, 299
  pets at, 220
Holiday Rental Vehicle Leasing, Inc., 85
Holland America Cruises, 92, 163
  contract for, 131-32
  tipping on, 279
Hollander, George, 220
Holy Land, 64
Homeric tours, 58
Homestead, the, 63
Hong Kong, 11-12, 284, 375, 376
Hornel, Graham A., 240
Hotel and Travel Index, 9
Hotel discount plans, 116-20
  alternatives to, 119
  directories from, 117, 118, 119
  in New York City, 117-19
  possible guests at, 119
  questionable value of, 116, 118
  restrictions on, 117-18, 119-20
Hotel phone bills, 297-300
  problems with, 299-300

Index • 403

Sightseeing tours, 273-76
American Sightseeing International, 274,
275
arranged through travel agents, 274, 275
cancellation of, 327
charter buses and, 78, 79
day of the week for, 276
Gray Line, 274-76
guidebooks for, 5
language of, 275
quaint back streets and, 276
selecting the best, 274
tape recording and, 276
SIMA Products Corporation, 250
Simoncelli, Morris G., 233
Singapore, 61, 385
Skiers, insurance for, 138-42
ARM Coverage Inc., 140-42
emergency evacuation, 141-42
example of coverage, 139-40
exclusions from, 140, 141
focus of, 140
rates, 141
supplementary, 141
Ski vacation, 329-30, 331
Skyward, 93
Skyway luggage, 203
Slade, Margot, 135, 164-70, 239, 349-58
Slotnick, Howard, 108-109
Smallpox, 258, 259
Small, remote resorts, 13
Smith, C. A., 238
Smoking on airplanes, 268-73
ASH and, 268-71, 273
C.A.B. and, 268, 269
foreign airlines and, 270
hands-off policies regarding, 272-73
regulations on, 269-71
smoking and nonsmoking sections, 270
when "no smoking" pays off, 271-73
Snizek, Edith, 198
Sobek Expeditions Inc., 367-68, 369
South Africa, 182, 183, 284
South America, 165, 168, 177, 256,
366-69
air fares to, 366-67
crossing borders in, 368
described, 366
entry requirements, 368
maps of, 201
paying bills, 369
safety, 368
suggested reading, 369
tours, 369
tour operators and, 367-68

visas to travel to, 181, 183
when to go, 368-69
see also specific countries
South American Handbook, 369
South America on a Shoestring (Crowther), 369
South-East Asia on a Shoestring (Wheeler),
195
South Korea, 283
Southward, 93
Southwest Airlines, 36, 272
Soviet bloc, *see* Eastern Europe
Soviet Union, 58, 222, 249, 377-84
areas off-limits to Americans, 380
being followed in, 378
car rentals in, 383, 384
group tours of, 379, 380
independent tours of, 379, 380
isolation of tourists in, 377
photography in, 384
visas for, 180, 182, 380, 381
Spain:
credit card currency conversion and,
157-58
crime in, 241, 244, 245, 246
driving in, 107, 283
government-operated hotels in, 121
guidebooks to, 193, 244
Spanish National Tourist Office, 245, 248
Special Expeditions, 372
Special Tours for Special People, 374, 375
Spiewak, Robert L., 332
Sporting equipment as baggage, 312
Spur of the Moment Tours and Cruises, 92
Sri Lanka, 136, 284, 350-51
Stand-Buys Ltd., 92
Standby travel:
airlines, 31, 49, 323
sea cruises, 93
Star Report, 9
Starward, 93
State Laws on Importing Alcoholic Beverages,
361
Steinbicker, Earl, 197
Sternik, Hans, 335
Survival Kit guidebooks, 195
Swan tours, 57, 58
Sweden, 285
Swedish National Tourist Office, 285
Swine fever, 358, 359
Swissair, 386
Swiss cog line, 71
Swiss Federal Railways, 71
Switzerland, 339, 340-41
Sydorko, Roberta, 241, 242
Syria, 237

Index • 407